teach yourself...

C

Charles Siegel

BPB PUBLICATIONS
B-14, CONNAUGHT PLACE, NEW DELHI-110001

FIRST INDIAN EDITION - 1989

SECOND REVISED INDIAN EDITION - 1994

Distributors:

BPB BOOK CENTRE
376, Old Lajpat Rai Market, DELHI-110006

BUSINESS PROMOTION BUREAU
8/1, Ritchie Street, Mount Road, MADRAS-600002

BUSINESS PROMOTION BUREAU
4-3-268-C, Giriraj Lane, Bank Street, HYDERABAD-500195

COMPUTER BOOK CENTRE
12, Shrungar Complex, M. G. Road, BANGALORE-560001

COMPUTER BOOK CENTRE
SCF No.-65, Sector-6, PANCHKULA-134109, CHANDIGARH

COMPUTER BOOK CENTRE
Shanti Niketan Building, 8, Camac Street, CALCUTTA-700017

Printed in India under arrangement with:
MIS: Press, Inc., USA.

ISBN 81-7029-016-3

Published by Manish Jain for BPB Publications, B-14, Connaught Place, New Delhi-110001 and Printed by him at Pressworks, Delhi.

Dedication

This book is dedicated to my mother, Ethel Navasky Siegel, with all my love.

Acknowledgements

Thanks to the people who helped bring out the second edition of this book, Steve Berkowitz, Cary Weinberger, Patricia Wallenburg and Dawn Erdos.

Special thanks for technical criticism and advice to Joe Walton, an excellent programmer and an even better friend.

Contents

Introduction

Over the past few years, C has become the most popular computer programming language. C's speed and power have always made it a favorite language for operating systems and engineering applications. Now C—along with its extension, C++—has also become the most popular language for software development and for everyday business applications. It has also become very accessible to the general public, because there are excellent, low cost compilers available.

Beginning programmers often want to start by learning C as their first language, but teachers and friends usually tell them that C should not be studied as a first language because it is too obscure and complex. As a result, many people spend six months or more learning BASIC, Pascal, or some other educational language before they can start working with C—the language they really want to learn.

The fault is not with the C language. It is with the approach most books take to teaching C.

It is possible to introduce C in a simple way—simple enough that it can be studied by beginners who have never used any other programming language. You can learn to program in C and can write many useful programs without bothering with the features that made C unsuitable as a first programming language. In fact, in some ways, C is ideal as an introduction to programming, because it shows you the way that computers really work.

Is This Book for You?

This book is aimed at beginners. All it requires is that you know how to use the computer keyboard for typing and that you have a C compiler to use. It uses a general form of the C language that works with virtually any compiler you may have.

This book is intended to introduce beginners to programming concepts while teaching the C language.

C has many advanced features that the beginning programmer should not have to deal with. For example, you can manipulate individual bits in C as you often do if you program in Assembly Language.

Even books that claim to make C easy generally start out by teaching many of the advanced features of the language before the user gets down to actual programming. The first chapter might contain a long list of *operators* including not only *logical operators* and *arithmetic operators*, but also *bitwise operators*. The chapters that follow include equally detailed discussions of the language's other features and equally long lists to memorize. You do not look at any programs except trivial example programs until you have learned all of the features of the language.

Beginning programmers must learn the essential facts about what programming languages do—such as defining variables, looping, and getting input from the user—rather than memorize long lists of operators. Beginners should be allowed to concentrate on the basics and to actually get practice using the basics, rather than getting lost in long lists of details.

The obscure abbreviations sometimes used by C are another obstacle for beginning programmers. These abbreviations save you time if you are already familiar with programming, but using them is too much of a burden when you are beginning. Your early programs should be written in an explicit style of code, which spells everything out.

For this reason, the code in this book is written in an educational style, specially designed to be clear. Abbreviations are introduced in the last chapters of the book. By then, you will welcome them because they let you save a few keystrokes when you are entering code that you already understand.

Instead of introducing all of the language's features before allowing you to do any real programming, this book does just the opposite. You begin writing small but useful programs in Chapter 1. By the end of the book, you develop complex programs, such as an address book. You do all of this using a specially clear, easy-to-understand version of the language.

You learn C in the same way you would learn a foreign language. You are not expected to learn all of the language's grammatical rules before you do any speaking or reading. Before you learn the past tense, you are given stories to read that use only the present tense.

Likewise, this book has you writing interesting C programs before you learn the whole language, and it introduces you to the basics of programming such as structured (or modular) programming, defining variables, redirecting program control through loops and if-else statements, handling strings, using arrays—to all the basics that you would normally learn in a book that is an introduction to programming using BASIC or Pascal.

The Advantage of C for Beginners

Approached in this spirit, C is actually a much better introduction to programming than BASIC, Pascal, and other high-level languages. C gives the new programmer more insight into how the computer actually works than these high-level languages do.

C is a a middle-level language, because it is closer to the way that computers actually work than languages such as BASIC and Pascal. Programmers usually talk about two classes of programming language:

- **Low-level languages**, such as Assembly Language, go through every step of what the computer hardware does. This type of language is very powerful but difficult to learn and use.
- **High-level languages**, such as BASIC and Pascal, are farther from how the computer actually works. They are designed to fit in with the way people think rather than with the way computers operate.

C has some of the advantages of both of these. It is low level in the sense that it works more like the computer than most high-level languages do, and it is high-level in the sense that its programs are structured like the programs of high-level languages, so their logic is easy to follow.

C's Closeness to the Hardware

Beginning programmers usually read books or take introductory courses to learn how computers actually work, but they learn high-level languages that do not illustrate the principles covered in these introductory courses.

For example, most beginning programmers are puzzled by the fact that words and other forms of text are referred to as *strings*. In introductory courses, they learn that computers use bytes to represent individual characters, and it follows logically that text must be treated as a sort of list or string of bytes. Yet the way that high-level languages such as BASIC handle strings is so far from the way the computers actually handle strings that programmers never get a practical grasp of what a string is.

In C, on the other hand, it is very apparent that, for the computer, text is simply a string of characters.

Likewise, beginning programmers learn in their introductory courses that computer memory consists entirely of binary digits, and that the computer can look at those digits either as numbers or as characters. Most high-level languages, though, separate the two types of data so completely that the beginning programmer never gets a practical grasp of the fact that they are both made up of the same bits.

In C, on the other hand, it is very clear that the computer looks at the same bits of data in different ways. It is so easy to understand that you use it as one of your first examples of programming in this book.

In introductory classes, the beginner learns that a computer has an **address** for every byte in its memory. But most high-level languages never let you use these addresses. Here, again, C makes it clear how the computer works. The list could go on.

C as a Structured Language

Despite their closeness to the hardware, however, C programs are far easier to understand than Assembly Language programs, and can be easier to understand than many BASIC programs.

To see why this is true, consider a brief history of computers and of programming, which is a useful background to what you learn in the first few chapters of this book.

Binary Data

Computers work with ones and zeros, but they must use this data in three different ways:

- ✦ They must have a cheap way to store the data for long periods of time. This is called *secondary storage.*
- ✦ They must have a very fast way to store and retrieve the data for immediate use when the computer is running. This is called *primary storage* or *main memory.* On personal computers, it is almost always called *random access memory (RAM).*
- ✦ They must have a way to manipulate and change the data. This is called the *central processing unit (CPU)* and in microcomputers, it is called the *microprocessor.*

Historically, several different forms of hardware have been invented to perform each of these tasks.

Computers once used punch cards for long-term storage; now they use magnetic disks. Computers once used magnetic cores wired by hand for main memory; now they use microchips. CPUs were once built of vacuum tubes that blinked on and off as the data changed, now they consist of tiny microprocessors.

All of these forms of hardware handle only binary data. Data can be represented by locations on a floppy disk that are magnetized or not magnetized, but vacuum tubes that are on or off, or by locations on a card that are punched out or not. In any case, each bit of data has just two possible values—a 1 or a 0. This most basic unit of data—which can just be 1 or 0, on or off—is called a *binary digit* or, for short, a *bit.*

Because they store data in the form of bits, computers naturally use binary arithmetic.

Letters and other characters on the keyboard are also represented by patterns of ones and zeros. The idea is the same as Morse Code, which was also invented because a technology (the telegraph) could only use two values—dots and dashes—to represent all of the letters.

The code that has become the overwhelming favorite for representing characters on computer systems is referred to as *ASCII,* which stands for *American Standard Code for Information Interchange.* Apart from the normal twenty-six alphabetic characters, in both upper and lower case, there are also codes for special characters, such as the question mark and exclamation point, and for control characters, such as the carriage return, the form-feed, and the beep.

Computer scientists adopted the convention of using 8 bits to represent these characters, which allows for 2^8 (256) characters. Standard ASCII includes 128 characters, but IBM-PC compatible computers use an extended form of ASCII with 256 characters to allow for foreign characters and special characters used for drawing lines and boxes.

The group of eight bits used to represent one character is really the basic unit of information that the computer handles—the *byte.* If a computer is working with text, it is processing a list of bytes, each representing a character.

Like data, instructions—statements that tell the computer to add two numbers of to manipulate data in any other way—are also represented by ones and zeros.

Each brand of CPU has its own *instruction set*—the pattern of ones and zeros that it recognizes as instructions about how to manipulate its data. Every CPU has *registers,* which are temporary holding places for data that it is working on, an *arithmetic-logic unit,* which is circuitry designed to perform the operations in its instruction set on this data, and a *control unit,* which tells the arithmetic-logic unit what to do next.

To add two numbers, for example, you must first put into the control unit the binary instructions for moving the numbers to be added from RAM into the registers that are used for addition. Then you must put in the control unit the binary instruction that makes the system add the numbers in those registers and store the answer in another register. Finally, you must put in the control unit the binary instruction that makes the system move the answer from that register to a location in RAM.

Computer Languages

At first, people actually wrote entire programs that were lists of these instructions, each written as a pattern of ones and zeros. This is *machine language.*

Because long lists of ones and zeros can rapidly cause strain to your eyes (and your brain), programmers soon invented *symbolic* languages. They used an English-like word, such as ADD or MOV to represent each binary control code in a computer's instruction set, and they wrote an program to read these words and replace each one with the proper binary number. This sort of symbolic language is still used when programmers must be in direct touch with the hardware: it is called *Assembly language,* and the program that translates the words to binary control codes is called an *assembler.*

Though it is a great improvement over writing lists of binary codes, programming in Assembly Language is difficult and requires considerable technical knowledge. You must go through all of the steps the computer goes through, and must know which registers can be used for addition (and for other operations), and in which register the answer ends up.

In the late 1950s and 1960s, big businesses began to use computers for massive amounts of data processing, and there was no chance of finding enough programmers with the technical training needed to program in Assembly Language.

Instead, computer scientists invented what they called ***high-level languages***, such as BASIC (Beginner's All-purpose Symbolic Instruction Code) and COBOL (COmmon Business Oriented Language).

COBOL was simple enough that, during the 1960s, companies could hire people who had never used a computer before, put them through a four-week training course, and then put them to work writing business programs.

The new programmer would write something like ADD AMOUNT-A TO AMOUNT-B GIVING AMOUNT-C. The COBOL compiler would automatically translate this into Assembly Language code that used the proper registers dealt with other details of the hardware.

There are two types of programs that let you use high-level languages:

- **Compilers** permanently translate the program into machine language, and produce a stand-alone program that can be run at any time.
- **Interpreters** translate the source code one line at a time, each time the program is run. The interpreter must be available in order to run the program.

Needless to say, compiled programs run much more quickly than interpreted ones. Interpreted programs require less memory than compiled ones, and so they were sometimes used on early PCs. But they are becoming obsolete now that memory is cheap and abundant.

Structured Programming

The original versions of BASIC and COBOL suffered from the typical problem of early high-level languages: they were unstructured.

Most computer programs perform relatively complex tasks and must do many things. For example, a typical early business program would read a list of employees' names, select employees who have been working less than a year, sort them alphabetically, produce a report that lists them in alphabetical order, sort them by date, and produce a second report that lists them in the order they were hired.

Each of these functions is complex in itself. To produce a report, you might need to count how many lines have been printed until you find a page is full, then skip lines for the lower margin of the page and upper margin of the next page, then print a header for the new page that includes its page number and the name of the report, then skip a line, and then go back to printing the report again.

Of course, you do not want to write the same code twice to produce the two reports you need. Instead, each time the file is sorted and ready to be printed, you redirect control of the program to the code that prints reports. This is called *control flow.*

In Assembly language, control is redirected using the instruction JMP (short for JUMP) or BR (short for Branch) or some similar instruction that directs control to continue in some other point in the program.

Early high-level languages adopted this command. For example, BASIC used the GOTO command. If the report-printing feature began at line 10300 of a BASIC program, for example, you had to use the GOTO 10300 when it was time to print.

Now, suppose that, a year later, a new programmer is hired to modify that program. When you are reading through a program and trying to understand how it works, a command such as GOTO 10300 is not much more helpful than the old string of binary digits. The programmer used to flip through the pages of the print out, looking for that line number, keeping one finger on the starting point as a reminder of what happened last. A few dozen lines after 10300, there would probably be another GOTO and another search through the program.

Programmers named this sort of code *spaghetti code,* because it gets so tangled up. This type of program was possible to understand when you were writing it. It became more difficult when you were going though it again to debug it. And it was virtually incomprehensible to someone who was hired a few years later make changes in it.

Problems with this type of code led computer scientists to develop *structured,* or *modular programming.* The program is written as a set of separate modules or procedures. The code to print the report, for example, is in a procedure that is separate from the rest of the program, and when you need to use it, you use a command such as PERFORM PROCEDURE PRINT-REPORT or DO PRNT-REPORT.

Even if you have never programmed, you can imagine how hard it is to follow a program that begins with several pages of code that includes all of the details about how to read the file and select the names according to the date they were hired and then directs you to the location, several pages farther down, of the code that sorts the names alphabetically, and then to the location of the code that prints the program.

You can imagine how much easier it is to read a structured program that begins:

```
PERFORM PROCEDURE READ-FILE
PERFORM PROCEDURE SELECT-NAMES
PERFORM PROCEDURE SORT-ALPHA
PERFORM PROCEDURE PRINT-REPORT
```

Structured programs are also much easier to debug, because you can test the modules one at a time and make sure each one does what you expect it to. Obviously, you can pinpoint your error much more quickly if you know what module it is in—rather than knowing that there is something wrong somewhere in your fifty-page program.

Structured programming was so obviously superior that new versions of BASIC and of COBOL have incorporated it with more or less success.

The next step in the evolution of programming after structured programming was *object-oriented programming*. The extension of the C language called C++ is the most important language for object-oriented programming.

This type of programming has become popular because it can be used to support a Windows or Macintosh-like interface that includes pop-up menus and dialog boxes with radio buttons, check boxes, push buttons, and other controls. This sort of interface is generally easy to use but difficult for the programmer, because there are many different events that can happen at any time: the user can click a push button, make a menu selection, click a check box, enter text in a text box, and the programmer must anticipate the result of all of these events.

It is best to learn programming using the linear, step-by-step logic of structured programming, and C has two advantages that other learning languages lack. It is close to the hardware, so it can be an ideal introduction to how computers actually work. More important, it is now the language that people ultimately want to use in practical applications.

If it is taught correctly, using a style that avoids advanced features and unnecessary obscurity, C can be the ideal introduction to computer programming.

Chapter

1

Talking with the User: printf( ) and scanf( )

As the introduction stated, the early chapters of this book use programs written in a format that is specially designed to be easy to understand. By the end of this book, you will be working with more conventional—and more obscure—C code. The "educational" style of code that you begin with, however, lets you write and understand useful C programs quickly.

In this chapter you learn enough about formatted input/output to write a small utility program that looks up the ASCII value of any character you enter. To develop this program, the chapter discusses:

- the basic form of a C program
- using functions, comments, and precompiler commands in programs
- how to declare a variable

- how to assign a value to a variable
- printing output to the screen with formatted variables using **printf( )**
- getting input from the user using **scanf( )**

Your First Program: Printing to the Screen

You will begin with a traditional program used to introduce C, which is very easy to understand. All the program does is print the words "Hello, world" on the computer screen. It is important as an introduction to the basic form of the C language.

The program reads as follows, though this initial version is not quite complete:

```
main()                       /* your first program*/
{
printf("Hello, world.\n");
}
```

The Basic Form of A Program

The first point to notice is the title at the top of this function—**main( )**. C uses such functions as the building blocks of its programs, and every C program must have a function entitled main( ), which is the first section to be executed when the program runs. If the function listed above were used as one module of a larger program, you would give it a descriptive title—you might call it **greet( )** because it greets the world—and other functions would call it simply by using the statement **greet( );**. You will soon examine a program with more than one function.

Second, notice that the body of the function is surrounded by curly brackets, or braces: { and }. C is a free-form language, which gives the programmer a great deal of flexibility when deciding whether items should be written with extra spaces or new lines. It is possible to write this program as follows,

```
main(){
printf("Hello,world.\n");
}
```

with the opening bracket on the same line as the module name. In more complex programs, however, things look clearer if each curly bracket is on a separate line, and this book adopts that convention. It is much easier to see that brackets are paired up properly if they line up one above another. In later chapters, you will see how this convention can clarify longer programs.

Adding Comments

Third, notice the words **/* your first program */**. Text surrounded by /* and */ is a comment, which is ignored by the C compiler and included purely for the benefit of future programmers who must read through and try to understand your program. Even if you return a year later to a program you wrote, you may find that it is often impossible to remember what you were doing. Good programming style includes many comments.

The compiler ignores new lines for comments also, and comments often are long enough to require many lines. The previous program could be written as follows:

```
main()                           /* your
                                 first
                                 program */

{
printf("Hello, world.\n");}
}
```

Or you could even write it as follows:

```
main()
{/*your
          first
                                 program*/
printf("Hello, world.\n");}
```

You can see how jumbled things can become in a free-form language such as C if you do not voluntarily adopt good style.

In this book, all comments are fully marked as follows for the sake of greater clarity, even though all the slashes and asterisks might not be required:

```
/* your */
/* first */
/* program */
```

The printf( ) Function

Next, notice the instruction **printf( )**, the first function of the C language that you will learn. Note the most obvious point about it first—it ends with a semicolon (;) as do most C statements.

The name of the function **printf( )** stands for PRINT with Formatting. Soon, you will examine some of the ways that this instruction can format variables. In this case, you just see it doing its basic job of printing text to the screen.

The text to be printed is placed in quotation marks within the parentheses of **printf( )**, and, as you can see, a control character is also placed in the quotation marks. **\n** within the **printf( )** statement stands for "new line". When the backslash character (\) appears within the quotation marks of **printf( )**, the character following it is called an *escape character* and is not read like the other characters in quotation marks.

Usually, the escape character instructs the computer what to do rather than functioning as a character of text that is printed to the screen. Because C is a rather low-level language, it does not do much for you; you must explicitly put the new line into the instruction.

Using C Functions

Notice that **printf( )** has the same basic form as the statement main( )—a word followed by parentheses. This is the form of all C functions, and C is made up largely of functions. The parentheses can be empty, as **main( )** is, or they can contain something that the function does something to, as **printf( )** does in this program.

The item in the parentheses is usually called an *argument* by C programmers. An argument is much like the object of a verb in ordinary English. You can say "Print," or you can say "Print a word," using the verb with or without an object. Likewise, you can use functions with or without arguments in C. Either way, though, you must include the parentheses at the end of a function word to let the compiler know it is a function.

You can invent functions like this at will, which is why C is so well-suited to structured programming. Suppose, for example, that you wanted a program that printed both "Hello, world" and "Goodbye, world" on the screen. You could write the program as follows:

```
main()                      /* your second program */
{
printf("Hello, world.\n");
printf("Goodbye, world.\n");
}
```

Or you could write a program that does the same thing as follows:

```
main()                 /* third sample program */
{
greet();               /* use function to print hello */
farewell();            /* use function to print goodbye */
}

greet()                /* function to print hello */
{
printf("Hello, world.\n");
}

farewell()             /* function to print goodbye */
{
printf("Goodbye, world.\n");
}
```

You can actually create functions out of blocks of existing commands, and then you can use those newly created functions just as if they were a part of the language. This feature of C not only makes it well-suited for structured programming, it also makes it indefinitely extensible.

You can buy packages at the computer store that contain specialized libraries of C functions that give the language the capacity for easy database management, for easy creation of windows and other fancy screen displays, or for just about any other purpose you have in mind. You can use the new functions in these libraries just as if they were part of the language.

The Standard Input/Output Header

There is still one missing element in the first sample program at the beginning of this chapter, which you learned above was not quite complete. The full program must contain the statement **#include <stdio.h>** as follows:

```
                    /* Chapter 1, Example 1 */

#include <stdio.h>                          /*your first program */
main()
{
printf("Hello, world.\n");
}
```

The **#** sign indicates that this statement is an instruction for the precompiler. Your compiler actually goes through your program several times as it compiles the program. The first time through, before it attempts to translate any code, it simply looks for **#** signs and make any substitutions in the program that are required by the statements that follow.

Notice that the precompiler instruction does not end with a semicolon as ordinary commands do. Also notice the new comment added at the top—**/* Chapter 1, Example 1 */**. This book uses this type of heading at the beginning of any program that is complete and ready to compile—but not for fragments that are used for illustration.

<stdio.h> is short for "standard input-output header." When the compiler sees the statement **#include <stdio.h>**, it reads this header into the program. When the compiler begins translating source code, the header is present, just as if you had typed it in. You probably will notice that, when they are compiling, Turbo C and QuickC tell you what line they are currently on, and even if you typed in a small six-line program, they tell you that they are working on lines with numbers in the hundreds because all of the lines in stdio.h have been added to the six lines that you entered.

One item included in this header is a declaration of the function **printf( )**, which is in a library of functions called the standard input-output package.

When it is finished compiling the program, your C compiler reads any needed functions from this library and links them with the program you wrote. The word *compiling,* in its strict sense, only refers to the process of producing a file with an OBJ extension. Linking is necessary to produce an executable file with an EXE extension. Most newer C compilers, such as Turbo C and Quick C, perform this linking automatically after they are done compiling. If you are using an older compiler, you must link the functions with the programs yourself with a linker program.

Declaration of any library functions you use must be present, or the compiler gives you an error message telling you that a function it needs is missing.

The declaration is a reassurance that the compiler will find this function when it arrives at the linking stage.

The cryptic statement **#include <stdio.h>** must be added, then, because **printf( )**, although it is one the most commonly used statements in C, is technically not part of the language. It belongs to a special library.

C's original designers preferred simplicity and elegance over features. They were designing a language for systems programming (and using it to implement the Unix operating system), so they considered speed, efficiency, and power all-important, and they ignored many more mundane features—even features as basic as input/output.

You could almost say that they wrote a language with grammar but with no vocabulary. The vocabulary was added by later developers who wrote libraries of functions. Developers of compilers have written extensive libraries of I/O functions, but this book uses only those that have become standard and are included in stdio.h in every C compiler.

Running the Program

Now that you have the entire program laid out, you can compile and run it. Enter the program into a file named **greet.c**. If the compiler produces error messages, make sure your program is identical to the listing.

Keep one point in mind when you are correcting errors, particularly later in the book when you are writing longer programs. If the compiler's error message does not make sense to you, it is probably caused by a mistake you made earlier in the program, which the compiler does not consider an error.

For example, if the error message tells you that a statement is not terminated by a semicolon, you might actually have left off the semicolon by mistake, so you can just make the correction the compiler indicates. On the other hand, your compiler will probably give you the same message if you leave off the final curly bracket of one of the functions in a program. For example, if you make this error in the sample program you just examined:

```
main()                  /* third sample program */
{
greet();                /* use function to print hello */
farewell();             /* use function to print goodbye */


greet()                 /* function to print hello */
```

```
{
printf("Hello, world.\n");
}
```

the compiler also says that you have a statement that is not terminated with a semicolon. Because the final curly bracket is missing in the **main( )** function, the compiler thinks that the second use of **greet( )** is another statement in **main( )** rather than the name of a new function.

When you receive this sort of irrelevant error message, look above the error that the compiler indicates to find the actual error you made, and also remember that the compiler ignores indentation and spacing.

As you will see when you write longer programs, a single minor error, such as leaving out a curly bracket, can make the compiler misinterpret most of the statements that follow and produce a long list of error messages. After you correct such an error, recompile the program rather than taking the time to go through all the mistaken error messages.

After you have successfully compiled the source code in the file **greet.c**, you will have created a new command that you can enter at the DOS prompt, much like the commands that are part of DOS or any other software. Simply type in greet at the DOS prompt, and your computer prints "Hello, world."

Assigning Values to Variables

So far, you have learned to make the program "talk" to the user by printing output to the screen. Before you are able to make a program "listen" to the user by receiving input from the keyboard, you must learn about variables. Anything the user types in must be stored in a variable so the rest of the program can use it.

What is a Variable

Variables are a basic feature of any programming language and are easy enough to understand that an example should make the idea clear without any special explanation.

The following statement,

```
x = 10;
```

assigns the value 10 to the variable x.

This instruction actually makes the computer place the value 10 (in binary form) in the area of memory that has been set aside to hold the variable x. Whenever x is mentioned later in the program, the program thinks of it as representing the number 10.

Of course, a later statement can change the value. You can use x to represent 10 for part of the program and then use the following statement.

```
x = 20;
```

so that x represents 20 for the rest of the program. Note that, like most statements in C, these assignment statements end with a semicolon..

The Assignment Operator

It is important to emphasize that the symbol = is used for assignment. It is called the *assignment operator*, since it is used to perform the operation of assigning a value to a variable.

The statement in C that you just examined is not at all the same as the statement x = 20 in algebra, which tells you that x equals 20.

In C, as in most computer programming languages, x = 20 assigns x the value of 20, no matter what x equals to begin with. It is probably best to read x = 20 as "let x equal 20" or "make x equal 20."

Names of Variables

Another note on programming style is desperately needed here, since you have just seen a blatant example of bad style. As a general rule, it is not a good idea to give variables names like x or y, which do not explain what they represent. It is much kinder to users who must later figure out the program—and also kinder to yourself as a programmer—to give variables meaningful names.

For example, if x in the previous examples is intended to stand for the number of workers, then the statements should be something like numWrkrs = 10; and numWrkrs = 20;. Likewise, if it stands for the amount paid, use names like amtPaid = 10 and amtPaid = 20;.

Variable names cannot include spaces, or the compiler reads them as more than one word. They also cannot include hyphens, or the compiler tries to subtract one variable from another. If it saw amt-paid, for example, it would want to subtract the variable paid from the variable amt.

It used to be most common to use the underscore character (_) to make names easier to read by showing divisions between words, such as **num_wkrs** and **amt_paid**. A more recent convention, which this book uses, is to use an uppercase letter at the beginning of each new word within the variables.

Remember also that the compiler distinguishes between lowercase and uppercase letters in variable names. If you receive error messages that seem particularly unreasonable to you, such as those telling you that a variable does not exist when you know that it does, check the capitalization of the variable's name.

Data Types

Before assigning a value to a variable within a program, you must define the variable's data type. Though there are more data types in C, all that are needed for most purposes are these three: *character*, *integer*, and *floating decimal-point number*, which C names char, int, and float, respectively:

- **char:** A char is a single ASCII character. These characters generally represent the characters on your keyboard—letters of the alphabet, numbers, or special characters such as $ and @—but they also can represent other ASCII characters, such as those that make the computer beep or instruct the printer to eject a sheet of paper.
- **int:** An int is a whole number such as 1, 2 or 25,000.
- **float:** A float is a number with a decimal point, such as 1.5 or 2.0.

You might already have a few questions. Why is it that the numbers on the keyboard are characters and also integers? Why is the float 2.0 different from the int 2?

The answer lies in the way the computer works. Remember, computer memory represents information as a long string of ones and zeros, which is divided into bytes, each of which is comprised of 8 bits. The computer finds individual bytes by giving each byte an address. Bytes are numbered from 1 up to the number of total bytes in memory.

When you assign a value to a variable, the program reserves a portion of memory for that variable. Then, whenever you mention the name **amtPaid** or **numWrkrs** or **x** or **y**, the program examines the portion of memory reserved for that variable and determines what value it contains.

The computer with two problems when it works with variables in this way:

- deciding how much memory to reserve for the variable and what form to store it in when it is creating the variable.
- deciding how to interpret the ones and zeros it finds there when it is reading the value of the variable.

Different variables require different amounts of storage.

The char

A char requires just one byte.

ASCII code (as you have seen) was designed so each character could be represented by a binary number that is no more than one byte long. When you assign a character value to a variable, ones and zeros that make up the binary form of the ASCII number of that character are stored in the one-byte-long memory location reserved for that variable.

The int

The amount of space that C reserves for an int depends on the machine that the compiler was designed for. The size of an int depends on the size of the machine's register. Older 16-bit systems use two bytes; and newer 32-bit systems use four bytes.

A little binary arithmetic tells you the maximum value of the integer that can be held in this space. Start with two and begin doubling. Soon, you will see numbers that are familiar to anyone who has read about computers: 2^6 is 64, 2^7 is 128, and 2^8 is 256. Now you know why early microcomputers had 64K or 256K or memory: the addresses of memory locations are kept using binary numbers (like everything else in a computer).

Continue doubling: 2^9 is 512, and 2^{10} is 1024. The fact that 210 is just over 1,000 is very convenient for humans, who are accustomed to thinking in terms of decimal numbers. That is why programmers refer to 1024 bytes as 1K. 1K does not mean 1,000, though it is used loosely to mean approximately 1,000.

Continue doubling: 2^{11} is 2K, 2^{12} is 4K, and finally (you can fill in the intermediate steps yourself), 2^{16} is 64K—the number that can be stored in a 16-bit integer. Because integers can be positive or negative, the maximum value for an int in a 16 bit system is 32K (more than 32,000), and the minimum value for an integer is negative 32K (less than -32,000). On a 32 bits system the range of an int is over 1,000,000,000.

The float

The third major data type that you must learn is the float—a number that can take non-integer values—which gets its name from the floating decimal point that divides the integer and the fractional part of this number. The number of bytes that C reserves for a float varies with the system and is usually four. In any case, a float is actually stored in the form of a number called a *mantissa*, plus an exponent that tells you what power of ten the mantissa is multiplied by. It commonly has a range of more than 1038—large enough that you usually do not have to think about it.

You do not need to worry about memorizing all of these details about variable storage and length. Just remember that the data types are char, int, and float

Using printf( ) to Format Variables

Next, you will see how much trouble you can get yourself into when you begin using the **printf( )** function to print variables of different data types.

Formatting an Integer Variable

Consider first a simple program that prints an integer variable:

```
                        /* Chapter 1, Example 2 */
#include <stdio.h>

main()                          /* sample program: */
{                               /* printf with int */
int smplNum;

smplNum = 9;
printf("The sample number is %d.\n", smplNum);
}
```

The only difference between this program and the previous program is that a variable is included in this program as part of the **printf( )** function, but this addition requires a few more steps.

First, the statement **int smplNum;** is needed to instruct the compiler to reserve a memory location long enough for an integer and to give the contents of this location long enough for an integer and to give the contents of this location the name **smplNum**. This is called *declaring the variable.*

In this book, for the sake of easier reading, programs always include a blank line after all of the variables are declared. You must declare the variable before you do anything else with it. Then, you can assign a value to that variable with the statement **smplNum = 9;**, which puts the binary number 9 in the 16-bit memory location reserved for **smplNum;**. That memory location then looks like the following:

```
0000000000001001
```

Finally, in the **printf( )** statement itself, you use another special character, **%d**, in place of the variable within the quotation marks, and then you insert a comma and the name of the variable whose value you want in that position after the quotation marks. When you run the program, it replaces the special character **%d** with an integer interpretation of the variable following the comma.

Compile and run this program so you become accustomed to working with variables. You might name your source code file **SAMPLNUM.C**. After it is compiled, enter the command **SAMPLNUM** at the DOS prompt. As you might expect, it prints the following on the screen:

```
The sample number is 9.
```

Note that there are two different types of special characters used by **printf( )**.

- The escape sequence that begins with a backslash, such as **\n**, which you looked at earlier in this chapter.
- The formatting code that begins with a percent sign, such as **%d** does. It represents a variable and instructs the compiler to print the variable in a certain format.

You use several of these special formatting characters in this book.

As you have already seen, **%d** tells **printf( )** that the variable should be printed as an integer. The letter **d** stands for integer because **printf( )** can format integers as hexadecimal (base 16) or octal (base 8) numbers as well as ordinary decimal (base 10) numbers. Remember, what **printf( )** actually must work with is a binary number. **%d** stands for "decimal."

printf( ) also uses the obvious special characters **%f** for floats and **%c** for characters.

Formatting a Character Variable

Now look at how to declare and print another data type:

```
                        /* Chapter 1, Example 3 */
#include <stdio.h>

main()                  /* sample program */
                        /* printf with char */
{
char smplLtr;

smplLtr = 'a';
printf("The sample letter is %c.\n",smplLtr);
}
```

This program prints the following:

```
The sample letter is a.
```

Note that you use the word char plus the name of the variable to declare a character variable, and note also that when you assign a value to a character variable, you must place that value in single quotation marks.

Formatting Multiple Variables

You can also use **printf( )** to print more than one variable, as in the following program:

```
                        /* Chapter 1, Example 4 */
#include <stdio.h>

main()          /* sample program */
{               /* printf char and int */
char smplLtr;
int smplNum;
smplLtr = 'a';
smplNum = 9;
printf("The samples are %c and %d.\n", smplLtr, smplNum);
}
```

This program prints the following:

```
The samples are a and 9.
```

You simply place the names of the variables after the final quotation mark of the **printf( )** statement with commas between them, and **printf( )** puts values in place of the special **%** formatting characters in the order in which they appear.

Consider the following program:

```
                    /* Chapter 1, Example 5 */

#include <stdio.h>

main()                  /* sample program */
{                       /* printf two chars */
char smplLtr, othrLtr;

smplLtr = 'a';
othrLtr = 'b';
printf("The samples are %c and %c.\n", smplLtr,othrLtr);
}
```

By now, it should be obvious that this program prints the following:

```
The samples are a and b.
```

The new point to note here is that you can declare more than one variable in one statement. Just list the variables after the word char (or int or float) with commas between them and a semicolon at the end of the entire statement, and they are all defined as members of that data type.

Formatting a Float Variable

Finally, try using **printf( )** with a float (to prove that programming is not always as simple as it seems):

```
                    /* Chapter 1, Example 6 */

#include <stdio.h>

main()                  /* sample program */
```

```
{                               /* printf with float */
float smplNum;

smplNum = 9;
printf("The sample number is %f.\n", smplNum);
}
```

This program does not print what you expect. It prints the following:

```
The sample number is 9.000000.
```

The default display for floats includes six decimal places.

Methods for controlling this display more precisely are summarized in Chapter 8 because they involve more details than you should bother with at this point.

The Power of printf( ) Formatting

The discussion of **printf( )** and variables in this chapter ends with a cautionary note and an indication of C's power.

Be careful not to think of a char as being identical to a letter and an int as being identical to a number. Consider the following program, for example:

```
                         /* Chapter 1, Example 7 */
#include <stdio.h>

main()                          /* sample program */
{                               /* printf with number */
char smplNum;

smplNum = '9';
printf("The sample number is %c.\n", smplNum);
}
```

This program prints exactly the same thing as the first of the formatted **printf( )** programs you looked at:

```
The sample number is 9.
```

There is, however, a difference in the way the computer handles the two programs.

In the earlier program, where you defined **smplNum** as an integer, the program assigned the value of 9 to it by putting the binary number for nine, 0000000000001001, in its two-byte memory location, as you have already seen. When **printf( )** sees the **%d**, it interprets this number in decimal format as 9.

In the later program, on the other hand, where you defined **smplNum** as a character, the program assigned the value 9 to it by writing the ASCII code for the character 9 in its one-byte memory location. 9 is ASCII character number 57, so the program places 00111001 (57 in binary) in that location. Then, when **printf( )** sees the **%c** format for this variable, it moves to its location, retrieves the value, and interprets it as ASCII character 57, which is 9.

You can take advantage of this feature of **printf( )** with programs such as the following:

```
                    /* Chapter 1, Example 8 */
#include <stdio.h>

main()                  /* print ASCII value of char */
{
char smplChr;

smplChr = '9';
printf("The ASCII value of %c is %d.\n",smplChr,smplChr);
}
```

Both of the special formatting characters in the **printf( )** statement read the variable **smplChr**. First, the **%c** reads the variable as a character. Then, the **%d** goes to the same place in memory and reads the same value as a decimal integer, so the program prints the following:

```
The ASCII value of the character 9 is 57.
```

You almost have a useful program here. It could be very handy to have a small utility that allows you to type in a character and then gives you the ASCII value of that character. You have not yet learned how to get a character from the keyboard and assign it to a variable, but before the end of this chapter, you will write such a program.

The flexibility of **printf( )**—the fact that it can display a variable in any format—is one reason for the power and speed of C. It allows you to do things like this ASCII conversion.

But this flexibility can also lead to problems. Other computer languages give you error messages and refuse to run if you mix up data types. If you use a character as if it were an integer in most languages, for example, you must use a special function to explicitly convert the character to its ASCII value before using it that way.

C, on the other hand, is sometimes called a *robust language*. It assumes that you know what you are doing and runs the program you have written even if there is an error.

You can imagine what sort of confusion it could cause if you mix data types in the middle of a prolonged mathematical calculation. It is important to watch your data types. If your program produces unexpected results, look through it to see if the data types are what they should be.

Getting Input from the User

The function **scanf( )** is used by C to receive input from the user. The function works very much like **printf( )** in reverse and should be easy for you to learn. Consider the following program:

```
                  /* Chapter 1, Example 9 */
#include <stdio.h>

main()                   /* sample program */
{                        /* using scanf and printf */.
int smplNum;;

printf("What sample number do you want to display? ");
scanf("%d",&smplNum);
printf("\nThe number you typed is %d.\n",smplNum);
}
```

First, this program prints the following:

```
What sample number do you want to display?
```

Note that this first **printf( )** function includes an extra space after the question mark and does not include a **\n** to create a new line after this message because you want the cursor to remain on the same line, with one space between it and the question mark, waiting for the user's input.

The program stops at this point and waits for the user to press one or more keys followed by the Enter key (also known as the Return key). Then, it assigns the value of the keys you pressed to the variable named in **scanf( )** in the format given in **scanf( )**.

Reading a Variable into scanf( )

One important point to notice is that the variable named in **scanf( )** must have an **&** before it.

In C, **&** followed by a variable name refers to the address of that variable in memory. For example, **&smplNum** is the address of the variable **smplNum**. As you learned earlier, all bytes in a computer's memory are numbered sequentially, and the number of a cell is called its *address*.

You will learn why the ampersand is needed when you look at addresses in C in more detail in Chapter 6. At this point, you should just remember that **scanf( )** must use the **&** before the name of the variables to which it assigns values.

The **scanf("%d",&samplNum)** statement in this program, then, reads the keyboard input as a decimal number and assigns that value to the variable smplNum. For example, if you type

```
9
```

and then press the Enter key, **smplNum** would contain the value 9, and the final **printf( )** statement displays the following:

```
The sample number you typed is 9.
```

You could also type

```
123
```

and press the Enter key. **scanf( )** takes numbers more than one character long. After all, when you declared the variable as an int, the program set aside enough memory for numbers as large as 32K.

Using scanf( ) with a float

Likewise, if **smplNum** had been declared as a float, you could enter floats of almost any length. Consider the following program:

```
                              /* Chapter 1, Example 10 */
#include <stdio.h>

main()                         /* sample 2 of */
{                              /* scanf and printf */
float smplNum;

printf("What sample number do you want to display? ");
scanf("%f", &smplNum);
printf("The number you typed is %f.\n", smplNum);
}
```

If you type

```
123.456789
```

and press Enter, the final **printf( )** statement displays the following:

```
The sample number you typed in is 123.456789.
```

Using scanf( ) With a char

On the other hand, if you declare the variable as a char, the program only accepts one character from the keyboard.

For example, consider the following programs:

```
                              /* Chapter 1, Example 11 */
#include <stdio.h>

main()                         /* sample program 3 */
{                              /* scanf and printf */
char smplChr;

printf("What character do you want to display? ");
```

```
scanf("%c",&smplChr);
printf("The sample you typed is %c.\n", smplChr);
}
```

If you type

```
ABCD
```

and press the Enter key, the program displays the following:

```
The sample character you typed is A.
```

Only the first character typed is assigned to the variable **smplChr** because a char is defined as a single character. The other characters are lost.

It is also possible to use **%s** with **scanf( )** to get an entire string of characters, such as ABCD, from the user in the same way that you get a char, int or float. It is more difficult to declare strings in C, however, so they are covered in Chapter 5.

Control Characters in scanf( )

One other point about **scanf( )** comes in handy. The way **scanf( )** handles control strings is also the reverse of **printf( )**.

For example, the statement **printf("%c\n",smplLtr)** prints the variable **smplLtr** plus a carriage return. The statement **scanf("\n%c,smplLtr)** reads any character into the variable **smplLtr** except a carriage return.

The same is true of any other characters used in the control string. **scanf( )** simply ignores those characters if they are entered by the user. This feature can be useful when you are getting characters or strings from the user and want to filter out certain characters.

An ASCII Chart Program

Now, you have learned enough to write your first really useful program, a small utility to give you the ASCII value of any character.

This program is very similar to the program you wrote earlier to print out the ASCII value of a variable, but, now that you have learned **scanf( )** also, you can ask the user what character he or she wants to look up as follows:

```
                        /* Chapter 1, Example 12 */
#include <stdio.h>

main()                          /* print ASCII value of */
{                               /* char asked by user */
char smplChr;

printf("\nWhat character do you want the ASCII value of > ");
scanf("%c", &smplChr);
printf("The ASCII value of %c is %d \n", smplChr, smplChr);
}
```

This program should be quite easy for you to understand. The only question is what command you would like to enter at the DOS prompt to look up ASCII values—something such as **ASCCHRT**. Just enter this program into the file **ASCCHRT.C**, and compile it.

Now, you have a small stand-alone utility that you can use any time you want to look up the ASCII value of a character. Just enter **ASCCHRT** at the DOS prompt, and you will be able to look up the value of one character.

Summary

C programs have the following general form:

```
#include <stdio.h>
main()                          /* generalized sample */
{
statemt1;
statemt2();
statemt3();
}

statemt 2()                     /* generalized subroutine */
{
statemt4;
statemt5();
}
```

Functions are the modular building blocks of the program. Each function consists of its name plus one or more statements enclosed in curly brackets. There must be one function named **main( )**, and it can execute instructions that are built into the language, included as functions in libraries, or written as functions by the programmer. In this case, the function **statemt2( )** is written by the programmer and used within **main( )** just like any other statement.

The name of a function must end with parentheses, which may be empty or may include arguments. All statements are terminated by semicolons. Comments, which are surrounded by /* and */, are ignored by the compiler and included for the benefit of the programmer. **#include <stdio.h>** is a precompiler instruction that reads in the standard input/output header. .

Three data types in C are **char** (character), **int** (integer), and **float** (number with a floating decimal point). The data type of a variable must be defined using a statement such as the following,

```
char smplVar;
```

before it can be used by other statements in the program. A value can be assigned to a variable, using a statement such as the following:

```
SmplVar = 'A';
```

The **printf( )** function prints output to the screen with formatting of variables; its general form is as follows:

```
printf("\n The variable is %c", SmplVar);
```

Ordinary characters within the quotation marks are printed on the screen. Special characters may follow a backslash. For example, **\n** prints a new line. Special characters that refer to variables follow a percent sign and format the variables named after the comma following the final quotation mark. In this case, **%c** means that **SmplVar** should be interpreted as a character. **%d** formats a variable as a decimal integer, **%f** formats it as a float, and **%s** formats it as a string.

The **scanf( )** function receives input from the keyboard; its general form is as follows:

```
scanf(%c,&SmplVar);
```

The characters used following the percent sign are the same as in **printf( )**. The name of the variable to which they are assigned must be preceded by the ampersand,(**&**), which is used to refer to an address.

Chapter 2

Controlling Program Flow

The small ASCCHRT utility you wrote in the last chapter is useful by itself, but most actual programs do not just do one thing for you and then dump you back in the operating system as ASCCHRT does. Most programs redirect the flow of program control, in order to repeat the same code and in order to let the user choose among options.

In this chapter, you rewrite the ASCCHRT utility to add a simple menu to it. To do this, you have to learn about control flow. This chapter covers:

- the forms of control flow used in structured programming: sequence, selection, and iteration
- using the **while** loop for iteration
- using the **if-else** statement for selection
- using the **if-else ladder** to choose among a larger number of options
- the logical operators
- special commands used in control flow, such as **break;** and **continue;**

Control Flow

A simple menu system begins by displaying a main menu with several options. When you select one option, it lets you do whatever it is that you have chosen, and after you are finished, the program returns you to the main menu and allows you to make another choice. You leave the program only when you choose Quit from the menu.

This type of menu system illustrates, in an understandable way, the three basic ways of controlling the flow of the program.

In the Introduction, you saw how confusing programs were when they used GOTO to direct program flow. Structured (or modular) programming was introduced to make programs easier to understand. The theoretical foundation for structured programming was a theorem, first proven in 1964 by two mathematicians named Bohm and Jacopini, that GOTOs are not needed for programming. Everything can be done using the three other methods of control flow:

- sequence
- selection
- iteration

In this chapter, you rewrite the ASCCHRT program as a menu-driven system that uses all three methods of controlling program flow.

You have already used one of these methods—sequence—in the ASCCHRT program. *Sequence* simply means that the program executes one instruction after another in the order in which the instructions appear.

Selection means choosing among two or more possible courses of action; it is generally done using an **if-else** statement (which you will soon examine). A simple menu-driven program, for example, first presents the menu of choices to the user and then uses a prolonged **if-else** statement to direct the flow of the program to one of the several routines that perform the program's different functions.

Finally, after the chosen routine is performed, the program brings you back to the menu you started with. This is *iteration.* Iteration simply means repeating—or reiterating—the same sequence of commands. It is more commonly referred to as *looping.*

The While Loop

It is easy to use iteration in C by using the **while** loop, which takes the following form:

```
while(condition)
     {
     statement;
     statement;
     statement;
     }
```

The program performs that series of statements over and over again, as long as the condition is true.

Of course, one of the statements must do something that eventually makes the condition false. Otherwise, the program will be stuck in the loop forever.

This sort of *infinite loop* is a bug that often comes up when you are developing programs. The program does the same thing over and over again, or it simply seems to "die" and do nothing if the loop is doing something that is not displayed on the screen. Sometimes, you must turn the computer off to get out of the loop.

Adding a While Loop to the Ascchrt Program

All of this should become clear when you rewrite the ASCCHRT program so that it repeats using a **while** loop.

To compile this program, you can simply copy the earlier ASCCHRT.C program into a new file called ASCCHRT2.C. Working from the DOS prompt, enter the the following command:

```
COPY ASCCHRT.C ASCCHRT2.C
```

Then, use your editor to make the following changes needed to convert the original into the new version.

To introduce basic concepts in a thorough way, the early chapters of this book includes a number of programs, such as the following one, that are similar to each other but with new features added. You can compile all of these programs if you would like the extra experience, or you can simply read some of the programs and compile only the crucial ones.

It is not difficult to compile all the programs if you simply copy and modify the previous one each time, and you might find that watching all the programs run makes it easier to understand the concepts they illustrate.

```
                        /* Chapter 2, Example 1 */
#include <stdio.h>

main()                          /* print ASCII value of char */
{                               /* with option to repeat */
char smplChr, again;

again = 'A';
while(again == 'A')
    {
    printf("\nWhat char do you want the ASCII value of > ");
    scanf("\n%c",&smplChr);
    printf("\nThe ASCII value of %c is %d\n",
    smplChr,smplChr);

    printf("\n\nEnter A to look up another ");
    printf("\nor any letter to quit ");
    scanf("\n%c",&again);
    }
}
```

The ASCCHRT program from the last chapter is now placed within a **while** loop.

Note that the condition following the word **while** is placed in parentheses and that there is no semicolon following it (because it is not a statement in itself—just an introduction to the statements in the brackets that follow).

When the program first encounters this **while**, it checks to see if the condition is true. Because the condition is true, all statements within the loop are executed. Then, when the program reaches the final } of the **while** loop, the program goes back to the **while**. If the condition is still true, the program performs the statements in the **while** loop again. If the condition is untrue, the program skips the statements in the loop and executes the statement following the closing } of the **while** loop.

Getting an Extra Keystroke

Because there is no other statement after the closing }, the program simply ends when the condition of the **while** loop becomes untrue, and control returns to the operating system.

Instead, you could require the user to press another key before continuing by defining an extra variable and adding a few extra lines between the end of the **while** loop and the end of the program:

/* Chapter 2, Example 2 */

```
#include <stdio.h>

main()                          /* print ASCII value of char */
{                               /* with option to repeat: ver 2 */
char smplChr, again, dummy;

again = 'A';
while(again == 'A')
      {
      printf("\nWhat char do you want the ASCII value of > ");
      scanf("\n%c,&smplChr);
      printf("\nThe ASCII value of %c is %d\n",
      smplChr,smplChr);
      printf("\n\nEnter A to look up another ");
      printf("\nor any letter to quit ");
      scanf("\n%c",&again);
      }
printf("\nEnter any letter to continue . . . ");
scanf("\n%c",&dummy);
}
```

If you do not enter an 'A' when the program asks you whether you want to look up another value, the program returns to the top of the loop and find that the condition is false. Then, it skips all of the statements within the **while** loop and executes the next statement, asking you to press the Enter key and then waiting for the variable that the program calls **dummy** because it is never actually used for anything.

There are a few important new points in these programs.

Limitations of scanf( )

Note that you now use **scanf(\n%c)** rather than just **scanf(%c)**.

scanf( ) can be used with **%s** (for strings), **%f** (for floats), or **%i** (for ints). It reads everything entered up to the carriage return and discards the carriage return.

When you use **scanf( )** with **%c**, however, it is more precise. It reads any single character—including the carriage return.

In the examples in Chapter 1, where there was no looping, reading everything up to the carriage return did not cause any problem. The carriage return was simply lost after the program ended.

In this case, however, the carriage return would be read by **scanf( )** the second time through the loop and assigned to the variable **smplchr** if the **\n** were not there to head it off. You might want to try an example program without the **\n** and see that the second time through the loop it will not wait for input from the user but will give you the ASCII number for the character carriage return—with a carriage return printed right in the middle of the statement.

You are seeing what is called the *keyboard buffer*—a small amount of memory the computer reserves to save any keystrokes that you type so they can be passed to the program when the program is ready for them. The buffer can be very handy, for example, if you are a fast typist and tend to get ahead of your programs.

Using **scanf("%c")** with **\n** is not the ideal way to handle the keyboard buffer, however.

If the user enters a long word instead of just one character, for example, **scanf( )** reads every character in the word, and the program loops dozens of times until it is done reading each of those characters.

On the other hand, if the user enters just a carriage return when the program asks for input, the program ignores the carriage return and keep waiting for input. If this happens, enter a letter to make the program continue.

After you learn about strings in Chapter 5, you will be able to handle this type of problem more gracefully, and the experience of handling a stream of characters at a very low level is valuable.

Indentation

Note that statements within the **while** loop are indented, and the brackets of the main program and of the **while** loop are lined up one above the other. Although this format is not required by the compiler, it is stylistically useful to help the programmer keep track of the logic.

The == Operator

Note the double equal sign (==) in the statement **while(again == 'A')**.

This symbol should not be confused with the single equal sign (=), which assigns a new value to a variable. The double equal sign tests the current value of the variable.

This sign is one of the famous *logical operators*, which means that, when C sees the ==, it evaluates the statement to see if the statement is true or false.

The opposite of the sign == (which means "is equal to") is the sign != (which means "is not equal to"). Statements that include these signs can be used in combination with each other if you use the sign **&&** (which means "and") or the sign || (which means "or") between them.

For example, it would be useful to change the condition in the program you have just looked at to the following:

```
while(again == 'A' || again == 'a')
```

When you put the "or" sign, ||, in the conditional statement, the entire condition is true if the condition on either side of the || is true. This can be read as "while **again** equals uppercase A or **again** equals lowercase a."

In cases where the conditions are more complicated, it often clarifies things if you add "it is true" to each statement when you read it in your own mind. You could read the above statement as "while it is true that **again** equals uppercase A or it is true that **again** equals lowercase a." Stating it this way makes it obvious that the condition is satisfied if either half is true.

What if you used **&&** instead and wrote the condition as **while(again == 'A' && again == 'a')**? You can read this in your own mind as "while it is true that **again** equals uppercase A and it is true that **again** equals lowercase a." Whey you use **&&**, the condition is satisfied only if both halves are true. In this case, the condition can never be satisfied because **again** cannot be both uppercase A and lowercase a simultaneously.

Using Nested Loops

Now try making this program a bit more precise and, in the process, gaining more experience with looping and with logical operators.

It is obviously not ideal to have the user type in one letter or one character to perform a task again or any other key to quit. It is fairly common practice to make the user enter either a 'Y' if he or she wants to perform a task again or an 'N' if he or she wants to quit, and not to accept any other input.

If you have formatted disks working from the DOS prompt on an IBM-PC, for example, you know that, when the system is done with one disk, it will ask you, "Do you want to format another (Y/N)?" If you enter any other letter, it repeats the same question again until it gets a Y or N for an answer.

You can make your program do the same thing by modifying it as follows:

/* Chapter 2, Example 3 */

```
#include <stdio.h>

main()                  /* print ASCII value of char */
{                       /* with option to repeat: ver 3 */
char smplChr, again;

again = 'Y';
while(again == 'Y' || again == 'y')
    {
    printf("\nWhat char do you want the ASCII value of > ");
    scanf("\n%c",&smplChr);
    printf("\nThe ASCII value of %c is
    %d\n",smplChr,smplChr);
    again = "x";
    while(again != 'Y'&& again != 'y'
                            && again != 'N' && again !='n')
        {
        printf("\nDo you want to look up another (Y/N) > ");
        scanf("\n%c",&again);
        }
    }
}
```

Instead of asking whether the user wants to perform a task **again** and getting the again variable from the keyboard within the normal sequence of the program, you put the question and answer within a **while** loop of its own, which is inside the **while** loop you already have. This technique is known as *nesting* one loop within the other.

You keep asking this question "while it is true that **again** does not equal uppercase Y *and* it is true that **again** does not equal lowercase y *and* it is true that **again** does not equal uppercase N *and* it is true that **again** does not equal lowercase n." Because you are using **&&**, all of these conditions must be true for the loop to execute. If **again** equals any of these four characters, the loop does not execute and the program continues.

Before entering the loop, you make **again** equal 'x'. If you had not done this, **again** would still be equal to uppercase Y, (which you made it equal to at the beginning of the program), and the loop would not execute. Because you have made it 'x', however, the condition is true, and the statements in this inner loop are executed.

The program asks "Would you like to look up another (Y/N?)" and gets the **again** variable from the user. Then, it goes back to the top of this inner loop and checks the condition again. If the user enters a Y or an N, either uppercase or lowercase, the condition is not satisfied and the inner loop does not execute a second time.

If the user enters any other letter, however, the condition is satisfied: "it is true that **again** does not equal uppercase Y *and* it is true that again does not equal lowercase y *and* it is true that **again** does not equal uppercase N *and* it is true that **again** does not equal lowercase n." The inner loop is executed. It asks the same question a second time and continues asking it until it gets a Y or N answer.

Once the user inputs a Y or N and gets out of the inner loop, the program reaches the final } of the outer loop. This makes it return to the top of the outer loop and tests the condition there again to see if "it is true that **again** equals uppercase Y or it is true that **again** equals lowercase y." If so, the program will execute that outer loop again and give the ASCII value of another character. If not, it will skip the outer loop and reach the end of the program.

All of this might seem obvious to some readers and obscure to others. In either case, it is valuable to actually follow the flow of the program's control carefully, step by step, when you are first learning about looping. You should look at the example once more, starting at the first line and following the way that the program control flows line by line as the user makes different choices. Be sure you understand just how the flow of logic works.

Using a While Loop with a Counter

There is one other thing that you can do to make this program a bit fancier and learn another very common way of using the while loop.

Most programs clear the screen before executing. C compilers generally have a built-in function to clear the screen, but you can write a simple one of your own as follows:

```
clrscrn()                    /* clear the screen */
{
int counter;
counter = 0;
while(counter != 25)
    {
    printf("\n");
    counter = counter + 1;
    }
}
```

This function simply prints a new line twenty-five times, and (because the computer screen displays twenty-five lines) it scrolls anything that is being displayed off the top of the screen.

Incrementing a Counter

The function **clrscrn( )** illustrates a very common programming practice—the use of a loop with a counter to make the program perform some task a given number of times.

The counter starts at zero. The **while** loop that performs the task you want repeats "while it is true that counter is not equal to 25" (or to whatever number happens to be the number of times that you want something done). The counter is incremented each time through the loop, so that after twenty-five times through, the condition no longer is true and the loop is not executed again.

Incrementing the loop involves a statement that sometimes shocks new students of computer programming:

```
counter = counter + 1;
```

This statement goes against everything you ever learned in algebra, where the equation $x = x + 1$ would be an absurdity. It is another reminder that the = sign in C stands for assignment—not for equality—and the statement should be read as "make the value of **counter** equal the (current) value of **counter** plus 1."

The Final Program

The function **clrscrn( )** also illustrates the fact that C is an extensible language. It is possible to write new functions of your own and use them like any other functions of the language.

Even if you have not been compiling all of the earlier versions of this program, you should compile this final version, which uses the new **clrscrn( )** function within the **main( )** function as follows:

/* Chapter 2, Example 4 */

```
#include <stdio.h>

main()                              /* print ASCII value of char */
{                                   /* with option to repeat: ver 4 */
char smplChr, again;

again = 'Y';
while(again == 'Y' || again == 'y')
    {
    clrscrn();
    printf("\nwhat char do you want the ASCII value of > ");
    scanf("\n%c",&smplChr);
    printf("\nThe ASCII value of %c is %d\n",
    smplChr,smplChr);
    again = 'x';
    while(again != 'Y' && again != 'y'
                            && again != 'N' && again !='n')
        {
        printf("\n\nDo you want to look up another (Y/N)> ");
        scanf("\n%c",&again);
        }
    }
clrscrn();
}

clrscrn()                                   /* clear the screen */
{
int counter;
```

```
counter = 0;
while(counter != 25)
      {
      printf("\n");
      counter = counter + 1;
      }
}
```

Note that **clrscrn( )** can be used just like any other function of the language (**printf( )** or **scanf( )**, for example).

When the **main( )** module reaches **clrscrn( )**, it transfers control to the **clrscrn( )** function. After **clrscrn( )** is done, control returns to the place where it left the main function, and the program continues with the next statement after **clrscrn( )** in **main( )**.

By writing **clrscrn( )** as a separate function, you save yourself work because you type in the steps needed to clear the screen only once, although the program uses the steps twice. Also you actually make the **main( )** module easier to read by writing **clrscrn( )** in it instead of putting in all of the steps each time they are used and forcing someone who is trying to read the program to figure out each time that all you are doing is clearing the screen

Selection: if-else

Now that you have looked at sequence and iteration, selection is the only other major type of program control that you must learn about.

Selection in C usually takes the following form:

```
if(condition)
      {
      statement;
      statement;
      }
else
      {
      statement;
      statement;
      }
```

There can be any number of statements in the brackets following the **if** and the **else**. If the condition is true, the statements following the **if** are executed. Otherwise, the statements following the **else** are executed.

The **else** and the statements that follow it are optional. You can just have an **if** clause. The statements that follow it are executed if the condition is true, and nothing is done if the condition is false.

Using If-Else To Add Options to the ASCCHRT Program

You can use **if-else** to expand the ASCCHRT program. Instead of just letting the user input a character to find out what its ASCII number is, you can also let the user input the ASCII number and find out what the corresponding character is.

To do this, you will write a new **main( )** module that provides a small menu screen that allows the user to choose whether he or she wants to look up the ASCII number of a character, look up the character for a number, or quit the program. Then, depending on the choice, the program branches to a module that is like the ASCCHRT program you have already looked at or to a module that does the same thing in reverse.

There are more elegant ways to do the same thing, but this way gives you good practice in building a program out of modules and uses the sort of simple menu system that illustrates the basic methods of control flow.

To write this program, use the DOS COPY command to copy the final ASC-CHRT program you wrote in the last section to a new file. Then use your editor to edit the file. Copy the old **main( )** function so it appears twice. Type over the title **main( )** and replace it with a**sctoint( )** in one case and with **inttoasc( )** in the other.

The function **asctoint( )** does the same thing that the former program did. It gives you the ASCII integer value of the character you enter. You need only modify a few commands in the **inttoasc( )** version to make it give you the character of the ASCII integer you enter. It is easy to understand the changes if you look carefully at the next listing.

Improving the Program

Now you just need to figure out what the new **main( )** module that holds these programs together will look like. It must be some sort of a menu.

As a first try, you might just list the three choices, require the user to input one of the choices you have provided (by using a **while** loop, as you did previously), and then use a series of **if** statements to execute whatever choice the user makes, as follows:

/* Chapter 2, Example 5 */

```
main()                                  /* menu for ASCII chart program */
{
char menu Opt;

clrscrn();
printf("MENU  - ASCII CHART PROGRAM");
printf("\n-------------------------");
printf("\n\n\n1 - Look up the character for an ASCII number");
printf("\n\n2 - Look up the ASCII number of a character");
printf("\n\n3 - Quit");
menuOpt = ' ';
while(menuOpt != '1' && menuOpt != '2' && menuOpt != '3')
    {
    printf("\n\n\nWHAT IS YOUR CHOICE > ");
    scanf("\n%c",&menuOpt);
    }
if(menuOpt == '1')
    }
    inttoasc() ;
    }
if(menuOpt == '2')
    {
    asctoint() ;
    }
clrscrn() ;
}

asctoint                                /* print ASCII number for */
{                                       /* a given character */
char smplChr, again;
again = 'Y';
while(again == 'Y'; || again == 'y')
```

```
    {
    clrscrn() ;
    printf("\nWhat char do you want the ASCII value of > ");
    scanf("\n%c",&smplChr);
    printf("\nThe ASCII value of %c is %d\n", smplChr, smplChr);
    again = 'x';
    while(again != 'Y'; && again != 'y'
                                && again != 'N' && again ! = 'n')
        {
        printf("\nDo you want to look up another (Y/N) > ");
        scanf("\n%c",&again);
        }
    }
}

inttoasc()                              /* print character for a */
{                                       /* given ASCII number */
int smplInt;
char again;

again = 'Y';
while(again == 'Y' || again == 'y')
    {
    clrscrn();
    printf("\nWhat number do you want the ASCII char of > ")
    scanf("%d",&smplInt);
    printf("\nThe ASCII char for %d is %c\n",smplInt,smplInt);
    again = 'x';
    while(again != 'Y' && again != 'y'
                                &&again != 'N' && again ! = 'n')
        {
        printf("\n\nDo you want to look up another (Y/N) > ");
        scanf("n%c",&again);
        }
    }
}

clrscrn()                               /* clear the screen */
{
```

```
int counter;
counter = 0;
while(counter != 25)
     {
     printf("\n");
     counter = counter + 1;
     }
}
```

Take a while to examine the logic of this entire program before compiling and running it.

The Logic of the Program

With a program this long, it is often best to print the program file so you can line up the entire listing, one page above another. Then, examine the listing you printed and follow the program's logic.

The menu prints a title and three choices and forces you to enter a 1, 2, or 3. (Note that these numbers are treated as characters and always placed in a single quotes).

If you enter a 1, the program executes **inttoasc( )**, which takes an integer, gives you the ASCII character for it, and gives you the opportunity to do the same thing again.

When you finally choose not to do it again, you return to the location in which you left off in the **main( )** module—i.e., after the **if** statement that made the program execute **inttoasc( )**. Rather than having the statement **clrscrn( )** at the end of both **inttoasc( )** and **asctoint( )**, as in the earlier version of the program, this version uses a single **clrscrn( )** at the end of **main( )**, which is executed after the program returns from either of the other two functions. Because the condition of the second **if** statement is false, the program skips it, clears the screen, and control returns to the operating system.

The same sort of thing happens if you choose Option 2.

Option 3 is there in case the user changes his mind. After seeing the menu, the user might decide this is not the program he thought it was and therefore does not want to look up anything. The program accepts the user's input of 3 and exits from the **while** loop. Then it does not execute either of the following **if** statements. It simply falls through to the end of the program, clears the screen, and returns to the operating system.

Now, compile the program and run it. Test the three menu options and make sure the program flow is what it should be. This program flow is probably quite adequate for an ASCII chart program. People want to look up the ASCII values of characters or the characters for ASCII numbers but generally do not want to do both at once.

The If-Else-If Ladder

In most simple menu systems, however, you return to the main menu after executing one of the choices and must explicitly choose Quit after executing one of the options.

It makes sense to modify this program to make it more like a conventional simple menu system, both for illustrative purposes and just in case someone wants to look up both characters and values. You could also eliminate the "press any key to continue..." message from the **asctoint( )** and **inttoasc( )** modules. Instead, the user would return to the main menu and press 3 to quit the program.

To write a conventional menu system, you will use what is sometimes called an **if-else-if** ladder, which has the following form:

```
if(condition)
     {
     statement;
     statement;
     }
else if(condition)
     {
     statement;
     statement;
     }
else if(condition)
     {
     statement;
     statement;
     }
else
     {
     statement;
```

```
    statement;
    }
```

It is obvious what this listing does. If any of the conditions is true, the program executes the statements under that **if** or **else if**. If none of the conditions is true, the program executes the statements under the final **else**. (The final **else** is optional; if it is left out, the **if-else-if** ladder does nothing if none of the conditions is true.)

Adding an Error Message

This final **else** is very handy for giving error messages. If the user does not choose any of the correct options, the final **else** is executed automatically.

This simplest way of indicating an error, one that is very common in professional programs, is to have the computer beep and give the user the list of options again.

The beep is actually an ASCII character itself, ASCII character number 7. The statement **printf("%c",7)** "prints" 7 in ASCII "character" form: that is, it makes the computer beep.

Using \t

In addition, you can make the menu look better by using the special character **\t** in the **printf( )** statements. **\t** represents tab, as **\n** represents newline, and it can be used to indent a line.

For example, the statement **printf("\t\t\tMENU - ASCII CHART PROGRAM")** approximately centers the heading of the menu, and adding a few tabs before each choice makes the menu look more attractive.

Modifying the Code

To modify the program, then, copy the previous version to a new file, and edit the **main( )** module as follows. The menu is placed within a **while** loop—so it repeats until option 3 is entered--the **if/else** ladder is used, and a beep is added.

The entire program now looks like the following:

```
                    /* Chapter 2, Example 6 */
#include <stdio.h>

main()                          /* menu for ASCII chart program */
```

```
{
char menuOpt;

menuOpt = 'x';
while(menuOpt != '3')
    {
    clrscrn();
    printf("\t\t\tMENU - ASCII CHART PROGRAM");
    printf("\n\t\t\t--------------------------");
    printf("\n\n\n\n\n\n\n\n\t\t");
    printf("1 - Look up the character for an ASCII number");
    printf("\n\n\n");
    printf("\t\t2 - Look up the ASCII number of a character");
    printf("n\n\n\t\t3 - Quit");
    printf("\n\n\n\n\n\n\n\t\tWHAT IS YOUR CHOICE > ");
    scanf("n%c",&menuOpt);
    if(menuOpt == '1')
        {
        inttoasc();
        }
    else if(menuOpt == '2')
        {
        asctoint();
        }
    else if(menuOpt == '3')
        {
        clrscrn();
        }
    else
        {
        printf("%c",7);
        }
    }
clrscrn();
}

asctoint()                          /* print ASCII number for */
{                                   /* a given character*/
char smplChr, again;
```

```
again = 'Y';
while(again == 'Y' || again == 'y')
    {
    clrscrn();
    printf("\nWhat char do you want the ASCII value of > ");
    scanf("\n%c",&smplChr);
    printf("\nThe ASCII value of %c is %d\n",smplChr, smplChr);
    again = 'x';
    while(again != 'Y' && again != 'y'
                        && again != 'N' && again != 'n')
        {
        printf("\nDo you want to look up another (Y/N)> ");
        scanf("\n%c",&again);
        }
    }
}

inttoasc()                          /* print character for a */
{                                   /* given ASCII number */
int smplInt;
char again;
again = 'Y';
while(again == 'Y' || again == 'y'
    {
    clrscrn();
    printf("\nWhat number do you want the ASCII char of > ");
    scanf("%d",&smplInt);
    printf("\nASCII char %d is %c\n", smplInt, smplInt);
    again = 'x';
    while(again != 'Y' && again != 'y'
                        && again != 'N' && again !='n')
        {
        printf("\n\nDo you want to look up another (Y/N) > ");
        scanf("\n%c",&again);
        }
    }
}

clrscrn()                           /* clear the screen */
```

```
{
int counter;

counter = 0;
while(counter != 25)
    {
    printf("\n");
    counter = counter + 1;
    }
}
```

Compile and run this program.

You will notice that it handles errors in a much more professional-looking way than the last version did. Instead of just asking you "WHAT IS YOUR CHOICE >" over and over again if you do not enter 1,2, or 3,—and scrolling up the screen each time so that the menu eventually disappears entirely—the program beeps to call your attention to the fact that you have made an error, and it rewrites the entire screen so that the menu looks just as it did before.

You can play around with the **\n** and **\t** special characters in the **printf( )** statements until the screen looks just the way you want it to look.

A Note on Screen Control

This program is actually emulating full-screen control by rewriting the entire screen whenever a change is needed. You may find that it rewrites the screen slowly. Notice also that the **scanf( )** that receives user input must be at the bottom of the screen. In this program, that location is a good place for user input. In later programs in this book, user input looks a bit clumsy in that location.

The standard input-output package that comes with C includes relatively primitive I/O capabilities. The way the computer naturally works is by printing one line of text to the screen and then scrolling the whole screen up when it prints another line. In the bad old days before computers used the cathode ray tube—the television-like display that you have on your computer—they used a teletype to interact with the user, and it would type out instructions or error messages one line at a time and would require a carriage return and line feed after each line, like a typewriter.

You can still use MS-DOS in this way: though versions after DOS 4 also have a shell, you do not have to use it. You can simply type in commands one at a time, and the computer reads your input and print out error messages, directory listings, or whatever, one line at a time, scrolling the screen up after each line.

When you use most programs, however, you usually see an entire screen. A menu, a spreadsheet, a record from a database, or a page from a word-processing document is arranged attractively on the screen, and the user can move the cursor or click the mouse anywhere to select options or make changes. Of course, this interface is usually a great advantage: there are few things more tedious, for example, than using an old-fashioned line editor that requires you to select one line at a time to edit rather than having the full-screen editing capacity that is now standard for text editors and word processors.

Some computer languages have a built-in capacity to work with the full screen. BASIC for example, includes the LOCATE command. The statements

```
LOCATE 10,5
PRINT '*'
```

move the cursor down ten lines from the top of the screen and five lines in from the left and then prints an asterisk in this location. This feature allows you to receive input from the user anywhere on the center of the screen.

Because C is a low-level high-level language, its standard I/O package uses the computer's native mode of writing to the screen one line at a time, scrolling the screen up as it goes along. Controlling thê screen at a low level with C requires some rather detailed and technical commands.

There are many developers, however, who have taken advantage of the fact that C is an extensible language and have written libraries of routines for screen control, sometimes called *programmer's toolboxes.* You can buy packages that give you capacity not just for the simple cursor control provided by BASIC but also for creating enhanced text, blinking text, windows, multiple windows, popup menus, mouse support, and virtually anything else anyone would ever want to do in terms of screen control. Several low-cost shareware packages are available.

Because it teaches a generic version of C, however, this book uses only the standard input-output package for I/O in its sample programs, and, in fact, only uses some of the functions in that package.

It is generally not a good idea for beginners to spend much time learning C functions. When you are working on a project, you can find the functions you need in some library and learn them immediately, but when you are first studying C, learning one function after another is just a distraction from learning the concepts of the language. In any event, there is no way of predicting what library of screen-control functions you will finally decide to use.

Thus, the programs in this book just scroll up the screen one line at a time. As a result you can control the full screen only by clearing it and rewriting it entirely; and whenever you pause for user input, the cursor will be on the last line. Just remember that you have the potential for incomparably greater control of the screen when you start using additional libraries that extend the language.

A Few Extra Tricks

Writing this menu system has taken you a long way. Professional programmers used to spend much of their time writing menu systems that work very much like the one you have just written—in dBASE, Pascal, and many other languages, as well as in C.

The basic ideas about control flow apply to almost any structured programming language. Once you have learned concepts such as these, it becomes easy to learn new languages.

Testing

After a program is developed, it usually goes through a long period of testing. Ideally, programs should not be tested by the programmers who write them. The programmers already have a fixed idea of how the program logic works and what cases it should cover, and they tend to test for those cases. If other people perform the testing, they are much more likely to look at possibilities that the original programmers ignored. In practice, however, particularly in the world of microcomputers, custom programs are often written by consultants who work on their own and must do their own testing.

When you are testing, it is good to imagine that you are an inexperienced user who might want to do unexpected things. Run the program and try to make every conceivable choice that a user might make.

Be sure to test the most extreme possibilities. If you are working with text, for example, enter a very long string and see what the program does with that string, and enter a string that has no letters in it at all (just press Enter) and see what the program does with that information. If you are working with numbers, enter a very large number, enter zero, and enter a negative number, and see what the program does with each of them. These extreme cases will most likely turn up the bugs in your program.

Try testing each of the menu options in your ASCII chart program. You should not have any major difficulties entering a character and getting its ASCII number. There will be minor errors if you enter more than one character or a carriage return without a character, which you will learn to deal with after you have learned about strings.

Errors with Numeric Input

On the other hand, when you try entering numbers and getting ASCII characters for them, you will find the program works perfectly well for medium range numbers but gives you bizarre results if you enter a letter or if you enter small, large, or negative numbers.

To correct the first problem by screening out letters and accepting only numbers from the user, you would need to make the program read the number as a string and then check that string and use it only if all digits were entered.

Though it is not difficult, you cannot perform this type of error checking until you have learned to work with strings. For that reason, such error checking is omitted from the sample programs in this book but is covered in more detail in Chapter 8.

Errors with ASCII Input

It is easier to correct the other problems, which occur because there are only 128 standard ASCII characters, as you have seen, and 256 characters (numbered from 0 to 255) in the extended ASCII character set used by the IBM-PC.

Telling the computer to print the ASCII character for any number larger than this limit is telling it to do something impossible.

In addition, the ASCII characters numbered 00 through 31 are control characters. If you enter some of these characters, the program completes the statement you are printing to the screen with a symbol that stands for a control character, such as a smiling face. In other cases, the program performs the action that the character represents. For example, if you enter a 7, it completes the statement by beeping. In some cases, it just ends the statement with a blank.

ASCII character 32 is a space, and having the chart print it would only confuse the reader. Character 255 is unprintable.

To protect users of your program from being confused by this sort of screen display, you must write what are called *error-trapping routines*—parts of the program that anticipate any errors people might make and give them relatively user-friendly messages telling them, in essence, that they are not allowed to do what they are attempting. To trap errors in this program, you must bypass the **inttoasc( )** function when the user enters a number that is less than 33 or greater than 254 (on the IBM-PC).

The Logical Operators

This routine requires new logical operators, representing "less than" and "greater than," that will probably look familiar to you.

All of the logical operators are summarized in the following chart, with the new operators at the end:

<table>
<tr><th>Symbol</th><th>Meaning</th></tr>
<tr><td>&&</td><td>and</td></tr>
<tr><td>| |</td><td>or</td></tr>
<tr><td>!</td><td>not</td></tr>
<tr><td>==</td><td>is equal to</td></tr>
<tr><td>!=</td><td>is not equal to</td></tr>
<tr><td>></td><td>is greater than</td></tr>
<tr><td><</td><td>is less than</td></tr>
<tr><td>>=</td><td>is greater than or equal to</td></tr>
<tr><td><=</td><td>is less than or equal to</td></tr>
</table>

Sometimes, only the first three of these symbols are called logical operators and the rest are called relational operators. On the other hand, sometimes the first three are called *Boolean*, and logical operators is often used as a general term that includes them all.

The four new operators in this chart are identical to the symbols used in algebra and should be easy to understand. For example, the condition **if(counter > 10)** is true if the variable named **counter** has a value that is greater than 10 and false if that variable has a value that is less than or equal to 10.

Trapping Errors

Using these new operators, you can easily screen out the errors in the **inttoasc( )** module. You receive the number from the user as always, but you must take the part of the module that prints the character for that number and make sure it executes only if the number is within the right range. To do this, you must place this part of the module within an **if-else** statement in the following form:

```
if(smplInt < 33 || smplInt > 254)
     {
     PRINT SOME ERROR MESSAGE
     }
else
     {
     PRINT THE ASCII CHARACTER FOR smplInt
     }
```

Note that the condition uses || (or). You want to print the error message if either of the conditions is true (if the number entered is less than 33 or the number entered is greater than 254).

If you are working on a computer other than an IBM-PC, you may have only 128 ASCII characters, numbered from 0 to 127, and you should modify this program accordingly. For you, the condition is as follows:

```
if(smplInt < 33 || smplInt > 126).
```

With this error-trapping added, the **inttoasc( )** module reads as follows:

```
                    /* Chapter 2, Example 7 */
           /* use as replacement of inttoasc( ) in Example 6 */

inttoasc()                          /* print character for a */
{                                   /* given ASCII number */
int smplInt;                        /* with error trapping*/
char again;

again = 'Y';
while(again == 'Y' || again == 'y')
```

```
    {
    clrscrn();
    printf("\nWhat number do you want the ASCII char of > ");
    scanf("%d",&smplInt);
    if(smplInt < 33 || smplInt > 254)
        {
        printf("\nThe number must be between 33 and 254");
        }
    else
        {
        printf("\nASCII char %d is %c\n", smplInt, smplInt);
        }
    again = 'x';
    while(again != 'Y' && again != 'y'
                            && again != 'N' && again != 'n')
        {
        printf("n\nDo you want to look up another (Y/N)> ");
        scanf("\n%c",&again);
        }
    }
}
```

This is another example of nesting one form of program control inside another. In this case, the **if-then** is nested within a **while** loop.

Nesting seems complicated when it is described in this way, but it is very easy to understand if you have developed it logically one step at a time and if you indent properly, as in the example. Often, programs nest five or six loops and conditions within each other, and the logic is still not hard to understand.

Improving the clrscrn( ) Function

There is one other modification to the program that you can make now that you know these new operators.

In the **clrscrn( )** function, you used the condition **while(counter != 25)** to make the loop stop executing after it had printed a new line twenty-four times. This program is so simple that nothing can go wrong when you use this condition, but as a general matter of programming style, it is much better to use < (less than) or > (greater than) to control loops. It is always possible that, for some reason you did not foresee, the counter does not exactly equal that number before becoming greater than it.

The danger is particularly great if you have a condition that involves floating decimal point numbers because of the possibility of what are referred to as *rounding errors.* Remember that the computer uses binary numbers, and its fractions only approximately represent the decimal numbers that you use, so it may round off a fraction into decimal form in a way that the programmer did not anticipate, and the counter never exactly equals the condition the programmer set up to end the loop.

You should not even need to think about this sort of problem, and so it is best to use > or < for loop control. You should modify **clrscrn( )** by changing the condition from **while(counter != 25)** to **while(counter < 25)**.

Controlling Looping

There are a few other points of style that you should know about control flow. It is sometimes necessary and often useful stylistically to control looping explicitly using the statements **break;** and **continue;**. Even when they are not necessary, these statements can make the flow of logic clearer to the programmer.

break;

The statement **break;** will, as the name implies, simply break you out of a loop. The program continues executing with the next statement after the end of the loop.

Notice that **break;** does not end with parentheses. It is one of the relatively few commands in C that is actually part of the language—not a function in a library.

The statement **break;** can be used as a clearer way of writing menus. Instead of placing the condition for quitting the menu up at the top as part of the **while( )** statement, you can put the condition for quitting within the loop, where it is obviously parallel with the other choices. This strategy becomes very clear if you examine the menu in the last version of the ASCII chart program, which has the following general form:

```
menuOpt = 'x'
while(menuOpt != '3')
    {
```

```
    ...
    DISPLAY MENU AND GET OPTION 1, 2 OR 3
    ...
    if (menuOpt == '1')
            {
            inttoasc();
            }
    else if (menuOpt == '2')
            {
            asctoint();
            }
    else if (menuOpt == '3')
            {
            clrscrn();
            }
    else
            {
            printf("%c",7);
            }
    }
 clrscrn();
}
```

Reading through the **if-else** ladder, you will not immediately see why the screen is simply cleared if the choice is 3. You must return to the **while( )** function to see that you are not only clearing the screen but also exiting from the program, which can make longer menus more difficult to understand, modify, or debug.

Many programmers would prefer to rewrite this menu as something like the following:

```
while(1==1)
    {
    . . .
    DISPLAY MENU AND GET OPTION 1, 2 OR 3
    . . .
    if(menuOpt == '1')
           {
           inttoasc();
           }
```

```
        else if(menuOpt == '2')
                {
                asctoint();
                }
        else if(menuOpt == '3')
                {
                clrscrn();
                break;
                }
        else
                {
                printf("%c",7);
                }
        }
clrscrn();
}
```

First, you deliberately set up an infinite loop with the condition **while(1==1)**. Because it is always true that 1 is equal to 1, this loop would ordinarily continue forever.

Instead, the loop is interrupted when the statement **break;** is executed if the user chooses menu option 3. The flow of program control does not return to the top of the **while** loop to evaluate the condition again. It breaks out of the loop and continues with the next statement after the loop's final curly bracket. In this example, of course, there is no next statement, and the program simply ends.

Looking at these two versions of the menu, you can probably see that it is easier to take in at a glance what the program is doing in the version using **break;** because everything that is happening is within the **if-else** ladder.

exit( );

Another statement that is a bit like **break;** is **exit( );**. The difference is that, while **break;** only takes you out of the current loop, **exit( );** takes you out of the program entirely and returns you to the operating system.

In the example you just examined, there would be one difference if you used **exit( );** instead of **break;**. The program would not execute the **clrscrn( );** command that follows the final } of the **while** loop. Instead of just exiting the loop, it would exit the entire program.

continue;

The statement **continue;** is almost the opposite of **break;**. Rather than breaking you out of the bottom of the loop, it takes you immediately back to the top of the loop and checks the condition there again.

One place that this statement can be useful is when you are performing error-trapping and do not want to nest the entire program inside of an **if-else** statement. The difficult way to do this sort of error trapping would be as follows:

```
while(condition)
    {
    GET INPUT FROM USER
    if(errorCondition)
        {
        PRINT ERROR MESSAGE
        }
    else
        {
        DO 500 LINES OF CODE
        }
    }
```

Like the ASCII chart program, the previous program should not be executed if the user does the wrong thing. Because this is a much longer program, however, it is confusing to put it all within the **else** portion of an **if-else** statement. By the time you reach the end, you could forget why it is doubly indented. The program is easier to read and understand in the following form:

```
while(condition)
    {
    GET INPUT FROM USER
    {
    if(errorCondition)
        {
        PRINT ERROR MESSAGE
        continue;
        }
    DO 500 LINES OF CODE
    }
```

In case of an error a message is displayed and the statement **continue;** directs the flow of the program back to the **while( )** at the top of the loop, bypassing the 500 lines of code you want to avoid (without nesting the 500 lines within an **if-else** statement).

goto labelname;

Finally, most discussions of controlling program flow in C end with a slightly shame-faced confession that C does actually contain a **goto** statement, which must be used in combination with a **label**, as follows:

```
if(condition)
     {
     goto nextstep;
     }
50 LINES OF CODE
nextstep:
500 MORE LINES OF CODE
```

If the condition is true, the program's flow of control skips over the fifty lines of code and moves to the label **nextstep:**. C knows this is a label because it ends with a colon.

You will see similar use of **goto** and labels in Assembly Language and in some other programming languages, so it is good to be familiar with it.

As you know, the use of **goto** has been generally discredited by the rise of structured programming, and most C programmers never use it. The example you just looked at is terrible programming style.

Yet there are times when **goto** can be useful. You can use it to escape from a deeply nested series of loops, for example, as follows:

```
while(condition}
     {
     DO CODE
     while(condition}
          {
          DO MORE
          while(condition)
               {
               DO YET MORE
```

```
            while(condition)
                {
                DO EVEN MORE
                if(errorCondition)
                {
                goto end;
                }
            DO YET MORE .
            }
        DO MORE
        }
    DO CODE
    }
end:
```

If you used **break;** instead of **goto end;** that would only take you of the innermost loop, and you would need to write some tricky code in four places to break out of all four loops.

Only in a situation like this are you beginning to reach a point at which you might be justified in considering using a **goto** statement.

Summary

In this chapter, you learned the basic forms of control flow used in structured programming.

Structured programming uses the following three methods of controlling program flow:

- sequence
- selection
- iteration

Sequence means performing one statement after another in the same order in which the statements appear in the program.

Iteration means repeating (or reiterating) the same procedure and can be done in C using the **while** loop, which takes the following form:

```
while(condition)
     {
     statement;
     statement;
     }
```

If the condition is true, the program performs the statements within the curly brackets. When it encounters the final bracket, it loops back up to the condition. If the condition is still true, the program performs these statements again. If the condition is false, the program continues to whatever statements follow the final curly bracket. There must be some statement within the curly brackets that eventually makes the condition false, or else the loop will continue indefinitely.

Selection can be performed using the **if-else** statement, which takes the following form:

```
if(condition)
     {
     statement;
     statement;
     }
else
     {
     statement;
     statement;
     }
```

If the condition is true, the statements in the curly brackets following it are executed. If it is false, the statements in the curly brackets following **else** are executed. The **else** may be omitted, and nothing is done if the condition is false.

You may choose among a larger number of options, using the **if-else-if** ladder.

In either the **while** loop or the **if-else** statement, the conditions must include logical operators, which are evaluated as true or false. The following chart summarizes these operators:

Symbol	**Meaning**
&&	and
||	or
!	not
==	is equal to
!=	is not equal to
>	is greater than
<	is less than
>=	is greater than or equal to
<=	is less than or equal to

You may combine other operators in a single condition, using **&&** or **||**. If **&&** is used, both (or all) conditions must be true for the entire statement to be true. If || is used, either (or any) condition may be true and the entire statement is true.

The following statements are used for controlling program flow:

- **break;**—breaks out of the loop and executes the command following its final curly bracket.
- **exit( );**—terminates the program and returns the user to the operating system.
- **continue;**—immediately returns to the **while** at the beginning of loop and checks its condition again.
- **goto labelName;**—must be used in combination with a label followed by a colon elsewhere in the program and should be avoided.

while loops and **if-else** statements may be nested within one another, and—though the compiler does not require it—it is very important to indent them properly in order to follow their logic.

Chapter 3

Numbers and Arrays

In this chapter, you develop a sample program that tests the user in arithmetic: The user select from the main menu whether to be tested in addition, subtraction, multiplication, or division.

This sample program is more complex than any you have developed so far, and requires several new techniques. In addition to giving you practice in what you have already learned, it teaches you about:

- creating and using arrays, groups of variables that have the same name but use different numbers as subscripts
- using the arithmetic operators for addition, subtraction, multiplication, division, and modulo division
- understanding precedence of operation in arithmetic
- using parentheses to change the precedence of operation
- knowing when to use global and local variables

The Array

The *array* is a basic element of computer programming and is particularly important in the C language. Yet it is really nothing more than an easy way to keep track of lists.

Keeping track of long lists—for example, of data about all of a business's employees or all of an organization's members—is one of the most common uses of computers, but it would be very unwieldy to keep track of this information by using the sorts of variables you have already learned about.

Imagine, for example, that you need a program that lets you enter an employee's weekly wages for every week of the year. To create this program using ordinary variables, you would need to begin by declaring 52 variables, with names like **wageWk1**, **wageWk2**, **wageWk3**, and so on, and then you would need to write over 100 lines of code to allow your data entry person to enter an amount for each week. The program would look like the following:

```
main()                        /* enter wages for each week */
{                                   /* written the hard way */
float wageWk1, wageWk2, wageWk3 . . .
         FORTY SEVEN MORE VARIABLES
         . . . wageWk51, wageWk52;

printf("\nEnter the wage for week 1 > ");
scanf("%f", &wageWk1);
printf("\nEnter the wage for week 2 > ");
scanf("%f", &wageWk2);
printf("\nEnter the wage for week 3 > ");
scanf("\n%f", &wageWk3);
. . .
NINETY-FOUR MORE LINES OF CODE
. . .
printf("\nEnter the wage for week 51 > ");
scanf("%f", &wageWk51);
printf("\nEnter the wage for week 52 > ");
scanf("%f", &wageWk52);
}
```

This program requires a great deal of unnecessary work, and it is just the sort of repetitive work that the computer can do for you.

Declaring an Array

All you need to do to make your life easier is declare all of these variables as an array, using the following statement:

```
float wageWk[52];
```

This statement automatically creates fifty-two variables, with names ranging from **wagewk[0]** through **wageWk[51]**. Each of these variables is called an *element* of the array. The number in brackets is sometimes called a *subscript*, and you can read these names as wageWk "sub zero" and "wageWK sub fifty-one."

You must declare the array as one of the ordinary data types so the compiler knows how much space to reserve in memory for each element of the array. You use **float** in this case because you are keeping track of money, but in other cases, you would create arrays of **int**s, and **char**s. Then, to tell the compiler how many elements the array has, you must give the array a name that ends with a number in square brackets.

The one slightly tricky thing about working with arrays in C is that the number in the declaration is one greater than the index number of the highest numbered variable you create. In this example of weekly wages, for instance, the variable is declared as **wageWk[52]**, but the elements are numbered up to **wageWk[51]**. The declaration tells you the actual number of elements in the array, but because numbering begins with **wageWk[0]**, the program only needs to go up to **wageWk[51]** for the array to have fifty-two elements all together.

In more advanced applications, it is often very convenient to have the numbering of arrays begin with 0. When you are first learning, it is a bit tricky, but you get used to it rather quickly.

A Sample Program with an Array

Note how much easier it is to write the weekly wage program you just looked at, if you use an array:

```
                          /* Chapter 3, Example 1 */

#include <stdio.h>

main()                          /* enter wages for each week */
```

```
{                                       /* written the easy way */
float wageWk[52];
int cntr, numofwks;

printf("\nHow many weeks of wages do you want to enter? ");
scanf("%d",&numofwks);
cntr = 0;
while (cntr < numofwks && cntr < 52)
     {
     printf("\nEnter the wage for week %d > ", cntr+1;)
     scanf("%f",&wageWk[cntr]);
     cntr = cntr + 1;
     }
```

You simply use a **while** loop to go through all of the elements of the array. The same variable, **cntr**, that you use for controlling the number of times you pass through the loop can also be used to index the array and give it values from **wageWk[0]** through **wageWk[51]**.

This example also lets you enter a smaller number of weeks, so you can test the program without having to go through the loop fifty-two times. Note that the condition of the **while( )** statement requires the number of times through the loop both to be smaller than fifty-two and to be smaller than the number of weeks you entered.

A Simpler Version of the Sample Program

The one slightly tricky thing about this program is its use of **cntr+1** as the number of the week. Again, this is because you begin numbering the array with 0, but you want to ask the user to enter values beginning with week number 1. If you find this a bit confusing, look at this slightly longer version of the program, which is easier to understand:

```
                    /* Chapter 3, Example 2 */
#include <stdio.h>

main()                              /* enter wages for each week */
{                                   /* the easy-to-understand way */
float wageWk[52];
```

```
int cntr, numofwks, weekNmbr;

printf("\nHow many weeks of wages do you want to enter? ");
scanf("%d", &numofwks);

cntr = 0;
weekNmbr = 1;
while(cntr < numofwks && cntr < 52)
     {
     printf("\nEnter the wage for week %d > ", weekNmbr);
     scanf("%f", &wageWk[cntr]);
     cntr = cntr + 1;
     weekNmbr = weekNmbr + 1;
     }
}
```

Here, you create a separate variable, **weekNmbr**, which is only used in the **printf( )** statement that asks the user to enter the wages for a given week, numbered from 1 to 52. If the first version of this program puzzled you, look at this version carefully, and you will see that the variable **weekNmbr** is always one greater than the variable **cntr**.

The Power of Arrays

Using an array saved you the trouble of writing close to 100 lines of code in this sample program alone. Of course, in an actual program, you would not just be getting the figures for each week's wages, but you would be doing things with these figures as well, and you would save yourself the same trouble each time you worked with them.

Perhaps later in the program, you will need to add all of the weekly wage figures in order to get a figure for the total yearly wages. You could do that very easily by adding a few extra lines to the program, as follows:

```
                        /* Chapter 3, Example 3 */
#include < stdio.h>

main()                         /* enter wages for each week */
{                              /* and calculate yearly wage */
float wageWk[52];
```

```
int cntr, numofwks;
float yrlyWage;

printf("\nHow many weeks of wages do you want to enter? " ) ;
scanf("%d", &numofwks);

cntr = 0;                    /* get each week's wages */
while(cntr <numofwks && cntr <52)
    {
    printf("/nEnter the wage for week %d > ",cntr+1);
    scanf("%f", &wageWk[cntr]);
    cntr = cntr + 1;
    }

yrlyWage = 0;                    /* add all weekly wages */
cntr = 0;
while(cntr < numofwks && cntr < 52)
    {
    Yrlywage = yrlyWage + wageWk[cntr];
    cntr = cntr + 1;
    }
printf("n\nThe total yearly wage is %f" ,yrlyWage);
}
```

The new addition to the program starts with a yearly wage of 0. Then it adds the wage for week 0, the wage for week 1, and so on through week 51 to get the entire year's wage.

When you test this program, you may find more examples of rounding errors, which occur when the computer converts the binary numbers it uses into the decimal numbers it displays; for example, if you enter a wage of **10.10** per week for four weeks, the program might say the total is **40.400002**. This degree of precision is adequate for working with money. Chapter 8 explains how to use double-precision floats and how to use **printf( )** to make floats display only two decimal points.

Remember that simply adding the wages for the year would take over fifty lines of extra code if you were using ordinary variables instead of an array, and you can begin to appreciate how much programming time and effort you can save by using arrays.

An Arithmetic Quiz Program

Arrays are most often used for going through a list from top to bottom, as in the previous example, but they can also be used in more creative ways. In the rest of this chapter, you develop a simple arithmetic quiz program, using an array of ten numbers to simulate a much longer list of numbers.

The program begins with a menu that gives users the choice of whether they want addition, subtraction, multiplication, or division problems. Because this is a simple program, the problems all use one-digit numbers—that is, numbers from zero to nine.

The Programming Problem

The problem for the programmer is how to give a long series of these problems without there being any obvious repetition.

Your first impulse might be to use a long list of numbers, perhaps a list of 100 numbers between zero and nine, arranged in random order, so the program could go through this whole list for its examples. You would begin the program by declaring an array, a counter to take you through the array, and a variable to get the answer from the user:

```
int nmbr[100];
int cntr;
int answer;
```

Then you would need a module to *initialize* the array—to give each of the variables from **nmbr[0]** to **nmbr[99]** a value.

Displaying the Test for the User

The modules that test the user could then contain loops that look something like the following:

```
cntr = 0
while(cntr<98)
     {
     printf("%d + %d = ", nmbr[cntr], nmbr[cntr+1]);
     scanf("%d", &answer);
     if(answer==nmbr[cntr]+nmbr[cntr+1])
```

```
                {
                printf("\nRIGHT!!");
                cntr = cntr + 2;
                }
        else
                {
                printf("\nwrong");
                }
    }
```

Note that when you use the symbols + and = here as parts of the string within quotation marks displayed by the **printf( )** statement, the program simply uses them as characters and does not use them to perform any arithmetic operations.

If **nmbr[cntr]** happens to equal 6, for example, and **nmbr[cntr+1]** happens to equal 3, the statement.

```
printf("%d + %d = ", nmbr[cntr], nmbr[cntr+1]);
```

simply displays the following on the screen,

```
    6 + 3 =
```

and the **scanf( )** statement that follows the **print( )** statement displays the cursor where the answer should go and waits for the user's response.

This example is a stripped-down version of the program. The actual program would include a title at the top of the screen and could also give clues in case of a wrong answer. This version simply shows how you would go through the list of numbers to use them in your problems.

Avoiding Repetition in Other Modules

More repetition becomes possible when you start to write the other modules.

If you begin them with **nmbr[0]** and go right through the list, as you did with addition, what you are doing will be fairly obvious even to children who are still learning arithmetic. They will not be overly impressed when they see that the first addition problem is, say, 7 plus 4, the first subtraction problem is 7 minus 4, the first multiplication problem is 7 times 4, and the first division problem is 7 divided by 4—and that there is the same mysterious correspondence among the other problems.

The obvious solution is to begin each different module with a different value of **cntr** so each begins at a different point in the list, and to make some modules work with **nmbr[cntr]** and **nmbr[cntr+2]** or **nmbr[cntr+3]**, rather than having all of them use **nmbr [cntr]** and **nmbr[cntr+1**.

One Solution

Now, you can actually apply this idea of varying the value of **cntr** more generally and make this program easier to write. Instead of using an array of 100 numbers, use an array of just ten numbers: all of the numbers from zero to nine arranged in random order. Then you can go through that list over and over again, varying the value of the counters so that it is not obvious that you are just going through the same array of nine numbers each time.

The module to initialize the values of the nine variables in the list would not be difficult to write. It would look something like the following:

```
initlze()
{
nmbr[0] = 3;
nmbr[1] = 5;
nmbr[2] = 0;
nmbr[3] = 9;
nmbr[4] = 6;
nmbr[5] = 1;
nmbr[6] = 7;
nmbr[7] = 2;
nmbr[8] = 8;
nmbr[9] = 4;
}
```

That strategy is much less work than initializing 100 variables and trying to make sure that the numbers are random while you are doing it.

It is easy to go through the list over and over again. If you add the following bit of code within the loop you use to go through the array of 100 variables,

```
if(cntr>9)
      {
      cntr = cntr - 10
      }
```

then the program keeps increasing the value of **cntr** by two each time through the loop, as it did before. But when the value of **cntr** reaches 10, this extra bit of code makes it equal to zero and start again at the beginning of the array, with **nmbr[0]**.

A Better Solution

You also need to worry about **cntr+1** being greater than nine. And it would be good to vary the spacing between the two numbers that the problems use. There is no need to always work with **nmbr[cntr]** and **nmbr[cntr+1]**. The program would do better at avoiding repetition if it could switch to working with **nmbr[cntr]** and **nmbr[cntr+2]** and later to working with **nmbr[cntr]** and **nmbr[cntr+3]**.

The easiest way to deal with these problems is by using two counters, **cntrA** and **cntrB**, along with a third variable, which could be called **diff**, (for difference). Then, it would not be difficult to vary the value of **diff**, to make **cntrB** equal **cntrA** plus **diff**, and to check **cntrA** and **cntrB** separately to see if either of them is greater than 9. Of course, you would also need to check **diff** to make sure it did not become too large.

With these changes, the stripped-down version of the addition module that you looked at previously would be as follows:

```
cntrA = 0;
diff = 1;
cntrB = cntrA + diff;

while(1==1)
    {
    printf("%d + %d = ", nmbr[cntrA],nmbr[cntrB]);
    scanf("%d",&answer);
    if (answer==nmbr[cntrA]+nmbr[cntrB])
        {
        printf("\nRIGHT!!");
        }
    else
        {
        printf("\nwrong");
        continue;
        }
```

```
cntrA = cntrA + 2;
if(cntrA>9)
        {
        cntrA = cntrA - 10;
        diff = diff + 1;
        }
if(diff>9)
        {
        diff = 2;
        }
cntrB = cntrA + diff;
if(cntrB>9)
        {
        cntrB = cntrB - 10;
        }
```

The logic here is not all that difficult to follow, but it is worthwhile to look at it carefully because much of what computer programmers do involves thinking up clever ways of writing code to eliminate repetitious programming work, as this code does.

The first half of the module does the same thing as the earlier fragmentary example: It displays the problem with the current values of the variables, for example,

```
3 + 5 =
```

followed by a blinking cursor, and then it waits for the answer and checks if the answer is right or wrong.

The entire second half of the program is devoted to changing the value of the variables.

The first time through, the program just makes **cntrA** equal 2 and **cntrB** equal 3, and the other conditions would not apply.

The fifth time through, however, after the program goes through the entire list once, **cntrA** is equal to 10, so the first **if( )** condition does not apply. As a result, **cntrA** would be made 0 again, and **diff** is made 2. The second **if( )** condition does not apply, so **cntrB** remains 9, and the problem is **nmbr[0]** plus **nmbr[9]**, a combination you did not have before.

The next time through, **cntrA** would be incremented by the usual 2. The statement **cntrB = cntrA + diff;** makes **cntrB** equal to 4 this time, so that the problem is **nmbr[2] + nmbr[4]**, another combination you did not have before.

So the program would go, with new combinations coming up all of the time. Trace in your own mind how the combinations go as **diff** becomes larger at the end of every five loops.

Again, this is just a stripped-down version of the addition module, used to show its logic. The actual module will have a better screen display, and the user will even have the option of exiting rather than remaining in this infinite loop forever.

The Arithmetic Operators

Before you write this program, you need to learn the **arithmetic operators** in C. Most of these operators will look familiar to you: in fact, you have already been using one, + for addition, without even thinking about it. The arithmetic operators are as follows:

+	addition
-	subtraction
*	multiplication
/	division
%	modulo division (remainder)

These same symbols are used in most computer languages and in programs such as spreadsheets.

The symbols for the four basic operations are for the most part the same ones you used in elementary arithmetic, the exception being that the asterisk * is used for multiplication instead of the usual times sign (**x**) to avoid confusion with the letter 'x'.

Modulo division is the only symbol that needs any explanation, and it simply gives you what elementary school teachers call the "remainder" from division. For example, 20 % 6 is equal to 2. That is, 20 divided by 6 is 3 with a remainder of 2, and the equation **20 % 6** gives you just the remainder from the division equation.

Displaying the Results of Division Problems

Keep in mind that the result of the division problem depends on whether the number you are dividing is declared as an integer or a float.

For example, the following program prints **10.000000/3.000000 = 3.333333** on the screen, which is just what you would expect if you remembered that the default display for floats is six decimal points.

```
                        /* Chapter 3, Example 4 */
#include <stdio.h>

main()                  /* sample of float division */
{
float dividend, divisor, answer;
dividend = 10;
divisor = 3;
answer = dividend/divisor;
printf("\n%f / %f = %f",dividend,divisor,answer);
}
```

On the other hand, this next program prints **10 / 3 = 3** on the screen. It works only with integer values and drops any decimals.

```
                        /* Chapter 3, Example 5 */
#include <stdio.h>

main()                  /* sample of integer division */
{
int dividend, divisor, answer;
dividend = 10;
divisor = 3;
answer = dividend/divisor;
printf("\n%d / %d = %d",dividend,divisor,answer);
}
```

There are times when programmers actually want only integer results, but in this simple quiz program, you use a method that gives the remainder as well, something like the following:

```
                    /* Chapter 3, Example 6 */
#include <stdio.h>

main()                          /* sample of integer division */
{                                            /* with remainder */
int dvidnd, dvisr, answr, remndr;
dvidnd = 10;
dvisr = 3;
answr = dvidnd / dvisr;
remndr = dvidnd % dvisr;
printf("\n%d / %d = %d R %d", dvidnd, dvisr,. answr remndr);
}
```

This program prints **10 / 3 = 3 R 1** on the screen.

Precedence of Operation

There is one other term about computer arithmetic that probably needs clarification. In computer jargon, this term is *precedence of operation*, which means deciding what operation is performed first.

In ordinary arithmetic, for example, you might interpret the problem **3 * 4 + 1** in two different ways:

- Multiply 3 times 4 first, getting 12, and then add 1 for a final answer of 13.
- Add 4 plus 1 first, getting 5, and then multiply by 3 for a final answer of 15.

Precedence makes a difference. If you multiply first, you do not get the same answer you get by adding first.

In arithmetic, you can either add or multiply first. In algebra, however, there is a set order of precedence, which you probably know without thinking about it. For example, if you knew that **n = 4** you would, without any hesitation, say that the value of **3n + 1** is equal to 13. In algebra, you generally perform multiplication and division before addition and subtraction.

The same is true in C and in most computer languages and applications you will ever come across. The problem **3 * 4 + 1** does not have two different answers: the answer is 13 because C gives precedence to multiplication and division over addition and subtraction. First it multiplies 3 times 4 to get 12, then it adds 1 to that result for a final answer of 13.

You can alter this order of precedence in C by using parentheses, just as you can in ordinary mathematics.

For example, in mathematics, if the problem were **(3 * 4) + 1**, you would know that you had to perform the multiplication first so that the answer is 13. But if the problem were **3 * (4 + 1)**, you would know that you had to perform the addition first, with the result being 15. You can also use parentheses this way in C and in most computer languages and applications to control precedence. If you rewrote the previous C formula as **3 * (4 + 1),** the answer would be the expected 15.

It is generally better programming style to use parentheses in any complex calculation, even if they just tell the computer to do things in the same order as it would through its normal order of precedence. Such notation make things easier to understand for any humans who must read the program at a later time For example, **(3 * 4) + 1** is better style than **3 * 4 + 1**, even though the answers are the same.

Incidentally, you can also use parentheses with logical operators to alter precedence.

For example, **if (x==1 && (y==2 || z==3))** is true only if it is true that **x==1** *and* it is also true that either **y==2** or **z==3**. On the other hand, **if((x==1 && y==2) || z==3)** is true if it is true both that **x==1** and that **y==2** or it is true that **z==3**. Without parentheses, the **&&** has precedence, but with logical conditions, it is always better to use parentheses to reduce—if not avoid—confusion.

Global and Local Variables

Before you begin to write the arithmetic quiz program, there is one more very basic programming concept you must know to handle this program's variables. In all of the programs you have looked at so far, each variable has been used by only one function. In this program, there are variables that are used by many functions.

The array of numbers must be given values by the **initlze( )** function and must also be accessible to the functions that display the addition, subtraction, multiplication, and division problems.

Local Variables and Structured Programming

Ordinary variables, the type you have used so far, are not shared between modules in this way, and the reason is fairly obvious. Because C is a structured language, it is necessary to keep modules as independent from each other as possible.

This is particularly important in making it an extensible language, which you can add to by writing libraries of new functions. Often, programmers work with libraries of functions that they have not studied in detail, just as you have used the functions such as **printf( )** and **scanf( )** without looking at the details of how they are written. What if one of these functions happens to have a variable with the same name as one of the variables in another module you were writing?

If the variables in each function were not strictly segregated from each other, the results could be disastrous. For example, consider the program from the beginning of this chapter, which had the user enter a worker's wages for each week of the year. Imagine that you suddenly remember that you wrote a function called **clrscrn( )** for another project a few months before and put it into a library, that you decide the wage entry program would look nicer if it cleared the screen after each week's wages, and that you write an **#include** statement so you can use that library and function in the program.

If you wrote both the new program and the library function together, so you could look at them more closely, the code would look like the following:

```
                              /* Chapter 3, Example 7 */
#include <stdio.h>

main()                /* enter wages for each week */
{                     /* written with clrscrn() */
float wageWk[52];
int cntr, numofwks;

printf("\nHow many weeks of wages do you want to enter? ");
scanf ("%d", &numofwks);

cntr = 0;
while(cntr < numofwks && cntr < 52)
    {
    printf("Enter the wage for week %d > ",cntr+1);
    scanf("%f",&wageWk[cntr]);
```

```
        cntr = cntr + 1;
        clrscrn();
        }
}

clrscrn()                        /* clear the screen */
{
int cntr;
cntr = 0;
while(cntr < 25)
        {
        printf("\n");
        cntr = cntr + 1;
        }
}
```

Within this program, you have set up a nice little loop to read the wage for every week, incrementing the variable **cntr** each time through to control the loop, but you cannot be expected to remember that **clrscrn( )** also used the variable **cntr**.

If variables in different modules were not segregated from each other, this program would be a mess.

At the end of each loop in the **main( )** module, **clrscrn( )** would be used and would leave **cntr** equal to 25. Starting with the second time through, the program would go on endlessly asking for the wages for week twenty-six and storing the input in **wageWk[25]**. It would always satisfy the condition of the main loop, **while(cntr < 52)**, so it would never terminate.

Alternatively, if the user entered a number of weeks that is less than 25, the other half of the condition of the main loop, **while(cntr < numofwks)**, would not be satisfied, and the program would end without getting wages for a second week.

The problem is easy to see in this short program, but you can imagine how difficult it could be to find and debug problems like this in a program that is fifty pages long, if variables in different functions were not strictly segregated from each other.

In reality, however, these variables are segregated from each other, so anything done to a variable in one function has no effect on its value in other functions, and this example program does not have any problems at all. The value of the variable **cntr** in the **clrscrn( )** module has absolutely no effect on the value of the variable **cntr** in the **main( )** module, so **main( )** runs just as it was intended to.

You should compile and run this program—even though it just gets fifty-two numbers from you and does nothing else with them—to impress that fact on your mind. Intuitively, you would tend to think that every time the variable **cntr** is used in this program, it refers to the same thing. It is important to fully realize that, in this program, **cntr** is the name of two entirely different variables.

Variables of this type, which exist only within their own functions, are called *local variables* for the obvious reason that they exist only locally in one part of the program.

Global Variables

The opposite of a local variable is a *global variable,* which can be used by any module of the program.

The way in which you make a variable global is quite simple and straightforward. As you have seen many times, a local variable, which is used only by one function, is declared in the function after its opening curly bracket. By contrast, a global variable, which can be used by the whole program and is not confined to one function, is declared outside of any function, before the program begins, above the **main( )** function.

Look again at the example of local variables in the program that was just given to enter weekly wages for a year. In both modules of that program, the statement **int cntr;** that declares the variable is enclosed within the curly brackets of the function, and the declaration creates a local variable that exists only in that function and has no connection with any other variables of the same name that might exist in other functions.

By contrast, when you are writing the arithmetic quiz program, you need to begin it with the following:

```
int nmbr[10]

main()
{
DECLARATION OF VARIABLES
MANY LINES OF CODE
}

addtest()
{
```

```
DECLARATION OF VARIABLES
MANY LINES OF CODE
}
```

The variables declared within each function are local, but the declaration **int nmbr[10];** creates an array of global variables that can be used by any function. It should be easy for you to remember that if a variable is declared within a function, it works only in that function, and if a variable is declared at the top of the program, it applies to all functions.

A Note on Parameters

There are times when you want more precise control over which modules can use a variable that you get by declaring a global variables, which is available to all of the modules of the program. It is possible to create a local variable and then make it available only to the other module or modules that you select by passing it to them as a *parameter*.

Parameters are not needed in the sample program you are developing in this chapter, however, and they are covered in the next chapter.

Writing the Code

You have already written a version of the **initlze( )** module of this program, which gives values to the variables in the array. The other modules should be easy to write.

The Main Module

The **main( )** module is just a menu similar to the one used by the ASCCHRT program. It gives users the choice of taking tests in addition, subtraction, multiplication, or division or quitting the program. It then uses a **scanf( )** statement to get the user's input and assign that input to a variable. The program then uses an **if-else-if** ladder to branch to the program that runs the test that the user chose. As in the final ASCCHRT program. this menu is placed within a loop so that, after finishing one test, the user has the option of choosing another test or quitting the program.

The only new point about this part of the program is that an array of global variables is declared before the main module begins and the variables are initialized before the menu is presented, as follows:

```
/* An Arithmetic Quiz Program */
nmbr[10]              /* array of numbers used by all */
                      /* modules */

main()
{
char choice;
initlze();            /* initialize array of numbers */
while(1==1)
    {
    printf("\n\n\n\t\t\tARITHMETIC QUIZ");
    printf("\n\n\n\n\n");
    printf("\t\t1 - Addition test\n\n");
    printf("\t\t2 - Subtraction test\n\n");
    printf("\t\t3 - Multiplication test\n\n");
    printf("\t\t4 - Division test\n\n");
    printf("\t\t5 - Quit\n\n");
    printf("\n\n\n\n\n\n\t\t\tWHAT IS YOUR CHOICE > ";
    scanf("\n%c" ,&choice);

    if(choice=='1')
        {
        addtest();
        }
    else if(choice=='2')
        {
        subtest();
        }
    else if(choice=='3')
        {
        multest();
        }
    else if(choice=='4')
        {
        divtest();
```

```
            }
        else if(choice=='5')
            {
            break;
            }
        else
            {
            printf("%c",7);
            }
        }
}
```

The final **else** of the **if-else-if** ladder is handy for error testing, as always. If the user's choice is not 1., 2., 3., 4. or 5, the computer simply beeps and the program's flow of control loops back up to **while (1==1)** and displays the menu again.

If any of the tests is chosen, then after that test is done, the program's flow of control returns to **main( )** at the point right after the point where the program left it, falls through all of the other conditions to the bottom of the **while** loop, loops back to the top, and displays the menu again.

The program **breaks** out of the loop and return to MS-DOS (or whatever other operating system is being used) only if 5 is chosen from the menu.

The Addition Module

You have already developed a stripped-down version of the module that tests for addition while looking at how to change the value of the counters that take you through the array. Look at this fragment again carefully and be sure you understand it:

```
cntrA = 0;
diff = 1;
cntrB = cntrA + diff;

while(1==1)
    {
    printf("%d + %d = ",nmbr[cntrA],nmbr[cntrB];
```

```
    scanf("%d" ,&answer);
    if(answer==nmbr[cntrA]+nmbr[cntrB]
        {
        printf("\nRIGHT!!");
        }
    else
        {
        printf("\nwrong");
        continue;
        }
    cntrA = cntrA + 2;
    if(cntrA>9)
        {
        cntrA = cntrA - 10;
        diff = diff + 1;
        }
    if(diff>9)
        {
        diff = 2;
        }
    cntrB = cntrA + diff;
    if(cntrB>9)
        {
        cntrB = cntrB - 10;
        }
    }
```

If you have forgotten the logic behind this fragment, look again at the discussion of it earlier in this chapter.

Once you understand this fragment, it should be easy for you to grasp the rest of this program. The module that gives the addition test simply adds a better screen display and gives the user the option of quitting after each problem:

```
addtest()                    /* test of addition */
{
int cntrA, cntrB, diff, answer;
char again;

cntrA = 0;
```

```
diff = 1;
cntrB = cntrA + diff;

while(1==1)
    {
    printf("\n\n\n\n\n\n");
    printf("\t\t\tADDITION QUIZ");
    printf("\n\n\n\n\n\n\n\n\n\n\n\n\n\n\n\n\n\n");
    printf("\t%d + %d = ",nmbr[cntrA],nmbr[cntrB]);
    scanf("%d",&answer);
    if(answer==nmbr[cntrA]+nmbr[cntrB])
        {
        printf("\nTHAT IS RIGHT!!");
        }
    else
        {
        printf("\nThat is wrong\n");
        printf("\The answer is %d",nmbr[cntrA]+nmbr[cntrB]);
        }
    printf("\n\nDo you want to try another ? Y/N > ");
    scanf("\n%c",&again);

    if(again != 'Y' && again != 'y')
        {
        break;
        }
    else
        {
        cntrA = cntrA + 2;
        if(cntrA>9)
            {
            cntrA = cntrA - 10;
            diff = diff + 1;
            }
        if(diff>9)
            {
            diff = 2;
            }
        cntrB = cntrA + diff;
```

```
            if(cntrB>9)
                {
                cntrB = cntrB - 10;
                }
            }
        }
}
```

If the answer is wrong, the program displays the right answer.

Whether the answer is right or wrong, the program asks users whether they want to try another problem. Then, if the user does not enter a 'Y', either upper- or lowercase, the program's flow of control **break**s out of the loop and returns to the menu in **main( )**. If the user does enter a 'Y', the program makes the changes in the value of the counters that were described earlier, and the flow of control loops back to let the user go again.

To give the user this choice, you nest the **if** statements used to change the values of the counters within a larger **if-else** that checks whether or not the user wants to go again. This series of nested **if** statements might seem a bit confusing at first, but if you begin by understanding the **if** statements that are used to change the value of the counters, it is not difficult to also understand why the larger **if-else** is added around them.

The Subtraction Module

The subtraction module is almost identical to the addition module. So that the subtraction problems do not just look like repetitions of the addition problems, the initial value of **cntrA** and of **diff** is changed. Also, because a simple arithmetic test should not have questions with negative answers, you use problems only if **nmbr[cntrA]** is larger than **nmbr[cntrB]**. You can do this by using an **if** statement to make the part of the module that displays the problem conditional, as follows:

```
subtest()              /* test of subtraction * /
{
int cntrA, cntrB, diff, answer;
char again;

cntrA = 2;
diff = 3;
```

```
cntrB = cntrA + diff;

while(1==1)
     {
     if(nmbr[cntrA]<nmbr[cntrB])
          {
          again = 'Y';
          }
     else
          {
          printf("\n\n\n\n\n\n\n\n\n");
          printf("\t\t\t\SUBTRACTION QUIZ);
          printf("\n\n\n\n\n\n\n\n\n\n\n");
          printf("\t%d - %d = ",nmbr[cntrA], nmbr[cntrB]);
          scanf("%d",&answer);
          if(answer==nmbr[cntrA]-nmbr[cntrB])
               {
               printf("\nTHAT IS RIGHT!!");
               }
          else
               {
               printf("\nThat is wrong\n");
               printf("The answer is %d",
                              nmbr[cntrA]+nmbr[cntrB]);

               }
          printf("\n\nDo you want to try another? Y/N > ");
          scanf("c%",&again);
          }
      if(again != 'Y' && again != 'y')
          {
          break;
          }
      else
          {
          cntrA = cntrA + 2;
          cntrB = cntrA + diff;
          if(cntrA>9)
               {
               cntrA = cntrA - 10;
```

```
            diff = diff + 1;
            }
        if(cntr>9)
            {
             cntrB = cntrB - 10;
            }
        if(diff>90)
            {
             diff = 2;
            }
        }
}
```

If **nmbr[cntrA]** is less than **nmbr[cntrB]**, you do not display that problem or get the answer. Instead, you just make **again** equal to 'Y' so that the program changes the value of the counters and loops back to the top again. You run through the program as usual only if **nmbr[cntrA]** is greater than **nmbr[cntrB]**. Thus, all of the problems that would have a negative answer are filtered out, and only those with a positive answer are displayed.

The Multiplication and Division Modules

The multiplication module is virtually identical to the addition module.

The division module is similar to the subtraction module but has one more possibility that it must filter out: You do not want users of this simple test to divide a number by a larger number, as with subtraction, and you also must avoid division by zero, which is meaningless mathematically. Furthermore, the division module must get two answers from the user, the answer and the remainder. Look for these changes in the listing of the entire program, which follows:

```
                        /* Chapter 3, Example 8 */
                      /* An Arithmetic Quiz Program */
#include <stdio.h>

nmbr[10];               /* ARRAY OF NUMBERS USED BY ALL */
                        /* MODULES */

main()
```

```
{
char choice;
initlze();            /* INITIALIZE ARRAY OF NUMBERS */
while(1==1)
     {
     printf("\n\n\n\t\t\tARITHMETIC QUIZ");
     printf("\n\n\n\n\n");
     printf("\t\t1 - Addition test\n\n");
     printf("\t\t2 - Subtraction test\n\n");
     printf("\t\t3 - Multiplication test\n\n");
     printf("\t\t4 - Division test\n\n");
     printf("\t\t5 - Quit\n\n");
     printf("\n\n\n\n\n\n\t\t\tWHAT IS YOUR CHOICE > ");
     scanf("\n%c",&choice);

     if(choice=='1')
          {
          addtest();
          }
     else if(choice=='2')
          {
          subtest();
          }
     else if(choice=='3')
          {
          multest();
          }
     else if(choice=='4')
          {
          divtest();
          }
     else if(choice=='5')
          {
          break;
          }
     else
          {
          printf("%c",7);
          }
```

```
    }
}

initlze()
{
nmbr[0] = 3;
nmbr[1] = 5;
nmbr[2] = 0;
nmbr[3] = 9;
nmbr[4] = 6;
nmbr[5] = 1;
nmbr[6] = 7;
nmbr[7] = 2;
nmbr[8] = 8;
nmbr[9] = 4;
}

addtest()           /* test of addition */
{
int cntrA, cntrB, diff, answer;
char again;

cntrA = 0;
diff = 1;
cntrB = cntrA + diff;

while(1==1)
    {
    printf("\n\n\n\n\n\n");
    printf("\t\t\tADDITION QUIZ");
    printf("\n\n\n\n\n\n\n\n\n\n\n\n\n\n\n\n");
    printf("\t\t\t\t%d + %d = ",nmbr[cntrA],nmbr[cntrB]);
    scanf("%d",&answer);
    if(answer==nmbr[cntrA]+nmbr[cntrB]
        {
        printf("\nTHAT IS RIGHT!!");
        }
    else
        {
```

```
          printf("\nThat is wrong\n");
          printf("The answer is %d",nmbr[cntrA]+nmbr[cntrB]);
          }
     printf("\n\nDo you want to try another ? Y/N > ");
     scanf("\n%c",&again);

     if(again != 'Y' && again != 'y')
          {
          break;
          }
     else
          {
          cntrA = cntrA + 2;
          if(cntrA>9)
               {
               cntrA = cntrA - 10;
               diff = diff + 1;
               }
          if(diff>9)
               {
               diff = 2 ;
               }
          cntrB = cntrA + diff;
          if(cntrB>9)
               {
               cntrB = cntrB - 10;
               }
          }
     }
}

subtest()           /* test of subtraction */
{
int cntrA, cntrB, diff, answer;
char again;

cntrA = 2;
diff = 3;
cntrB = cntrA + diff;
```

```
while(1==1)
    {
    if(nmbr[cntrA]<nmbr[cntrB])
        {
        again = 'Y';
        }
    else
        {
        printf("\n\n\n\n\n\n");
        printf("\t\t\tSUBTRACTION QUIZ");
        printf("\n\n\n\n\n\n\n\n\n\n\n\n\n\n\n\n\n");
        printf("\t\t\t\t%d - %d = ",nmbr[cntrA],nmbr[cntrB]);
        scanf("%d",&answer);
        if(answer==nmbr[cntrA]-nmbr[cntrB]);
            {
            printf("\nTHAT IS RIGHT!!");
            }
        else
            {
            printf("\nThat is wrong\n");
            printf("The answer is %d",
                                        nmbr[cntrA]+nmbr[cntrB]);
            }
        printf("\n\nDo you want to try another ? Y/N > ");
        scanf("\n%c",&again);
        }

    if(again != 'Y' && again != 'y')
        {
        break;
        }
    else
        {
        cntrA = cntrA + 2;
        if(cntrA>9)
            {
            cntrA = cntrA - 10;
            diff = diff + 1;
            }
```

```
            if(diff>9)
                {
                diff = 2;
                }
            cntrB = cntrA + diff;
            if(cntrB>9)
                {
                cntrB = cntrB - 10;
                }
            }
        }
}

multest()       /* test of multiplication */
{
int cntrA, cntrB, diff, answer;
char again;

cntrA = 4;
diff = 5;
cntrB = cntrA + diff;

while(1==1)
        {
        printf("\n\n\n\n\n\n");
        printf("\t\t\tMULTIPLICATION QUIZ");
        printf("\n\n\n\n\n\n\n\n\n\n\n\n\n\n\n\n\n");
        printf("\t\t\t\t%d x %d = ",nmbr[cntrA],nmbr[cntrB]);
        scanf("%d",&answer);
        if(answer==nmbr[cntrA]*nmbr[cntrB])
            {
            printf("\nTHAT IS RIGHT!!");
            }
        else
            {
            printf("\nThat is wrong\n");
            printf("The answer is %d",nmbr[cntrA]*[cntrB]);
            }
        printf("\n\nDo you want to try another ? Y/N > ");
```

```
     scanf("\n%c",&again);

     if(again != 'Y' && again != 'y')
          {
          break;
          }
     else
          {
          cntrA = cntrA + 2;
          if(cntrA>9)
               {
               cntrA = cntrA - 10;
               diff = diff + 1;
               }
          if(diff>9)
               {
               diff = 2;
               }
          cntrB = cntrB + diff;
          if(cntrB>9)
               {
               cntrB = cntrB - 10;
               }
          }
     }
}

divtest()            /* test of division */
{
int cntrA, cntrB, diff, answer, remaindr;
char again;

cntrA = 3;
diff = 4;
cntrB = cntrA + diff;

while(1==1)
     {
     if(nmbr[cntrA]<nmbr[cntrB] || nmbr[cntrB] == 0)
```

```
        {
        again = 'Y';
        }
    else
        {
        printf("\n\n\n\n\n");
        printf("\t\t\tDIVISION QUIZ");
        printf("\n\n\n\n\n\n\n\n\n\n\n\n\n\n\n\n\n\n\n");
        printf("\t%d / %d = ",nmbr[cntrA], nmbr[cntrB]);
        printf("\nWhat is the answer > ");
        scanf("%d",&answer);
        printf("\nWhat is the remainder > ");
        scanf("%d",&remaindr);
        if(answer==nmbr[cntrA/nmbr[cntrB]
                && remaindr ==nmbr[cntrA]%nmbr[cntrB])
            {
            printf("\nTHAT IS RIGHT!!");
            }
        else
            {
            printf("\nThat is wrong\n");
            printf("The answer is %d remainder %d"
              nmbr[cntrA]/nmbr[cntrB],nmbr[cntrA]%nmbr[cntrB]);
            }
        printf("\n\nDo you want to try another ? Y/N > ");
        scanf("\n%c",&again);
        }
    if(again != 'Y') && again != 'y')
        {
        break;
        }
    else
        {
        cntrA = cntrA + 2;
        if(cntrA>9)
            {
            cntrA = cntrA - 10;
            diff = diff + 1;
```

```
          }
     if(diff>9)
          {
          diff = 2;
          }
     cntrB = cntrA + diff;
     if(cntrB>9)
          {
          cntrB = cntrB - 10;
          }
     }
  }
}
```

This program should be quite easy for you to understand, largely because it is repetitious.

Making Your Code More Compact

Up to now, this book has generally used this repetitious style of programming—a **main( )** menu module calling several similar subordinate modules—as a teaching device because it makes programs easy for beginners to grasp.

It is better programming style, however, to break down the modules further and create separate functions to perform repeated tasks.

In this program, for example, it would be better style to have a separate function to change the values of the counters, rather than repeat the same code four times (though it would require techniques that you do not learn until Chapter 6). This is not only because it would be more elegant but also because it would make the program easier to modify and maintain. If you had to change this aspect of the program, you would be able to modify the code in only one place, rather than modifying the same code four times in the four places where it is repeated.

Now that you have had practice with repetitious code that is easier to understand, you learn to develop more compact and elegant—and sometimes more cryptic—code in the rest of this book.

One thing you will notice when you run this program is that its screen display leaves something to be desired. As in all of the programs in this book, the display simply scrolls up the screen one line at a time, and the **scanf( )** that gets user input is on the bottom line of the screen. In some cases, the screen looks good even with this condition, but in this program, where there is only a heading and an arithmetic problem, the screen looks empty and unbalanced. This is the sort of problems that would be very easy for you to fix after you get a library of screen control functions.

Summary

To declare an *array*, you can use a statement such as the following:

```
char samplAry[100];
```

This statement creates 100 character variables, with names ranging from **samplAry[0]** to **samplAry[99]**. Each of these variables is called an *element* of the array.

It is important to remember that, because the declaration gives the total number of elements in the array and the elements are numbered beginning with 0, the subscript of the highest numbered element of the array is 1 less than the number in the declaration.

You can create arrays of any data type. The declaration simply consists of the data type and the name of the variable with the number of elements in the array enclosed in square brackets (and ends with a semicolon, like any declaration).

The arithmetic operators are as follows:

+	addition
-	subtraction
*	multiplication
/	division
%	modulo division (remainder)

Modulo division (**%**) gives the remainder of integer division.

When arithmetic operations are evaluated, multiplication and division are given precedence over addition and subtraction, so **3 * 4 + 1** is evaluated as 13. It is possible to alter the precedence by using parentheses: **3 * (4 + 1)** is evaluated as 15. The addition would have precedence because it is enclosed in parentheses.

Parentheses can also be used to alter the precedence of logical operators. For example, **x==1 && (y==2 || z==3)** is evaluated as true only if it is true that **x** equals 1 *and* it is true that either **y** equals 2 or **z** equals 3. On the other hand, **(x==1 && y == 2) || z==3** is evaluated as true if it is true that **x** equals 1 and **y** equals 2 *or* it is true that **z** equals 3. If **x==3** is the only one of these three statements that is true, then the first example is evaluated as false and the second is evaluated as true. Without parentheses, **&&** has precedence over || in C, but it is best to always use parentheses in complex logical conditions to minimize confusion.

Earlier programs in this book used only *local variables*, which are known only to the module that declares them. It is also possible to create *global variables* that are known to all the modules of a program. Global variables are declared at the beginning of the program, before the **main( )** module begins; local variables are declared within the curly brackets of the module they are used by. If two modules have local variables with the same name, the program considers them to be totally different variables. This makes C a more structured and extensible language.

Chapter

4

Two-Dimensional Arrays: Tic-Tac-Toe

The sort of arrays that were discussed in the last chapter, with only one index number for each variable, were relatively easy to understand. But C also lets you create arrays with several index numbers for each variable, which are more powerful but more complex.

In this chapter, in order to get experience with more complex arrays, you develop a program that plays tic-tac-toe. To develop this program, you also have to learn how to pass parameters and how to do the preliminary analysis that normally precedes programming. This chapter covers:

- using two-dimensional arrays
- using higher-dimensional arrays
- analyzing a programming problem using a top-down approach
- writing pseudocode to begin developing a program
- declaring parameters and passing them between modules

Two-Dimensional Arrays

The arrays you looked at in the last chapter were just lists, but it is also possible to create arrays that represent tables.

For example, the beginning of the last chapter talked about keeping employees wages in an array you declared using the statement:

```
float wageWk[52];
```

Because this array has only one index number, it is called a *one-dimensional array.*

But imagine that you do not just want to keep a list of the employee's wages for each week, but instead you want a more complete list of the employee's weekly wages, tax deductions, social security deductions, net wages after deductions, and the amount the employer paid for benefits.

You want to keep a record of five different figures for each of the fifty-two weeks, and you can declare an array to keep track of them as follows:

```
float wageTot[52][5];
```

This creates an array of floats that you can think of as a table that is 52 down and 5 across. This is a *two-dimensional array.*

Conventionally, the first index number is thought of as the row number and the second as the column number, so this array represents a table with 52 rows and 5 columns.

In reality, the computer's memory just consists of a sequence of bytes, each with its own address number. When you declare this two-dimensional array, the compiler simply reserves enough of these addresses—all in a row—to accommodate all of the variables being created. But it is convenient for humans to think of it as a two-dimensional table that looks like the following.

	WAGES	TAXES	FICA	NET PAY	BENEFITS
WEEK 1					
WEEK 2					
WEEK 3					
WEEK 4					

and so on, down to week fifty-two. Once you visualize the array as having two dimensions, it becomes easier to write programs for it.

A Sample Two-Dimensional Array

You can revise the program for entering each week's wages that you looked at in the beginning of last chapter, for example, by thinking in terms of columns (that hold figures for WAGES, TAXES, etc.) and rows (that hold the different weeks).

Remember, the one tricky point is that an array declared as **wageTot[5]** is numbered from **wageTot[0]** to **wage[4]**. Then look back at the program at the beginning of the last chapter, and it should be easy to understand how the program is revised as follows:

```
                    /* Chapter 4, Example 1 */
#include <stdio.h>

float wageTot[52][5];
int numofwks;

main()              /* enter wages, taxes, FICA */
{                   /* and benefits for each week */
int cntr;

printf("\nHow many weeks of data do you want to enter? ");
scanf("%d",&numofwks);

cntr = 0;
while(cntr < 52 && cntr < numofwks)
```

```
    {
    printf("Enter the gross wages for week %d > ",cntr+1);
    scanf("%f",&wageTot[cntr][0]);

    printf("Enter the taxes deducted for week %d > ",cntr+1);
    scanf("%f",&wageTot[cntr][1]);

    printf("Enter the FICA deducted for week %d > ",cntr+1);
    scanf("%f",&wageTot[cntr][2]);

    wageTot[cntr][3] = wageTot[cntr][0] - wageTot[cntr][1]
    wageTot[cntr][2];

    printf("Enter the benefits paid for week %d > ",cntr+1);
    scanf("%f",&wageTot[cntr][4]);

    cntr = cntr + 1;
    }
}
```

Note that the array that holds the wages and the variable that holds the number of weeks are declared as global variables, so other modules added to this program can have access to the data. The net wages for each week **(wageTot[cntr][3])** are calculated by taking the gross wages for that week **(wageTot[cntr][0])** and subtracting from it the tax deductions for that week **(wageTot[cntr][1])** and the FICA deductions for that week **(wageTot[cntr][2])**.

Working With a Two-Dimensional Array

It becomes easier to manipulate the figures when you think of them as being in the form of a table. For example, if you wanted to total an employee's FICA deductions for the year, you could do it by adding this module to the previous example, and adding the command **totfica( );** before the final }.

/* Chapter 4, Example 2 */

/* to be used with Chapter 3, Example 9 */

```
/* add the statement totfica(); before its final } */
/* and add this function after its final } */
```

```
totfica()
{
int cntr;
float sum;

cntr = 0;
sum = 0;
while(cntr < 52 && cntr < numofwks)
    {
    sum = sum + wageTot[cntr][2];
    cntr = cntr + 1;
    }
printf("\n\nTotal FICA is %f\n\n",sum);
}
```

This example takes advantage of the fact that **wageTot[52][5]** was declared as a global array, not as part of the **main( )** module, so that all modules can access it.

Similarly, it is easy to look up the record for an employee for a particular week, as follows:

/* Chapter 4, Example 3 */

/* to be used with Chapter 3, Example 9 */

```
/* add the command lookupwk(); before its final } */
/* and add this function after its final } */

lookupwk()
{
int wkToFind;

printf("\nWhat number week do you want to find > ");
scanf("%d",&wkToFind);
if(wkToFind < 1 || wkToFind > 52 || wkToFind > numofwks)
    {
    printf("%c",7);
    }
else
    {
    wkToFind = wkToFind - 1;
```

```
    printf("\nGross Wages: %f",wageTot[wkToFind][0]);
    printf("\nTaxes: %f",wageTot[wkToFind][1]);
    printf("\nFICA: %f",wageTot[wkToFind][2]);
    printf("\nNet Wages: %f",wageTot[wkToFind][3]);
    printf("\nBenefits: %f",wageTot[wkToFind][4]);
    }
}
```

Again, the only trick about this program is remembering to subtract 1 from the week number the user enters to get the week number the computer uses, because humans begin numbering with 1 and the computer begins numbering with 0.

An actual program would not just get the wages, then sum the FICA payments, then let the user look up one week, then terminate. These steps are put in sequence purely as an example of ways of using two-dimensional arrays. As an exercise, you might want to rewrite the program as a menu-driven system.

Using Variables as Both Index Numbers

So far, these examples have used a variable to represent the row and constants to represent the columns. Things do get more complicated when you want to use two counters, one for the rows and one for the columns of the array. For example, imagine that you wanted to print out all of the wage data for one employees for a year. You could declare two variables as follows:

```
int rowCntr, colCntr;
```

Then, after printing out a heading that includes the words GROSS WAGES, TAXES, FICA, NET WAGES, and BENEFITS, carefully spaced so they will appear above the proper columns, you could print out the entire year's figures in tabular form with the following code:

```
rowCntr = 0;
while(rowCntr<52)
{
printf("\n\nweek %d:",rowCntr+1);
colCntr = 0;
while(colCntr<5)
```

```
    {
    printf("\t\t%f",wageTot[rowCntr][colCntr]);
    colCntr = colCntr + 1;
    }
rowCntr = rowCntr +1;
}
```

This program is elegant and concise. The first time through, when **rowCntr** equals 0, it begins by printing **week 1:** on a new line. Then it makes **colCntr** equal 0 and prints, on the same line but after tabs, **wageTot[0][0]**, the gross wage for the first week. Then the program makes **colCntr** equal 1 and prints, on the same line but after tabs, **wageTot[0][1]**, the taxes for the first week. The program keeps incrementing **colCntr** and prints all of the values for the first week across the first line. Then, when **colCntr** equals 5, the program breaks out of the inner loop, makes **rowCntr** equal to 1, loops back up to the top of the outer loop, prints **week 2:** on a new line, and goes through the inner loop another five times, printing the values for the second week across the line. And it keeps doing this until **rowCntr** equals 52, meaning that it has printed out all fifty-two weeks worth of data.

Higher Dimensional Arrays

You can see how powerful a two-dimensional array can be, and how much it can do with just a few lines of programming. But you can also see that a two-dimensional array can be a bit hard to follow.

Beyond that, there are higher-dimensional arrays. For example, this company probably does not have just one employee. If the company has 100 employees and you want to keep these same records for each employee, you could declare the following three-dimensional array:

```
float wageTot[100][52][5];
```

That declaration creates 100 of the 5-column-by-52-row tables you have been working with. You would be able to print out yearly records for all of the workers, using the same program you just looked at with only a few lines added to create an outer loop that prints the worker number (from 1 to 100) and a heading and, after all fifty-two rows were printed for that worker, adds 1 to the worker number, and does it again and again until all 100 tables are printed out.

Just a few extra lines of code, less than two dozen lines in all, and you have a program that prints out hundreds of pages of data.

Tic-Tac-Toe

Because two-dimensional arrays and other higher dimensional arrays are powerful but a bit difficult to master, this chapter gives you extensive practice with them by developing a program that plays tic-tac-toe.

You simply use a two-dimensional array of nine characters—**char sqr[3][3];**—to represent the nine squares of the tic-tac-toe board. Before the game begins, the program initializes each of the nine elements of the array with a blank. As the game goes on, it makes these elements equal to Xs and Os, and it will check to see if either side won the game. If **sqr[0][0]**, **sqr[1][0]**, and **sqr[2][0]** are all equal to X, for example, then X wins.

Analyzing the Programming Problem

In addition to being more fun to write than a program that keeps records of workers' wages, a tic-tac-toe program is more complex than any of the programs you have worked on so far in this book. Earlier programs in this book were simple enough to write off the top of your head, without planning them out in advance. This tic-tac-toe program is complex enough to serve as a good introduction to the type of analysis programmers generally perform before beginning the actual work of writing code.

In some large-scale corporate applications, analysis is a complex process performed by many people using an elaborate division of labor. Often analysis takes more time than the programming itself does. But most work with microcomputers uses a relatively simple and natural method of analysis based on a *top-down* approach using *pseudocode.*

The Top-Down Approach

The top-down approach involves looking at the problem as a whole and breaking it up into its larger component parts before breaking it down further and looking at the details of how each part works.

Earlier chapters in this book tended to develop programs using a *bottom-up* approach, looking at individual details first—for example, at the addition module of the arithmetic flashcards or at the utility that gives the ASCII value of characters—and building them up into more complex programs. Often, this strategy resulted in repetitive code, with many modules that were copied from one another with only slight variations.

The bottom-up method is an excellent way of introducing programming concepts to beginners, who need to study some of the individual trees before they can look at the whole forest. By now, you are advanced enough that you can learn to analyze the program as a whole and come up with a final version of it that is more complex, more elegant, and easier to modify and maintain than earlier programs.

Pseudocode

Writing pseudocode is simply a matter of thinking about the problem you have to work on in the same step-by-step way that you use in computer programming, but without worrying about every detail the program has to take care of or about the exact syntax of the programming language.

It is very much like an artist drawing a rough sketch of a painting that she will be working on: the idea is to get all of the basic shapes in the right place without worrying about the fine details or the colors. It is easy for the artist to modify the sketch as she sees what the composition of the whole picture will be. And it is easy for programmers to modify the pseudocode as they see what the whole program will look like and how best to break it down into modules. In any real programming job, the time you spend in analysis is amply repaid in the time you save in debugging and rewriting your final program.

A Rough Sketch of the Program

Using a top-down approach, you would start with pseudocode that describes the flow of the whole program, and then you would work out more and more detailed pseudocode, which might ultimately need very little adjustment to be translated into the final program—just as the artist might work on more and more detailed sketches that come closer and closer to the final picture.

This process naturally fits in with structured programming, which encourages a top-down approach. The first rough sketch of the program corresponds to the **main( )** module, and the details are handled in the other modules.

What, then, does a tic-tac-toe program need to do? Much of it, obviously, is a matter of getting moves from the opponent, making moves yourself, seeing if the opponent has a chance to win, and seeing if there is a chance for you to win. Think about what you do more clearly, in terms of the step-by-step logic that computers use, and your first attempt at pseudocode could look like the following:

```
Repeat until the end of the game:
    Get a move from the opponent
    Check to see if the opponent has won
    If so
        display the updated board
        congratulate him
        end the game
    Otherwise
        Check to see if you can win
        If so
            make the move that wins
            display the updated board
            end the game
        Otherwise
            Check to see if opponent can win
            If so
                block him
            Otherwise
                make some move
            Display the updated board.
```

Writing this pseudocode is simply a matter of thinking systematically about what you actually do when you are playing tic-tac-toe and it is your turn to move.

First, you see if the opponent has won. If not, you see if there is anywhere you can move to win. If not, you see if the opponent is threatening to win and if you need to block him. Only after doing all of these things do you look for another possible move. Add to these thoughts the things the computer must do, such as displaying the screen, and you create a sketch of the program.

When you are playing tic-tac-toe yourself, though, you do all of the thinking you need in an instant, and you do not even know what sequence you are considering these issues in. You need to think for a while about what you actually do in a game before you realize, for example, that you check if you can win first and then see if you need to block your opponent from winning.

When you first are working on pseudocode, you might well jot the tasks down in the wrong order or leave out a task. Then, as you look through the pseudocode again, you will suddenly realize that you made a mistake and will correct it. Do not let this worry you. It is a trait you share with virtually every other computer programmer in the world.

It is important to remember that analysis is what is called an "iterative" process—just the programmer's way of saying that you need to go through the pseudocode again and again and figure out more things about it each time.

Adding More Details

Even from the bit of pseudocode you have already developed, you can see that there should probably be a separate module to display the board and another that can check for an actual or potential win for either X or O so that you do not need to write the same code twice.

As you consider the pseudocode and think about what to do next, it becomes clear that you must choose whether you want the program to be able to play both X and O or just one. For the sake of simplicity, make it play only X for now.

It is also obvious that you need to start off the pseudocode by filling all of the squares with blanks.

And it is obvious that there is no need to check for wins after the first move: The opponent can threaten to win only after his second move, and you can have the chance of winning only when your third move comes. Thus, you can have a separate set of commands for the earliest moves—beginning with the best initial move, which is to place your X in the center square.

As you think more about the details of the program, you will notice that, in addition to checking for wins, you must handle the possibility of a draw—which is actually more than just a possibility because most tic-tac-toe games do end in a draw.

One way of checking for a draw would be to scan the whole board and see if all of the spaces are filled, but it is easier just to count the moves. If you and your opponent make nine moves and fill all of the squares without either of you winning, then you have a draw. Because you have X and make the first move, any draw would occur after your move, so that is when the program should check the number of moves.

At some point, perhaps after you have rewritten the pseudocode several times, you will realize that when you get the opponent's move in the program, it might be an error: either because it is a number greater than 8 or because it is the number of a square that is already filled. So you not only need to get the move, but you do need to check it for validity and, if it is invalid, give the user an error message and get another move.

You could become aware of this type of problem at any time. You simply must go back to your editor and revise the pseudocode accordingly. Analysis really just means looking at the problem again and again, and writing down your ideas until you have the process all clear in your mind. It is easier to correct your errors in the planning phase than when you are actually writing code.

Finally, the program should end by asking the opponent if he or she wants to play another game. To do this, you put the whole program inside of a loop—a second, larger loop in addition to the central loop that Repeats until the end of the game. If the opponent wants to play another game, you loop the opponent back to the beginning. If not, you **break;** the opponent out of the large loop.

If you add these features to the pseudocode, you get the following:

```
Repeat while the user wants to keep playing:
    Make all nine squares equal to blank
    Put an 'x' in the central square
    Display the board
    Get a move from the opponent
    Make some move
    Display the board
    Make the move counter equal to three
    Repeat until the end of the game:
        Get a move from the opponent
        Add one to the move counter
        Check to see if the opponent has won
        If so
            display the updated board
            congratulate him
            end the game
        Otherwise
            check to see if you can win
            If so
                make the winning move
                display the updated board
                end the game
            Otherwise
                check to see if opponent can win
                If so
```

```
        block him
    Otherwise
        make some move
    Display the updated board.
    Add one to the move counter.
    If the move counter equals nine
        End the game as a draw
After the end of the game,
ask if the opponent wants to play another game.
```

Some programmers would then analyze the program in more detail and write more specific pseudocode, but most would consider the pseudocode above to be adequate for a program as simple as this one.

Now, you need to analyze some of the repeated tasks that go into separate modules.

Displaying the Board

To display the board, it is probably best to use the underline and the "pipe" character (|), which is above the backslash on your keyboard. The program would actually look better if you used the graphics characters that are in the extended ASCII character set of the IBM-PC, but using the underline and pipe is a bit simpler and is portable to other systems. The board looks something like the following when it is time for the opponent's first move:

```
                COLUMN
             1    2    3
      1          |    |
 R            -----------
 O    2          | X  |
 W            -----------
      3          |    |
Which row do you put your 'O' in?
          Enter a number from 1 to 3 >
```

After the column number is entered, the program asks for the row number in the same way.

Analysis in this case consists mainly of fiddling around with your editor until you get a nice looking screen and then counting how many tabs, spaces, and skipped lines you used to get the effect you wanted. In the program, you simply use a series of **printf( )** statements to display this screen line by line.

Checking for a Win

Once you have sketched out the screen, it is very easy to see how you write the module to check if the opponent has actually won. You just need to write a long series of conditions, similar to the following:

```
If sqr[0][0] = 'o' and sqr[0][1] = 'o' and sqr[0][2]] = 'o'
    'o' wins
Otherwise,
if sqr[1][0] = 'o' and sqr[1][1] = 'o' and sqr[1][2] = 'o'
    'o' wins
```

Continue the list with the other row and the three columns and end with the diagonals:

```
Otherwise,
if sqr[0][0] = 'o' and sqr[1][1] = 'o' and sqr[2][2] = 'o'
    'o' wins
Otherwise,
if sqr[0][2] = 'o' and sqr[1][1] = 'o' and sqr[2][0] = 'o'
    'o' wins
```

You also need to have this module check for 'X' winning as well as for '0' winning. When you actually write the code, you will see how to check for a winner, and you will also use loops to replace some of the repetition in the pseudocode.

Getting a Move

The module to get a valid move is similar enough to parts of other programs you have looked at that the pseudocode should come easily:

```
Repeat until the move is valid:
    Get a move
    Of the column is less than 'o' or more than '2'
      or if the row is less than 'o' or more than '2'
      or if the square is not a blank
```

give the user an error message

Otherwise

the move is valid

You simply do not let the user out of the loop if there is something wrong with the move he or she enters.

Other Features of the Program

To make it easier to develop this program, begin by developing a dumb version of it, which just makes any move when its turn comes. Then add more features to make it a bit smarter. Thus, the module to check for future wins is developed later in the chapter, when you are developing the smarter version of the program.

The only other statement that is repeated in the pseudocode frequently enough that it obviously needs a module of its own is the vague Make some move, which is executed when none of the other conditions applies.

The module that does this in the dumb version of the program can simply go through all of the squares on the board and put an 'X' in the first blank square it finds. Because it is usually a better strategy to move in the corner squares, the Make some move module looks at these squares first.

Finally, though it is not repeated, the code is clearer if you write a separate module to Make all nine squares equal to blank. This module also just goes through all of the squares and assigns the value of a blank space to each.

Passing Parameters

The pseudocode is now at a point where you can begin translating it into an actual C language program. First, however, you must learn one more basic programming concept, which you need to handle the variables in this program.

So far, you have learned about global and local variables. In this program, the variables that represent the board, **sqr[0][0]** through **sqr[2][2]**, must be used by almost all of the modules in the program and should be global. Most variables within the modules will be local.

But there are also variables in this program that need to be used by only two modules.

For example, instead of writing one set of modules to check for wins and potential wins for 'X' and another set to check for 'O', suppose the analysis came up with the idea of using a variable called **toCheck**, which can be made to equal either 'X' or 'O', so the same modules can check both. This **toCheck** variable would need to be given the value of 'X' or 'O' by the **main( )** module, which controls the order in which wins are checked, and then that value would need to be passed to the module that does the checking. This value passing could be done by making **toCheck** a global variable, but it is much better programming style to use what is called a *parameter*, a local variable that is passed between functions.

The way parameters are passed from one function to another in C may seem a bit strange at first, but it should ultimately become clear that such parameter passing is necessary, like the segregation of local variables, to make the language fully structured and extensible.

Imagine, for example, that for some reason you wanted to write a function that would add integers, which might be called **addint( )**. Following is how the function would be used with a simplified **main( )** module.

/* Chapter 4, Example 4 */

```
#include <stdio.h>

main()                          /* sample program */
{                               /* passing parameters */
int numbr1, numbr2, total;
numbr1 = 5;
numbr2 = 3;
total = addint(numbr1,numbr2);
printf("%d plus %d equals %d",numbr1,numbr2,total);
}

addint(x,y)                     /* add two integers */
int x,y;
{
return x + y;
}
```

Note that you declare the parameters of **addint( )**—the variables that appear within the parentheses of the function—after the name of the function but before the opening curly bracket that begins the body of the function. These variables are known as *formal arguments.* (Chapter 8 discusses another way of declaring these formal arguments.) By contrast, the arguments of **addint** that are used within **main( )** (or within any function that calls **addint( )**) are known as *actual arguments,* and are declared within the curly brackets of the function, like any other variables.

You now know all three locations where variables can be declared

- **Local variables**, used only in one function, are declared within the body of that function.
- **Global variables**, used by all functions, are declared at the very top of the program, outside of any function.
- **Parameters**, which are passed between functions, appear between the name and the body of the to which function they are passed.

These declarations are all in plausible places. Their locations pretty much convey how that type of variable fits in the program.

Note that parameters are actually ordinary local variables within the function that passes them (the **main( )** function in the example) and are parameters of the function they are passed to, where they appear within the parentheses following the function to which they are passed.

Parameters are declared as ordinary local variables within the function that calls another function. The names of the variables in the two functions are not related to each other. The values of the variables in the calling function are copied into the parameters of the function that is called.

What initially seems strange about passing parameters is that the names of the variables in the function that does the passing (**main( )** in the example) are different from the variable names in the function to which they are passed. If you think about it, you will see that this difference is absolutely necessary for C to work as an extensible, structured language.

If you write a library of functions to perform special mathematical calculations, for example, the people who use this library should not be forced to change the names of all of the variables in their programs to match the variable names in your library. Even if you are developing a large program by yourself, it is very handy to be able to concentrate on the module you are writing without having to worry about all of the variable names in the rest of the program. It might be useful to be able to borrow a function from a program you wrote before without needing to change the variable names. COBOL is a miserable language to program in because it requires you to declare all the of variables for the entire program before you begin writing any of its modules. It has only global variables, which is why it is not a genuinely structured language.

You could use the same name for the parameter in both modules if you wanted to, and the program would work, but the compiler would not be affected by the fact that the parameters have the same name. The variables in the two modules are segregated from each other, like local variables. The program would work regardless of the fact that the variables had the same name, just as the example that used local variables to enter weekly wages worked regardless of the fact that variables in two modules both happened to be named **counter**. It is best to use different names for stylistic reasons, to remind you that variables in different modules are segregated from each other and that parameters must be passed back and forth explicitly.

The example of **addint( )** makes it very clear how variables are passed to a function as its parameters: you simply use that function (in this case, **addint( )**) with the variables you want it to work on, and the compiler automatically copies those variables into the variables declared as the function's parameters. Likewise, it is clear from the example that a value is passed back, using the statement **return**. The function itself takes on the value that is returned, so you can then use that value by making other variables equal to the value returned by the function, as in the example.

If nothing else is specified, a function returns an integer. It is possible to declare a function to make it return another data type, and you will look more closely at this and other special features of functions later in Chapter 8. You already know enough about functions to complete the tic-tac-toe program and the other sample programs in this book.

Developing the Tic-Tac-Toe Program

Your analysis of the tic-tac-toe program has gone far enough that you can almost translate directly from pseudocode to the C language. You still need to learn a bit more about passing parameters to complete a few places where the **main( )** module works with other modules, but you can just leave these areas as pseudocode for now, and you see precisely how the parameters are passed as you write the modules they work with.

A Dumb Version of the Program

Look again at the pseudocode listed earlier in this chapter, and most of the **main( )** module should be easy to write.

You need to begin by declaring the global variable that represents the board. You could either put the entire program in a loop headed **while(again=='Y')** or else put it in a **while(1==1)** loop and use **break;** at the bottom of the program to get out of the loop. Putting it in a **while(1==1)** loop and using **break;** at the bottom makes the program a bit easier to read and gives you more experience with this sort of loop control. It is obvious from the start that you must declare the **again** variable within the **main( )** module. Other variables this module uses become apparent as you write the program.

You should use more comments here than you have used so far because this program is more complicated and could be difficult for other programmers to understand. The pseudocode itself is the best tool for making the code clearer, and you can use it as the basis of your comments as you run through the pseudocode and translate it into C code.

The only parts of the program that may be a bit difficult for you are the modules to check for a win or potential win. These modules must get parameters from the main module and return values to it. So you can be introduced to this concept gradually, the first version of the program only includes one of these modules: the module to check for a win. The module to check for a future win is added later, and the parts of the program that call it is left as comments in pseudocode in the first version.

This gives you a dumb tic-tac-toe program that cannot block the opponent's win or even see if it can win itself. In the first version, this program simply get the opponent's move and make its own move in the first empty space available.

Using a Flag to Check for a Win

To check for the opponent's win, the program uses the command **checkwin('O');**. After writing the **main( )** module, you write the **checkwin( )** function to receive parameters from **main( )** and to return information to the **main( )** module about whether O won or not.

This version of **main( )** uses what programmers call a *flag*, which is simply a variable that is set to one value until a certain condition applies, and then it is changed to act as a signal that this particular condition is in effect. **winFlag** would be a good name for this variable. **main( )** gets information back from

checkwin( ) by using the command **winFlag = checkwin('O');**. Then, it can test the value of winFlag to see whether or not the opponent won.

Different languages use different data types as flags. COBOL one is the simplest: It is usual to use characters as flags and start off by setting them equal to 'N' (for "no") or 'F' (For "false"). When the condition comes into effect, the flag is changed to 'Y' (for "yes") or 'T' (for "true"). Then the condition is checked using the easy-to-understand statement **IF WINFLAG EQUALS 'T'** or **IF WINFLAG EQUALS 'Y'**.

In C, for reasons that become clear in Chapter 7, it is common to use integers as flags and to make them equal to 0 if the condition is false and equal to 1 if the condition is true.

The main( ) Module

One other point must be added to what was sketched out in the pseudocode. Because this first "dumb" version of the program is not checking for its own potential wins—and making its move and claiming a win on the basis of the result—the program needs to check after it moves, to see if it has won. The program simply needs to issue the command **winFlag = wincheck('X');** after its move to see if, by chance, it has made a move that won the game. This should be clear when you look at the code of the **main( )** module:

```
                    /* Chapter 4, Example 5A */
          /* (to be combined with Examples 5B, 5C, 5D, 5E, 5F) */
                 /* Tic-Tac-Toe: Dumb Version */
#include <stdio.h>

char sqr[3][3];                  /* array used as board   */

main()
{
char again;
int moveCntr, winFlag;

while(1==1)                      /* repeat as long as the */
    {                            /* user wants to play */

    initliz();                   /* make squares equal blank */
```

```
    sqr[1][1] = 'x';            /* put X in central square */
    dispbord();                 /* display the board */
    getmove();                  /* get a valid move */
    makemove();                 /* make some move */
    moveCntr = 3;               /* three moves made */

    while(1==1)                 /* repeat till end of game */
        {
        dispbord();
        getmove();
        moveCntr = moveCntr + 1;

        winFlag = checkwin('O');
        if(winFlag==1)          /* see if opponent won */
            {                   /* if so end the game */
            dispbord();
            printf("Congratulations!! You win.\n");
            break;
            }

/* TO BE INCLUDED IN NEXT VERSION                                */
/*                                                               */
/*              OTHERWISE                                        */
/*                  CHECK TO SEE IF YOU CAN WIN                  */
/*                  IF SO                                        */
/*                      MAKE THE WINNING MOVE                    */
/*                      DISPLAY THE UPDATED BOARD                */
/*                      END THE GAME                             */
/*                  OTHERWISE                                    */
/*                      CHECK IF OPPONENT CAN WIN                */
/*                      IF SO                                    */
/*                          BLOCK HIM                            */
/* TO BE INCLUDED IN NEXT VERSION                                */

        else
            {                   /* otherwise make some move     */
            makemove();

/*INCLUDED IN "DUMB" VERSION ONLY                                    */
```

```
/*                                                      */
/*                                                      */
            winFlag = checkwin('X');
            if(winFlag==1)          /* see if program won   */
                {                   /* if so end the game   */
                dispbord();
                printf("I win.\n");
                break;
                }
/*                                                      */
/*                                                      */
/*INCLUDED IN "DUMB" VERSION ONLY                       */
            }

        moveCntr = moveCntr + 1;
        if(moveCntr==9)             /* if nine moves without   */
            {                       /* a win, end game: draw   */
            dispbord();
            printf("It's a draw. Good game.\n");
            break;
            }
        else                        /* otherwise, do */
            {                       /* the loop again */
            continue;
            }
        }
                                    /*** game over ***/

    printf("\nDo you want to play again (Y/N)? ");
    scanf("\n%c",&again);

    if(again=='Y'|| again=='Y')
        {                           /* if user wants to */
        continue;                   /* play again, loop */
        }                           /* back to beginning */
    else
        {                           /* Otherwise, */
        break;                      /* end the program */
```

```
        }
    }
}
```

The logic of the main, inner loop of this module should be clear if you simply ignore what will be added in the smarter version of the program. First, this module gets a move from the opponent and checks to see if the opponent won. If so, it congratulates the opponent and breaks out of the loop, ending the game. Then it makes a move and checks to see if it won. If so, it claims the win and breaks out of the loop. Then it sees if the move counter equals 9. If so, it says the game is a draw and breaks out of the loop. Once the flow of control has broken out of the inner loop, the program asks if the user wants to play again.

The checkwin( ) Module

The one problem you still have is to write the **checkwin( )** module that gives **main( )** the information on whether or not a player won. You could declare another global variable to carry back to the main module information from the modules that check for wins, but it is more elegant and is really not difficult to pass the parameter directly from one module to another.

The module **checkwin( );** simply goes through all of the rows, columns, and diagonals of the board to see if there are three of the same letter in any of them. Because the module must work for either 'O' or 'X', it will be written in the general form **checkwin(ltr)**, which checks for any **char** you pass to it.

Remember the example of **addint(x,y);** that you looked at early in this chapter. The **addint** module is written using the variables **x** and **y**, but the module that calls it can use any variables. If you use the command **addint(numbr1,numbr2)**, the **addint** module does the same thing it always does, using the values of **numbr1** and **numbr2** in place of **x** and **y**.

Likewise, the module **checkwin** is written in general form, using the variable **ltr**, so that other modules are able to use the commands **checkwin('X');** or **checkwin('O');** to check for these specific letters. (Note that the letters must be surrounded by single quotation marks because they are constants rather than variables.)

The program then must send back to the **main( )** module information about whether or not that letter won.

As you have seen, the program does this by using the statement **winFlag = checkwin('O')**, which also is very similar to the statement used in the first example of parameters you looked at: **total = addint(numbr1,numbr2);**. There, you wrote the **addint** module to **return x+y;**, so you were able to use an assignment statement to make **total** equal **x** plus **y**. Here, you simply write the **checkwin( )** module to return a 0 if there is no win and a 1 if there is a win, so you can use the assignment **winFlag = checkwin('O')** to make **winFlag** equal to 1 or 0, as follows:

```
                        /* Chapter 4, Example 5B */
                       /* to be added to Example 5A */

checkwin(ltr)
char ltr;
{
int ct;
ct = 0;
while(ct < 3)
    {
    if (sqr[ct][0]==ltr && sqr[ct][1]==ltr && sqr[ct][2]==ltr)
        {
        return 1;
        }
    else                                /* read thru all rows */
        {
        ct = ct + 1;
        }
    }
ct = 0;
while(ct < 3)
    {
    if(sqr[0][ct]==ltr && sqr[1][ct]==ltr && sqr[2][ct]==ltr)
        {
        return 1;
        }
    else                                /* read thru all columns */
        {
        ct = ct + 1;
        }
    }
```

```
if(sqr[0][0]==ltr && sqr[1][1]==ltr && sqr[2][2]==ltr)
    {
    return 1;                          /* read thru diagonals */
    }
if(sqr[0][2]==ltr && sqr[1][1]==ltr && sqr[2][0]==ltr)
    {
    return 1;                          /* and return 1 if all */
    }                                  /* three squares have */
return 0;                              /* same letter: a win */
}                                      /* Otherwise, return 0 */
```

This module simply goes through all of the possible combinations that win and, if any of these conditions applies, the program returns 1. Otherwise, it returns 0. The first loop in the module uses a counter to go through all three columns of each row and to see if any row has **ltr** in all three of its squares. The second loop reads through all three rows of each column. The final two statements check the diagonals.

One important point to note here is that the **return** statement not only determines what value is passed back, it also breaks out of this function entirely and returns the program flow to the calling function without any other code in this function being executed. Thus, if any of the tests shows there is a win, this function returns a 1 and also returns control to **main( )** without executing the other statements.

In fact, you can use the statement **return;** alone, without any value, simply to redirect program flow. This use of **return;** is a bit like **break;**, except that **return;** breaks you out of the entire function rather than just out of a loop.

The variable **winFlag** in the **main( )** function is made equal to whatever value **checkwin( )** returns: to 1 if there is a win or to 0 if the module goes through all of the tests without finding a win and manages to reach its final statement.

The Remainder of the Program

With this module out of the way, the other modules of this "dumb" version of tic-tac-toe should be easy for you to write.

Writing the final program is often actually easier than performing the analysis. After you have developed good pseudocode, you just need to go through the pseudocode, filling in extra little details and changing the wording to conform to the C language. It would be equally easy to translate the pseudocode into almost any computer language. Once you understand the sort of step-by-step logic that computers use, the details of individual languages are not hard to pick up.

The initiliz( ) Module

Write the other modules in the order in which they appear in the program. **initliz( )** uses two nested **while( )** loops to make all of the squares equal to a blank at the beginning of the program:

```
                          /* Chapter 4, Example 5C */
                          /* to be added to Example 5A */

initliz()                           /* make all the squares */
{                                   /* equal to blank */
int rowCntr, colCntr;

rowCntr = 0;
while(rowCntr < 3)
    {
    colCntr = 0;
    while(colCntr < 3)
        {
        sqr[rowCntr][colCntr] = ' ';
        colCntr = colCntr + 1;
        }
    rowCntr = rowCntr + 1;
    }
}
```

First, to make the first three squares blank, the row counter is 0 as the column counter increases from 0 to 2. You can think of the program as going across the three columns of the first row. Then, the row counter is increased to 1 and to 2, and the column counter goes across all of the columns or the second and third rows to make the squares blank. This module is a very typical example of how two-dimensional arrays are manipulated.

The dispbord( ) Module

The module to display the screen is even simpler to write. Look again at the model screen that was laid out early in this chapter. All you need to do is count the new lines, tabs, and spaces and write a series of **printf( )** statements to display this model on the screen, along with the contents of each square, depending on whether the variable is 'X' or 'O' or a blank:

/* Chapter 4, Example 5D */
/* to be added to Example 5A */

```
dispbord()                              /* display the board */
{
printf("\n\n\n\n\n\n\n");
printf("\t\t\t\t   COLUMN\n");
printf("\t\t\t\t 1    2    3\n\n");
printf("\t\t\t      1   %c | %c | %c\n",
                           sqr[0][0],sqr[0][1],sqr[0][2]);
printf("\t\t\t   R       -----------\n");
printf("\t\t\t   O 2    %c | %c | %c\n",
                           sqr[1][0],sqr[1][1],sqr[1][2]);
printf("\t\t\t   W       -----------\n");
printf("\t\t\t      3   %c | %c | %c\n",
                           sqr[1][0],sqr[1][1],sqr[2][2]);
printf("\n\n\n\n\n\n\n");
}
```

If you do not like the screen layout here, you can design one of your own. Just remember that, after this **dispbord( )** function runs, the function that called it needs to display four more lines on the screen that ask for another move, announce the end of the game, or tell the user his move is invalid. That is why the module above only displays twenty lines instead of the total of twenty-five lines on the screen. You must not display the board so close to the top of the screen that it scrolls off when the extra lines are displayed.

The getmove( ) Module

The module to get a valid move from the opponent should also be easy for you to understand because the method of checking for validity is very similar to what you used in previous programs. You simply put the **scanf( )** statement that gets the move within a **while** loop, and you do not let the user out of that loop unless the move is valid.

```
                    /* Chapter 4, Example 5E */
                  /* to be added to Example 5A */

getmove()                          /* get a valid move */
{
int rowNmbr, colNmbr;

while(1==1)                          /* get opponent's move */
    {
    printf("\nWhat row will you put O in?");
    printf("\nEnter a number from 1 to 3 > ");
    scanf("%d",&rowNmbr);
    printf("\nWhat col will you put O in?");
    printf("\nEnter a number from 1 to 3 > ");
    scanf("%d",&colNmbr);

    rowNmbr = rowNmbr - 1;
    colNmbr = colNmbr - 1;

    if(rowNmbr < 0 || rowNmbr > 2 || colNmbr < 0 || colNmbr > 2
                           || sqr[rowNmbr][colNmbr] != ' ')
        {
        printf("%c",7);              /* if move is invalid */
        dispbord();                  /* beep, redisplay */
        continue;                    /* board and loop back */
        }                            /* to get new move */
    else                             /* if valid, put an o */
        {                            /* there */
        sqr[rowNmbr][colNmbr] = 'O';
        break;
        }
    }
}
```

After the row and column numbers are entered, 1 is subtracted from them to convert them to the actual subscripts used in the array (which, of course, run from 0 to 2 instead of 1 to 3).

This function checks for two errors the user can make: entering numbers that are not between 1 and 3 or entering the number of a square that is not blank. (Like the other programs you have looked at so far, this program does not check for the entry of a non-numeric character.)

In case of an error, the program redisplays the board before looping back and asking for the move again. Otherwise, the board would scroll up the screen an extra two lines each time the user makes an invalid move, and could ultimately disappear completely if the user makes enough errors.

The statement **continue;** is not really needed to loop back to the beginning of the module. Even without it, program control would bypass the **else** half of the condition and then flow back to the top, but it is useful stylistically to make clear what is happening here.

If the move is valid, the square whose numbers were entered is made to equal 'O'. You do not even need to think about passing this value back to the **main( )** module because all of the **sqr[ ][ ]**s are global variables, which are automatically accessible to all modules.

The makemove( ) Module

All you have left to do is to write the **makemove( )** module to MAKE SOME MOVE if none of the other possibilities applies, which is just a matter of going through all of the squares, given priority to the corner squares, and looking for a blank:

/* Chapter 4, Example 5F */
/* to be added to Example 5A */

```
makemove()
{
if(sqr[0][0]==' ')
    {
    sqr[0][0] = 'X';
    }
else if(sqr[0][2]==' ')
    {
```

```
        sqr[0][2] = 'X';
        }
    else if(sqr[2][0]==' ')
        {
        sqr[2][0] = 'X';
        }
    else if(sqr[2][2]==' ')
        {
        sqr[2][2] = 'X';
        }
    else if(sqr[0][1]==' ')
        {
        sqr[0][1] = 'X';
        }
    else if(sqr[1][0]==' ')
        {
        sqr[1][0] = 'X';
        }
    else if(sqr[1][2]==' ')
        {
        sqr[1][2] = 'X';
        }
    else if(sqr[2][1]==' ')
        {
        sqr[2][1] = 'X';
        }
}
```

The program skips **sqr[1][1]**, which cannot be blank because the program put an X there as the first move.

It would be nice if the program could have a final **else** statement that declares a draw if none of the squares is blank. In this initial version of the program, this **else** statement would work as the function is used to make all of X's moves. In the final version, however, this function does not run each time the program goes through the loop, as you can see by looking at the pseudocode left in the **main( )** function above. The program needs to check for a draw separately, by seeing if **moveCntr** is equal to nine.

That completes the first, "dumb" version of the tic-tac-toe program. Put Program Examples 2A, 2B, 2C, 2D, 2E, and 2F in a single file and compile and run it. It plays a legal, though decidedly not an inspired, game.

A Smarter Tic-Tac-Toe Program

To become a bit smarter, the program needs a function to look for possible wins on the next move.

This function must do two things. First, it must check if X can win, and, if so, it must make the winning move and end the game. Second, it needs to check if O can win and, if so, put an X in the square that blocks the win.

In either case, the function needs to scan the board only until it finds one square that satisfies the condition it is looking for. This is the way the computer's logic naturally works, using the **return;** statement, and this logic is perfectly appropriate here because there is really no need to see if there is a second square where you can move to win and no point to seeing if there is a second square where you need to move to block the opponent.

If there are two squares where the opponent can move to win, the program blocks the one that it comes across first. Then, if the opponent moves in the other square and wins, the program notices the move when it is scanning the entire board to see if the opponent has won--one of the first things the program does as it goes through the repeated central loop of its **main( )** function.

Checking for Future Wins: the Pseudocode

You could write the module to search for future wins by checking whether any possible combination of two Xs (or two Os) and a blank exists on the same line, which would take three lines for each row, column, and diagonal on the board. Fortunately, there is an easier way to search for future wins: make each blank space an 'X' (or an 'O', depending on which you are checking) temporarily, and then run the **checkwin( )** module. Then make the square a blank again.

The pseudocode would look like the following:

```
For every square
    If the square is a blank
        make the square an 'x'
        check for a win (using checkwin( ))
        If there is a win
```

            leave the x there
            stop checking other squares
        Otherwise
            make the square a blank again
            keep checking other squares
    If no wins were found in any square
        make some move

If you are checking for 'X', simply leave the X there to make the winning move if this module shows there is one. Otherwise, make the square blank again and keep checking.

Checking Future Wins for Both X and O

There is only one difference when using the module to check a future win for O: When the module shows there is a win, put an X in that square in place of the O that you put there temporarily in order to block the win. Otherwise, make the square equal to blank again and keep checking.

```
canwin(xoro)
char xoro;
{
int rowCntr, colCntr;
int winFlag;

rowCntr = 0;
while(rowCntr < 3)
    {
    colCntr = 0;
    while(colCntr < 3)
        {
        if(sqr[rowCntr][colCntr]==' ')
            {
            sqr[rowCntr][colCntr] = xoro;
            WinFlag = checkwin(xoro);
            if(WinFlag==0)
                {
                sqr[rowCntr][colCntr] = ' ';
                }
```

```
            else
                {
                if(xoro == '0')
                    {
                    sqr[rowCntr][colCntr] = 'X';
                    }
                return 1;
                }
            }
        colCntr = rowCntr + 1;
        }
    rowCntr = rowCntr + 1;
    }
return 0;
}
```

This function is powerful but not too hard to understand. It uses the familiar nested **while( )** loops, with a row counter and a column counter, to go through all of the squares on the board. If a square is blank, the program makes it either 'X' or 'O', depending on which is being tested, and runs the **checkwin( )** function.

Normally, there will be no win. **checkwin( )** returns a 0, and the program makes the square a blank again and goes on to try an 'X' or 'O' in the next square.

On the other hand, sometimes **checkwin( )** finds there is a win, making **winFlag** equal to 1. Then, the program does not make **sqr[rowCntr][colCntr]** a blank again. If the ltr being checked is X, the program simply returns a 1, returning control to **main( )** and letting that function know it should display the board and declare a victory. If the **ltr** being checked is O, the program puts an X in the square to block the win and returns a 1, letting **main( )** know that it does not need to make a move.

Finally, if the program goes through all of the squares without finding a win, it returns a 0, letting **main( )** know that no move has been made and that the program must go on to the next step.

A Stylistic Shortcut

This part of the program should be clear when you look at the entire program listing. There is one other shortcut in the final listing: It cuts out the use of the **winFlag**. Instead of the following:

```
winFlag = checkwin('O');
if(winFlag==1)
```

the program simply uses

```
if(checkwin('O')==1);
```

When you were first learning this program, it was easier to understand if this part of the program was in two steps: first, to check for the win and second, to use the result in a condition. Now that you are used to the program, however, you should be able to see without any trouble that you were able to give **winFlag** the value of 1 or 0 by making it equal to **checkwin('O')** only because **checkwin('O')** itself had the value of 1 or 0. So why not cut out the middleman and use **checkwin('O')** itself in the condition. (You see this type of nesting of parentheses frequently in C code, and if it is confusing, just break it up into two parts by inventing some variable to represent the innermost function, as **winFlag** did above.)

The Final Program

The entire program is long enough that there is an advantage to putting the modules in alphabetical order to make them easier to follow. The complete listing follows:

```
                    /* Chapter 4, Example 6 */
        /* program to play tic-tac-toe: smarter version */

#include <stdio.h>

char sqr[3][3];                 /* array used as board */

main()
{
char again;
int rowCntr, colCntr;
int moveCntr;
while(1==1)                     /* repeat as long as the */
```

```
{                               /* user wants to play */

initliz();                      /* make squares equal blank */
sqr[1][1] = 'X';                /* put X in central square */
dispbord();
getmove();                      /* get a valid move */
makemove();                     /* make some move */
moveCntr = 3;                   /* three moves made */

while(1==1)                     /* repeat until end of game */
     {
     dispbord();
     getmove();
     moveCntr = moveCntr + 1;

     if(checkwin('O')==1)               /* if opponent won */
          {                             /* end the game */
          dispbord();
          printf("Congratulations!! you win.\n");
          break;
          }

     else                               /* if you can win */
          {                             /* end the game */
          if(canwin('X')==1)
               {
               dispbord();
               printf("I win.\n");
               break;
               }
          else                          /* if opponent can */
               {                        /* win, block him */
               if(canwin('O')==0)
                    {                   /* otherwise make */
                    makemove();         /* some move */
                    }

               }

          }
     moveCntr = moveCntr + 1;           /* if nine moves */
     if(moveCntr==9)                    /* without a win */
```

```
                {                               /* end game : draw */
                dispbord();
                printf("It's a draw. Good game.\n");
                break;
                }
            else                                /* otherwise, do */
                {                               /* the loop again */
                continue;
                }
            }                                   /*** game over ***/
        printf("\nDo you want to play again (Y/N)? ");
        scanf("\n%c",&again);
        if(again=='Y' || again=='Y')
            {                                   /* if user wants to */
            continue;                           /* play again, loop */
            }                                   /* back to beginning */
        else
            {                                   /* Otherwise, */
            break;                              /* end program */
            }
        }
}

canwin(xoro)
char xoro;
{
int rowCntr, colCntr;

rowCntr = 0;
while(rowCntr<3)                        /* loop through all squares */
    {                                   /* if one is blank, make it */
    colCntr = 0;                        /* x or 0 temporarily */
    while(colCntr < 3)
        {
        if(sqr[rowCntr][colCntr]==' ')
            {
            sqr[rowCntr][colCntr] = xoro;
            if(checkwin(xoro)==0)       /* if no win, make */
                {                       /* it blank again */
```

```
                    sqr[rowCntr][colCntr] = ' ';
                    }
               else                     /* if there is a win */
                    {                   /* either block O or */
                    if(xoro == 'O')     /* just leave X */
                         {
                         sqr[rowCntr][colCntr] = 'X';
                         }
                    return 1;           /* and return 1 to */
                    }                   /* let main() know */
               }                        /* a move was made */
          colCntr = colCntr + 1;
          }
     rowcntr =  rowCntr + 1;
     }                                  /* if no move was */
return 0;                               /* made, return 0 */
}

checkwin(ltr)
char ltr;
{
int ct;
ct = 0;
while(ct < 3)
     {
     if(sqr[ct][0]==ltr && sqr[ct][1]==ltr && sqr[ct][2]==ltr)
          {
          return 1;
          }
     else                           /* read thru all rows */
          {
          ct = ct + 1;
          }
     }
ct = 0;
while(ct <3)
     {
     if(sqr[0][ct]==ltr && sqr[1][ct]==ltr && sqr[2][ct]==ltr)
          {
```

```
            return 1;
            }
        else                                     /* read thru all columns */
            {
            ct = ct + 1;
            }
        }
    if(sqr[0][0]==ltr && sqr[1][1]==ltr && sqr[2][2]==ltr)
        {
        return 1;                                /* read thru diagonals */
        }
    if(sqr[0][2]==ltr && sqr[1][1]==ltr && sqr[2][0]==ltr)
        {
        return 1;                                /* and return 1 if all */
        }                                        /* 3 squares have same */
                                                 /* letter: there is win */
    return 0;
    }                                            /* Otherwise return 0 */

    dispbord()                                   /* display the board */
    {
    printf("\n\n\n\n\n\n\n");
    printf("\t\t\t\t   COLUMN\n");
    printf("\t\t\t\t 1   2   3\n\n");
    printf("\t\t\t     1  %c | %c | %c\n",
                                 sqr[0][0],sqr[0][1],sqr[0][2];
    printf("\t\t\t    R    -----------\n");
    printf("\t\t\t    O 2  %c | %c | %c\n",
                                 sqr[1][0],sqr[1][1],sqr[1][2]);
    printf("\t\t\t    W   ------------\n");
    printf("\t\t\t      3  %c | %c | %c\n",
    s sq
                                 sqr[2][0],sqr[2][1],sqr[1][2]);
    printf("\n\n\n\n\n\n\n");
    }

    getmove()                                    /* get a valid move */
    {
    int rowNmbr, colNmbr;
```

```
while(1==1)                         /* get opponents move */
     {
     printf("\nWhat row will you put O in?");
     printf("\nEnter a number from 1 to 3 > ");
     scanf("%d",&rowNmbr);
     printf("\nWhat column will you put O in?");
     printf("\nEnter a number from 1 to 3 > ");
     scanf("%d",&colNmbr);

     rowNmbr = rowNmbr - 1;
     colNmbr = colNmbr - 1;

     if(rowNmbr < 0 || rowNmbr > 2 || colNmbr < 0
               || colNmbr > 2 || sqr[rowNmbr] [colNmbr] != ' ')
          {
          printf("%c",7);           /* if move is invalid */
          dispbord();               /* beep, redisplay */
          continue;                 /* board and loop back */
          }                         /* to get new move */
     else
          {
          sqr[rowNmbr][colNmbr] = 'O';
          break;
          }
     }
}

initliz()                           /* make all the squares */
{                                   /* equal to blank */
int rowCntr, colCntr;
rowCntr = 0;
while(rowCntr < 3)
     {
     colCntr = 0;
     while(colCntr < 3)
          {
          sqr[rowCntr][colCntr] = ' ';
          colCntr = colCntr + 1;
          }
```

```
     rowCntr = rowCntr + 1;
     }
}

makemove()                                  /* make some move */
{
if(sqr[0][0]==' ')
     {
     sqr[0][0] = 'X';
     }
else if(sqr[0][2]==' ')
     {
     sqr[0][2] = 'X';
     {
else if(sqr[2][0]==' ')
     {
     sqr[2][0] = 'X';
     }
else if(sqr[2][2]==' ')
     {
     sqr[2][2] = 'X';
     }
else if(sqr[0][1]==' ')
     {
     sqr[0][1] = 'X';
     }
else if(sqr[1][0]==' ')
     {
     sqr[1][0] = 'X';
     }
else if(sqr[1][2]==' ')
     {
     sqr[1][2] = 'X';
     }
else if(sqr[2][1]==' ')
     {
     sqr[2][1] = 'X';
     }
}
```

It is interesting that the logic of the **main( )** module of this program obviously requires three nested **if-else** statements. If the opponent wins, congratulate him. Otherwise, look for a potential win. If that win is found, make the winning move. Otherwise, see if the opponent, can win. If he can win, block him. Otherwise, make some move.

The use of nested **if-else** statements is much more intuitive here than in most cases, and if you study this example closely, looking especially at the indentation and the reverse-indentation of the closing brackets, you should find it easy to work with nested **if-else** statements in the future.

Future Improvements in the Program

More conditions could be added to this series of **if-else** statements if you wanted to make the program even smarter. This program just checks for a win on the next move. If it does not find anything, it uses the **makemove( )** function and simply occupies the first open square it finds. By adding more conditions here, you could make the program look even farther ahead to find the best move.

If you were writing a program to play a difficult game, such as chess, much of the programming would be devoted to developing heuristics to make the best move. *Heuristics* are programs that use "rules of thumb" to guide you toward the best possibility when there is no precise, step-by-step way of getting to your goal, and they are a major subject of research in artificial intelligence. In tic-tac-toe, the game is simple enough that heuristics are not needed. You can work entirely with what are called *algorithms,* the step-by-step procedures to reach a precise goal that computers most often use.

If you wanted to do the extra work, you could develop a module to check whether it was possible to create what is called a "fork", or a position where you can win in two ways. For example, in the following position:

```
  | O | X
-----------
  | X |
-----------
O |   |
```

the program could be intelligent enough to put the X in row 3, column 3 so that it could win on the next move by going in either row 2, column 3 or in row 1, column 1.

This would involve looking ahead two moves instead of just one. It is not hard to do in theory. It is simply a matter of putting in 'X' in each blank square temporarily and then using the module that checks for potential wins, **canwin( )**, to see if any of those moves creates two different potential wins. If two potential wins were possible, the program would leave the 'X' there. Otherwise, it would make the square blank again.

Finally, you could write a module to set up future forks, looking ahead three moves. Then, the program would be as good as any human tic-tac-toe player, which is really no great achievement for artificial intelligence.

You can begin to see that when people talk about computers becoming more intelligent and imitating human thought, what they really mean is that programmers are becoming more intelligent and developing sets of rules that let the computer imitate some of the forms of thinking that people do. The intelligence is built into the program, and all that more advanced computers do is execute the programs more quickly.

Summary

In additional to the one-dimensional arrays covered in the previous chapter, it is also possible to create higher dimensional arrays. For example, the declaration:

```
char samplAry[100][5];
```

would create a *two-dimensional array* with 500 elements, numbered from **samplAry[0][0]** to **samplAry[99][4]**. It is easiest to think of two-dimensional arrays as tables. The example above could be visualized as a table with 5 columns across and 100 rows down.

Likewise, the declaration:

```
char samplAry[20][100][5];
```

would create a *three-dimensional array* with 10,000 elements.

Local variables are used by one function. *Global variables* can be used by all functions. *Parameters* are variables that are passed between two functions.

Local variables are declared within the function they are used in, as follows:

```
main()
{
int samplVar;
MORE CODE
}
```

Global variables are declared outside of any function, before the **main( )** module, as follows:

```
int samplVar;
main()
{
MORE CODE
}
```

Parameters are declared after the name of a function and before its opening bracket as they are received by that function from outside:

```
smplfunc(a,b)
int a,b;
{
MORE CODE
}
```

(Chapter 8 covers another, newer way of declaring parameters in the function that receives them.)

Parameters are declared as ordinary local variables within the function that calls another function. The names of the variables in the two functions are not related to each other. The values of the variables in the calling function are copied into the parameters of the function that is called.

Using the statement **return;** plus some value within the called function makes the program return that value to the calling function. That is, the called function assumes that value in the calling and the value can be assigned to a variable as follows: **samplVar = smplfunc(1,2);**. This example assigns to **samplVar** the value that **smplfunc** returns if its parameters a and b have the values 1 and 2.

The statement **return;** also redirects the flow of program control back to the calling function, without any of the remaining instructions of the called function being executed. It can be used without any value simply to redirect control flow in this way.

Chapter

5

Working with Words

So far, you have written programs that work with numbers and with individual letters, but you have not been ready until now to work with continuous text. This chapter teaches you to work with *strings* of characters, and it teaches you to group these strings into structures (or structs) to make them easier to handle. Finally, you write a flash-card program to give you experience working with strings and structs. You learn about:

- declaring and initializing strings
- working with individual letters of strings
- using functions to compare strings, find the length of strings, and change the capitalization of strings
- using input/output functions with strings
- declaring and using the struct, a package of different types of data
- using arrays of structs

Strings of Characters

Now that you have experience working with arrays, you are ready to work with strings—that is with words and texts—because, in C, a string is an array of characters.

The Null Character

To be more precise, a string is an array of characters terminated by the *null* character.

The null is the first ASCII character, which has a value of zero. The eight bits that represent this character are set to 00000000. It is not to be confused with the character zero (0), which is ASCII character 48.

The null character is not actually used in any text in the way that ordinary characters such as '0' or 'A' or '?' and even carriage returns are used. For this reason, the null can be used as a signal to let the compiler know when the text has ended.

In C, null is represented by the special escape character **\0**, which is similar to the special characters **\n** (for a new line) and **\t** (for tab) that have been discussed previously.

Declaring a String

Having this sort of marker to tell you when the string ends is useful because it allows you to work with character strings of different lengths. Say, for example, that you are working with names. You can declare the array of characters that will hold a name as follows,

```
char name[16];
```

assuming that the maximum length of a name is fifteen characters and adding one more character for the final null.

The String as Array

Then, if the program must work with the name "Sam," you can initialize that array as follows:

```
name[0] = 'S';
name[1] = 'a';
name[2] = 'm';
name[3] = '\0';
```

name[4] through **name[15]** are either empty or contain random values they happened to hold when the program began. However, when other parts of the program work with this string, they simply read the characters until they reach the null. Then they know the string is over.

In the previous example, other parts of the program read 'S', 'a', and 'm' and then stop. Later in the program, if you want to use the name "Amadeus," for example, you can initialize the same string, char **name[16];**, as follows:

```
name[0] = 'A';
name[1] = 'm';
name[2] = 'a';
name[3] = 'd';
name[4] = 'e';
name[5] = 'u';
name[6] = 's';
name[7] = '\0';
```

Using the null terminator allows you to use the same array to hold strings of different lengths, which in turn allows you to give the strings different values—regardless of the strings' lengths—and to use strings more or less like other variables.

Initializing a String

It is important to emphasize, however, that a string cannot be initialized like other variables. In general, you cannot say

```
name[16] = "Sam";
```

Sometimes, with some compilers, you can initialize entire strings by using the equal sign as you do with other variables. However the general rule is that each element of an array—in this case, each character of a string—is a separate variable. If you want to initialize using the equal sign as you do with other variables, the logic of the C language dictates that initialize each character in a string individually, as you always do when you initialize an array.

Fortunately, there are standard functions in C that provide easy ways to work with strings. The most common way of initializing a string is using the function **strcpy( )** (short for "string copy"), which takes the following form:

```
char name[16]; strcpy (name,"Amadeus");
```

This code copies the string "Amadeus" into the array **name[16]** and automatically places the null terminator after the string: In just one line, this code accomplishes the same task as the previous seven-line program.

Note that, as in most string-handling functions, you enter the name of the target string that is being changed first. You can also copy one variable into another. For example, if you had another string declared as char **musician[16];** that had already been given the value **"Amadeus"**, then you could use the statement

```
strcpy(name, musician);
```

to copy the value that is now in the string **musician[16]** into the string **name[16]**.

Delimiters for Strings

Note also that strings that are constants, such as **"Sam"** and **"Amadeus"**, are surrounded by double quotation marks, unlike individual **chars,** such as 'S', 'a', and 'm', which are surrounded by single quotation marks.

Of course, a character can be surrounded by double quotes if that character happens to be a one-letter string. For example, the statement

```
strcpy(name,'I');
```

is equivalent to the following:

```
name[0] = 'I';
name[1] = '\0';
```

The string **"I"** is made up of the **char 'I'** plus the **char '\0'**

The Names of Strings

Finally, note the one tricky thing about the names of the strings that are variables within the **strcpy( )** function: the arrays **name[16]** and **musician[16]** are referred to simply as **name** and **musician**, without any brackets after them.

The name of an array, without the brackets, refers to the address of the beginning of that array. When you learned the **scanf( )** function, you looked briefly at the symbol **&**, which means "the address of." In this example, **name** means **&name [0];** it is the address of the beginning of the array.

You learn more about addresses in Chapter 6. Here, you must simply note that because you generally do not know the exact length of a string, the functions that work with strings must be given the address of each string's first character, so the functions can act on all of the characters—from this beginning character's address to the null terminator.

Because you need the beginning address of the string so often, being able to refer to the string's name without entering the brackets and the ampersand is a handy shortcut.

Working with the Letters of a String

Of course, you can still access the letters as individual elements of the string.

For instance, if you expanded the last example as follows,

```
                    /* Chapter 5, Example 1 */
#include <stdio.h>

main()                            /* sample program */
{                                 /* initializing a string */
char name[16];

strcpy(name,"Amadeus");
printf("%c%c%c",name[3],name[4],name[5]);
}
```

the program would print **deu**. Here, you can begin to see the convenience of treating words as arrays. Treating words as arrays makes it easy to manipulate them letter by letter.

Screen Output Using Strings

Another easy way of handling strings is to use the **printf( )** and **scanf( )** functions, both of which can use the special character **%s** to work with strings, just as they use **%d**, **%f**, and **%c** to work with integers, floats, and characters.

For instance, you can make the previous example more meaningful as follows:

```
                                   /* Chapter 5, Example 2 */
#include <stdio.h>

main()                                     /* sample program */
{                                          /* string handling */
char name [16];

strcpy(name,"Amadeus");
printf("The second letter of %s is %c.",name,name[1]);
}
```

This example prints **"The second letter of Amadeus is m."**

Screen Output of Individual Letters of Strings

If you want to get fancier, you can combine this technique with a loop, as follows:

```
                                   /* Chapter 5, Example 3 */
#include <stdio.h>

main()                                     /* sample program */
{                                          /* using a counter */
char name[16];                             /* with a string */
int cntr;

cntr = 0;
strcpy(name,"Amadeus");
while(name[cntr] != '\0')
     {
     printf("\nLetter %d of %s is %c.", cntr+1,name,name[cntr]);
     cntr = cntr + 1;
     }
}
```

As usual, you must add 1 to the counter when you are talking to the user, who starts counting at 1 rather than at 0. Thus, the first time through the loop, the program prints **"Letter 1 of Amadeus is A."** The program prints a similar message for each letter in the name until it reaches the null terminator. After the program reaches the null terminator, the condition at the top of the loop, **while(name[cntr] != '\0')**, is no longer true, so the program stops executing.

You need to use similar methods of loop control in most functions you write that work with strings.

Input/Output with Strings

You can use both **printf( )** and **scanf( )** with strings to personalize the **"Hello, world"** program you wrote in Chapter 1 so it greets the individual user:

```
/* Chapter 5, Example 4 */
#include <stdio.h>

main()                              /* sample program */
{                                   /* talking with the user */
char name[21];
printf("\nWhat is your name? ");
scanf("%s",name);
printf("\nhello, %s.\n",name);
}
```

Note that when it is used with strings, the **scanf( )** function does not need the ampersand (**&**) before the name of the variable. Remember, **scanf( )** needs the **&** operator before the names of most variables because **scanf( )** expects an address. However, when the name of an array is not followed by brackets, that name already represents an address, so the ampersand is not needed.

Changing Capitalization

If a user of the program you just looked at entered "John," the program would print "Hello, John" on the screen. But if John happened to have his Caps Lock key on and entered "JOHN," the program would display the rather unprofessional looking message: "Hello, JOHN."

Here, the problem is just a matter of appearance, but there are many programs in which a name that is entered must be matched up with a name on a list (for instance, so the program can look up the person's address or telephone number). Remember that a computer considers the upper- and lower-case versions of the same letter to be two totally different symbols, each with its own ASCII code, and would not find a match between 'h' and 'H,' for example.

There are two C functions to deal with the problem of capitalization:

- **toupper( )** returns the uppercase version of a letter but does not affect character symbols that are not letters. For example, **ltr = toupper('c');** makes the variable **ltr** equal 'C', and **ltr = toupper('$');** makes **ltr** equal **'$'**.
- **tolower( )** makes letters lowercase but, like toupper( ), does not affect ASCII characters other than letters.

When you are manipulating a piece of text, it is useful to be able to make certain letters upper- or lower-case without having to worry about mutilating the rest of the text.

Properly Capitalizing a String

To change the program so it does not print **"Hello, JOHN,"** add a loop to adjust the case of whatever letters are entered:

/* Chapter 5, Example 5 */

```
#include <stdio.h>

main()                              /* sample program */
{                                   /* talking with the user */
char name[21];                      /* a better way */
int counter;
printf("\nWhat is your name? ");
scanf("%s",name);
name[0] = toupper(name[0]);
counter = 1;
while (name[counter] != '\0')
     {
     name[counter] = tolower (name[counter]);
     counter = counter + 1;
     }
printf ("\nHello, %s.\n",name);
}
```

First, the program makes the first letter of the name uppercase. Then, the loop makes each of the following letters lowercase, until it comes to the null terminator and stops.

(If statements such as **name[0] = toupper(name[0]);** make you uncomfortable, just remember that these statements are also assignment statements, similar to **counter = counter + 1**. The statement **name[0] = toupper(name[0]);** can be read as "make the first letter of name equal to the uppercase version of the current first letter of name.")

Capitalization in Menus

The function **toupper( )** is particularly useful in the sort of menus that you have used in the sample programs of this book.

By now you are probably tired of statements such as the following:

```
choice = ' ';
while (choice!='n' && choice!='N' && choice!='y' && choice!='Y')
       {
       printf("\nWhat is your choice?");
       scanf("\n%c",&choice);
       }
```

The repetition could really become tiresome if you were writing a program with a menu that included numerous letter choices and you had to write a prolonged **if-else-if** ladder and include both the lower-and upper-case letters in each condition.

Fortunately, this approach is not necessary. Instead, the program can just make the choice uppercase when the user enters the letter. The previous example could be converted to the following:

```
choice = ' ';
while(choice!='N' && choice!='Y')
      {
      printf("\nWhat is your choice? ");
      scanf("\n%c,&choice);
      choice = toupper(choice);
      }
```

Of course, you save even more work in the code that follows because you can see what the program should do next by using the condition **if(choice=='Y')** rather than **if(choice=='Y' || choice=='y')**.

Special String-Handling Functions

The importance of another string-handling function becomes apparent if you notice that Program Example 5, shown previously, capitalizes only the first name. It contains no commands to capitalize the first letter of the last name. When you test this program, you see that it only gets the first name because **scanf( )** used with **%s** reads only up to the first blank of the string.

More precisely, when **scanf( )** is used with any formatting character except **%c**, it does not read any blank space characters—including tabs, newline characters, or blank spaces, all of which create blank space on the screen.

Of course, this feature of **scanf( )** is often useful, but it does mean that **scanf( )** cannot be used to read a string that contains blank spaces. Though **printf( )** is quite adequate for printing string output, it is better to use a different I/O function to get string input from the user.

Unformatted I/O Functions

So far, you have used only the formatted I/O functions **printf( )** and **scanf( )** with the special characters **%c**, **%f**, **%i**, and **%s** to print and to access different data types. There is also a set of unformatted I/O functions with a different function for each date type. Each type uses **put** or **get** plus some abbreviation of the data type handles.

The most standard unformatted I/O functions are **putchar( )** and **getchar( )**, used to print and read characters, and **puts( )**, and **gets( )**, used to print and read strings.

One reason these functions are sometimes used is that because they are less powerful than **printf( )** and **scanf( )**, they use less memory. The compiled program can be smaller if its code does not need the formatted I/O functions and can substitute one of the unformatted functions for the I/O it does use.

Even apart from the saving in memory and the fact that it is easier to type, **putchar(7);** is simply a far more common way of creating a beep than **printf("%c",7);**—so much so that is seems more natural—and it is used in the rest of this book.

Using gets( ) to Read Strings

One reason that **gets( )** is one of the most useful functions in the C language is that it reads strings that include blank space characters.

Using **scanf('%',name);** you can only get the user's first name. To read the user's entire name into the string, you can use the statement **gets(name);**.

Thus, you can rewrite the example used earlier in this example so that it gets an entire name and capitalize it properly, as follows:

```
                         /* Chapter 5, Example 6 */
#include <stdio.h>

main()                                /* sample program */
{                                     /* talking with the user */
char name[21];                        /* an even better way */
int counter;
printf("\nWhat is your name? ");
gets(name);
name[0] = toupper (name[0]);
counter = 1;
while(rame[counter] != '\0')
    {
    if (name[counter-1] == ' ')
        {
        name[counter] = toupper(name[counter]);
        }
    else
        {
        name[counter] = tolower(name[counter]);
        }
    counter = counter + 1;
    }
printf("\nHello, %s.\n",name);
}
```

This program gets an entire name, capitalizes the first letter, and then goes through the rest of the name letter by letter and makes any letter that follows a blank uppercase and any other letter lowercase. If you enter "james a. smith," for example, it capitalizes the 'J' and then go through the name and capitalizes the 'A' and the 'S.' (Unfortunately, it does not handle names that have capital letters in the middle, such as "Ponce DeLeon," which are the bane of a computer programmer's existence.)

Using gets( ) to Read a Single Character

The function **gets( )** is also useful for getting menu choices and other forms of single-character input from the user.

Up to this point, you have been using **scanf("\n%c")** to avoid having **scanf("%c")** read two characters for each input. Remember that if a loop uses **scanf("%c")** without the **\n**, there will be an echo. The first time through the loop, the program reads the character that the user entered, and the second time through, the program reads the newline character, which is still in the buffer.

One problem this approach creates, however, is that the programs do not react if the user simply presses the Enter key.

The function **gets( )** does not have this problem. If the user presses Enter, **gets( )** simply makes **'\0'** the first **char** of the array. If the user presses a letter key first, **gets( )** will make that letter the first **char** of the array.

To use **gets( )** to read a single character entered as a menu choice, then, you must declare the variable that accepts the menu choice as a string. Then, after accepting the input from the user, you must check for just the first **char**, element **[0]** of the array.

Now that you have learned how to use strings, you can make user input work more smoothly when you are designing this sort of menu—and in many other situations.

Other String-Handling Functions

There are two additional string-handling functions that are very common and that you should know:

- **strcmp( )**, compares strings.
- **strlen( )**, checks the length of a string.

As you will see, these functions are invaluable when you are working with strings.

Comparing Two Strings

The function **strcmp( )** (short for "string compare") checks to see if two strings are identical. If the strings are the same, the function returns a 0.

If the strings differ, what this function does differs in various versions of C. Some compilers return the position of the first letter that is different and some return a negative number if the character that differs is lower or a positive number if the character is higher in the ASCII chart than the character in the string it is being checked against.

Because the function is generally used to see whether two strings are identical, the important point to remember is simply that all compilers return a 0 if the strings are the same.

A program that uses a password to keep out unauthorized users provides a typical example of this function. The following version of a password module makes input easier for the user by accepting the password in either upper- or lowercase.

/* Chapter 5, Example 7 */

```
#include <stdio.h>

main()                              /* sample password program */
{
password();
printf("Correct password. You may begin the program");

/* MORE CODE FOR MAIN PROGRAM */
}

password()                          /* get and check password */
{
int ltrCntr, tryCntr;
char userWord[11];

tryCntr= 0;                         /* loop to give user three */
while(1==1)                         /* tries to enter password */
    {
    printf("What is the password? ");
    scanf("%s",userWord);
                                    /* capitalize user's entry */
    ltrCntr = 0;
    while(userWord[ltrCntr] != '\0')
        {
```

```
        userWord[ltrCntr]   = toupper(userWord[ltrCntr]);
        ltrCntr = ltrCntr + 1;
        }
    if(strcmp(userWord,"OPENSESAME")==0)
        {
        break;                  /* if entry is right */
        }                       /* continue with main program */
    else
        {
        tryCntr = tryCntr + 1;
        if(tryCntr==3)
            {                   /* if three tries are wrong */
            exit();             /* do not let user in program */
            }
        }
    }
}
```

First, the password module gets the password from the user. Then, it goes through the entry one letter at a time, capitalizing each letter until it reaches the final null. Then the module compares the entry with **"OPENSESAME,"** which this program uses as the password.

Note how one set of parentheses is nested inside another in this condition: if **(strcmp(userWord,"OPENSESAME")**. If the two strings are the same, the program returns a 0 so that the condition then is equivalent to **if (0==0)** and is true. As mentioned in Chapter 4, a beginner might find it easier to perform this task in two steps by declaring an integer variable called, say, **compRslt** to hold the result of the comparison and making the comparison and the condition into two separate lines:

```
compRslt = strcmp (theWord, "OPENSESAME");
if (compRslt == 0)
```

Once you become used to the fact that a function such as **strcmp( )** returns a value, however, you will find it easy to perform this type of task in a single statement.

If the word entered is **"OPENSESAME"**, the program **break;**s out of the loop and returns to the **main( )** module so the user can go on with the rest of the program.

If the wrong word is entered, though, the program increments the **tryCntr** and loops up to the top of the **password( )** module again to give the user a second try. Before looping, however, the program checks to see how many tries the user has already had. If there have already been three attempts, it **exit( )**s so users cannot just keep trying passwords until they find the right one. This example is an excellent illustration of the difference between **break;** and **exit( );**.

Finding the Length of a String

One final string-handling function you should understand is **strlen( )**, which returns the length of a string.

This function is useful for error checking because it can help you screen out data that does not fit into the space a program allocates for it.

For example, in the program that says "Hello" to the user, which you wrote earlier in this chapter, an array of twenty-one characters is used to hold the user's name, so it can hold a name that is a maximum of twenty characters long (plus the null character). If a name longer than this is entered, some operating systems simply lose the data at the end, but most (including MS-DOS) would save this data in the keyboard buffer—the memory reserved to hold input from the keyboard—and would it to the next **scanf( )** (or any other keyboard input function).

Of course, passing this excess data to the next keyboard input function could create serious problems, so programs must check to make sure that strings entered are of a valid length.

You can check string length by creating your own buffer—a longer array that you read the string into before copying it into the array where it belongs. Then use **strlen( )** to check whether the string is longer than the array that is meant to hold it. Finally, put the string in that array only if it is not too long.

You can modify the program that says "Hello" to the user to incorporate this type of error trapping as follows:

/* Chapter 5, Example 8 */

```
#include <stdio.h>

main()                                  /* sample program */
{                                       /* talking with the user */
char name [21];                         /* the best way */
char buffer [80];
int counter;
```

```
printf("/nwhat is your name? ");
gets (buffer);
if (strlen(buffer)>20)
      {
      printf("sorry. That name is too long.");
      }
else
      {
      strcpy(name,buffer);
      name[0] = toupper(name[0]);
      counter = 1;
      while(name[counter] != '/0')
            {
            if(name[counter-1]==' ')
                  {
                  name[counter] = toupper(name[counter]);
                  }
            else
                  {
                  name[counter] = tolower(name[counter]);
                  }
            counter = counter + 1;
            }
      printf("\nHello, %s.\n",name);
      }
}
```

It really does not make sense, however, to have this type of error checking in this program. Instead of adding a second array to use as a buffer, you can make the name array itself longer. This is an instructive example but not a practical one.

There are cases, though, in which this error checking would be appropriate. For example, if you are dealing with long lists of words and storing them on disk, as you learn to do in Chapter 6, you must limit the space each word is allowed so the total list does not waste too much space on the disk. In such a case, you would have good reason to make sure that none of the words entered is longer than the space allocated for it.

The Struct: a Package of Data

Because one word is an array, a list of words is a two-dimensional array. If you wanted your program to say "Hello" to ten users, for example, instead of just one, you could declare the array that holds the users names as follows: **char name [21][10];**. Think of this example as an array of ten names, each of which can hold a maximum of twenty characters (plus the null terminator) as did the single name that the last program worked with. If you wanted to list both the first and last name for each user, you might try a three-dimensional array. To add the address, you could use a four-dimensional array.

It is easy for the computer to follow this sort of list, in which the elements are distinguished by changes in one out of three or four index numbers. But for the programmer, following this type of list is even more confusing than following a program with variables that have names such as **x**, **y**, and **z** rather than descriptive names. Also, it is impossible to combine data types by using higher dimensional arrays. Such arrays won't allow you to keep track of employees' names, addresses, and salaries, (at least, not if you want the salaries in number form so that you can perform calculations on them).

Fortunately, in C you can create a package of data called a *structure* or *struct* that lets you combine different data types in a way that is easier to follow.

Declaring a Struct

To declare the struct, you simply declare each of its elements after its name.

For example, you might declare a struct to keep track of employees as follows:

```
struct employee
     {
     char fname[21];
     char lname[31];
     char address[31];
     char city[21];
     char state[3];
     char zip[6];
     char sex;
     int age;
     float salary;
     };
```

This declaration essentially creates a new data type, **employee**, by packaging together a list of existing data types. It includes strings of varying lengths to hold the employee's name and address, a character for the sex code ('M' or 'F', an integer for the age, and a float for the salary.

Note that the **struct** declaration must end with a semicolon as must any other statement. The semicolon comes after the entire declaration, following the final curly bracket.

Declaring Variables

The other slightly tricky point to remember about the declaration of a **struct** is that the declaration does not create an actual variable.

The previous definition of **struct employee**, for example, did not create a variable named **employee**. It essentially created a new data type named **struct employee** that can be used in declarations of variables such as **struct employee smith;** or **struct employee jones;**. Once the type **struct employee** has been declared, these declarations create new variables named **smith** and **jones**, each of which contains slots for name, address, sex code, age, and salary, as outlined in the declaration of the **struct**.

The declaration of the **struct** and of the variables can also be combined, as follows:

```
struct employee
    {
    char fname[21];
    char lname[31];
    char address[31];
    char city[21];
    char state[3];
    char zip[6];
    char sex;
    int age;
    float salary;
    }smith, jones;
```

This declares the **struct employee** and also declares two variables of that type, **smith** and **jones**.

Referring to Elements of the Variables

To refer to any of the elements (name, address, sex code, etc.) of one of these variables (**smith** or **jones**), simply use the name of the variable, a period (.), and the name of the element. For example, you could use **smith.age** or **jones.address**. These elements can be manipulated in the same way as any other variables of the same data type. To find the total salary of the two workers, for example, you can add the following lines at the appropriate places in the program:

```
float totSal;
totSal = smith.salary + jones.salary;
```

To make sure all of the letters in Jones's last name are capitalized, you can add the following lines, just as if you were working with any other string;

```
int counter;
counter = 0;
while(jones.lname[counter] != '\0')
    {
    jones.lname[counter] = toupper(jones.lname[counter]);
    counter = counter + 1;
    }
```

Note that the words **struct employee** are left out of all of these statements. Only the names, such as **smith** and **jones**, that you gave to particular variables of this type are used to refer to their elements.

Arrays of Structs

It is not exactly convenient, however, to create a separate variable to store the data for each employee in your company.

As you saw when you first learned about arrays, creating a separate variable for each employee means that you must write code for each employee means that you must write code for each employee whenever you do anything to the data. It is much easier to use an array, so you can just change the index number to refer to all of the employees.

You can also create arrays of structs that let you manipulate the data in structs as easily as you manipulate the data in any array. For example, if you had to keep track of the 100 employees in the Acme Company, you could declare an array with the following statement,

```
struct employee acmeEmp[100];
```

This statement creates 100 variables, with names from **acmeEmpl[0]** to **acmeEmpl[99]**, each of the type **struct employee** (assuming, of course, that you declared **struct employee** earlier in the program).

Working with Arrays of Structs

You can work with this array in much the same way as with any array. For example, you can add up the total salaries of all of the workers with the following module:

```
total()
{
int counter;
float sumOfSal;
sumOfSal = 0;
counter = 0;
while(counter < 100)
    {
    sumOfSal = sumOfSal + acmeEmp[counter].salary;
    counter = counter + 1;
    }
printf("\ntotal salary is %f:",sumOfSal);
}
```

You refer to each employee's salary just as you would with any array, using a variable name, a period, and the name of the element—**salary**. The only difference here is that the variable name includes a counter because it is part of an array of structs. (Note that this module assumes that the array was declared earlier in the program as a global variable and that values for the salaries have been entered in another module.)

Working with Strings in Arrays of Structs

Likewise, it is quite easy to look up the name of a particular employee and capitalize it properly. Even though you are working with two arrays—the array that holds the name of a particular employee and the array of structs that holds data on all of the employees—there is none of the potential confusion that would arise if you were working with a two-dimensional array.

For example, you can capitalize the last names of all the employees as follows:

```
capitliz()
{
int empCtr, ltrCtr;

empCtr = 0;
while(empCtr<100)
    {
    ltrCtr = 0;
    while(acmeEmp[empCtr].lname[ltrCtr] != '\0')
        {
        acmeEmp[empCtr].lname[ltrCtr] =
                toupper(acmeEmp[empCtr].lname[ltrCtr];
        ltrCtr = ltrCtr + 1;
        }
    empCtr = empCtr + 1;
    }
}
```

The first time through the outer loop, **empCtr** is equal to 0 so that the program looks at **acmeEmp[0]**. The inner loop capitalizes all of the letters of the last name, starting with **acmeEmp[0].lname[0]** and adding 1 to **ltrCtr** until it reaches the final null of the last name. Then the outer loop increments **empCtr** and the same is done for **acmeEmp[1]** and all of the other employees up to **acmeEmp[99]**. This program would obviously be more confusing if it simply used a two-dimensional array to keep the records and didn't include the index numbers connected with the words **acmeEmp** and **lname** to remind you of what they are referring to.

Language Flashcards

To give you experience working with strings, structs, and arrays of structs, in this section you develop a language flashcard program to test students in French vocabulary. This program is similar to the arithmetic quiz in Chapter 3 but has some major differences.

First, because the program cannot "calculate" the English meaning of a French word as it calculates the answer to an arithmetic problem, it stores the French and English words together in an array of structs. In the version of this program that you develop in this chapter, these structs simply are initialized by a function of the program. In Chapter 6, however, you learn to store these words in files on disk and create a more generalized version of the program that lets the user expand the vocabulary list available on disk.

Second, the arithmetic quiz had separate functions for addition, subtraction, multiplication, and division. It is generally easier for beginners to understand a program if it duplicates code to perform similar functions in separate modules, as did the ASCCHRT program and the arithmetic quiz, in which you used your editor to copy one function and modify it to create the others.

This approach gives you a program with an easy-to-understand block structure in which the **main( )** menu function simply branches to one of the other functions, depending on the user's choice, but it also gives you a program that is difficult to modify and maintain. If any change is needed in the screen display, for example, all functions must be changed accordingly. It is easy to create four copies of the original, but it is much more difficult to modify and test all four functions than to modify and test one.

Normally, programs are modified considerably as they are developed and tested by potential users because it takes quite a while for programmers to figure out what users really want. And even when a program is complete, it continues to be modified in later versions. In general, then, even though doing so creates a block structure that is easy to understand, it is not good programming style to create similar functions with slight variations.

By now, you have reached the point where you can use more sophisticated techniques that let a single function replace several slightly varied functions. What you learned in Chapter 4 about passing parameters—along with a few new points that you need to learn now about using strings as parameters—lets you use a single function to display all of the different types of flashcards in this program.

Analyzing the Programming Problem

Before programming, of course, you must analyze what the program should do.

All language flashcards—computerized or not—give people the choice of translating from their native language (in this case, English) to the foreign language (in this case, French) or from the foreign language to their native language.

In addition, you should allow users to retest the words they got wrong the last time through and to test only nouns, only verbs, or only other parts of speech (such as adjectives or prepositions). To do this, you must store the vocabulary in a **struct** that includes the English word, the French word, the part of speech (noun, verb, or other) and some sort of flag to show whether or not there was an error on this word the last time through the cards.

The Struct To Hold the Data

To do what you want, the program must use the following data:

- ✦ words in both French and English, which you might decide should be up to fifteen letters long (plus the final null)
- ✦ the part of speech, which can be represented by a single letter, 'N' for noun, 'V' for verb, or 'O' for other
- ✦ the retest flag, which will be an **int**.

You could easily create a flag that is a **char** that is set to 'Y' or 'N', depending on whether or not resting is needed, but (as you learned earlier) it is more common to use **ints** as flags in C. In this chapter, you learn how C programs refer to an **int** as if it were a logical variable.

Given the data that is needed, it is clear that the program can use a **struct** that is declared as follows:

```
struct flshcard
    {
    char English[16];
    char French[16];
    char spchPart;
    int errorFlg;
    };
```

Pseudocode for the main( ) Module

The pseudocode for the **main( )** module is simple and is similar to many menu modules that you have written previously.

There is only one additional refinement. You should give users the option of retesting the words that they got wrong the last time only if there are words to be retested (that is, only if they actually got one or more words wrong).

Some flashcard programs always give users this option, even when they first start the program, and simply tell them that there are no errors to retest if they choose the retest option the wrong time, but you can improve on that sloppy technique by creating a global variable that is a flag to tell you if there are any errors to retest, setting the flag equal to 0 at the beginning of the program, and setting it to 1 when an error is made.

The program displays the retest option only if this flag is equal to 1. It sets the flag to 0 again if another menu option is chosen so, that the next time the menu appears, the program again would only display the retest option if there had been an error the last time that the user went through the stack of cards.

Bearing this retest option in mind, you can write the pseudocode for the main module as follow:

```
Initialize the array with french, english words, etc.
Initialize the global retest flag with zero.
Repeat as long as the user wants to continue:
    Print a heading on the screen.
    Print these options for testing on the screen:
    -French to English for all words,
    -French to English for nouns,
    -French to English for verbs,
    -French to English for others,
    -English to French for all words,
    -English to French for nouns,
    -English to French for verbs,
    -English to French for others.
    If the global retest flag equals one
        print the option of retesting errors
    Print the option of quitting
    Get the user's choice
    If the user did not choose retesting errors
```

make the retest flag equal zero
Perform the option the user chose.

It may seem odd that this function repeatedly sets the global retest flag to 0 and never gives it any other value, but remember that the function that actually displays the flashcards will set the flag to 1 as soon as the user makes an error.

Passing a Parameter To Determine Part of Speech

The final line of the pseudocode, perform the option the user chose, is a bit enigmatic. The programs you have written in the past would branch to different functions, depending on the user's choice, but how can you make a single function perform a variety of options? The answer is that you can pass the user's choice to the function as a parameter.

The more obvious way to make this function perform different options is by including **if-else** statements that depend on the parameter passed to the function. **main( )** uses this method to pass the option about what part of speech will used. Name the function that displays the flashcards **testword( )** and give it the parameter **pos** (short for "part of speech"). The function has the following general form:

```
testword(pos)
char pos;
{
MORE CODE
}
```

Then, depending on whether the user chooses to test nouns, verbs, other words, or all words, **main( )** can call the function as **testword('N');** or **testword('V');** or **testword('O');** or **testword ('A');**.

When **main( )** calls the function in this way, the value 'N', 'V', 'O', or 'A' is copied into the variable **pos** in the **testword( )** module. Then, while it is testing, that module bypasses any word whose part of speech is not the same as **pos**.

At this point, the pseudocode for **testword( )** looks like the following:

Repeat while there are still more words in the list:
If the part of speech called for is not "all"
and the part of speech called for is not the
same as the part of speech of the word,
Go to the next word in the list.

Otherwise,

Display the heading.

Display the (English or French) word.

Get the user's (French or English) meaning.

If the meaning is correct,

congratulate the user.

Otherwise,

tell the user the correct meaning.

mark the word for retesting.

Go to the next word.

Tell the user there are not more words in the list.

Note how economical it is to pass the part of speech to this function as a parameter and use one **if-else** statement in this function to handle the choice of parts of speech, instead of creating four separate functions for the four choices.

Passing Parameters To Determine Language Tested

Is there any equally economical way to handle the choice of French-English or English-French translation? Your first impulse might be to handle it in a similar way by using a parameter that has eight values to represent each of the four possibilities you have already looked at in either English-French or French-English. This approach leads to a very complex series of **if-else** statements, however.

There is a simpler way to accomplish the same task—you can use three parameters. One represents which part of speech is being used, as you have already seen, and the other two represent the names of the two languages. The **testword( )** function, then, would have the following general form:

```
testword(lang1,lang2,pos)
char pos;
char lang1[];
char lang2[];
{
MORE CODE
}
```

The **testword( )** module could, for example, use the following line as the heading of its screen display:

```
printf("\t\t\tTranslating from %s to %s", lang1, lang2);
```

When **main( )** calls **testword( )**, it uses a command such as a the following:

```
testword("English", "French",'n')
```

Then **testword( )** gives **lang1** the value **"English"** and **lang2** the value **"French"** so that it would print the heading as **"Translating from English to French."**

String Handling

Note the declaration of a string as a parameter. Earlier in this chapter, you used string variables as arguments of functions such as **strlen( )** and **strcmp( )** by simply using the name without any brackets. But this is the first time that you are actually writing a function that takes a string as its argument, so you should examine the function again:

```
testword(lang1,lang2,pos)
char pos;
char lang1[];
char lang2[];
{
MORE CODE
}
```

Note also that, within the parentheses of the function, the names of the string variables **lang1** and **lang2** are simply used without any brackets following them, like string variables within the parentheses of the string-handling functions discussed earlier in this chapter. The declaration of the variables, however, has empty brackets following the variable name. Chapter 6, which includes a discussion of pointers to address, explains the meaning of these uses of string names.

This flashcard program uses the function **gets( )** to read the user's input. As you saw previously, **scanf("%s")** only reads a string up to a blank space character. Because many vocabulary words must contain blanks (for example, French nouns must include the article), **gets( )** is the only way to accept these words.

This program also takes advantage of **gets( )** to accept menu choices from the user. Later in this chapter, after you have compiled the program, try pressing the Enter key when the menu screen is displayed, and you will see the advantage of **gets( )** over **scanf( )** in menus. This program uses the character array **choice[2]** to hold the menu choice, so that if the user enters a long string as a menu choice, the program loops until it has read all of the characters. This is done even in some commercial programs, but if you want to bullet-proof this menu completely and avoid this problem, you can declare the array that gets the menu choice as **char choice [128];** instead.

Refining the Program

Now, you have reached the point in the analysis where you should look at preliminary code for the program, which deals with the issues described above.

After you have examined the preliminary code and you understand the relationship between the modules of the program, you can add further refinements to the code.

Preliminary Code

Look carefully at the relationship between the **main( )** and the **testword( )** modules in the following incomplete version of the program:

```
struct flshcard
        {
        char English[16];
        char French[16];
        char spchPart;
        int errorFlg;
        } enFr[10];
int retstFlg;

main()
{
char choice[2];

initlze();
while(1==1)
        {
        printf("\n\t\t\tLanguage Flashcards\n\n"),
        printf("\n\n\t\t1 - English to French, nouns");
        printf("\n\n\t\t2 - English to French, verbs");
        printf("\n\n\t\t3 - English to French, others");
        printf("\n\n\t\t4 - English to French, all");
        printf("\n\n\t\t5 - French to English, nouns");
```

```
printf("\n\n\t\t6 - French to English, verbs");
printf("\n\n\t\t7 - French to English, others");
printf("\n\n\t\t8 - French to English, all");
if(retstFlg==1)
     {
     printf("\n\n\t\t9 - Errors from last test");
     }
printf("\n\n\t\t0 - Quit");
if(retstFlg!=1)
     {
     printf("\n\n");
     }
printf("\n\n\t\t\tWhat is your choice > ")
gets(choice)
if(choice[0]=='1')
     {
     testword("English","French",'N');
     }
else if (choice[0]=='2')
     {
     testword("English","French",'V');
     }
else if(choice[0]=='3')
     {
     testword("English","French",'o');
     }
else if(choice[0]=='4')
     {
     testword("English","French",'A');
     }
else if(choice("[0]=='5')
     {
     testword("French","English",'N');
     }
else if(choice[0]=='6')
     {
     testword("French"."English",'V');
     }
else if(choice[0]=='7')
```

```
            {
            testword("French","English:,o;);
            }
        else if(choice[0]=='8')
            {
            testword("French","English",'A');
            }

        /* ELSE IF CHOICE == 9  */
            /* NOT YET IMPLEMENTED  */

        else if(choice[0]=='0')
            {
            break;
            }
        else
            {
            putchar(7);
            }
        }
}

testword(lang1,lang2,pos)
char pos;
char lang1[];
char lang2[];
{
int wrdCntr, ltrCntr;
char answer[16];
char yorn[2];

wrdCntr = 0;
while(wrdCntr<10)
    {
    if(pos!='A' && pos!=enFr[wrdCntr].spchPart)
        {
        wrdCntr = wrdCntr + 1;
        continue;
        }
```

```
printf"\n\n\n\n");
printf("\t\t\tTranslation from %s to %s", lang1,lang2);
printf("\n\n\n\t\t\t\ttest of ");
if(pos=='N')
    {
    printf("nouns");
    }
else if(pos=='V')
    {
    printf("verbs");
    }
else if(pos=='O')
    {
    printf("other words");
    }

else if(pos=='A')
    {
    printf("all words");
    }

if(lang1[0]=='F')
    {
    printf("\n\n\n\n\n\n\n\n\n\n");
    printf("\t\t\t\t%s", enFr[wrdCntr].French);
    printf("\n\n\n\n\n\n\n\n\n);
    printf("What is the English translation > ");

    gets(answer);

    ltrCntr = 0;
    while(answer[ltrCntr] != '\0')
        {
        answer[ltrCntr] = toupper(answer[ltrCntr]);
        ltrCntr = ltrCntr + 1;
        }
    if(strcmp(answer,enFr[wrdCntr].English)==0)
        {
        printf("\n\nCongratulations.  That is right.");
```

```
                printf("\nDo you want to try another (Y/N) > ");
                gets(yorn);
                if(toupper(yorn[0]=='N')
                {
                return;
                }
            }
        else
            {
            enFr[wrdCntr].errorFlg = 1;
            retstFlg = 1;
            printf("\n\nThe correct answer is %s.",
                                    enFr[wrdcntr].English);
            printf("\nDo you want to try another (Y/N) > ");
            gets(yorn);
            if toupper(yorn[0])=='N')
                {
                return;
                }
            }
        wrdCntr =wrdCntr + 1;
        }

    else
        {
        printf("\n\n\n\n\n\n\n\n\n");
        printf("t\t\t\t%s", enFr[wrdCntr].English);
        printf("\n\n\n\n\n\n\n\n");
        printf("What is the French translation > ");

        gets(answer);

        ltrCntr = 0;
        while(answer[ltrCntr] != '\0')
            {
            answer[ltrCntr] = toupper(answer[ltrCntr]);
            ltrCntr = ltrCntr + 1;
            }
         if(strcmp(answer,enFr[wrdCntr].French==0)
```

```
          {
          printf("\n\nCongratulations. That is right.");
          printf("\nDo you want to try another (Y/N) > ");
          gets(yorn);
          if(toupper(yorn[0]=='N')
               {
               return;
          }
     }
          else
               {
               enFr[wrdCntr].errorFlg = 1;
               retstFlg = 1;
               printf("\n\nThe correct answer is %s.",
                                             enFr[wrdCntr].French);
               printf("\nDo you want to try another (Y/N) > ");
               gets(yorn);
               if(toupper(yorn[0])=='N')
                    {
                    return;
                    }
               }
         wrdCntr =wrdCntr + 1;
         }
     }
}
```

Note that the program begins by declaring the struct named **flshcard**, which contains the elements already discussed, and simultaneously declaring an array of variables of that type named **enFr[10]** (short for English-French Word List). This array only has ten elements (which means that there will only be ten vocabulary words to test) because, in this chapter, you will simply initialize it by using a series of **strcpy** O commands within the program. In Chapter 6, when you learn to work with disk files, you create a much longer word list.

After the initial definitions and declaration of global variables, **main( )** displays a menu with nine choices, accepts the user's choice, and then begins a prolonged **if-else-if** ladder to call the **testword( )** module with parameters that depend on the user's choice.

Then **testword( )** uses these parameters to determine what it displays.

Note that, toward the beginning of **testword( )**, there is an **if-else-if** ladder to display the heading on the screen as "test of nouns," "test of verbs," etc. depending on whether pos is 'N', 'V', etc.

Furthermore, before displaying the screen to test for a word, **testword ( )** checks to make sure the part of speech of the word **wrdCntr** is currently pointing to is the same as **pos**.

If the current word's part of speech is not the same as **pos** *and* if **pos** is not equal to 'A' (indicating that all words should be tested), then **testword( )** adds 1 to **wrdCntr** and loops back to the beginning with the statement **continue;** to try again with the next word in the list and see if it is the right part of speech.

If the current word's part of speech is the same as **pos** or if all words are being tested, the program displays the English or French word, and gets the user's answer. Then it uses a **while** loop to capitalize the user's response (so the user can enter it in either upper- or lower-case letters), compares the user's translation with the French or English word in the database, and tells the user if it is right or wrong.

Then it gives the user the option of entering an 'N' to stop the quiz and **return;** to the main menu. If any other letter is entered, the program loops back to the beginning and goes through the steps again, after checking the condition in the **while( )** to make sure that the **wrdCntr** is not equal to 10, which would mean that you have reached the end of the list.

The use of parameters here is a bit tricky, so you should look at the preliminary code carefully. Once you understand it, you can consider some other refinements that will be added to the program.

Using the Precompiler Command #define

Remember that the preliminary code began by declaring the struct named **flshcard** and declaring an array of variables of that type named **enFr[10]**. Though this array only has ten elements now—because will simply initialize it by using a series of **strcpy( )** commands within the program—you will be able to use a longer list of words in Chapter 6, after you learn to work with disk files.

C includes a feature that makes it easy to modify the program in this way when you need to.

It is generally good programming style in any computer language to list values that might be changed when the program is modified as variables at the beginning of the program. Then, when you modify the program, you only need to change one statement at the beginning rather than look through the entire program for every occurrence of a particular value.

C performs this task even more efficiently with the precompiler command **#define**, which lets you define a word (or any string of characters) as representing a value.

The next version of this program, for example, contains the statement **#define MAXWORDS 10**. (Note that like other precompiler commands, this command does not end with a semicolon.) Throughout the program, wherever the counter must be less than 10, you test whether it is less than **MAXWORDS** instead.

As the # sign indicates, this command is processed by the precompiler, as is the command **#include**. Before actual compilation begins, the value 10 is substituted for the word **MAXWORDS** wherever **MAXWORDS** appears in the program.

Because this program uses this constant, it runs more efficiently than programs in languages that use variables for values, such as this one, that may eventually be changed. This program does not require extra memory to store a variable or extra time to retrieve it. Yet it is as easy for the programmer to change the value of this constant as it would be to change the value of a single variable at the beginning of the program.

It is conventional to give this type of defined constant a name that is in all upper-case letters to distinguish it from a variable.

Retesting Words

Option nine on the menu, the option of retesting words that were missed the last time through, has not been discussed yet in order to simplify the development of the program up to this point.

To implement this option, you must add another conditional **if( )** statement toward the beginning of **testword( )**. Just after the **if( )** that checks for part of speech (and, if it is not right, adds one to the counter and loops back to the beginning to try again), you need another **if( )** that checks to see if the **errorFlg** for that word is equal to 1 and, if it is not, loops back in just the same way to try the next word.

In addition, you must add a line of code farther down in the program (where it prints an error message if the user gets the word wrong) to set **errorFlg** to 1 in case of error. If the user does not choose retesting from the menu, you would have to make all of the **errorFlgs** equal to O again, to keep a record of the errors on the next round, as in the pseudocode.

One intriguing thing about the retest option is that the program must record which languages were used the last time through in order to implement that option. The program must know whether to use the **wordtest("English","french",'R');** statement or the **wordtest("French","English",'R');** statement. The words that need to be retested are marked, because the **errorFlg** has been made equal to 1, but the program has no way of knowing whether to retest by asking the user these words in English and getting a French translation, or vice versa.

The obvious way to solve this problem is to create two new string variables, which you could call **toAsk** and **toAnswer**. When the user chooses any option, the program stores the word **"English"** in **toAsk** and **"French"** in **toAnswer** if the user is translating from English to French, and the program stores **"French"** in **toAsk** and **"English"** in **toAnswer** if the user is translating from French to English. Then, if the user chooses the option of retesting, you can simply use the command **wordtest(toAsk, toAnswer,'R');**, and the program interprets that command to mean **wordtest("English","French",'R',)** or **wordtest("French","English",'R')**, depending on which of type of test was taken the last time.

Simplifying the Program

Once you think about creating these new string variables to solve the problem of retesting, you should also begin to have a larger idea about how to simplify that prolonged **if-else-if** ladder in the **main( )** module of the program.

Why not use the same variables, **toAsk** and **toAnswer**, for all of the options? You can give them their values in just one brief **if-else** statement rather than in a prolonged **if-else-if** ladder. This strategy is easier to understand if you look at the listing that follows. You must also create a new variable for the final parameter, which represents the part of speech or retest option. This variable can be called **whchWrds**.

Now that you have seen the longer version of this choice, you should not have much trouble understanding the shorter but slightly more complex version that follows.

```
                    /* Chapter 5, Example 9 */
#include <stdio.h>

#define MAXWORDS 10       /* English-French Flashcard program */

struct flshcard
```

```
    {
    char English[16];
    char French[16];     /* struct to hold flashcard data */
    char spchPart;
    int errorFlg;
    } enFr[MAXWORDS];

int retstFlg;

main()                                          /* main menu */
{
char ch[2];
char toAsk[8], toAnswer[8], whchWrds;

initlze();
retstFlg = 0;
while(1==1)                                /* display the menu */
  {
  printf("\n\t\t\tLanguage Flashcards \n\n");
  printf("\n\n\t\t1 - English to French, nouns");
  printf("\n\n\t\t2 - English to French, verbs");
  printf("\n\n\t\t3 - English to French, others");
  printf("\n\n\t\t4 - English to French, all");
  printf("\n\n\t\t5 - French to English, nouns");
  printf("\n\n\t\t6 - French to English, verbs");
  printf("\n\n\t\t7 - French to English, others");
  printf("\n\n\t\t8 - French to English, all");
  if(retstFlg==1)
    {
    printf("\n\n\t\t9 - Errors from last test");
    }

    printf("\n\n\t\t0 - Quit");
    if(retstFlg!=1)
        {
    printf("\n\n\");
        }
    printf("\n\n\t\t\tWhat is your choice > ");
    gets(ch);
```

```
                             /* get user's choice and */
                             /* set parameters accordingly */

    if(ch[0]=='1' || ch[0] == '2' || ch[0] == '3' ||
                                          ch[0] == '4')
       {
       strcpy(toAsk,"English");
       strcpy(toanswer,"French");
       }
    if(ch[0] == '5' || ch[0] == '6' || ch[0] == '7' ||
                                          ch[0] == '8')
       {
       strcpy(toAsk,"French");
       strcpy(toAnswer,"English");
       }
    if(ch[0] == '1' || ch[0] == '5')
       {
       whchWrds = 'N';
       }
    else if(ch[0] == '2' || ch[0] == '6')
       {
       whchWrds = 'V';
       }
    else if(ch[0] == '3' || ch[0] == '7')
       {
       whchWrds = 'O';
       }
    else if(ch[0] == '4' || ch[0] == '8')
       {
       whchWrds = 'A;
       }
    else if(ch[0] == '9' && retstFlg == 1)
       {
       whchWrds = 'R';
       }
    else if(ch[0] == '0')
       {
       break;
       }
```

```
        else
             {
             putchar(7);
             continue;
             }
        testword(toAsk,toAnswer,whchWrds);
        }
 }

initlze()                          /* create list of English */
{                                  /* and French words: to be */
int counter;                       /* improved in Chapter 6 */

counter = 0;
while(counter<MAXWORDS)
     {
     enFr[counter].errorFlg = 0;
     counter = counter = 1;
     }
strcpy(enFr[0].English,"TO SPEAK");
strcpy(enFr[0].French,"[PARLER");
enFr[0].spchpart = 'V'
strcpy(enFr[1].English,"TO SELL");
strcpy(enFr[1].French,"VENDRE");
enFr[1].spchPart = 'V';
strcpy(enFr[2].English,"TOGO");
strcpy(enFr[2].French,"ALLER");
enFr[2].spchPart = 'V'
strcpy(enFr[3].English,"THE BOY");
strcpy(enFr[3].french,"LE GARCON");
enFr[3].spchPart = 'N';

strcpy(enFr[4].English,"THE PEN");
strcpy(enFr[4].french,"LA PLUME");
enfr[4].spchPart = 'N';
strcpy(enFr[5].English,"THE GIRL");
strcpy(enFr[5].French, "LA FILLE");
enFr[5].spchPart = 'N';
strcpy(enFr[6].English, 'IN');
```

```
strcpy(enFr[6].French,"DANS");
enFr[6].spchPart = 'O';
strcpy(enFr[7].English, "ON");
strcpy(enFr[7].French, "SUR");
enFr[7].spchpart = 'O'
strcpy(enFr[8].English, "DURING");
strcpy(enFr[8].French,"PENDANT");
enFr[9].spchPart = 'O';
strcpy(enFr[9].English,"BEFORE");
strcpy(enFr[9].French,"AVANT");
enFr[9].spchPart = 'O';
}

testword(lang1,lang2,pos)                    /* test user */
char pos;
char lang1[];                                /* using parameters */
char lang2[];                                /* set in main() */

{
int wrdCntr, ltrCntr;
char answer[16];
char yorn[2];
int retestFlg;

wrdCntr = 0;
if(pos!='R')                           /* if not a retest, make */
     {                                 /* error flags 0 so they */
     while(wrdCntr<MAXWORDS)           /* can record new errors */
          {
          enFr[wrdCntr].errorFlg = 0;
          wrdCntr = wrdCntr + 1;
          }
     }

wrdCntr = 0;                           /* skip those that are */
while(wrdCntr<MAXWORDS)                /* wrong part of speech */
     {
     if(pos!+'A; && pos != 'R' && pos !=enFr[wrdCntr].spchPart)
          {
```

```
        wrdCntr = wrdCntr + 1;
        continue;
        }
    if(pos=='R' && enFr[wrdCntr].errorFlg!=1)
        {
        wrdCntr = wrdCntr + 1;
        continue;
        }
    printf("\n\n\n\n\n\n\n");
    printf("\t\t  Translation from %s to %s", lang1, lang2);
    printf("\n\n\t\t\t  test of ");
    if(pos=='N')
        {                                       /* display screen */
        printF("nouns");
        }
    else if(pos=='V')
        {
        printf("verbs");
        }
    else if(pos=='O')
        {
        printf("other words");
        }
    else if(pos=='A')
        {
        printf("all words")'
        }

    if(lang1[0]=='F')                           /* French-English */
        {
        printf("\n\n\n\n\n\n\n\n\n");
        printf("\t\t\t\t%d". enFr[wrdCntr}.French);
        printf("\n\n\n\n\n\n\n");
        printf("What is the English translation > ");

        gets(answer);                           /* get user's answer */
                                                /* and capitalize it */
        ltrCntr = 0;
        while(answer[ltrCntr] != '\0')
```

```
            {
            answer[ltrCntr] = toupper(answer[ltrCntr]);
            ltrCntr = ltrCntr + 1;
            }

        if(strcmp(answer,enFr[WrdCntr].English==0)
            {
            printf("\n\nCongratulations. That is right.");
            printf("\nDo you want to try another (Y/N) > ");
            gets(yorn);
            if(toupper(yorn[0]=='N')
                {
                return;
                }
            }                                /* message for right */
    else                                     /* or wrong answer */
            {
            enFr[wrdCntr].errorFlg = 1;
            retstFlg = 1;
            printf("\n\nThe correct answer is %s.",
                                          enFr[wrdCntr].English);
            printf("\nDo you want to try another (Y/N) > ");
            gets(yorn);
            if(toupper(yorn[0])=='N'
                {
                return;
                }
            }
            wrdCntr=wrdCntr + 1;
        }
    else                                     /* English-French */
        {

        printf("\n\n\n\n\n\n\n\n\n\n");
        printf("\t\t\t\t%s", enFr[wrdCntr].English);
        printf("\n\n\n\n\n\n\n");
        printf("What is the French translation > ");

        gets(answer);                        /* get user's answer */
```

```
                                        /* and capitalize it */
    ltrCntr = 0;
    while(answer[ltrCntr] != '\0')
         {
         answer[ltrCntr] = toupper(answer[ltrCntr]);
         ltrCntr = ltrCntr + 1;
         }
    if(strcmp(answer,enFr[wrdCntr].French)==0)
         {
         printf("\n\ncongratulations. That is right.");
         printf("\ndo you want to try another (Y/N) > );
         gets(yorn);
         if(toupper(yorn[0])=='N')
              {
              return;
              }
         }                         /* message for right */
    else                           /* or wrong answer */
         {
         enFr[wrdCntr].errorFlg  = 1;
         retstFlg = 1;
         printf("\n\nNo, the correct answer is %s.",
                                   enFr[wrdCntr].French);
         printf("Do you want to try another (Y/N) ");
         gets(yorn);
         if(toupper(yorn[0])=='N')
              {
              return;
              }
         }
    wrdCntr =wrdCntr + 1;
    }
  }
}
```

Compare this final version of the code in the second half of the **main( )** module, which assigns values to the variables used as parameters of the command

testword( );, with the first version of the program, which includes the prolonged **if-else-if** ladder that uses **testword( )** with eight different constants as parameters.

This may seem like more thinking than you should have to do to save just a few lines of code. Yet it is an excellent exercise in making programs more compact and, at the same time, it solves the problem of retesting that could not be handled in the first version of the program. If the user chooses option nine, to retest the errors he or she missed last time, the program does not assign any values at all to the variables that represent the names of the languages. It simply leaves them as they were the last time around.

When you start writing programs on your own, it is a good exercise to go over your code and see if it can be made more compact in this way.

It will take you more time to write the code at first. There is always a temptation to do things the quick-and-dirty way by using your editor to create one version after another of the same command or of the same module, each modified to do something slightly different from the last. But analyzing the program carefully and finding ways to eliminate duplication and make the code more compact—if more complex—makes you a much better and much faster programmer in the long run.

Summary

A *string*, which is used to manipulate words or text in C, is an array of characters terminated by the null character, **'\0'**. It is declared as an array of **chars** and must contain one element more than the maximum number of characters in the word that it will hold to leave a space for the null terminator. For example, the array declared as char **word[21];** holds a word of up to twenty letters.

It is possible to assign a value to a string by initializing each **char** of the string individually and adding the null terminator, but it is easier to use the function **strcpy( )**, which can copy a constant to a variable as follows:

```
char name [16];
strcpy(name,"Amadeus");
```

String constants are enclosed in double quotation marks, unlike **chars**, which are enclosed in single quotation marks.

As with most string-handling functions, the first argument of **strcpy( )** is the target that is changed. This function can also be used to copy one variable to another. For example, the statement **strcpy(name, musician);** copies the string already stored in the variable **musician[ ]** into the variable **name[ ]**.

The formatted I/O functions **printf( )** and **scanf( )** can be used with the special character **%s** to handle strings, but **scanf( )** only reads a string up to the first blank space character (space, newline, tab, or carriage return).

The unformatted I/O function **gets( )** can be used to read a string containing blank spaces. **gets( )** is one of a family of unformatted I/O functions that begin with **get** or **put**, including the functions **gets( )** and **puts( )** for strings and **getchar( )** and **putchar( )** for characters.

Other functions that are commonly used with strings include the following:

- **toupper( )** and **tolower( )**, both of which take one **char** as their argument and which make an alphabetic **char** uppercase or lowercase but have no effect on nonalphabetic characters.
- **strcmp( )**, which takes two strings as its arguments and returns a 0 if the two are identical.
- **strlen( )**, which takes one string as its argument and returns the length of that string.

The *structure* or *struct* can be thought of as a package of data that lets you combine different data types. The declaration of a structure includes each of its elements after its name, as follows:

```
struct employee
   {
   char fname[21];
   char lname[31];
   char address[31];
   char city[21];
   char state[3];
   char zip[6];
   char sex;
   int age;
   float salary;
   };
```

This declaration essentially creates a new data type, named **employee**, by packaging together a list of existing data types. It does not create an actual variable. To create variables of this type, you can use a declaration such as **struct employee smith;**. You can also create arrays of structs, with a declaration such as **struct employee acmeEmp[100];**.

You can also combine the declaration of the struct and of the variables as follows:

```
struct employee
    {
    char fname[21];
    char lname[31];
    char address[31];
    char city[21];
    char state[3];
    char zip[6];
    char sex;
    int age;
    float salary;
    }smith, jones, acmeEmp[100];
```

To refer to individual elements of a variable that is a struct, you must use the name of the variable, plus a period, plus the name of the element, for example, **jones.salary** or **acmeEmp[10].salary** or **acmeEmp[10].lname[10]**.

The precompiler command **#define** makes it easy to modify programs by letting you define a word (or any string of characters) as representing a constant value. For example, the statement **#define MAXWORDS 10** makes the precompiler substitute the value 10 whenever MAXWORDS appears. Note that, like other precompiler commands, this statement does not end with a semicolon. It is conventional to use all uppercase letters for the names of defined constants.

Chapter 6

Addresses and Disk Files

In Chapter 5, you developed a foreign language flash-card program, but its test included only a few words, because you were not able to store lists of words on disk.

In this chapter, you write a program that lets you enter a list of words and stores it in a disk file. You also modify the flash-card program that you already developed so that it reads this list of words from disk and uses it in its test. To do this, you learn:

- how to use pointers, which let you access addresses in memory
- how to make one function change the value of a local variable in another function
- how to access elements of an array using pointer arithmetic
- how to use a stream pointer to access a file
- the difference between C's high-level and low-level file-handling functions

A Warning

As you know, the main topic of this chapter is saving data in files on disk and reading them back into memory. Because this requires you to use what are called *pointers*—variables that "point" to addresses in memory—this chapter begins with a brief general overview of pointers.

This is a fairly advanced topic, and you should not necessarily try to master it before going on to the rest of the chapter. Virtually every advanced seminar on C programming covers pointers, because they can be one of the most difficult features of the language.

A few simple uses of pointers are included in this beginning book on C for two reasons:

- to help you understand the two different ways that one function of a structured program can manipulate variables in another function.
- to give you some general background on the way computers use addresses, which fill out your introduction to the concepts of computer programming.

Yet a warning is needed before you start compiling programs that use pointers.

Remember that C is a "robust" language. You have learned from the beginning of this book that C does what you tell it to do, whether your instructions make sense or not. C's robustness is the source of much of its power, but it is also potentially dangerous.

As you saw in Chapter 1, for example, if you tell C to print an integer as a character, it does so rather than warn you, as most languages would, that you are using an incorrect data type. This characteristic of C made it easy to write the ASCCHRT program, but it adds to your responsibility as a programmer.

For example, you can mix up a calculation horribly if you mistakenly define one of the numbers that you are using as a char and the program, without any error message, simply uses the ASCII value of that number rather than the number itself.

C is equally "robust" when it is working with addresses, which can cause even more problems.

Say, for example, that you declare an integer variable named x and give it some initial value. Later in the program, if you want to change the variable's value and mistakenly tell C to write a value in address number x, rather than in the address of variable x, your program places that value in that memory slot instead of assigning that value to the variable, just as you told it to.

When a program is running, the operating system, such as MS-DOS, remains in RAM and its services are available for use by the program. If you write a C program that mistakenly places variables in addresses that happen to be located in the area of RAM that holds the operating system, your program simply writes over MS-DOS and causes the system to fail.

This error does not happen if you write data into the addresses of the variables, but—as you see later in this chapter—it can happen if you leave out just one little **&** by mistake, so that the program writes data into the address whose number is the same as the value of the variable.

If you write over your operating system, you must simply turn the computer off, and then turn it back on. When the computer reboots, MS-DOS is comfortably installed in RAM again.

The real danger when you use pointers is that you might mistakenly write over data that is stored on your disk and lose it permanently. You could overwrite parts of an expensive program that you just installed on your hard disk, or overwrite data that is irreplaceable.

Even worse, there is a part of your disk that is called the File Allocation Table (or FAT), which is a chart showing where data is stored. The operating system cannot access any data from the disk without this table, and, unfortunately, if you make an error in typing your C program, you can conceivable overwrite this table and lose all of the data on your hard disk.

The most common way for beginners to lose all of their data is by formatting their hard drive when they are trying to format a new floppy drive: in early versions of DOS, entering the command **FORMAT** without the **A:** you are supposed to add after it, could cause DOS to wipe out your entire hard disk without even giving you a warning.

The most common way for more advanced users to lose the data on their hard disk is by making an apparently minor error in a C program that uses pointers. The obvious lesson is always to keep your hard disk backed up. Get into the habit of performing a routine backup at the end of every week.

While you are working on the rest of this book, back up any new data you add. Most important, be sure your hard disk is completely backed up before you compile and run any C programs that use pointers.

Pointers: The Basics

You have already learned about one operator that you need in order to work with pointers—the ampersand (**&**), which means "the address of."

The other operator that goes along with it is the asterisk (*), sometimes called the *indirection operator,* which means "the contents of address."

Look, for example, at the following program fragment:

```
pSamplVar = &samplVar;
*pSamplVar = 12;
```

The first line means "make pSamplVar equal to the address of samplVar," and the second line means "make the contents of address pSamplVar equal to 12." The contents of address pSamplVar is the variable samplVar, so this program makes samplVar equal to 12.

Note that the first line, which assigns the value of some variable's address to the pointer, must precede the second line. If you wrote a program that declared a pointer and placed, for example, 12 in that address without first assigning a value to that pointer, the program simply interprets whatever random value that pointer happened to have as an address and would put the value 12 there, possibly in some key memory location. This is is another good example of how you can make your system to crash.

Declaring a Pointer

The asterisk is also used in the declaration of a pointer. For example, the previous code fragment would need to be preceded by the declaration int ***pSamplVar;** because pSamplVar points to an integer.

You use this same kind of declaration to declare pointers to any data type. For example, a pointer to a character would be declared as **char *pSamplVar;**.

The fact that the asterisk is used as an operator in the code and is also used in the declaration is a bit confusing, because you should read it differently in these two places. Remember that:

- in the code, the asterisk means "the contents of address."
- in the declaration, the asterisk just means that the variable is a pointer: It holds the number that is the address of some memory slot.

Also remember that the declaration **char *pSamplVar;** or **int *pSamplVar;** does not mean that the pointer variable itself is a **char** or in **int.** It means that the pointer points to a **char** or an **int**.

The compiler needs to know what data type the pointer is the address of to know how many bytes to get to read the contents of that address. If the pointer points to a **char**, then the contents of that address is only one byte long. If the pointer points to an **int**, the contents of the address is two bytes long, and so on.

Using Pointers To Change the Value of a Variable

With this basic background, you can write your first program using pointers, which expands only slightly on the previous program fragment:

```
                        /* Chapter 6, Example 1 */
#include <stdio.h>

main()                          /* sample program */
{                               /* using pointers */
int samplVar;
int *pSamplVar;

samplVar = 10;
printf("\nThe sample variable is %d.",samplVar);
pSamplVar = &samplVar;
*pSamplVar = 2;
printf("\nThe sample variable is now %d.",samplVar);
}
```

First, this program makes **samplVar** equal to 10 and prints a message telling you its value. Then it uses pointers to make **samplVar** equal to 2 and prints a message telling you its new value. The important part of the program is the way it changes the value of the variable by using pointers. First it makes **pSamplVar** equal to the address of **samplVar**, and then it makes the contents of the address **pSamplVar** equal to 2. This example is meant to make the use of pointers more real to you by letting you use them to actually change the value of a variable, so make sure your hard disk is backed up, and then compile and run this program.

Changing the Value of a Local Variable in Another Function

The use of pointers in the previous example was just an illustration. The program could obviously accomplish the same task much more easily by saying **samplVar = 2;**.

But there is one very important case in which you do need to change the value of a variable in this roundabout way by using pointers: When the variable is a local variable declared in another function of the program.

Local variables in different functions are, as you have seen, strictly segregated from each other. Up to this point, you have written functions that can have variables passed to them as parameters by other functions, can perform operations using variables, and then can return values to the functions that called them. But these functions cannot create any permanent changes in the parameters passed to them.

Consider a slight variation in the program that uses **addint( )**, which was used as an example of parameters in Chapter 4. Imagine that you wanted a function that not only added the values of two integers but that incremented each of the integers by 1 first and then added them.

The Call by Value

If you did not understand how to do this using pointers, you might try writing the program in the following way:

/* Chapter 6, Example 2 */

```
#include <stdio.h>

main()                          /* sample program: the wrong way */
{                               /* to change parameters' values */
int numbr1, numbr2, total;

numbr1 = 5;
numbr2 = 3;
total = incadd(numbr1,numbr2);
printf("\n%d plus %d equals %d",numbr1,numbr2,total);
}

incadd(x,y)
```

```
int x,y;
{
x = x + 1;
y = y + 1;
return x + y;
}
```

When **main( )** calls **incadd( )**, the values of the variables **numbr1** and **numbr2** in **main( )** are merely copied into the variables **x** and **y** in incadd( ). Any operations performed by the function that is called affect only the copies of the variables that are passed to the called function and do not affect the original variables in the calling function.

In this example, then, **incadd( )** adds 1 to the 5 and adds 1 to the 3 passed to it. Then it adds the results, and it would finally return a value of 10. But unfortunately, **main( )** prints "5 + 3 = 10," rather than "6 + 4 = 10," as the programmer intended. **incadd( )** does not affect the values of the variables in **main( )**.

This way of passing parameters to a module is known as a *call by value* because only the values of the variables in the calling function are known to the function that is called—the called function cannot get at the variables themselves.

The Call by Reference

For the called function to be able to change the variables themselves, you must use what is known as a *call by reference*, which actually gives the called function the addresses of the variables so it can affect the variables directly, as in the following program:

```
                    /* Chapter 6, Example 3 */

#include <stdio.h>

main()                  /* sample program: the right way */
{                       /* to change parameters' values */

int numbr1,numbr2,total;

numbr1 = 5;
numbr2 = 3;
total = incadd(&numbr1,&numbr2);
printf("\n%d plus %d equals %d",numbr1,numbr2,total);
```

```
}

incadd(x,y)
int *x,*y;
{
*x = *x + 1;
*y = *y + 1;
return *x + *y;
}
```

This program does make sense if you simply translate the asterisks and ampersands into English.

First, the calling function, **main( )**, must pass the addresses of the variables it wants changed to the function it calls. **main( )** assigns values to **numbr1** and **numbr2**, and then it gives a command that can be translated as "let total equal the value that is returned when you perform **incadd( )** on the address of **numbr1** and the address of **numbr2**."

The module **incadd( )** then receives two parameters that are addresses. Because these parameters are addresses, they must be declared as pointers at the beginning of **incadd( )**, in the statement int ***x,*y;**. Then, **incadd( )** says "Let the contents of address x equal the contents of address x plus 1; let the contents of address y equal the contents of address y plus 1. Then return a value that is equal to the sum of the contents of address x plus the contents of address y."

Because **incadd( )** actually made a direct reference to the addresses of the variables in **main( )**, the value of these variables is changed, and the program prints "6 + 4 = 10," which is greatly preferable to the "5 + 3 = 10" result you received from the last version.

The Use of Addresses in scanf( )

Now you can understand why the function **scanf( )** must take an address as its argument. It is because **scanf( )** changes the value of a variable in the calling function.

For example, if **main( )** includes the statement

```
scanf("%d",&smplNmbr);
```

it is calling the function **scanf( )** and asking **scanf( )** to give some value to the variable smplNmbr, which was declared in **main( )**. But, as you know, to change the value of a variable in the calling function, you must use a call by reference, which passes the address of the variable to **scanf( )**.

The Use of Addresses with Strings and Arrays

At this point, you might be ready to object and say that you have already worked with other functions that altered the variables passed to them as parameters—the string-handling functions.

For example, if you use the command **strcpy(name,"Amadeus");** the function **strcpy( )** changes the value of the variable name in the function that calls **strcpy( )**. Why didn't you need to use the ampersand to pass the address of name to **strcpy( )**?

This function works because the name of a string (or of any array) without the brackets following it actually represents the address of the first element of that array. In the example just mentioned, name is equivalent to **&name[0]**. In the string-handling function itself, you can declare the parameter either this way,

```
strcpy(str)
str[]
{
CODE
}
```

or this way, which is equivalent:

```
strcpy(str)
*str
{
CODE
}
```

Declaring the parameter with the empty brackets following it seems to indicate that the parameter is an array, and declaring it with an asterisk seems to suggest that it is a pointer, but actually the two declarations mean the same thing to the compiler. C deals with an array by using the address of the array's first element. When you are working with a string or an array as a whole (rather than element by element), it is important to remember that the distinction between a call by value and a call by reference disappears. The function that is called can always change the value of the variable because the name of the string or the array is itself an address.

Accessing Elements of Arrays

Advanced C programmers often use pointers to access the elements of an array rather than refer to those elements by their index numbers.

The use of index numbers to refer to the elements of an array is a relatively high-level feature of C. Using pointers accomplishes the same task on a lower level, which is closer to the way the computer itself does it. Pointers are used because, like many programs written at a lower level, programs using pointers generally run faster than the higher-level equivalent, although they are more difficult to follow.

If you look briefly at this advanced use of pointers, you gains more insight into the way the computer actually works with arrays. You can actually see how the program reserves an area of its memory for the elements of the array.

Pointer Arithmetic

One feature of pointers makes it easy to use them to refer to arrays.

The pointer itself is a sort of integer because the locations in memory are numbered in sequence, and the pointer is the address number of one of these locations. But the pointer is an integer of a very peculiar sort.

If you add 1 to it, it gives you the address of the next location after the variable it points to, no matter how many slots in memory the variable occupies. If it is a pointer to a **char**, adding 1 to the pointer is just like adding 1 to any integer and gives you the very next memory address. But if it is a pointer to a **float**, then adding 1 to the pointer gives you the memory location four bytes beyond the location of the **float**, which is the location immediately after the four bytes that hold the **float** (assuming, of course, that the system uses a four-byte **float**).

If you make a pointer equal to the address of one element of an array of **ints** or **floats**, then adding 1 to that pointer gives you the address of the next **int** or **float** in the array. There is no need to think about how many bytes the elements of the array actually take up. Pointer arithmetic does that for you.

The High-Level Method

Consider as a simple illustration the same program written in two different ways. First, the high-level method is as follows:

```
                        /* Chapter 6, Example 4 */
#include <stdio.h>

main()                              /* printing an array */
{                                   /* higher level method */

int counter, smplArry[9];
counter = 0;
while(counter<9)                    /* give values to all */
     {                              /* elements of the array */
     smplArry[counter] = counter + 1;
     counter = counter + 1;
     }
nineprnt(smplArry);
}

nineprnt(arry)                      /* print the array */
int arry[];
{
int counter;

counter = 0;                        /* print each element */
while(counter<9)                    /* by index number */
     {
     printf("\nElement %d equals %d.",counter,arry[counter]);
     counter = counter + 1;
     }
}
```

After storing the numbers from 1 to 9 in an array, the previous program prints the array by using a counter as the subscript that refers to each element of the array.

The Low-Level Method

The second version of the **main( )** module is the same as the first, but the module that prints out the array uses pointers instead of the ordinary index numbers of the array elements:

```
                    /* Chapter 6, Example 5 */
#include <stdio.h>

main()                              /* printing an array */
{                                   /* lower level method */
int counter, smplArry[9];

counter = 0;
while(counter<9)                    /* give values to all */
    {                               /* elements of the array */
    smplArry[counter] = counter + 1;
    counter = counter + 1;
    }
nineprnt(smplArry);
}

nineprnt(arry)                      /* print the array */
int *arry;
{
int counter;

counter = 0;                        /* print each element */
while(counter<9)                    /* using pointers */
    {.
    printf("\nElement %d equals %d.",counter,*array+counter);
    counter = counter + 1;
    }
}
```

In this second version of the program, during the first time through the loop of **nineprnt( )**, when counter is equal to 0, the program is told to go to the address **arry (plus 0)** instead of to **element arry[0]**. The second time through, the program goes to the **address arry plus 1** instead of to **element array[1]**.

Of course, these locations are the same (for instance, arry plus 1 is the same as arry[1]). The only difference is that the locations in the second version are accessed by address rather than by the usual array index.

Pointer arithmetic ensures that when you add one to the address, you get the address of the next int in memory.

A Note on Higher-Dimensional Arrays

You can also refer to higher-demensional arrays on a low level by using pointers, but this use of pointers is a more advanced topic that is not covered in this book.

You should note, however, that when you are using a two-dimensional array with index numbers, you can write the program so either number changes more quickly.

For example, if you have an array with ten rows and twenty columns, declared as **float nmbrs[10][20]** within the program, you can refer to the array as **nmbrs[rowCntr][colCntr]** and use two nested **while( )** loops to go through the array, varying either **rowCntr** or **colCntr** more quickly, depending on where you place the inner loop.

As you learned earlier, the first subscript is conventionally said to refer to the rows and the second to the columns. Most applications are easier to understand intuitively if you go through an array row by row. First, you would go through all of the numbers in row zero, from **nmbrs[0][0]** to **nmbrs[0][1]** to **numbr[0][2]**, and so on until you got to **nmbrs[0][19]**. Then, you would start the second row, beginning with **nmbrs[1][0]** and continuing through **nmbrs[1][19]**, and so on until you got through the tenth row.

This is the order used in the tic-tac-toe program, for example, and is known as going through the array in *row-major order.* Note that the number that represents the columns (that is, the number on the right) must change more quickly than the number on the left in order to read the array in row-major order.

There is one common application, however, in which row-major order is not the easiest method to understand intuitively--that is, when the two-dimensional array represents a list of words. Say, for example, that you have a list of 100 names, each name with a maximum of twenty letters. It is natural to think of this list as **names[21][100]** because **names[21]** is the array to hold one name, and it seems sensible to add the **[100]** at the end to create a list of 100 of these names.

Notice, though, that when you go through this list, you must vary the number on the left more quickly. You start by reading the first letter of the first name, **names[0][0];** then you read the second and third letters, **names[1][0]** and **names[2][0]**, and you keep going until you get to the final **'\0'** Then you start reading the first letter of the second name, **names[0][1],** and its second and third letters, **names[1][1]** and **names[2][1]**, and so on. In this case, the index number on the left is varying more quickly, which is not row-major, but *column-major,* order.

Because row-major order makes the most sense for most applications, the compiler actually stores the array in memory in this order. To read the array as it is stored in memory, the index number on the right (the column number) must vary more quickly.

Working on a higher level, you can use either order whenever you are working with an array. Although column-major order causes the program to jump back and forth in memory to retrieve the elements of the array, the user does not notice this fact.

It is generally best, particularly for beginners, to use whichever order is easiest to understand, regardless of the way it is actually stored in memory, which is why this book has used column major order—a form similar to **names[21][100]**—to store lists of words.

Advanced programmers, however, would be more likely to declare this list of words as **names[100][21]** (row-major) so that the right index number would change more quickly as the program went through each word, and the left number would change more slowly as the program went through the words on the list. By going through the array of names in row-major order, as the compiler does, advanced programmers store the letters in memory in the same order as they are used in the program, which makes it easier to access them on a lower level.

The fact that lists of names or words are often indexed in this apparently reverse way is a bit puzzling at first, but it is not hard to get used to.

Working with Disk Files

As indicated in the beginning of this chapter, pointers are an advanced topic that a beginner need not master completely. The general background about pointers that has been covered here is meant to help you to understand the reasons behind some concepts you learned in earlier chapters and, most important, to help you see why pointers are used with disk files.

Like a string, a disk file is not a fixed length, and so it cannot be handled like an ordinary variable, such as a **float** or **char**, which has a fixed location set aside in memory.

A text file is handled in much the same way as a string. The program must refer to the disk file by using a name that is a pointer to the file's first byte (like the name of an array). And the program knows the file has ended when it finds an end-of-file mark (which works like the **'\0'** at the end of a string).

High- and Low-Level Disk Input-Output

C includes two different sets of standard functions to handle disk Input-Output.

There is a low-level I/O system that is powerful but does little for the programmer. It requires you to perform all of the basic housekeeping chores yourself.

This book uses only the higher-level I/O system that does some of the housekeeping for you.

The low-level disk I/O functions are useful to write complex routines for specific tasks. The high-level I/O system is actually written by using these low-level functions and is included as part of the standard input-output package to make it easy to perform the common task of buffered I/O of text files.

Buffered Input-Output

The most noteworthy built-in feature this high-level system is the fact that it provides a buffer for you.

This means that if a program reads a disk file one character at a time, the I/O system actually reads a group of characters into RAM and gives those characters to the program one at a time as they are needed, without the programmer specifically telling the I/O system to do so. This part of RAM that holds the characters until the program asks for them is the buffer.

By contrast, low-level file I/O not does create a buffer automatically. Low-level file I/O accesses the disk to find one new character each time it is supposed to read a character from a file, unless the programmer explicitly creates a buffer. Because accessing the disk requires physical movement, it is much slower than accessing RAM, and the programmer generally would have to do this extra housekeeping work.

High-Level I/O Functions

This chapter uses four basic functions of the high-level I/O system:

- **fopen( )** opens a file so it can be used and also returns a pointer to the beginning of the file.
- **fclose( )** closes a file after you are done using it.
- **getc( )** reads a single character from the file.
- **putc( )** writes a single character to the file.

The Stream Pointer

Before opening a file, you must declare the variable that is used as the pointer to the file, as follows:

```
FILE *filePtr;
```

As you know, the asterisk before the variable name means that the variable is a pointer.

FILE is essentially a new data type. It is written in uppercase because it is actually implemented using a **#define** statement (like **MAXWORDS** in Chapter 5), which is included in **stdio.h**. The details of the implementation are not important, though. You can simply think of this declaration as creating a new data type, a pointer to a file.

This type of pointer is often called a *stream pointer* because it keeps track of a stream of characters.

A Simple Memo Program

The following simple memo program should make C's high-level file I/O functions easier to understand:

```
                          /* Chapter 6, Example 6 */
#include <stdio.h>

main() /* write the user's input */
{      /* into a text file */

FILE *filePtr;
char userInpt;
filePtr = fopen("memo.txt","w");
printf("n\Enter memo > ");
while(userInpt != '\n')
     {
     scanf("%c",&userInpt);
     putc(userInpt,filePtr);
     }
fclose(filePtr);
}
```

First, this program declares the variable **filePtr** as a stream pointer and the variable **userInpt** as a **char**. Then, the program opens the file named **memo.txt**. There are two points you should notice about the statement **filePtr=fopen("memo.txt","w");** which opens the file:

- the function **fopen( )** takes two arguments: the name of the file that is being opened plus a letter that indicates the mode in which the file is being opened. Here, the mode **"w"** indicates that the file is being opened for the program to write to it. Other common modes are **"a"** for append and **"r"** for read.
- the function **fopen( )** returns the value of a stream pointer and, the program must assign this value to a variable of that type, such as **filePtr**, in order to use the file.

After opening the file, the program uses a **while( )** loop to keep reading characters from the keyboard and writing them to the disk file until the user enters a carriage return (making the condition of the **while( )** loop untrue). The function **scanf( )** reads the characters from the keyboard one at a time. The function **putc( )** writes one character to the disk location that **filePtr** indicates and, at the same time, **putc( )** automatically increases the value of **filePtr** so it points to the next character in the disk file and is ready for the next character the user inputs.

Compile and run this program (after making sure your hard disk is backed up). Enter a memo and look at the light that indicates if your disk is being used.

Note that the program does not actually write each character to the disk when you enter the character, as the code seems to say it should. The program accesses the disk only when you enter the carriage return and leave the loop that gets and writes characters.

You are seeing the automatic input buffer at work. Without your having to worry about creating a buffer in the program, the high-level I/O functions have created a buffer in RAM. The high-level I/O functions store the characters that the user enters in that buffer until it is full, and then they write those characters to disk.

The short memo the user inputs in this program does not fill the buffer, but the **fclose( )** function at the end of the program automatically flushes the buffer. That is, **fclose( )** writes any characters left in the buffer to the file before closing it.

The programmer only needs to think about reading characters from the key-board and writing them to the disk, and all of the housekeeping just discussed is performed automatically.

Other Features of fopen( )

After you run this program and enter a sample memo into it, you can use DOS's **DIR** command to confirm that the program has created a new file named **"memo.txt"** on your disk. You can display the contents of this file on your screen by entering the command **TYPE MEMO.TXT** at the DOS prompt to confirm that the file contains the same memo you typed into it.

Run the program again, enter a second sample memo, and use **TYPE** to display the contents of the file on your screen again. You will see that the first memo has disappeared. Only the second memo is now in the file **"memo.txt."** When **fopen( )** is used with the mode **"w," fopen( )** overwrites and destroys anything that is already in the file.

Appending Text to a File

You can rewrite the program to add new memos to what is already in the file **"memo.txt,"** by using the command **fopen( )** with the append mode as follows:

```
filePtr = fopen("memo.txt","a");
```

You will try this version of the command in the next version of the program.

Error Testing

The next version of the program also expands on the **fopen( )** command by adding a common form of error testing to it.

If **fopen( )** is not able to open a file, **fopen( )** returns the value **NULL**, which is defined in **stdio.h** to be a pointer to address zero, which is not a valid pointer in C.

The **fopen( )** function returns **NULL** if the program tries to write to a file that is on a floppy disk that has a write-protect tab on it, for example.

An Improved Memo Program

To see how these features work, try this new version of the program.

```
                    /* Chapter 6, Example 7 */
#include <stdio.h>

main()                          /* append the user's input */
{                               /* to a text file */
```

```
FILE *filePtr;
char userInpt;

filePtr = fopen("memo.txt","a");
if(filePtr == NULL)
    {
    printf("That file cannot be opened");
    exit();
    }
printf("\nAdd to memo > ");
while(userInpt != '\n')
    {
    scanf("%c",&userInpt);
    putc(userInpt,filePtr);
    }
fclose(filePtr);
}
```

Try this program a few times, and note that the new memos are appended to the file that contains the old memos.

Reading from a File

Finally, rather than using the MS-DOS **TYPE** command, you can write a program in C whose sole function is to read these memo files. The reading program looks like the programs that write the memo files, with a few significant variations.

First, of course, it opens the file in the read mode, by using **"r"** in **fopen( )** instead of **"a"** or **"w"**.

Second, it reverses the commands within the **while( )** loop. Instead of using **scanf( )** to get a character from the user followed by **putc( )** to write that character in the file, the read program uses **getc( )** to read from the file, followed by **printf( )** to write the information on the screen. (When you look at the code of the program, note the use of **getc( )** carefully: It returns a value that is then assigned to the variable **toWrite**.)

The one new concept in this program is the use of **EOF**, the end-of-file marker.

The use of **EOF** in files is parallel to the use of the null character in strings. Just as string-handling functions receive a pointer to the beginning address of the string and keep reading until they reach the **'\0'** character that terminates strings, functions that work with text files receive a stream pointer to the first character of the file and keep reading until they reach an end-of-file (**EOF**) marker.

In MS-DOS, text files are terminated with ASCII character 26. You can enter this character by holding down the Ctrl key and simultaneously pressing the Z key (Ctrl-Z). This control character is displayed on the screen as **^Z**, and some text editors actually let you see it at the end of files.

If you have a DOS compiler, **EOF** is defined in **stdio.h** to mean **^Z**. To make your programs more portable to other systems, it is best to use **EOF** rather than the actual character that DOS uses.

If you understood the examples of writing to a file, the way the following program works should be apparent:

```
                    /* Chapter 6, Example 8 */
#include <stdio.h>

main()                                  /* read the memo file */
{
FILE *filePtr;
char toWrite;

filePtr = fopen("memo.txt","r");
if(filePtr== NULL)
    {
    printf("The memo file cannot be opened");
    exit();
    }
while(toWrite != EOF)
    {
    toWrite = getc(filePtr);
    printf("%c",toWrite);
    }
fclose(filePtr);
}
```

Try running this program to print out the contents of the memo files you have already created. Then, delete the memo file (using the DOS command **DEL MEMO.TXT**) and try it again. If the file is not there, the program sends you an error message saying that it cannot open the file.

These memo programs begin to be useful if you could use them with what are called *command line arguments* to create files with names that you choose. Instead of just entering commands such as **writememo** and **readmemo** (or whatever you happened to named the C source-code files for these programs), it would be good if you could enter commands such as **writememo meeting.txt** or **readmemo monday** to create or read files with those specific names. The **writememo** and **readmemo** programs have served their purpose for now, but Chapter 8 shows you how to use them with this sort of command line argument.

Other Forms of File Input/Output

C includes a number of other functions for high-level file I/O that are not be used in this book.

There are several functions for unformatted file I/O that are similar to the functions for unformatted console I/O, for example, **fgets( )** and **fputs( )**, which work like **gets( )** and **puts( )**.

There are also two functions for formatted file I/O that you use in Chapter 7 and that will look very familiar to you: **fprintf( )** and **fscanf( )**. These functions use the same special formatting characters as **printf( )** and **scanf( )**, respectively. One important purpose of **fprintf( )** and **fscanf( )** is to format numerical information.

In MS-DOS systems, all of these high-level functions generally work only with text files, which means that if your program is working with floats, for example, it must place those floats on disk and read them from the disk in ASCII form. A float is actually handled as four bytes of binary numbers, including a mantissa and an exponent, but if you are storing, for example, the float "2.1415" in a text file, it must be stored as six characters—'2' in the first byte, '.' in the second byte, '1' in the third byte, and so on. The functions **fprintf( )** and **fscanf( )** are a handy way of making this conversion.

In addition to text files, MS-DOS also uses binary files, which can store ints or floats in their original form rather than converting them to ASCII strings. This capability is useful if you are actually working with mathematical data because the conversion to and from ASCII can involve rounding errors. These binary files, however, are handled in an entirely different way from text files. Instead of using an end-of-file marker, DOS keeps track of the total length of the files.

File I/O is covered in almost every advanced book on C because it is a complex and sometimes difficult topic. In an introductory book such as this, however, it is more appropriate to use only **putc( )** and **getc( )** with text files, the most basic forms of disk I/O.

Language Flashcards on Disk

You have already learned enough about disk I/O for some practical tasks—certainly enough to complete the flashcard program you began in the last chapter.

As you remember, the defect of that program was in its **initlze( )** function, which assigned values to the array of structs that contained a list of English and French words and their parts of speech. In that early version, the program used a series of **strcpy( )** statements to read words into this list, but this was such a tedious process that the program used a list only ten words long.

To make the flashcard system work properly, you need to write two new programs. The **initlze( )** function of the existing program must be rewritten to read words from a disk file and assign them to the elements of the struct. But first, you need a separate program to write the words into a disk file.

Storing Words in a Disk File

Entering the words into a disk file is relatively easy.

The program that follows declares variables that are equivalent to the elements of the struct of the flashcard program, **char English[16], char French[16]**, and **char spPrt[2]**. There is no need to make these variables part of a struct here, as it is easy enough to keep them in order.

The program opens the file **wordlist.txt** with error checking, just as earlier programs opened the file **memo.txt**. If there is no disk error, the program gets the English and French versions of the word from the user by using a routine series of **printf( )** and **gets( )** statements. The program then asks the user to confirm the fact that he or she wants to save entries on disk, so there is an escape in case the user wants to correct an error.

The only new thing about this program is what happens when the user confirms that the entry should be saved. The program uses a counter along with a **putc( )** statement to go through each of the sixteen characters of the arrays that hold the English and French words and write them on the disk. The program writes only the first letter of **spPrt** to disk. **spPrt** was declared with two letters only so it could be used with **gets( )** to get user input. Then the program asks if the user wants to enter another word. If the user does not, the program breaks out of the **while( )** loop that performs this data entry and closes the file before ending.

A Preliminary Version of the Program

This logic should be fairly easy to follow in this preliminary version of the program:

```
                    /* Chapter 6, Example 9 */
#include <stdio.h>

main()                          /* enter vocabulary words */
{                               /* into a disk file to be */
                                /* read by flashcard program */
FILE *filePtr;                  /* PRELIMINARY VERSION */

char English[16];
char French[16];
char spPrt[2];

char again[2], confirm[2];
int counter;

filePtr = fopen("wordlist.txt","a");
if(filePtr== NULL)
     {
     printf("Disk Error: the word-list file cannot be opened");
     exit();
     }

while(1==1)
     {
     printf("\n\n\n\n\n\n\n\n\n\n");
     printf("\t\t\tENTER VOCABULARY WORDS");
     printf("\n\t\t\t----------------------");
     printf("\n\n\n\n\n\n\n\n\n\n\n");

     printf("Enter the English Word > ");
     gets(English);

     printf("\nEnter the French Word > ");
     gets(French);

     while(1==1)
```

```
        printf("\nEnter the Part of Speech");
        printf("\n\tN-noun, V-verb, O-other > ");
        gets(spPrt);
        spPrt[0] = toupper(spPrt[0]);
        if(spPrt[0]=='N' || spPrt[0]=='V' ||
                                     spPrt[0]=='O')
            {
            break;
            }
        else
            {
            putchar(7);
            }
        }
    printf("\nDo you want to save this entry (Y/N) > ");
    gets(confirm);
    if(toupper(confirm[0]=='Y')
        {
        counter = 0;
        while(counter<16)
            {
            putc(English[counter],filePtr);
            counter = counter + 1;
            }
        counter = 0;
        while(counter<16)
            {
            putc(French[counter],filePtr);
            counter = counter + 1;
            }
        putc(spPrt[0],filePtr);
        }
    printf("\nWould you like to enter another (Y/N) > ");
    gets(again);
    if(toupper(again[0]) != 'Y')
        {
        break;
        }
```

```
    }
fclose(filePtr);
}
```

When you compile and run this program, watch the light that shows whether your disk is moving. Your disk does not move each time through the loop. Even though the program contains the **putc( )** commands that write to disk, the input is actually being held in the buffer.

The Left-Overs on Your Disk

Notice that this preliminary version of the program does not initialize all of the spaces in **English[16]** and **French[16]** with blanks before getting input from the user. The **gets( )** function fills up the beginnings of these arrays with the letters the user enters but does not do anything to the leftover spaces.

If you have been working on your computer for a while before running this program, your computer may well have used this part of memory for something else and left random garbage in these spaces. If you examine the file on the screen by using the DOS command **TYPE WORDLIST.TXT**, your screen may may resemble the following:

```
THE BOY R          LE GARCON          NTHE FISH          LE POISSON
NBEFORE H          AVANT SSON         OAFTER  H          APRES SSON
ONEAR H PRES DE ON OTO GO H ALLER E ON VTHE HAT LE CHAPEAU N
```

The **'R'** that follows **"BOY,"** the scattered **'H'**s, and the **"SSON"**s are all left-overs. It looks as if two earlier runs of the program stored **POISSON** in this general region, and **"AVANT"** and **"APRES"** wrote over the beginning of **"POISSON"** and just left the **"SSON"**.

You might also see graphic characters (lines used for drawing boxes) and control characters scattered among the words on screen.

Notice, however, that there is a blank space after every complete word that is stored. This space is where the **'\0'** null character that C uses to terminate strings is stored. **'\0'** is displayed as a blank. On the other hand, there are other no spaces following any of the part-of-speech symbols, **'N,' 'V,'** and **'O'** (except the final **'N'**) because these symbols are stored as characters--not as strings--and words a restored right after them.

For a reason that becomes clear later, the next version of this program initializes these strings with all blanks before getting words from the user. For the moment, however, the garbage is useful as an illustration of how strings work. You can write a program to read this file, even with all of the garbage there, and it prints out only the strings: the string-handling functions read only up to the null character that terminates the string and ignore the garbage that follows.

Reading Words from the Disk File

Try using a simple method of read the words from the disk file.

This short program (which is similar to the new **initlize( )** function that you will write soon for the flashcard program) just reads the file and then prints the words to screen to make sure they are right. Note how the program counts its way through the series of characters in the file and makes those characters meaningful by assigning the right number of characters to the right variable.

This sample program reads these characters into the same struct the flashcard program uses. After opening the file with the **"r"** read) option, with the usual error checking, it uses **getc( )** to read the characters one at a time as long as it does not reach the end- of-file marker.

Up to this point, the program is similar to the memo reading program discussed earlier in this chapter, but then it must use a complex **if-else-if** ladder, with three different counters, to assign these characters to the proper location in the struct. The **if-else-if** ladder assigns the first sixteen **chars** it reads to **English[16]**. After this counter reaches sixteen, the **if-else-if** ladder assigns the next sixteen **chars** to **French[16]**. After that counter runs out, it assigns one **char** to **spchPart**. Then the program sets all of these counters back to 0 and adds 1 to the entry-counter. It checks to see if the number of entries is greater than the maximum that the array can hold before it starts to read the next entry.

After reading all of the words, this sample program prints them all on the screen by using **printf("%s")**. Compile and run this program, and notice that it omits all of the garbage that follows the null terminators of the strings.

```
                    /* Chapter 6, Example 10 */
#include <stdio.h>

#define MAXWORDS 100

struct efWrdLst
   {
   char English[16];
```

```
     char French[16];
     char spchPart;
     }entry[MAXWORDS];

main()                                /* read word list */
{                                     /* high-level method */
FILE *filePtr;

char ltr;
int entrCntr, eLtrCntr, fLtrCntr, posCntr, testCntr;
if( (filePtr = fopen("wordlist.txt",'r') )== NULL)
     {
     printf("ERROR: The wordlist file cannot be opened");
     exit();
     }

entrCntr = 0;
eLtrCntr = 0;
fLtrCntr = 0;
posCntr = 0;
while(ltr != EOF)
     {
     ltr = getc(filePtr);
     if(eLtrCntr<16)
          {
          entry[entrCntr].English[eLtrCntr] = ltr;
          eLtrCntr = eLtrCntr + 1;
          }
     else if(fLtrCntr<16)
          {
          entry[entrCntr].French[fLtrCntr] = ltr;
          fLtrCntr = fLtrCntr + 1;
          }
     else if(posCntr<1)
          {
          entry[entrCntr].spchPart = ltr;
          posCntr = posCntr + 1;
          }
     if(eLtrCntr==16 && fLtrCntr==16 && posCntr==1)
```

```
            {
            entrCntr = entrCntr + 1;
            eLtrCntr = 0;
            fLtrCntr = 0;
            posCntr = 0;
            if(entrCntr > MAXWORDS)
                {
                printf("\nERROR: wordlist file is too long.");
                printf("\n\tThe program will work");
                printf("\n\twith %d words but must",MAXWORDS);
                printf("\n\tbe modified to use all the words");
                break;
                }
            }
        }
fclose(filePtr);

testCntr = 0;
while(testCntr < entrCntr)
    {
    printf("\n\n%s,entry[testCntr].English);
    printf("\n%s",entry[testCntr].French);
    printf("\n%c,entry[testCntr].spchPart);
    testCntr = testCntr + 1;
    }
}
```

One odd thing about this program is that it declares the array of structs that holds the words as a global variable, even though the program contains only one function.

However, there is a reason to make this variable global rather than local even though there is no other function to use it. C assumes that all local variables exist only as long as their function is running and are discarded when the function is over in order to save memory, and so it stores them in a special section of RAM, called the *stack*, that is reserved for temporary storage to make it easier to create and destroy these variables as the program proceeds. Though the stack has enough room for all of the local variables you would normally expect to be in use at one time, it does not have enough space for a large block of memory that an array of structs might demand.

If you try making this array of structs a local variable, you will find that if you **#define MAXWORDS** to be too large a number, the compiler gives you an error message saying that there is a *stack overflow.* Because global variables are not temporary, they are not stored in the stack, so this problem does not arise. (In Chapter 8, you will learn another way of making variables permanent and avoiding this problem.)

Working on a Lower Level

You should also notice that the **if** statement used to check whether it is time to set all of the counters back to 0 and start a new entry must be separate from the **if-else-if** ladder. It seems natural to make this statement into a final else on this ladder because it is true when all of the other conditions on the ladder are untrue. But this strategy would cause the program to go through the loop another time and read an extra **char** from the file (which would not be assigned to any variable) just to see if it was finished throwing itself out of sync by one char the next time through.

Obviously, this type of problem can be difficult to program and debug. In this case, if you want to work with lower-level input-output functions, you might actually find it easier to use the method of reading the file into the struct that is shown in Example 11 below.

A **struct**, like an **array**, is simply a block of memory. Rather than using an **if-else-if** ladder and three counters to refer to each element by its full name, a program that worked on a lower level could read right through the disk file one char at a time by using pointers.

The program in Example 11 declares a **char** pointer named **current** and, after opening the file in the usual way, initializes this pointer with the address of the first **char** of the array with the statement

```
current = &(entry[0].English[0]);
```

Then, it simply reads the disk file one **char** at a time (until it reaches **EOF**) and assigns that **char** to its proper place in the struct with the statement ***current = ltr;** ("make the contents of current equal to ltr"). It makes current equal to the next address slot in the struct by using the statement **current = current + 1;** before going on to read the next **char** from the file and assigning it to its proper place in the struct.

Note how much simpler this method is than the **if-else-if** ladder and three variables in the higher-level version of the program.

This low-level version also has a **ltrCntr** variable that it increments each time a letter is written to the file. This variable can take the place of the entry-counter in the high-level version. Because you know that each entry has thirty-three chars, you can check **if ltrCntr/33 > MAXWORDS**, and it is just the same as checking **if entrCntr > MAXWORDS** in the earlier version of the program.

```
/* Chapter 6, Example 11 */
#include <stdio.h>

#define MAXWORDS 100
struct efWrdLst
     {
     char English[16];
     char French[16];
     char spchPart;
     }entry[MAXWORDS];

main()                                    /* read word list */
{                                         /* low-level method */
FILE *filePtr;

char ltr;
char *current;
int ltrCntr = 0;
int testCntr = 0;

if( (filePtr = fopen("wordlist.txt","r") )== NULL)
     {
     printf("ERROR: The wordlist file cannot be opened");
     exit();
     }

current = &(entry[0].English[0]);

while(ltr != EOF)
     {
     ltr = getc(filePtr);
```

```
        *current = ltr;
        current = current + 1;
        ltrCntr = ltrCntr + 1;

        if( (ltrCntr/33) > MAXWORDS)
            {
            printf("\nERROR: wordlist file is too long.");
            printf("\n\tThe program will work");
            printf("\n\twith %d words but must",MAXWORDS);
            printf("\n\tbe modified to use all the words");
            break;
            }
        }
fclose(filePtr);

while(testCntr < (ltrCntr/33) )
        {
        printf("\n\n%s",entry[testCntr].English);
        printf("\n%s",entry[testCntr].French);
        printf("\n%c",entry[testCntr].spchPart);
        testCntr = testCntr + 1;
        }
}
```

This low-level version of the program uses exactly the same code to print out the words as the high-level version did. Of course, the results are the same because each **char** from the file has been read into the same address in the memory location that holds the struct in both versions.

This program is an elegant example of the fact that working on a lower level can sometimes actually make your life easier because the code is not nearly as hard to write and debug as the high-level program it replaces.

The Final Word Entry Program

Unless you are extremely unlucky, both of these programs read your garbage-filled file, **wordlist.txt**, and print out only the strings that you entered into it, proving that the null terminator of strings lives up to its name—that is, that the program reads the string until it gets to the **'\0'** and then terminates.

If you are very unlucky, though, one of the bits of garbage in the file will be DOS's end-of-file marker, ASCII character 26 or **^Z** (**[Ctrl-Z]**), which is not visible when you **TYPE** the file to screen. Because the programs that print the file keep reading characters only until they reach the end of the file, a stray end-of-file marker causes the programs to stop reading before they have read all of the words you entered.

The final version of the program to enter words eliminates this problem and makes the test file look a bit neater also. The only addition it makes to the preliminary version is that it simply blanks out the array with the statements:

```
strcpy(English,"
strcpy(French,"
```

before it gets input from the user. Both arrays are initialized as a string of fifteen blanks (plus a null terminator), so there is no garbage in that part of RAM when it gets its new value from the user.

Now that you have had the experience of working with files with garbage included, add these two lines to the preliminary version of the program to get the final version. If you were unlucky enough to get a stray end-of-file marker in the middle of the file when you used the last version of the program so that the two programs to read the file mysteriously malfunctioned, try them again after creating a new word file with the following program:

```
                              /* Chapter 6, Example 12 */
#include <stdio.h>

main()                          /* enter vocabulary words */
{                               /* into a disk file to be */
                                /* read by flashcard program */
FILE *filePtr;                  /* FINAL VERSION */

char English[16];
char French[16];
char spPrt[2];

char again[2], confirm[2];
int counter;

filePtr = fopen("wordlist.txt",'a');
```

```
if(filePtr== NULL)
     {
     printf("Disk Error: the word-list file cannot be opened");
     exit();
     }

while(1==1)
     {
     strcpy(English," ");          /* blank out */
     strcpy(French," ");           /* garbage */

     printf("\n\n\n\n\n\n\n\n\n\n\n");
     printf("\t\t\tENTER VOCABULARY WORDS");
     printf("\n\t\t\t---------------------");
     printf("\n\n\n\n\n\n\n\n\n\n\n\n");
     printf("Enter the English Word > ");
     gets(English);
     printf("\nEnter the French Word > ");
     gets(French);
     while(1==1)
          {
          printf("\nEnter the Part of Speech");
          printf("\n\tN-noun, V-verb, O-other > ");
          gets(spPrt);
          spPrt[0] = toupper(spPrt[0]);
          if(spPrt[0]=='N' || spPrt[0]=='V' || spPrt[0]=='O')
               {
               break;
               }
          else
               {
               putchar(7);
               }
          }

     printf("\nDo you want to save this entry (Y/N) > ");
     gets(confirm);

     if(toupper(confirm[0]=='Y')
```

```
            {
            counter = 0;
            while(counter<16)
                 {
                 putc(English[counter],filePtr);
                 counter = counter + 1;
                 }
            counter = 0;
            while(counter<16)
                 {
                 putc(French[counter],filePtr);
                 counter = counter + 1;
                 }
            putc(spPrt[0],filePtr);
            }
       printf("\nWould you like to enter another (Y/N) > ");
       gets(again);
       if(toupper(again[0]) != 'Y')
            {
            break;
            }
       }

fclose(filePtr);
}
```

Incidentally, if you wanted to make this program foolproof, you could create your own buffer of perhaps eighty characters in the program and have the user enter the words into that buffer. Then, you could use **strlen( )** to see if the words were more than the maximum fifteen letters that this program can handle.

You could also have the program automatically capitalize all of the letters entered. The flashcard program capitalizes the user's input before comparing it with the word on disk to make sure the user does not have any problems with upper- and lower-case. In the program to enter the words, however, the assumption is that the user knows to enter words that are not too long and are all upper-case letters because this program will actually be used by someone who is setting up a list of words to be distributed with the flashcard program to the final end-user.

The Final Flash-Card Program

Either of the programs you wrote to read the disk file—high-level or low-level—can be substituted with very little change for the **initlze( )** module in the flash-card program. In this book, the final code of the program incorporates the harder high-level version, but you can substitute the low-level version if you want.

There is one other change in the final flashcard program. It begins with the statement **#define FOREIGN French** and uses **FOREIGN** wherever the earlier version used French. Now, you can modify it into a flashcard program for any language you choose by simply changing that initial definition into **#define FOREIGN German**, **#define FOREIGN Italian**, or whatever language you want, and using the previous word entry program to enter the appropriate set of foreign and English words into the **wordlist.txt** file.

/* Chapter 6, Example 13 */
/* English-French Flashcard program */

```
#include <stdio.h>

#define MAXWORDS 100
#define FOREIGN French

struct flashcard
     {
     char English[16];
     char FOREIGN[16];          /* struct to hold flashcard data */
     char spchPart;
     int errorFlg;
     } enFr[MAXWORDS];

int retstFlg;

main()                                              /* main menu */
{
char ch[2];
char toAsk[8], toAnswer[8], whchWrds;
initlze();
retstFlg = 0;
while(1==1)                                    /* display the menu */
```

```
{
printf("\n\t\t\tLanguage Flashcards\n\n");
printf("\n\n\t\t1 - English to FOREIGN, nouns");
printf("\n\n\t\t2 - English to FOREIGN, verbs");
printf("\n\n\t\t3 - English to FOREIGN, others");
printf("\n\n\t\t4 - English to FOREIGN, all");
printf("\n\n\t\t5 - FOREIGN to English, nouns");
printf("\n\n\t\t6 - FOREIGN to English, verbs");
printf("\n\n\t\t7 - FOREIGN to English, others");
printf("\n\n\t\t8 - FOREIGN to English, all");
if(retstFlg==1)
    {
    printf("\n\n\t\t9 - Errors from last test");
    }
printf("\n\n\t\t10 - Quit");
if(retstFlg!=1)
    {
    printf("\n\n");
    }
printf("\n\n\t\t\tWhat is your choice > ");
gets(ch);
                                    /* get user's choice and */
                               /* set parameters accordingly */
if(ch[0]=='1' || ch[0]=='2' || ch[0]=='3' || ch[0]=='4')
    {
    strcpy(toAsk,"English");
    strcpy(toAnswer,"FOREIGN");
    }

if(ch[0]=='5' '' ~h[0]=='6' || ch[0]=='7' || ch[0]=='8')
    {
    strcpy(     k,"FOREIGN");
    strcpy     iswer,"English");
    }
if(ch[0]==     || ch[0]=='5')
    {
    whchW   , = 'N';
    }
else if(ch   ]=='2' || ch[0]=='6')
```

```
          {
          whchWrds = 'V';
          }
      else if(ch[0]=='3' || ch[0]=='7')
          {
          whchWrds = 'O';
          }
      else if(ch[0]=='4' || ch[0]=='8')
          {
          whchWrds = 'A';
          }
      else if(ch[0]=='9' && retstFlg == 1)
          {
          whchWrds ='R';
          }
      else if(ch[0]=='0')
          {
          break;
          }
      else
          {
          putchar(7);
          continue;
          }

      testword(toAsk,toAnswer,whchWrds);
      }
}

initlze()                                    /* read word list */
{
FILE *filePtr;
char ltr;
int entrCntr, eLtrCntr, fLtrCntr, posCntr, testCntr;

if( (filePtr = fopen("wordlist.txt",'r') )== NULL)
      {
      printf("ERROR: The wordlist file cannot be opened");
      exit();
```

```
    }
entrCntr = 0;
eLtrCntr = 0;
fLtrCntr = 0;
posCntr = 0;

while(ltr != EOF)
    {
    ltr = getc(filePtr);
    if(eLtrCntr<16)
        {
        enFr[entrCntr].English[eLtrCntr] = ltr;
        eLtrCntr = eLtrCntr + 1;
        }
    else if(fLtrCntr<16)
        {
        enFr[entrCntr].FOREIGN[fLtrCntr] = ltr;
        fLtrCntr = fLtrCntr + 1;
        }
    else if(posCntr<1)
        {
        enFr[entrCntr].spchPart = ltr;
        posCntr = posCntr + 1;
        }
    if(eLtrCntr==16 && fLtrCntr==16 && PosCntr==1)
        {
        entrCntr = entrCntr + 1;
        eLtrCntr = 0;
        fLtrCntr = 0;
        posCntr = 0;

        if(entrCntr > MAXWORDS)
            {
            printf("\nERROR: wordlist file is too long.");
            printf("\n\tThe program will work");
            printf("\n\twith %d words but must",MAXWORDS);
            printf("\n\tbe modified to use all the words");
            break;
            }
```

```
        }
    }
fclose(filePtr);
}

testword(lang1,lang2,pos)
char pos;                                  /* test user */
char lang1[];                              /* using parameters */
char lang2[];                              /* set in main() */

{
int wrdCntr, ltrCntr;
char answer[16];
char yorn[2];
int retestFlg;

wrdCntr = 0;
if(pos!='R')                             /* if not a retest, make */
    {                                    /* error flags 0 so they */
    while(wrdCntr<MAXWORDS)              /* can record new errors */
        {
        enFr[wrdCntr].errorFlg = 0;
        wrdCntr = wrdCntr + 1;
        }
    }
wrdCntr = 0;                             /* skip those that are  */
while(wrdCntr<MAXWORDS)                  /* wrong part of speech */
    {
    if(pos!='A' && pos!= 'R' && pos!=enFr[wrdCntr].spchPart]
        {
        wrdCntr = wrdCntr + 1;
        continue;
        }
    if(pos== 'R' && enFr[wrdCntr].errorFlg!=1)
        {
        wrdCntr = wrdCntr + 1;
        Continue;
        }
```

```
    printf("\n\n\n\n\n\n\n\n");
    printf("\t\t Translation from %s to %s", lang1,lang2);
    printf("\n\n\t\t\t test of ");
    if(pos=='N')
        {                                   /* display screen */
        printf("nouns");
        }
    else if(pos=='V')
        {
        printf("verbs");
        }
    else if(pos=='O')
        {
        printf("other words");
        }
    else if(pos=='A')
        {
        printf("all words");
        }

    if(lang1[0]=='F')                       /* French-English */
        {
        printf("\n\n\n\n\n\n\n\n\n");
        printf("\t\t\t\t%s", enFr[wrdCntr].FOREIGN);
        printf("\n\n\n\n\n\n\n");
        printf("what is the English translation > ");
        gets(answer);                      /* get user's answer */
                                           /* and capitalize it */
        ltrCntr = 0;
        while(answer[ltrCntr] != '\0')
            {
            answer[ltrCntr] = toupper(answer[ltrCntr]);
            ltrCntr = ltrCntr +1;
            }

        if(strcmp(answer,enFr[wrdcntr.].English)==0)
            {
            printf("\n\nCongratulations. That is right.");
```

```
            printf("\nDo you want to try another(Y/N) > ");
            gets(yorn);
            if(toupper(yorn[0]=='N')
                {
                return;
                }
            }                               /* message for right */
        else                                /* or wrong answer */
            {
            enFr[wrdCntr].errorFlg = 1;
            retstFlg = 1;
            printf("\n\nThe correct answer is %s.",
            enFr[wrdCntr].English);
            printf("\nDo you want to try another (Y/N) > ");
            gets(yorn);
            if(toupper(yorn[0])=='N')
                {
                return;
                }
            }
        wrdCntr =wrdCntr + 1;
        }

    else                                    /* English-French */
        {
        printf("\n\n\n\n\n\n\n\n\n\n");
        printf("\t\t\t\t%s", enFr[wrdCntr].English);
        printf("\n\n\n\n\n\n\n\n");
        printf("what is the FOREIGN translation > ");

        gets(answer);                       /* get user's answer */
                                            /* and capitalize it */
        ltrCntr = 0;
        while(answer[ltrCntr] != '\0')
            {
            answer[ltrCntr] = toupper(answer[ltrCntr]);
            ltrcntr = ltrCntr + 1;
            }
        if(strcmp(answer,enFr[wrdCntr].FOREIGN)==0)
```

```
                {
                printf("\n\nCongratulations. That is right.");
                printf("\ndo you want to try another (Y/N) > ");
                gets(yorn);
                if(toupper(yorn[0]=='N')
                    {
                    return;
                    }
                }                           /* message for right */
            else                            /* or wrong answer */
                {
                enFr[wrdCntr].errorflg = 1;
                retstFlg = 1;
                printf("\n\nNo, the correct answer is %s.",
                                      enFr[wrdCntr].FOREIGN);
                printf("do you want to try another (Y/N) ");
                gets(yorn);
                if(toupper(yorn[0]== 'N')
                    {
                    return;
                    }
                }
            wrdCntr = wrdCntr + 1;
            }
        }
    }
```

Summary

A *pointer* is a variable that is the address of another variable. Two operators are used to work with pointers: (**&**) means "the address of," and the asterisk (*), the indirection operator, means "contents of address."

A pointer is declared using the data type of the variable it points to plus an asterisk before its name. For example, **float *pSmplVar;** declares a variable that is a pointer to a float.

For one function to change the value of a local variable of another function, it is necessary to pass the address of that variable to the function that is to change the variable's value. This is a *call by reference.*

By contrast, if you just pass a function the name of the variable, it is a *call by value.* The value of the variable is copied into the parameter, and the called function can change only its copy of the variable, not the variable in the calling function itself.

The name of an array, used without any subscript, refers to the address of the first element of that array. For example, **smplArry** is equivalent to **&smplArry[0]**.

Functions that work with strings are always given the address of the first element of the array because an array does not have a fixed size, as ordinary variables do. Thus, functions that handle arrays are always called by reference.

Rather than accessing the elements of an array, using their index numbers (for example, as **smplArry[2]**, it is possible to access those elements by using their addresses (for example, as **smplArry+2**). Both forms refer to the same element of the array. Regardless of the data type a pointer points to, adding 1 to a pointer gives you the address that follows the memory needed to hold that data type. Pointer arithmetic lets you access the next element of an array by adding 1 to the address of the current element.

Low-level disk I/O functions are very powerful but difficult to use. High-level disk I/O functions do some of the routine housekeeping tasks for you. The following four high-level functions are used to work with text files:

- **fopen( )** opens a file so it can be used and also returns a pointer to the beginning of the file. This function can be used with the mode **"r"** (read), **"w"** (write), and **"a"** (append)
- **fclose( )** closes a file after you are done using it.
- **getc( )** reads a single character from the file.
- **putc( )** writes a single character to the file.

Before opening a file, you must declare the variable that is used as the pointer to the file, as follows: **FILE *filePtr;**. **File** can be thought of as a new data type, often called a *stream pointer.*

After this declaration, a value can be assigned to filePtr by using the statement **filePtr = fopen("filename","r");** so the file can be read one character at a time by using **variable = getc(filePtr);**, which assigns the character in the disk file to the variable (which should be declared as a char earlier in the program).

If the mode **"a"** or **"w"** is used, the file can be written to one character at a time by using **putc(variable,filePtr);** which will write the character stored in the character variable to the disk file. The mode **"w"** destroys any data already in the disk file. The mode **"a"** adds what is being written at the end of the disk file.

Chapter 7

A Practice Program: the Little Black Book

In this chapter, to consolidate your knowledge of the ideas you have learned in this book, you develop an address book and mailing list program. This program does not introduce you to any new concepts that are as basic as arrays, strings, structs, or disk files. It is a sort of "term-project," a fairly ambitious and complex program.

This chapter is intended to bring together the basic concepts you have already learned, and to improve your programming style. It covers:

- using the increment operator to speed up your program
- the difference between simple and compound statements
- using **1** and **0** as logical values
- understanding the difference between sequential and random files
- speeding the development of complex programs through stub testing
- sending text to your printer
- using the **bubble sort** algorithm, a classic method of sorting records

A Matter of Style

To sharpen your programming style, the program in this chapter incorporates some of the shortcuts that C programmers habitually use. Up to now, programs in this book have deliberately used a more verbose style than most C programs—an educational style designed to be easier to understand than conventional C programming.

By now, though, you are ready to use some of the more compressed ways of writing commands that are used routinely in C programs. This compressed style is a stumbling block for beginners, and it has given C the reputation of being cryptic. But is should be easy for you to now, as you use it in familiar places to do things you have already done in a simpler style.

The Increment Operator

One of the most common abbreviations in C is the increment operator, **++**, which adds 1 to a variable. For example, the statement **counter++;** is equivalent to the statement **counter = counter + 1;**.

For beginners, **counter = counter + 1;** is enough to grapple with. It also has the advantage of being similar to the way you increment the value of a variable in most other languages.

Even professional programmers sometimes object to the command **counter + +;** and use it as an example of the fact that C is weird and obscure compared to other programming languages.

Yet this statement is actually one of the most reasonable abbreviations in C. It is based on the fact that most computers' instruction sets include one instruction to add two numbers and (because adding 1 to a counter is so common) a separate instruction to increment a variable by 1. In Assembly Language, these instructions are represented by **ADD** and **INC**.

These two instructions work differently:

- The addition instruction needs to load the two numbers into two registers of the CPU before performing the operation on them. In this case, the instruction would load the variable **counter** into one register and the constant **1** into the other.
- The increment instruction only needs to load the variable into a register before performing the operation on it.

For this reason, it is faster to increment than to add 1, so the C statement **counter++;** runs faster than the statement **counter = counter + 1;**. You can test this for yourself with the following two programs:

```
                    /* Chapter 7, Example 1 */
#include <stdio.h>

main()
{
long counter;

counter = 0;
printf("start\n");
while(counter<10000000)
     {
     counter = counter + 1;
     }
printf("done\n");
}
```

Notice that these programs use a new data type, the long integer or **long** rather than the ordinary **ints** as their counters. This is because, if you have an older system, the largest **int** is just over 32,000, and the programs might count up to this maximum so quickly that they would be hard to time. As they are, they take long enough that you should be able to see if there is any difference using the + + operator.

Compile this program and time how long it takes it to count to ten million, and then compare it with the following program. If you have a older computer, you might want to change these programs to make them count up to one million, and if you have a very fast computer, you might want to make them count to one hundred million.

```
                    /* Chapter 7, Example 2 */
#include <stdio.h>

main()
{
long counter;

counter = 0;
```

```
printf("start\n");
while(counter<10000000)
     {
     counter++;
     }
printf("done\n");
}
```

Some compilers now perform extensive optimizing of code and are intelligent enough to use the **INC** operator to add 1, regardless of the original C source code. With many compilers, however, the program takes somewhere between two-thirds and four-fifths as long to run using the increment operator as it does using ordinary addition.

The **++** operator and its slightly less common counterpart, the **– –** operator, which subtracts 1 from a variable, are among the most frequently used symbols in C programs. These operators can also be used for pointer arithmetic. They are often used in compressed statements, and their usage in these cases is discussed at greater length in Chapter 8.

Simple and Compound Statement

This program also takes the shortcut of leaving out curly brackets that enclose only one statement. Up to this point, you have used the curly brackets following an **if else**, **if else if**, or **while**, even if there was only one statement to be executed following the condition, and this is not necessary.

Unnecessary Curly Brackets

The program menu in this chapter, for example, uses an **if-else-if** ladder that begins as follows:

```
if(choice=='a')
     append();
else if(choice=='m')
     prntmail();
else if(choice=='b')
     prntbook();
else if(choice=='l')
     lookup();
```

instead of using the following form that you used previously:

```
if(choice=='a')
     {
     append();
     }
else if(choice=='m')
     {
     prntmail();
     }
else if(choice=='b')
     {
     prntbook();
     }
else if(choice=='l')
     {
     lookup();
     }
```

The extra brackets set the statements off and make them easier to read, but by now, you should not have trouble understanding the first version, which sets them off using only indentation and saves you a bit of typing in the process.

To be precise, a one-line command terminated by a semicolon is a single simple statement, and all of the commands enclosed within a pair of curly brackets are a single compound statement.

A condition must be followed by a single statement that is executed if the condition is true.

If there is more than one command to be executed when the condition is true, those commands as a group must be enclosed in curly brackets to make them into a single compound statement. But if there is only one command, it is already a single statement, so the brackets are not needed.

The if-else-if Ladder

Once you know when brackets can be omitted, you can see that the **if-else-if** ladder is really nothing more than a convenient way of writing a series of **if-else** statements. Using the conventional indentation of **if-else** statements, you could write the previous menu as follows:

```
if(choice=='a')
    append();
else
    if(choice=='m')
        prntmail();
    else
        if(choice=='h')
            prntbook();
        else
            if(choice=='l')
                lookup();
```

The **if-else-if** ladder is actually just a series of nested **if-else** statements. Any condition lower down on the ladder is not executed if an earlier condition is true because the condition is nested within the **else** of that earlier conditional statement.

Because C is a free-form language that lets you use blank spaces, tabs, and carriage returns to make the code more understandable, the **if-else-if ladder** is ordinarily written with all of these nested **if-else** statements lined up along the left side of the screen (rather than indented) and with the **ifs** put on the same line as the **elses** that they follow, to make it easier for the programmer to read.

The compiler reads this code just as if it were a series of nested **if-else** statements.

1 and 0 as Logical Values

This chapter uses one more common stylistic shortcut, which also gives you more insight into the way that the computer actually works. It uses **1** and **0** to represent true and false—for example, in **if** and in **while** statements.

Flags

As you learned earlier, COBOL generally uses the easy-to-understand symbols **"Y"** and **"N"** or **"T"** and **"F"** as flags to keep track of whether a condition is true.

C programmers have a good reason for using the numbers 1 and 0 instead. The C compiler actually evaluates the number 0 as having the logical value of false and any other number as having the logical value of true.

The tic-tac-toe program in Chapter 4, for example, includes a **checkwin( )** function to see if either player had won. If this function finds a win, it will

return 1; otherwise, it will **return 0;**. The **main( )** function used **checkwin( )** to test for a win by using the condition **if(checkwin('O')==1)**.

But the program could just as well have simply used the condition **if(checkwin('O'))**.

If the function **checkwin('O')** returns a 1 (or any other number except 0), it is evaluated as true and the statements following this condition are executed. If it returns a 0, it evaluates as false, and the statements are not be executed.

Infinite Loops

One handy use of this feature of the compiler is to create infinite loops.

Programs in earlier chapters used the condition **while(1==1)** to create infinite loops (in combination, of course, with the statement **break;** within the loop).

Because the number 1 by itself means true, it is more common for C programmers to work at a lower level by simply using the condition **while(1)** to create an infinite loop instead.

strcmp( )

There is one important function that becomes a bit confusing when it is used in the way.

Remember that **strcmp( )** returns an integer showing where the difference between two strings begins if the strings being compared are different. If the strings are the same, **strcmp( )** returns a 0.

As a result, the condition **if(!strcmp(str1,str2))** is often used to test if two strings are the same.

This condition would normally be read as "if strcmp( ) of string1 and string2 returns not true", but it actually is true when the strings are identical and **strcmp( )** returns a 0.

In other words, **strcmp( )** works in a way that is just the opposite of what you would expect: **strcmp(str1,str2)** is false if the strings are identical and true if the strings are different. This apparent anomaly makes sense, however, if you remember why **strcmp( )** returns an integer (to show where the strings began to differ) or a 0 (to show that they did not begin to differ anywhere)

To keep this clear in your mind, you should not read **!strcmp(str1,str2)** as a logical statement. Instead, think of it simply a shorter way of saying **strcmp(str1,str2)==0**.

Creating the Address Book

Since this program does not introduce new concepts, its code is relatively easy to understand, and it is a fairly substantial project to fit into a single chapter, it is developed rather quickly. Its functions are explained before they are written but are not developed using pseudocode, so you have to study the code itself a bit more closely than in earlier chapters.

Analyzing the Programming Problem

The basic functions that an address book program must perform are fairly obvious.

To maintain a list of names, addresses, and phone numbers in a disk file, the program must let the user add new entries to the list, look up names in the list, and delete entries that are no longer needed from the list.

Most programs of this type also allow the user to edit entries that are already in the list, but this program does not include that feature because it is not possible to write a good editing function unless you have full screen control, which allows you to move the cursor over the existing entry and type over letters you want to change. You might want to try writing an editing function yourself after you get a library package that gives you good screen control capability.

In addition, this address book program should be able to print out a listing of its entries in alphabetical order, providing the user with a handy little pocket phone book. Because it can produce this sort of listing, this program is named **LBB - The Little Black Book**. It also allows the user to print out address labels for mailings.

Database Terminology

A bit of basic database terminology is used in this chapter, terms that are not specific to C but are used whenever databases are being discussed.

A *record* is the usual name for one meaningfully connected group of data that is part of a list of similar groups of data, such as name, address, and telephone number or all of the data on a single employee.

Each individual piece of data within the group—for example, the last name, city, or salary—is called a *field*.

The entire list of records is called a *file*.

Finally a collection of related files, which can be connected with each other, is called a *database*, although the term database is often used more loosely to refer to a single file of data.

Sequential and Random Files

One fact about disk files in C is crucial to this program. Many high-level computer languages let you use two kinds of disk files, called *sequential files* and *random files*:

- ✦ **Sequential files** can only be read from beginning to end and can only be added to by appending new data onto the end.
- ✦ **Random files** can be read or changed at any point (designated by its offset from the beginning).

Naturally, random files are best suited for an address book database application because you might want to search for and read a record located at any point in the file.

C works differently from higher-level languages. It offers programmers its low-level file-handling functions, which can be used to manipulate files in most any way you want and are much more powerful (but also more difficult to use) than random files in in a language such as BASIC.

Of course, it is possible to get libraries of C functions, for database manipulation that are written using these low-level functions, which makes it extremely easy to use very powerful forms of random file access. There are even packages of functions available that contain a C function that is equivalent to each of the common xBASE commands. These packages allow you to emulate xBASE, the most popular database programming language for the IBM-PC.

If you are interested in writing database management programs in C, you should get one of these packages after finishing this book—or, if you are more ambitious, you should get a book that teaches you to write this sort of function yourself.

As you have seen, however, the one set of easy-to-use file-handling functions that is included in the standard C Input/Output package is the high-level file I/O system discussed in Chapter 6. These functions allow only for sequential file handling—that is, for reading files from beginning to end and for appending new text onto the end of an existing file as you did in Chapter 6.

A professional database program would more advanced methods to give you access to records on disk.

The address book program in this chapter, however, uses these high-level file I/O functions that you have already learned about, and it uses a fairly simple trick to give the user random access to any record in the file.

The file consists of an array of structs, each with a name, an address, and soforth. When the program first begins, it reads this entire array into RAM, that is, every name and address is an active variable in memory, ranging from **entry[0]** up to **entry[99]** (or whatever you define the maximum number of entries to be). Then it is very easy for you to use **entry[10]** or **entry[20]** or any other random point in the file. Finally, before the program ends, it writes the entire file back onto the disk, using **putc( )** with the **"w"** mode, so the version of the file that was on the disk when you started is overwritten and destroyed, and the new version of the file in RAM (with any changes that the user has just made) is saved.

This method could not work with a very large database because here is only a limited amount of space in RAM. With a short address book of 100 names or so, however, it is actually better than performing the random access on the disk because accessing the disk requires physical motion, which takes more time than accessing RAM.

To use this method, the program needs an option to "initialize" the address book. Whenever it is started, the program must have all 100 entries in a file on the disk so they can be read into the array of structs in RAM—even the first time the program is used—before any data has been put into any of these entries. You will see how this works in more detail when you write the **initliz( )** function.

The main( ) Function

You already have enough background to write the **main( )** function, which is really a very simple menu program, similar to what you have written many times before.

Stub Testing

This **main( )** function makes use of a technique called *stub testing*, which is often used in developing complex commercial programs.

Because it would be very difficult to compile and test a complex program all at once, after the program is finished, it is common practice to write stubs of subordinate functions. For example, a stub of a function that test for some condition does not do the testing that the function actually needs to see if a condition is true or false. Instead, it just returns a 0 or a 1 to the **main( )** module. Then the main program could be complied and tested before the functions that handle all of the details are completed.

The Code for main( )

In this case, the program just contains functions to print "not yet implemented" if any of the menu options is chosen. Using these stubs lets you compile **main( )** and test it early in the process of development. Then you can add on all of the menu options and test them as they are written.

Note that this program is written using the ++ operator and the conditional statement **while(1)** and omitting unnecessary curly brackets.

```
                    /* Chapter 7, Example 3A */
                    /* LBB - Little Black Book */
              /* an address book and mailing program */
#include <studio.h>
#define MAXNAMES 100

struct nmAddrPh
     {                             /* declare an array to hold */
     char fname[21];               /* a hundred names, addresses */
     char lname[31];               /* and phone numbers */
     char addr[36];
     char city[21];
     char state[3];
     char zip[6];
     char areaCd[4]:
     char phone No[9]:
     } entry[MAXNAMES];

main()
{
char dummy[2], choice[2];
clrscrn();
printf("\n\n\n\n\n\t\t\t\tTHE LITTLE BLACK BOOK");
printf("\n\n\n\t\t copy right 1988 by My Own Development Group");
printf("\n\n\n\n\n\n\n\n\n\n\nPress ENTER to continue");
gets(dummy);
```

```
readbook();                 /* read entire book into RAM */

clrscrn();
while(1)                    /* create loop to display choices */
    {
    printf("\n\n\n\n\t\t\t\tMENU\n\n");
    printf("\n\n\t\tA - Add a New Entry");
    printf("\n\n\t\tM - Print Mailing Labels");
    printf("\n\n\t\tB - Print Alphabetical Address Book");
    printf("\n\n\t\tL - Look up a Name");
    printf("\n\n\t\tD - Delete an Entry");
    printf("\n\n\t\it - Initialize a New Address Book");
    printf("\n\n\t\tQ - Quit");
    printf("\n\n\n\n\n\tWHAT IS YOUR CHOICE > ");

    gets(choice);
    choice[0] = tolower[choice[0]);

    if(choice[0]=='a')
        append();
    else if(choice[0]=='l')
        lookup();
    else if(choice[0]=='d')
        delete();
    else if(choice[0]=='m')
        prntmail();
    else if(choice[0]=='b')
        prntbook();
    else if(choice[0]=='i')
        initliz();
    else if(choice[0]=='q')
        {                       /* only way to exit program is */
        savebook();             /* thru menu choice Q, which */
        break;                  /* automatically saves book */
        }
    else
        putchar(7);             /* if choice is invalid */
    }                           /* beep and loop back to menu */
}
```

```
append()
{
printf("not yet implemented");
}

clrscrn()
{
printf("not yet implemented");
}

delete()
{
printf("not yet implemented");
}

initliz()
{
printf("not yet implemented");
}

lookup()
{
printf("not yet implemented");
}

prntmail()
{
printf("not yet implemented");
}

prntbook()
{
printf("not yet implemented");
}

readbook()
{
printf("not yet implemented");
}
```

```
savebook()
{
printf("not yet implemented");
}
```

Testing main( )

Even at this early stage, you can test the program.

You only need to add the familiar **clrscrn( )** function to make the program's output meaningful:

```
                        /* Chapter 7, Example 3B */
              /* replaces the clrscrn( ) function in Example 3A */

clrscrn()                           /* clear the screen */
{
int counter;

counter = 0;
while(counter < 25)
     {
     printf("\n");
     counter++;
     }
}
```

With this addition, the program simply displays the menu, displays the message in the stubs when you make selections, and beeps if you makes an error. Nevertheless, it still is worthwhile to compile and test the program at this point.

You can correct any minor typographical errors, redesign the menu screen to your liking, and, if you were developing the program from scratch, you might also find errors to correct in the number of placement of curly brackets.

It is easier to find and correct these bugs now than to wait until later and try to find them while you are also struggling with more complex parts of the program.

Initializing the Address Book

It is not difficult to initialize the address book—that is, to start a new book filled with blank entries.

As a general rule, the program sees if the null terminator that C uses to end strings is in the first letter of a field in order to test whether the field is blank. For example, any functions that read the book check to see if the entry is blank by seeing if the first letter of **lname** is **'\0'**.

In essence, all the **initliz( )** function does is put this null in place, but it also adds bells and whistles to make sure it is not used by mistake.

Protecting Existing Data

It would be disastrous to use **initliz( )** by mistake, because you would essentially erase all of the entries that already existed in an address book. Once **initliz( )** puts in a **'\0'** as the first character of the entry, the function that looks up names considers that entry to be blank. You would not be able to look up names without patching the data file somehow to replace these nulls with some other character.

Even worse, if the user did not realize that there was already an address book on the disk or in the subdirectory being used and started a new one using **initliz( )**, the new address book would overwrite and totally destroy the data in the one already on disk when the program automatically saved it.

For this reason, **initliz( )** includes two levels of warning.

To guard against the possibility of the user entering 'i' by mistake instead of some other menu choice, whenever **initliz( )** is used, the program warns the user that it will overwrite any data in RAM and requests confirmation that the user wants to do this.

Even if the user does confirm that he or she wants to initialize a new address book, however, the program uses an **fopen( )** statement with the more **"r"** to see if there is already an address book file on the disk and, if there is, warns the user that it will be written over and destroyed if **initliz( )** is used. This warning guards against the possibility that the use might want to initialize a new file without realizing that there is already one in the current subdirectory.

The Code of initliz( )

With this background, you should find the code of the **initliz( )** function easy to follow:

/* Chapter 7, Example 3C */
/* replaces the initliz( ) function in Example 3A */

```
initliz()
{
int counter;           /* write \0 at the beginning of each */
char name[9];          /* entry, so other functions can see */
char yn[2];            /* which are empty */
FILE *filePtr;

clrscrn();
printf("This command is used to create a new address book.");
printf("\n\nIf it is used when an address book is being
used,");
printf("\nor when one exists in the current directory,");
printf("\nit will overwrite that address book.");
printf("\n\n ALL DATA WILL BE LOST.");
printf("\n\nEnter Y to continue or press any key to abort > ");
gets(yn);
if(toupper(yn[0]) != 'Y')
    return;

filePtr = fopen("LBB.txt",'r');
if(filePtr != NULL)
    {
    fclose(filePtr);
    clrscrn();
    printf("\n\n\nWARNING");
    printf("\n\nThere is already an ADDRESS BOOK FILE");
    printf("\n\nin this subdirectory or on this floppy disk!!");
    printf("\n\nALL DATA WILL BE DESTROYED!!!!!!!");
    printf("\n\nThe choice I - INITIALIZE should be selected");
    printf("\nONLY IN A SUBDIRECTORY OR ON A FLOPPY DISK");
    printf("\nWHERE THERE IS NO ADDRESS BOOK !!!!!!!!!");
    printf("\n\nEnter  !  to create a new address book and");
    printf("\n\tDESTROY the one already on disk");
    printf("\n\tor press any key to abort > ");
    gets(yn);
    if(yn[0] != '!')
```

```
        return;
    }
fclose(filePtr);

counter = 0;
while(counter<MAXNAMES)
    {                                   /* any entry must */
    entry[counter].lname[0] = '\0;      /* have a last name */
    counter++;
    }
clrscrn();
printf("Would you like to make entries now (Y/N) ?");
gets (yn);
if(toupper(yn[0]) == 'Y')
    append();                        /* otherwise, it returns */
}                                    /* to the menu */
```

This function takes advantage of the fact that **fopen( )** with the **"r"** mode returns **NULL** if it does not find the address book file on disk. This is like the error message in Chapter 6, but in reverse. In this case, there is a problem if **fopen** *can* find a file.

All address book files must be named **LBB.TXT** (short for "Little Black Book"), and only one file with the same name can exist in one subdirectory or on one floppy disk—though this program can be used to create address books in different directories or disks.

At the end of the function, the user is given the option of making entries immediately in the address book that has just been created. If this option is not chosen, the program returns to the menu. Remember, the user can only be allowed to quit the program through the menu, because changes in the address book are saved automatically when the user selects that menu option.

Note that the two levels of warning in this function cannot be combined because users might enter **'I'** from the menu by mistake the first time they are using the program, after entering data but before saving the address book to disk. Given the dire consequences of such an error, it is probably best to have two levels of warning anyway.

You might want to add this function to **main( )** and compile it just to correct any typographical errors, even though there is no way to test its performance yet.

Reading the File from Disk

Reading the file from disk into the array of structs is somewhat similar to reading the word list file in Chapter 6.

The function listed below uses a high-level method of reading the file with nested **while( )** loops. The inner loops read through each letter of each of the struct's elements, and the outer loop reads through each element of the array of structs (in other words, through each record of the file).

A Lower-Level Method

You might want to try using the easier but more advanced method instead, similar to the lower-level method of reading the word file that was described in Chapter 6. To do this, you must:

- declare only one counter and a character pointer named ***char begin;**
- make that pointer equal to the address of the beginning of the array of structs with the statement **begin = &entry[0].fname[0];**
- go through both the file and the array one byte at a time with the statements **counter = 0;**, ***(begin+counter)=getc( );** and **counter++;**.

Use the method described below to read until you reach the end of the file.

The End-of-File Marker

Note that in this program, you do not need to worry about the end-of-file marker with either the high-level method or the low-level method, because the file is a constant length.

The high-level method used in the listing below keeps reading until **rcrdCntr** is equal to **MAXNAMES**. To use the low-level method, you would need to count the characters and keep going until the total equals **MAXNAMES** multiplied by the total number of characters per record.

Because the end-of-file marker is not used here, you can leave all of the garbage you want in the file. The **initliz( )** function could just put a null in the first space of each **lname** and not blank everything else out, as the function to initialize the list of English and French words in Chapter 6 did.

If you prefer a neater text file, you can rewrite that function, using **strcpy( )** to copy blanks to all of the elements of each struct in the array and then to make the first space of each **lname** a null. If you were writing a commercial program, this would make your product look better, but it is not necessary in this case, and you will probably find it interesting to TYPE the file to screen and compare what is really there with the strings that the program reads.

The Code of readbook( )

Given the experience you had earlier with the flash card program, it should be easy for you to understand the listing for the **readbook( )** module in light of the discussion above. It would be an interesting challenge for you to modify this code to use the lower-level method of reading the file.

/* Chapter 7, Example 3D */

/* replaces the readbook( ) function in Example 3A */

```
readbook()              /* always used at beginning of program */
{                       /* to read entire address book into RAM */
FILE *fp;
int ltrCntr, rcrdCntr;
char dummy[2];

fp = fopen("lbb.txt",'r');           /* if there is none, user */
if(fp == NULL)                       /* should select I from */
    {                                /* menu to create one */
    clrscrn();
    printf("\n\nThere is no Address Book in this directory.");
    printf("\n\n\tYou must choose I - INITIALIZE");
    printf("\n\tfrom the menu to create one.");
    printf("\n\nPress any key to continue. . . ");
    gets(dummy);
    }

            /* if there is one, all entries are read */
            /* a char at a time and assigned to variables */
else
    {
    printf("\n\nREADING ADDRESS BOOK.  WAIT A MOMENT PLEASE.");
    rcrdCntr=0;
    while(rcrdCntr<MAXNAMES)
```

```
{
ltrCntr=0;
while(ltrCntr<21)
    {
    entry[rcrdCntr].fname[ltrCntr] = getc(fp);
    ltrCntr++;
    }
ltrCntr=0;
while(ltrCntr<31)
    {
    entry[rcrdCntr].lname[ltrCntr] = getc (fp);
    ltrCntr++;
    }
ltrCntr=0;
while(ltrCntr<36)
    {
    entry[rcrdCntr].addr[ltrCntr] = getc(fp);
    ltrCntr++;
    }
ltrCntr=0;
while(ltrCntr<21)
    {
    entry[rcrdCntr].city[ltrCntr] = getc(fp);
    ltrCntr++;
    }
ltrCntr=0;
while(ltrCntr<3)
    {
    entry[rcrdCntr].state[ltrCntr] = getc(fp);
    ltrCntr++;
    }
ltrCntr=0;
while(ltrCntr<6)
    {
    entry(rcrdCntr].zip[ltrCntr] = getc(fp);
    ltrCntr++;
    }
ltrCntr=0;
while(ltrCntr<4)
```

```
            {
            entry[rcrdCntr].areaCd[ltrCntr] = getc(fp);
            ltrCntr++;
            }
        ltrCntr=0;
        while(ltrCntr<9)
            {
            entry[rcrdCntr].phoneNo[ltrCntr] = getc(fp);
            ltrCntr++;
            }
        rcrdCntr++;
        }
    fclose(fp);
    }
}
```

Saving the File to Disk

The **savebook( )** function uses much of the same type of nested **while( )** loops as **readbook( )**, but in reverse. It goes through the address book in RAM character-by-character and writes it to disk.

In addition, **savebook( )** displays a fairly urgent warning if it cannot open the file for writing. This warning is in a **while( )** loop, so it is repeated until the user deliberately decides to sacrifice the session's work because of disk failure.

Like **readbook( )**, **savebook( )** prints a message to the screen telling the user to wait a moment while it is accessing the disk. In general, you will want to give users messages such as this when there is a delay in the program so they do not think the program has stopped working properly.

The Code of savebook( )

Enter the code of the **savebook( )** function, which is listed below.

/* Chapter 7, Example 3E */

/* replaces the savebook( ) function in Example 3A */

```
savebook()      /* automatically runs when user chooses Q */
{               /* from menu, writes book in RAM back to disk */
```

```
FILE *fp;
int ltrCntr, rcrdCntr;
char yn[2];

fp = fopen("lbb.txt","w");              /* error message if */
while( fp==NULL )                       /* file cannot be opened */
     {
     printf("ERROR: can not write to disk.\n");
     printf("If you cannot correct the error,\n");
     printf("\tthis sessions work will be lost.\n\n");
     printf("if you are using a floppy disk\n");
     printf("make sure it does not have a write protect tab\n");
     printf("SHOULD I TRY TO WRITE TO DISK AGAIN (Y/N) > ");
     gets(yn);
     if(toupper(yn[0]=='N')
          exit();
     else
          fp = fopen("lbb.txt","w");
     }

printf("SAVING ADDRESS BOOK. WAIT A MOMENT PLEASE.");
rcrdCntr=0;
while(rcrdCntr<MAXNAMES)                     /* save all records */
     {
     ltrCntr=0;
     while(ltrCntr<21)
          {
          putc(entry[rcrdCntr].fname[ltrCntr],fp);
          ltrCntr++;
          }
     ltrCntr=0;
     while(ltrCntr<31)
          {
          putc(entry[rcrdCntr].lname[ltrCntr],fp);
          ltrCntr++;
          }
     ltrCntr0;
     while(ltrCntr<36)
          {
```

```
            putc(entry[rcrdCntr].addr{ltrCntr],fp);
            ltrCntr++;
            }
        ltrCntr=0;
        while(ltrCntr<21)
            {
            putc(entry[rcrdCntr].city[ltrCntr],fp);
            ltrCntr++;
            }
        ltrCntr=0;
        while(ltrCntr<3)
            {
            putc(entry[rcrdCntr].state[ltrCntr],fp);
            ltrCntr++;
            }
        ltrCntr=0;
        while(ltrCntr<6)
            {
            putc(entry[rcrdCntr].zip[ltrCntr],fp);
            ltrCntr++;
            }
        ltrCntr=0;
        while(ltrCntr<4)
            {
            putc(entry[rcrdCntr].areaCd][ltrCntr],fp);
            ltrCntr++;
            }
        ltrCntr=0;
        while(ltrCntr<9)
            {
            putc(entry[rcrdCntr].phoneNo[ltrCntr],fp);
            ltrCntr++;
            }
            rcrdCntr++;
            }
    fclose (fp);
    }
```

Testing the Program

At this point, another meaningful test of the program is possible.

Make sure that you have added all of the functions listed so var to the **main( )** function. *After making sure that your hard disk is well backed up*, compile and run the program.

Test to see if it gives you the proper message telling you to initialize the book the first time you run it, when there is no address book file. See if it creates a new file named **LBB.TXT** on disk. In addition, make sure that it does not give you the message telling you to initialize the address book the second time you run it, when the file already exists.

Using the Address Book

You have already created the basic features of the Address Book program. Now you must add modules to let you use the address book: to add data, to delete data, and to look up data.

Adding Data

The **append( )** function, which lets the user enter new names, addresses, and telephone numbers, is not at all difficult to understand, though it is a bit lengthy.

It begins with a loop that increments a counter from 0 up to **MAXNAMES**, the total number of names allowed, and checks to see if it has **'\0'** as the first letter of the last name. If the counter equals **MAXNAMES** at the end of the loop, then the program has not found an empty slot, and it tells the user there is no more room in the address book.

Otherwise, the program breaks out of the loop when it finds an empty slot, leaving the value of the counter equal to that entry number. Then the program gets the name, address and other data from the user the puts that information into the entry with the index number. It checks to make sure the entry fits into the field by reading the entry into a buffer first. If the string the user entered is too long, the program prints an error message and forces the user to enter data that is the proper length.

In a professional program, there is more error checking than this. For example, the program would also make sure that the zip code was all numbers. Here, for the sake of brevity, the program only checks for the length of the data.

After all of the fields are entered, the program asks the user to confirm that the data should be entered in the address book.

Many database programs of this type read each of the fields into a temporary variable first and then copy them into the actual variables in the database only if the user confirms that they should be entered. Because of the way the database is being handled here, however, it is possible to enter the data into the actual variables. Then, if the user does not confirm that the information should be in the database, the program simply replaces the first letter of the **lname** field with the **'\0'** that indicates to other functions of the program that this record is empty.

Finally, notice that all of this is nested in a **while( )** loop, to allow for multiple entries. At end of an entry, the program asks if the user wants to make another entry. If so, the **'Y'** that the user enters makes the condition of the **while( )** loop true, so the it is executed again. Note that this **yn[2]** variable serves a number of different purposes in the function, saving the computer a tiny bit of memory, and saving the programmer the trouble of typing multiple declarations.

The Code of append( )

Read through the code of the **append( )** function and look back at the explanation of it above to make sure you understand it. Then enter and compile the program.

```
                 /* Chapter 7, Example 3F */
      /* replaces the append( ) function in Example 3A */

append()
{
int ctr;
char yn[2];
char buffer[80];

yn[0] = 'Y';                              /* create loop to */
while(toupper(yn[0])=='Y')                /* allow multiple entries
     {
     clrscrn();
     ctr = 0;
     while(ctr<MAXNAMES)                  /* find an empty entry */
          {
          If(entry[ctr].lname[0] == '\0')
          break;
```

```
        ctr++;
        }

    if(ctr==MAXNAMES)        /* if not found, error message */
        {
        printf("This address book is full.");
        printf("\nNo new entries may be made.");
        printf("\n\nPress enter to continue ");
        gets(yn);
        break;
        }
                            /* if found, get data and put in */
                                           /* address book */
    printf("ADD A NEW NAME AND ADDRESS\n");
    printf("--------------------------\n");
    while(1)
        {
        Printf("\nEnter the First Name > ");
        gets(buffer);
        if( strlen(buffer) < 21 )
            {
            strcpy(entry[ctr].fname,buffer);
            break;
            }
        else
            {
            printf("The first name cannot be more than");
            printf("\n\t20 letters long.");
            }
        }

    while(1)
        {
        printf("\nEnter the Last Name > ");
        gets (buffer);
        if( strlen(buffer) < 31 )
            {
            strcpy(entry[ctr].lname,buffer);
            break;
```

```
            }
        else
            {
            printf("\nThe last name cannot be more than");
            printf("\n\t30 letters long.");
            }
        }
    while(1)
        {
        printf("\nEnter the address > ");
        gets(buffer);
        if( strlen(buffer) < 36 )
            {
            strcpy(entry[ctr].addr,buffer);
            break;
            }
        else
            {
            printf("\nThe address cannot be more than");
            printf("\n\t35 letters long.");
            }
        }
    while(1)
        {
        printf("\nEnter the city > ");
        gets(buffer);
        if ( strlen(buffer) < 21 )
             {
             strcpy(entry[ctr].city,buffer);
             break;
             }
        else
             {
             printf("\nThe city name cannot be more than");
             printf("\n\t20 letters long.");
             }
        }
    while(1)
        {
```

```
        printf("\nEnter the state - two letters > ");
        get(buffer);
        if( strlen(buffer) == 2 )
            {
            strcpy(entry[ctr].state,buffer);
            break;
            }
        else
            {
            printf"\nThe state name must be");
            printf("\n\t2 letters long.");
            }
        }
    while(1)
        {
        printf("\nEnter the zip code - five digits > ");
        gets(buffer);
        if( strlen(buffer) == 5 )
            {
            strcpy(entry[ctr].zip,buffer);
            break;
            }
        else
            {
            printf("\nThe the zip code must be");
            printf("\n\t5 digits long.");
            }
        }
    while(1)
        {
        printf("\nenter the area code > ");
        gets(buffer);
        if( strlen(buffer) == 3)
            {
            strcpy(entry[ctr].areaCd,buffer);
            break;
            }
        else
            {
```

```
            printf("\nThe the area code must be");
            printf("\n\t3 digits long.");
            }
        }
while(1)
        {
        printf("\nenter the telephone number > ");
        gets(buffer);
        if( strlen(buffer) == 8 )
            {
            strcpy(entry[ctr].phoneNo,buffer);
            break;
            }
        else
            {
            printf("\nThe the telephone number must");
            printf("\n\thave 7 digits and a hyphen.");
            }
        }
while(1)
        {
        printf("\n\nDo you want to save this entry (Y/N)> ");
        gets(yn);
        yn[0] = toupper(yn[0]);
        if(yn[0] != 'Y' && yn[0] != 'N')
            putchar(7);
        else                /* force user to enter Y or N */
            break;          /* to escape from while loop */
        }
if(yn[0] == 'N')                /* if user does not confirm */
                                /* enter the \0 in lname */
   entry[ctr].lname[0]= '\0';           /* to show an */
                                        /* empty entry */

printf("Do you want to enter another (Y/N)> ");
gets(yn);
}
```

Testing append( )

Once you have this function running, you should enter a few names and then return to the DOS prompt and use the command **TYPE LBB.TXT** to look at the file that holds the names so you can make sure they are at least roughly what they should be.

If each entry has two last names and no first name, for example, then it is likely that you made a minor typographical error in **savebook( )** and had the program save **lname** twice for each record, rather than first saving **fname** and then **lname**. This is a good time to find and correct this sort of gross error. You can look for more detailed errors after you have written the program to look up a record.

Looking Up or Deleting a Record

There is one basic problem to grapple with before you write the program to look up a record: differences of upper- and lower-case letters.

If a user makes an entry for "Smith," for example, and tries to look up "SMITH" an hour later, it would be baffling (and would probably lead to errors) if the program said that there was no such name in the address book. One way around this problem would be to use the **toupper( )** function to enter names in all uppercase letters, but then the program prints out an address book and mailing labels that are all uppercase.

Comparing Strings Without Considering Case

Instead, you can write a special function for the **lookup( )** function to use that is similar to **strcmp( )** but that compares two strings without regard to case. Then the program will print out names just as the user entered them, but there are no problems if someone wants to look up a name and does not type it in with this precise capitalization.

The function is as follows:

```
                    /* Chapter 7, Example 3G */
                  /* to be added to Example 3A */

upstrcmp(str1,str2)
char str1[], str2[];
{
int cntr;

cntr = 0;
```

```
while(1)
    {
    if( toupper(str1[cntr]) != toupper(str2[cntr])
        return 1;
    if( str1[cntr] == '\0' && str2[cntr] == '\0' )
        return 0;

    cntr++;
    }
}
```

The **upstrcmp( )** function simply uses a counter to go through the two strings and compare the uppercase versions of each of their characters. If the function finds characters that are different, then it returns 1, and if it gets to the null terminators of both at the same time (without having found a difference and returned earlier), then it returns 0.

The function is called **upstrcmp( )** because it compares uppercase versions of strings. It uses the 0 and 1 return values in the same way that **strcmp( )** does, so **!upstrcmp(name1,name2)** would be true if the two names were the same.

The lookup( ) and find( ) Functions

Now it is easy to look up a record. Simply get the last name to be searched for from the user, and then to go through all of the records in the array, using **upstrcmp( )** to see if the last name in any record matches the name being looked up.

The only minor problem is that two or more people in the list might have the same last name. To get around this problem, when the program finds a name that matches, it displays all of the data on that person and asks the user if it is the right entry. If it is the correct entry, the program breaks out of the loop that does the searching, but if it is not the correct entry, the program keeps searching for another entry with the same last name.

This type of search must also be performed by the function that deletes a record. To delete a record, the program also needs to look through all the records for the last name requested and confirm that the record it found is correct before deleting that record, so this search procedure is written in a separate function, called **find( )**, that can be used by both **lookup( )** and **delete( )**.

With this search procedure removed, **lookup( )** is extremely simple. **lookup( )** prints a heading and calls **find( )** for as long as the user wants to keep looking up names.

find( ) is also fairly simple. **find( )** just keeps looking through the list until the user confirms that it has found the right record. It has one other bit of error-trapping as well. If the user just presses the Enter key, **find( )** returns to **lookup( )** without going through the list, so it does not find that each of the empty entries is a match for the empty string the user just entered.

The connection between these two functions is a bit tricky. **find( )** returns the number of the record the user confirms as correct so that **lookup( )** knows that the record has not been found if the number returned is equal to **MAXNAMES**. Look at this feature of the functions carefully as you enter the following code:

/* Chapter 7, Example 3H */

/* replaces the lookup( ) function in Example 3A */

```
lookup()          /* calls find() to search for a record */
{
int recnum;
char yn[2];

while(1)
     {
     clrscrn();
     printf("LOOKUP A RECORD\n");
     printf("---------------\n");
     recnum = find();
     if(recnum == MAXNAMES)
     printf("\n\nNOT FOUND!");
     printf("\n\nWould you like to look up another (Y/N) ");
     gets(yn);
     if( toupper(yn[0]) != 'Y' )
          break;
     }
}

find()                     /* locate a record a user wants */
{                          /* called from delete() & lookup() */
int ctr;
char lookName[31];              /* let him search by lname */
char yn[2];
```

```
printf("\n\n\nEnter the last name > ");
gets(lookName);
ctr=0;
while(ctr<MAXNAMES)                  /* search */
     {                               /* for lname */

     if(lookName[0] == '\0')         /* if user just presses */
          return MAXNAMES;           /* ENTER, no find */

     if( !strcmp(entry[ctr].lname,lookName) )
          {
          printf("\n\nFirst Name: %s",entry[ctr].fname);
          printf("\n\nLast Name: %s",entry[ctr].lname);
          printf("\n\nAddress: %s",entry[ctr].addr);
          printf("\n\nCSZ: %s, %s %s",
             entry[ctr].city,entry[ctr].state,entry[ctr].zip);
          printf("\n\n\nIs this the correct entry (Y/N) ");
          gets(yn);
          if(toupper(yn[0])=='Y')    /* if it is the one */
               break;                /* that is wanted */
          }                          /* break and use record */
     ctr++;
     }
                                /* if counter equals MAXNAMES */
return(ctr);                    /* record is not found */
}
```

Deleting a Record

The function to delete a record is very similar to **lookup( )**, and it is very easy to write now that **find( )** is already written.

Like **lookup( )**, this function tells the user the record is not found if **find( )** returns a value equal to MAXNAMES. Otherwise, it deletes the record whose number **find( )** returned—after double checking that the user wants it deleted.

```
                    /* Chapter 7, Example 31 */
            /* replaces the delete( ) function in Example 3A */

delete()                                  /* delete a record */
```

```
{
int recnum;
char yn[2];

while(1)
    {
    clrscrn();
    printf("DELETE A RECORD\n");
    printf("---------------\n");
    recnum = find();                       /* if find() reaches */
    if(recnum == MAXNAMES)                 /* MAXNAMES name was */
        printf("\n\nNOT FOUND!");          /* not found. */
    else
        {
        printf("\n\nDelete this record? (Y/N) > ");
        gets(yn);                          /* otherwise, delete */
        if( toupper(yn[0]) == 'Y' )        /* the record number */
            {                              /* that it returned */
            entry[recnum].lname[0] = '\0';
            entry[recnum].zip[0] = '\0';
            printf("\n\nThe record has been deleted");
            }
        else
            {
            printf("\n\nThe record has NOT been deleted");
            }
        }
        printf("\n\nFind another record to delete? (Y/N)> ");
        gets(yn);
        if( toupper(yn[0]) != 'Y')
            break;
    }
}
```

Testing the New Functions

Now you have a substantial portion of the program ready to be tested. To test the new features you have added, you should:

- ✦ Make several entries, some of which have the same last name.
- ✦ Look up names that are and are not in the database.
- ✦ Delete entries and then add more entries.

In addition, you should try entering more than **MAXNAMES** entries, to make sure you are receiving the right error message. To do this, you probably want do redefine **MAXNAMES** as 5 or 10. Note how much easier **#define** makes your life.

As you test the program, you might notice a few extra features that you would like to add to it. For example, it is not easy to cancel an entry while you are making it. You must enter all of the fields before the system gives you the option of cancelling. You can get through some fields easily by pressing Enter, but some fields require you to enter the right number of digits, making the task much more difficult.

As an exercise, you might want to modify the program so it accepts either entering the right number of digits or just pressing Enter for these fields. This modification also allows the user leave these fields empty.

After deleting entries and making new ones, you should return to the DOS prompt and try using the command **TYPE LBB.TXT** to see what the file looks like. Some deleted entries should be there with only the first letter missing, and others will be overwritten in part by new entries with the ends of some fields showing.

You can imagine that, if entries were very long, it would be useful to have an undelete command that could search through the database, looking for an **lname** that began with a **'\0'** and matched all of the letters except for the first letter of a name that the user entered. If the user confirmed that the command found the entry, the undelete command would replace the first letter, making the entire entry usable again.

In fact, there are well-known utilities to let you recover a file that you deleted by mistake, which work something like this imaginary utility for **LBB**.

Of course, to recover either a file or an entry in **LBB**, you would have to use the utility before something new is written over it.

Printing Reports

The remaining functions you must write for the address book program are reminiscent of what computer programmers spent much of their time doing in the

1960s. Before there were many packaged programs to manage databases, businesses had teams of programmers, usually working in COBOL, that were dedicated to producing printed reports in various formats and to and writing custom programs to sort and manipulate the data.

You will use one of the most famous of the early algorithms, the *bubble sort*, at the end of this chapter.

Printing Mailing Labels

You should start, however, with the function to print the most simple report that this program creates, the mailing labels.

Assuming that the printer is loaded with a single-column roll of mailing labels, this function simply needs to print out the first and last name on a single line, the address on the next line, the city, a comma, the state and the zip code on the next line, and then a few newline characters to get down to the next label before printing the next entry.

Using the Printer

This is the first time you have written a program that uses the printer, but you actually know how to use the printer already because MS-DOS treats the printer as a file.

Consider a few DOS commands for displaying data.

If you enter the command **ECHO HELLO WORLD** at the DOS prompt, the computer prints **HELLO WORLD** on the screen. The screen is the standard output—the place where output automatically goes.

It is also possible to redirect output to a file by using the > sign. If you enter the command **ECHO HELLO WORLD > SMPLFILE.TXT**, nothing appears on the screen. Instead, the system creates a new file named **SMPLFILE.TXT**, which contains the characters "HELLO WORLD."

Finally, you can send output to the printer by entering the command **ECHO HELLO WORLD > PRN**. This command works because DOS treats the printer as a file with the name PRN.

Using C Functions to Print

The functions that write reports take advantage of the way that MS-DOS treats the printer by using the statement **prPtr = fopen("prn","w");**. In just the same way that **fopen( )** opens any file so the program can write to it, this statement opens the printer so the program can write to the printer.

It is difficult to use **putc( )** to write to the printer in this case because you do not want any extra garbage in the **LBB.TXT** file to be printed. Instead, this function uses **fprintf( )** to print just the strings--and also to print needed new-line characters. **fprintf( )** works like **printf( )** except that it must include the name of the file pointer as its first argument, before the usual control string and variable names that you are very familiar with from using **printf( )**.

The prntmail( ) Function

The use of **fprintf( )** should be clear when you read the code:

```
                    /* Chapter 7, Example 3J */
          /* replaces the prntmail( ) function in Example 3A */

prntmail()                        /* print mailing labels */
{
char yn[2];
FILE *prPtr;
int cntr;

clrscrn();
printf("\nPRINT MAILING LABELS");
printf("\n--------------------");
printf("\n\n\nMake sure your printer is ready");
printf("\n\tand press ENTER to continue ");
gets(yn);

prPtr = fopen("prn",'w');
while(prPtr == NULL)
     {
     putchar(7);
     printf("\n\nPrinter is not working.");
     printf("\n Do you want to try again (Y/N) > ");
     gets(yn);
     if(toupper(yn)=='N')
          return;
     prPtr = fopen("prn",'w');
     }

cntr=0;
```

```
while(cntr<MAXNAMES)
     {
     if(entry[cntr].lname[0] != '\0')
          {
          fprintf(prPtr,"\n%s %s",
                    entry[cntr].fname,entry[cntr].lname);
          fprintf(prPtr,"\n%s",entry[cntr].addr);
          fprintf(prPtr,"\n%s, %s %s",
          entry[cntr].city,entry[cntr].state,entry[cntr].zip);
          fprintf(prPtr,"\n\n\n");
          }
     cntr++;
     }
fclose(prPtr);
}
```

Note that **fprintf( )** is identical to **printf( )** except for the addition of the stream pointer name.

A Formatted Report

After creating a simple report, such as **prntmail( )**, that just prints out raw data, you should not find it difficult to create a formatted report to print the address book itself.

The formatting in this report involves using two variables:

- A variable to count lines, so you know when the page is full. At this point, the program needs to skip a few lines for the bottom margin of the current page and the top margin of the next page and then to print a header for the new page.
- A variable to count page numbers, which are printed as part of each page header.

Most business reports would probably have footers in addition to headers. In addition, they might use a few more variables to keep subtotals of various numeric fields, such as total wages for the employees in each division, and include routines to print these subtotals at the appropriate places and a running total at the end. These variables would work in much the same way as the counters used in this function, which is kept simple for instructional purposes.

This function also uses the tab character to indent each line, and it prints pages that are 5.5" high (half as large as ordinary paper), so the user can cut them out and assemble them into a little pocket-sized address book.

In a short while, you will add a function to sort the names alphabetically, but for now, you can just use a stub of this function that prints "not yet implemented" until you get the printing working properly.

/* Chapter 7, Example 3K */
/* replaces the prntbook( ) function in Example 3A */

```
prntbook()                    /* print address book */
{
char yn[2];
FILE *prPtr;
int cntr, lineCntr, pageCntr;

clrscrn();
printf("\nPRINT ADDRESS BOOK");
printf("\n------------------");

printf("\n\nShould the names be alphabetized (Y/N) > ");
gets(yn);
if(toupper(yn[0])=='Y')
     {
     printf("\n\nSORTING: Wait a moment please . . .");
     sort();
     }

printf("\n\n\nMake sure your printer is ready");
printf("\n\tand press ENTER to continue ");
gets(yn);

prPtr = fopen("prn",'w');
while(prPtr == NULL)
     {
     putchar(7);
     printf("\n\nPrinter is not working.");
     printf("\n Do you want to try again (Y/N) > ");
```

```
          gets(yn);
          if(toupper(yn)=='N')
               return;
          prPtr = fopen("prn",'w');
          }

     cntr=0;
     lineCntr = 0;
     pageCntr = 1;
     while(cntr<MAXNAMES)
          {

          if(lineCntr==0)
               {
               fprintf(prPtr,"\n\n");
               fprintf(prPtr,"\tLITTLE BLACK BOOK: page %d\n",
                                                  pageCntr);
               fprintf(prPtr,"\t--------------------------\n\n\n");
               lineCntr = 6;
               }

          if(entry[cntr].lname[0] != '\0')
               {
               fprintf(prPtr,"\n\t%s, %s",
                         entry[cntr].lname,entry[cntr].fname);
               fprintf(prPtr,"\n\t%s",entry[cntr].addr);
               fprintf(prPtr,"\n\t%s, %s %s",
               entry[cntr].city,entry[cntr].state,entry[cntr].zip);
               fprintf(prPtr,"\n\t%s %s",
                    entry[cntr].areaCd,entry[cntr].phoneNo);
               fprintf(prPtr,"\n\n");
               lineCntr = lineCntr + 6;
               }
          if(lineCntr==30)
               {
               fprintf(prPtr,"\n\n\n");
               pageCntr++;
               lineCntr = 0;
               }
```

```
      cntr++;
   }
fclose(prPtr);
}

sort()
{
printf("not yet implemented");
}
```

The Bubble Sort

To sort the records, the program uses an algorithm called the *bubble sort*, which was invented in the early days of computer programming.

To understand how a bubble sort works, imagine that you have a list of ten names to sort. This algorithm begins by comparing names nine and ten and putting them in proper order. If ten comes before nine alphabetically, it reverses their places. Otherwise, it does nothing.

Then it compares names eight and nine and puts them in proper order, and so on until it reaches the top of the list.

Note that, somewhere along the line, the program gets to the name that should be first, and then swaps it with every name until it actually is first. After one time through the list, the first name is in its proper position, but the second name probably is not.

Imagine, for example, that before the program begins sorting, Aaron A. Aardvark happens to be the tenth name on the list and Abigail Abacus happens to be ninth. The program compares them and swaps them. Mr. Aardvark is now number nine, and he continues to be compared and swapped until he becomes number one. But Ms. Abacus becomes number ten after the swap, and she is not compared again on this pass through the list.

When you begin the second pass through the list, then, you can be sure that the name that should be first already is first, but you cannot say anything about the location of the second name.

At some point in the second pass, however, the program comes across the name that should be second and, now that the first name is out of the way, it keeps comparing and swapping that name until it reaches its proper place. After two times through the list, then, you can be sure that the first two names are both in their proper places.

Likewise, after going through the list a third time, you can be sure the third name is in its proper place. And after going through the list a number of times that is equal to the number of names on the list, you can be sure that all the names are in their proper places.

This algorithm is called the bubble sort because names rise to the top one at a time, like air bubbling up through water.

More Efficient Bubble Sorts

The bubble sort could be made more efficient in several ways.

For example, it could include a flag to let the program know the sorting is complete if the sort goes through the entire list without changing the place of any record. If only one name has been added since the last time you sorted, the sort program has to go through the list only once to put it in its proper place. The second time through the list, the program would find that it does not have to change the order of any records—proving that all of the records are already in the right order. At this point, the sort could simply terminate, rather than going through the list again and again until it has made a number of passes equal to the number of records in list—and not changing the order of the records each time it goes through.

In addition, you could cut sorting time in half by not comparing the records that are already properly sorted. Instead of comparing all of the names each time through, the program could omit the first name on the second pass through the list, the first two names on the third pass through the list, and so on.

In fact, the last pass through the list can be omitted entirely. If all of the names except the last one are known to be in the proper order, then obviously all the names are in the proper order.

The program uses this final improvement because it is so simple to go through the list a number of times equal to one less than the number of names.

It is not worthwhile to work too hard on improving the efficiency of this algorithm, however, because there are other sorting algorithms that are far more efficient. The bubble sort was popular on mainframe computers that were programmed during the day and were left running all night to process their data, and its main virtue was simplicity rather than speed.

Sort algorithms are an interesting exercise in computer programming. As an exercise, you might want to try on your own to add the improvements described above, and to think up other improvements on your own. You should be able to reduce average sort time to about one-quarter of what it is using the bubble-sort code listed below. If you find sorts interesting, you can try to research or invent other sort algorithms and program them in C.

Preliminary Code

Start by looking at a slightly abbreviated version of the final bubble-sort function the program will actually use.

This function uses three nested **while( )** loops.

The outermost loop simply repeats the process a number of times equal to **MAXNAMES-1**. Remember that you must go through the list comparing and exchanging names a number of times equal to one less than the number of items to be sorted in order to be sure the names are all in place.

The middle loop uses the variable **wrdCtr** to go through all of the names in the list, so the program can compare **entry[wrdCtr]** and **entry[wrdCtr-1]**.

The innermost loop uses the variable **ltrCtr** to go through the names in these two entries one letter at a time, comparing the uppercase versions of each letter in both.

As long as the letters in both words are the same, the program keeps comparing the next letter. As soon as it comes to a letter that is different, however, the program knows what order the names should be in:

- If the letter in the entry that is farther down the list, **entry[wrdCtr]**, is less than the entry that is higher on the list, the program changes the order of the two names and then **break**s out of the loop.
- If the letter in the entry that higher in the list, **entry[wrdCtr-1]**, is less, then the names are already in proper order, and the program simply leaves them by **break**ing out of the loop.

Be sure you understand the code in this version of the function before going on to the next version.

The variable **wrdCtr** starts being equal to **MAXNAMES** and is decremented each time through the loop. The program works just as well if **wrdCtr** started at zero and increased each time through the loop and if names that were higher alphabetically were swapped to the higher numbered entries at the end of the list.

The function **swap( )**, which changes word order, will be added in a moment, as you will be ready for it after you understand this preliminary version of the code:

```
sort()
{
int timesCtr, wrdCtr, ltrCtr;

timesCtr = 0;

while(timesCtr < MAXNAMES-1)
    {
    wrdCtr = MAXNAMES-1;
    while(wrdCtr > 0)
        {
        ltrCtr = 0;
        while(1)
            {

            if(toupper(entry[wrdCtr].lname[ltrCtr]) <
                    toupper(entry[wrdCtr-1].lname[ltrCtr]) )
                {
                swap(wrdCtr);
                break;
                }
            if(toupper(entry[wrdCtr].lname[ltrCtr]) >
                    toupper(entry[wrdCtr-1].lname[ltrCtr]) )
                break;

            ltrCtr++;
            }
        wrdCtr--;
        }
    timesCtr++;
    }
}
```

The sort( ) Function

The preliminary version of the bubble sort that you just looked at takes account of only two possible results of comparing last names letter by letter. Either one name or the other comes first.

But there is actually a third case that is very common in the real world. What happens, for example, if the program must sort a list that includes both Aaron A. Smith and Xavier X.Smith? If the two last names are the same, a sort program must also alphabetize on the basis of first name.

The final version of the program deals with this problem by adding a third condition in the inner loop. If the letter of both first names is a **'\0'**, then the program does the same sort on the first name that it just did on the last name. So that time is not wasted on empty entries, it only performs this sort if the **'\0'** is not the first letter of the last name.

Adding this new innermost **while( )** loop to sort by first name adds a few new problems. When the program **breaks** out of this loop, for example, it is still trapped in the last name sorting loop. There is a definite temptation to use a **goto** to solve this problem, but instead, this program adds a flag called **frstFlg**, which is set ON if the first name must be sorted and used to break the program out of the inner loop.

What if the first names are also the same? The program tests for this by seeing if **ltrCtr** is greater than 20, the maximum length of a first name, without any differences. This is a rather complex series of nested loops, but it is not hard to follow if you take the loops one step at a time.

The final version of the program also adds a **swap( )** function to exchange the positions of two entries. To swap records, it creates a temporary entry to hold one name while the other is being copied into its location. You cannot simply copy entry two into entry one and then copy entry one into entry two because entry one would be destroyed before it was copied.

/* Chapter 7, Example 3L */

/* replaces the sort( ) function in Example 3K */

```
sort()
{
int timesCtr, wrdCr, lrCr;
int frstFlg = 0;

timesCtr = 0;
while(timesCtr < MAXNAMES)
     {
     wrdCr = MAXNAMES-1;
     while(wrdCr > 0)
```

```
{
lrCr = 0;
while(1)
    {

    if(toupper(entry[wrdCr].lname[IrCr]) <
            toupper(entry[wrdCr-1].lname[lrCr]) )
        {
        swap(wrdCr);
        break;
        }

    if(toupper(entry[wrdCr].lname[lrCr]) >
            toupper(entry[wrdCr-1].lname[lrCr]) )
        break;

    if(entry[wrdCr].lname[lrCr] == '\0' &&
        entry[wrdCr-1].lname[lrCr] == '\0'&&
        lrCr != 0)
        {
        frstFlg = 1;
        lrCr = 0;
        while(1)
            {
            if(toupper(entry[wrdCr].lname[lrCr])
                    < toupper(entry[wrdCr-1].lname[lrCr]))
                    {
                    swap(wrdCr);
                    break;
                    }

            if(toupper(entry[wrdCr].lname[lrCr])
                    > toupper(entry[wrdCr-1].lname[lrCr]))
                    break;

            if(lrCr > 20)
                    break;

            lrCr++;
```

```
                    }
                }
            if(frstFlg)
                {
                frstFlg = 0;
                break;
                }
            lrCr++;
            }
        wrdCr--;
        }
    timesCtr++;
    }
}

swap(nmbr)
int nmbr;
{

struct nmAddrPh temp;
strcpy(temp.lname , entry[nmbr].lname);
strcpy(temp.lname , entry[nmbr].lname);
strcpy(temp.addr , entry[nmbr].addr);
strcpy(temp.city , entry[nmbr].city);
strcpy(temp.state , entry[nmbr].state);
strcpy(temp.zip , entry[nmbr].zip);
strcpy(temp.areaCd , entry[nmbr].areaCd);
strcpy(temp.phoneNo , entry[nmbr].phoneNo);
strcpy(entry[nmbr].lname , entry[nmbr-1].lname);
strcpy(entry[nmbr].lname , entry[nmbr-1].lname);
strcpy(entry[nmbr].addr , entry[nmbr-1].addr);
strcpy(entry[nmbr].city , entry[nmbr-1].city);
strcpy(entry[nmbr].state , entry[nmbr-1].state);
strcpy(entry[nmbr].zip , entry[nmbr-1].zip);
strcpy(entry[nmbr].areaCd , entry[nmbr-1].areaCd);
strcpy(entry[nmbr].phoneNo , entry[nmbr-1].phoneNo);

strcpy(entry[nmbr-1].lname , temp.lname);
strcpy(entry[nmbr-1].lname , temp.lname);
```

```
strcpy(entry[nmbr-1].addr , temp.addr);
strcpy(entry[nmbr-1].city , temp.city);
strcpy(entry[nmbr-1].state , temp.state);
strcpy(entry[nmbr-1].zip , temp.zip);
strcpy(entry[nmbr-1].areaCd , temp.areaCd);
strcpy(entry[nmbr-1].phoneNo , temp.phoneNo);
}
```

Note that there is no problem sorting a pair of names such as "Smith" and "Smithson." When this function compares the **'\0'** following the 'h' in "Smith" and the 's' following the 'h' in "Smithson," it simply considers the null a lower value character—because it is ASCII value zero—and puts the shorter name before the longer one, where it should be.

Refining the Address Book Program

That completes the code needed for a quick-and-dirty address book program, but consider how many refinements could be added to it.

Think about adding a field for an organization name as well as a person's name, for example.

If you did this, you might want to add a few **if-else** statements to the sorting function to check if an entry's **lname** is blank and alphabetize the entry in combination with those that have names. For example, AAA Acme Co. would come even before Mr. Aardvark.

When you were printing the address book, you would have some entries that had only a name or an organization and some that had both. You might want to add code to omit these blank lines. And there would be cases where you would want to have a page break if a longer entry followed but not if a shorter entry followed.

Think about a simpler refinement: Adding a page break whenever a new letter occurs in the address book. The program would check to see if an entry's first letter is the same as the first letter of the previous entry and, if it is not, add enough new lines to fill out that page and printing a heading for the next.

Or think about making the mailing program more useful. It could sort the entries by zip code to print out labels for bulk rate mailings. It could print labels for only certain states or certain zip codes or add other fields that would let users add criteria of their own for mailings. It could give the user an entire menu of different label forms, such as two or three columns as well as one column, with tab and newline characters used to get the spacing needed by all of the popular sizes of commercial labels.

Finally, think about making the program more complex by rewriting it to record contributions that are sent in response to mailings. The best way to do this is to use what is called *database normalization*: to have two files, one with names and addresses and a code number for each person, the other with just the code number and the amount and date of the contribution. Then you could write functions to sort both files on the code number, to read both files simultaneously, to skip through the name file until you found a record that had the same code number as the first code number in the contribution file, to print out that name and address and to continue to print out the contributions until the code number in the contribution file changed, to print out the total of that person's contributions, and to continue this process (with occasional interruptions for page breaks) until you printed out a report with the names and addresses of everyone who contributed.

You now know enough about the C programming language to add these features if you want.

Summary

The ++ operator increments (adds 1 to) a variable, and the -- operator decrements (subtracts 1 from) a variable. With most compilers, the statements **variable++;** and **variable - -;** run faster than **variable = variable + 1;** and **variable = variable - 1;**.

A one-line command terminated by a semicolon is a single simple statement. All of the commands enclosed within a pair of curly brackets make up a single compound statement. A condition must be followed by a single statement, either simple or compound. Thus, if there is more than one instruction to be executed if the condition is true, the instructions must be enclosed in curly brackets to make them into a single compound statement. If there is only one instruction, it is already a single statement, and the brackets can be omitted.

The C compiler evaluates the number 0 as having the logical value of false and any other number as having the logical value of true. Thus, instead of **if(checkwin('O')==1)**, you can simply say **if(checkwin('O'))**. If the function has a value of 1, it is evaluated as true by itself. Likewise, instead of **if(checkwin('O')==0)**, you can simply say **if(!checkwin('O'))**. Instead of using the condition **while(1==1)** to create an infinite loop, you can use **while(1)**.

A *record* is a connected group of data that is part of a repetitive list, for example, a name, address, and telephone number, or all the data on a single employee. A *field* is an individual piece of data within the group, for example, the last name, the city, or the salary. A *file* is the entire list of related records. A *database* is a group of related files that can be connected with each other, though the term database is often used more loosely to refer to a single file of data. These terms are all used generally to refer to databases and are not specific to C.

Most high-level computer languages let you use two kinds of disk files: *sequential* files, which can only be read from beginning to end and can only be added to by appending new data onto the end; and *random* files, which can be read or changed at any point (designated by its offset from the beginning). The high-level file-handling functions that are built into C's standard input/output package can only access files sequentially. C's low-level file-handling functions can be used to write libraries of functions for special uses, such as database programming.

MS-DOS treats the printer as a file with the name **prn**. You can print text by using the high-level file-handling functions to open the printer and write to it just as if it were a file. The statement **prPtr = fopen("prn","w");** opens the printer so the program can write to it, just as **fopen( )** opens any file so the program can write to it.

Chapter

8

Continuing Your Study of C

As you know, the goal of this book is to get you writing C programs as quickly as possible. To do this, it uses an instructional style in its early programs that was easy to read, and it left out features of the C language that were not necessary for you to begin writing programs.

This chapter fills other aspects of the language that you should know about before you continue your study of C. It covers:

- using other data types in C
- declaring the storage class of a variable
- using other features **printf( )**—for example, printing memory addresses
- iteration using the the **do while** loop and the **for( )** loop
- selection using the **switch( )** statement
- using numeric functions
- passing command line arguments to programs
- understanding the condensed style of C programming

How to Study a Computer Language

The best way learn a computer language—to get a real feeling for the language that will make you fluent in it—is to study actual programs.

Once you know the basics, reading programs can eventually enable you to write code for simple applications, such as menus, almost as easily as you speak your native language. Reading actual programs is also the best way to learn what computer programming can accomplish. You learn what you can accomplish by looking at what is being accomplished.

Of course, you also need a manual on the language to use as a reference book when you have to figure out difficult code. The manual should be your secondary source, and the actual programs should be your primary source.

Fortunately, there are many excellent books available for intermediate programmers, with useful examples of C code—ranging from screen control to database management to graphics to artificial intelligence.

Before you can go on to study these examples, however, you must fill some of the gaps that this book has left in your knowledge. This book introduced you to the basics of computer programming by using a somewhat simplified subset of the C language. While you are learning basic techniques, such as looping or working with variables, it is best to avoid most of the abbreviations and shortcuts that make the language easier to use once you are an experienced programmer.

When you are learning to control program flow, for example, it is best to learn one or two methods of selection and iteration—not to be forced to spend time learning all of the other instructions that can perform the same tasks. Having to memorize all of these instructions before starting to program is a major obstacle to learning C.

However, when you go on to study code in intermediate books on C, you will be faced with these other instructions. This chapter outlines briefly the frequently used C techniques that were left out of the main text. It does not attempt to be comprehensive but just to teach you the statements that are commonly used in C, so you can go on to study actual programs. Now that you know what a computer language can do, should not be difficult for you to pick up these new ways of performing the same tasks.

Declaring Variables

First, look at some added techniques that you can use when you declare variables. In addition to using some data types that have not been covered earlier, you can specify the storage class of a variable when you declare it.

Data Types

C includes a few other data types in addition to the types of variables used in this book, the **char** (character), **int** (integer), and **float** (number with a floating decimal point).

The Double

The **double** (double-precision, floating decimal-point number) is just like the **float** except that most compilers reserve 8 bytes to hold it instead of the 4 bytes used for a float. The extra width makes it precise to approximately one-trillionth of a unit, while the ordinary float is precise only to about one-millionth of a unit.

In Chapter 3, Program Example 3 illustrated a rounding error. If you entered a wage of 10.10 per week for four weeks, the program might say the total is 40.400002. Because it uses binary arithmetic, the computer necessarily creates rounding errors such as this when it is converting numbers to and from decimal form. The **float** in Chapter 3 gave a result that was off by two-millionths of a unit. A **double** would give an error of only a few trillionths. The accuracy of the **float** is adequate for dealing with money. The double is used for more precise calculations.

Types of Integer

C also includes three types of integers: the **int**, the **long**, and the **short**.

The size of the **int** generally depends on the size of what is sometimes called a "word" of the computer that the compiler is designed for—that is, the amount of data normally used by a register.

Compilers designed for older 16-bit processors have a 2-byte **int**, with a range of 64K: from -32K to +32K. Compilers designed for 32-bit processors have a 4-byte **int**, with a range of over one billion.

Regardless of the size of the **int**, the **short** is assigned 2 bytes, and the **long** is assigned 4 bytes. Thus, the **short** can be used instead of the **int** on 32-bit systems to save memory, and the **long** must be used instead of the **int** on 16-bit systems to handle large numbers.

Storage Class

The declaration of a variable can also include a modifier before the data type, which indicates the *storage class* of that variable. Storage classes include **unsigned**, **register**, **extern**, and **static**.

Unsigned

The modifier **unsigned** can be used before any type of integer to declare an unsigned integer of that type. The word **unsigned** can also be used alone to declare an **unsigned int**.

Ordinarily, the first bit of an integer indicates its sign, so an **int** can have positive and negative values. By declaring an integer as **unsigned**, you double the maximum value it can hold, by eliminating the negative values.

On the IBM-PC (though not on all systems), pointers to addresses are unsigned integers, and you will see how to print one out shortly.

Register

Declaring a variable with the modifier **register** simply gives it priority to be stored in a register rather than in RAM so that it can be processed more quickly.

As you learned in the Introduction, variables that are stored in RAM must be moved to the registers of the Central Processing Unit (CPU) before they can be manipulated. It is possible to store a frequently used variable in a register rather than in RAM to speed up the program.

Most compilers try to optimize the performance of their code by storing some variables in registers automatically, but they are not always good at guessing which variables it is best to store there. By using the modifier **register**, you determine which variables have priority to be stored in registers.

It is best to use this modifier sparingly. Because the computer has a limited number of registers, there is no guarantee that the variable can be kept in a register.

If you declare several variables of this type, you make it less likely that the variable that really needs to be processed quickly will actually get in a register. If you are writing a program with six counters, and one of them (**cntrF**, for example) is used frequently to count up to a high number while the other five are used infrequently to count up to lower numbers, then you could declare these variables as follows:

```
int cntrA, cntrB, cntrC, cntrD, cntrE;
register int cntrF;
```

to make it more likely that the counter that gets the most use will be stored in the register and processed most quickly.

Extern

The modifier **extern** is used if you want to repeat the declaration of a global variable within a function.

It is necessary to use **extern** if you are compiling several files separately and intend to link the object files that are produced after compiling is finished. When you compile a file that uses a global variable declared in another file, the compiler gives you an error message saying that the variable has not been defined unless you declare it within that file as external.

If you declare it without the modifier **extern**, the compiler creates a new, local variable. If a program uses the same name for both a local and a global variable, then the local variable overrides the global one. That is, a global variable is not accessible to a function that uses a local variable with the same name. Thus, this modifier is necessary to let you compile one file that uses a global variable declared in another file.

This is a rather advanced concept that you should not worry about, but you will see the modifier **extern** occasionally in code you examine, and you can just remember that it means the variable is actually defined elsewhere.

Static

The modifier **static** causes a local variable to remain in memory throughout the execution of a program.

Most local variables exist only when the function that contains them is executing, but there are times, when you need one that remains between calls of the function.

If a function is keeping a running total of salaries for an entire company, for example, and is called by several other functions that give it totals for one division or another to add onto the company total, the variable this function uses to accumulate the running total must be declared as **static**. Without this declaration, the total already accumulated would disappear as soon as the function was no longer being used.

The storage type **static** can also solve a problem you encountered in Chapter 6, Program Example 10. There, the array of structs that held a list of English and French words was declared as a global variable to avoid a stack overflow error, even though the program that used it had only one function.

While they are active, most local variables are kept on the stack, an area of RAM used for temporary storage. But the stack in this example did not have enough room for this array, so you had to declare the array as global to make the storage permanent.

It would work equally well and would make more sense to declare the array within the function as **static**, as follows:

```
                              /* Chapter 8, Example 1 */
                    /* an improvement on Chapter 6, Example 10 */
#include <stdio.h>
#define MAXWORDS 100

main()                          /* read word list */
{                               /* high-level method */
static struct efWrdLst
    {
    char English[16];
    char French[16];
    char spchPart;
    }entry[MAXWORDS];

FILE *filePtr;

char ltr;
int entrCntr, eLtrCntr, fLtrCntr, posCntr, testCntr;

filePtr = fopen("wordlist.txt",'r');
if(filePtr== NULL)
    {
    printf("ERROR: The wordlist file cannot be opened");
    exit();
    }

entrCntr = 0;
eLtrCntr = 0;
```

```
fLtrCntr = 0;
posCntr = 0;

while(ltr != EOF)
      {
      ltr = getc(filePtr);
      if(eLtrCntr<16)
            {
            entry[entrCntr].English[eLtrCntr] = ltr;
            eLtrCntr = eLtrCntr + 1;
            }
      else if(fLtrCntr<16)
            {
            entry[entrCntr].French[fLtrCntr] = ltr;
            fLtrCntr = fLtrCntr + 1;
            }
      else if(posCntr<1)
            {
            entry[entrCntr].spchPart = ltr;
            posCntr = posCntr + 1;
            }
      if(eLtrCntr==16 && fLtrCntr==16 && posCntr==1).
            {
            entrCntr = entrCntr + 1;
            eLtrCntr = 0;
            fLtrCntr = 0;
            posCntr = 0;

            if(entrCntr > MAXWORDS)
                  {
                  printf("\nERROR: wordlist file is too long.");
                  printf("\n\tThe program will work");
                  printf("\n\twith %d words but must",MAXWORDS);
                  printf("\n\tbe modified to use all the words");
                  break;
                  }

            }
      }
fclose(filePtr);
```

```
testCntr = 0;
while(testCntr < entrCntr)
     {
     printf("\n\n%s",entry[testCntr].English);
     printf("\n%s",entry[testCntr].French);
     printf("\n%c",entry[testCntr].spchPart);
     testCntr = testCntr + 1;
     }
}
```

Declaring this **struct** as **static** lets you use it as a local variable without stack overflow rather than declare it as a global variable as you did in Chapter 6. Declaring this **struct** as static makes its storage permanent and takes it off the stack, without implying that it is used by more than one function.

Automatic

By default—that is, if they are not explicitly declared as being in any storage type—local variables are **automatic**, meaning that (as you have seen) they automatically come into existence when their function is used and go out of existence when their function is done.

Some programmers declare this fact explicitly by using the storage type **auto** for most local variables.

Declaring Functions: the ANSI Standard

It is becoming more common stylistically to make all declarations explicit, rather than simply letting the compiler use the default. Most important, it is becoming common to always declare the data type that functions return.

For the sake of simplicity, this book did not declare the data type of functions. It used only functions that returned **int** values, which C functions return by default if there is no declaration.

Look at a simple example of a function that you can create with or without declaring its data type.

Chapter 4 included this function to add two **ints**:

```
addint(x,y)
int x,y;
{
return x+y;
}
```

The value it returns is an **int** by default, simply because no other type was declared, but it is now becoming a more common practice to declare the function's data type explicitly even when it is an **int** and the declaration is not necessary.

You must declare the type of the function if you want it to return any data type other than an **int.**

A function's data type is declared in two places: along with the variables within the calling function and before the name of the function that is called.

For example, if you wanted to write a separate function to add two double-precision floats (similar to the one used to add two **ints**), you could use a program like the following:

```
/* Chapter 8, Example 2 */
#include <stdio.h>

main()                          /* add two doubles - old style */
{
double nmbr1, nmbr2, total, adddbl();

nmbr1 = 2.6;
nmbr2 = 2.7;
total = adddbl(nmbr1,nmbr2);
printf("\n%f + %f = %f",nmbr1,nmbr2,total);
}

double adddbl(x,y)
double x,y;
{
return x + y;
}
```

Note that the type of **adddbl( )** is declared along with all of the other variables of **main( )**. Its declaration looks just like the declaration of any other variable, except that it includes the final parentheses that indicate it is a function. The type is also declared in the function **adddbl( )** itself. It simply precedes the name of that function.

Void

In addition, it is possible to declare a function as void if it does not return any value, and many would consider doing so to be good style.

void is a new data type that is used only with functions, as follows:

```
void clrscrn()
{
int cntr;
while(cntr<25)
    printf("\n");
}
```

This declaration makes it obvious that the function that clears the screen does not return a value. The **void** function declaration makes it easier to decipher a complex program.

The ANSI Standard

Much of older code that you see will not include these unnecessary declarations of functions that return **ints** or **voids**. Leaving them out is another one of those shortcuts that C programmers take.

In the future, however, declarations of all functions should become more common, because they are part of the ANSI standard for C.

The American National Standards Institute (ANSI) has defined standard versions of many computer languages. Until very recently, though, the standard version of C was defined in the book *The C Programming Language* by Brian Kernighan and Dennis Ritchie (Prentice-Hall, 1978), who developed the language at Bell Laboratories.

After more than five years of study, beginning in 1983, ANSI came out with a standard for C. Kernighan and Ritchie have produced a second edition of their book that brings it into conformity with the ANSI standard.

Function Prototyping

The most important innovations in ANSI C have to do with the declaration of functions. Within the calling function, ANSI C allows what is called *function prototyping*. You declare not only the type of the function itself but also the type of its variables.

For example, **adddb1( )** is declared in the old-fashioned way in the **main( )** function above. In ANSI C it would be rewritten as follows:

/* Chapter 8, Example 3A /*

/* to be used in combination with Example 3B */

```
#include <stdio.h>

main()                            /* add two doubles: ANSI style */
{
double nmbrl, nmbr2, total, adddbl(double a,double b);

nmbrl = 2.6;
nmbr2 = 2.7;
total = adddbl(nmbrl,nmbr2);
printf("\n%f + %f = %f",nmbrl,nmbr2,total);
}
```

Instead of merely declaring the function as **double adddb1( );**, ANSI standard C includes a complete prototype of the function in the declaration **double adddb1(double a, double b);**, including the function's parameters and their data types, which lets the compiler do more error checking.

In the previous example, if **nmbr1** and **nmbr2** were mistakenly declared as ints, the compiler would be able to tell that the statement **total = adddb1(nmbr1,nmbr2);** contained an error, that is that the parameters are not the same data type as the function's prototype says they should be.

This type of error checking was impossible with the older version of C.

Declaring Parameters

This same sort of prototyping is carried to the declaration of the parameters of the function that is called, as in the following:

/* Chapter 8, Example 3B /*
/* to be used in combination with Example 3A */

```
double adddbl(double x, double y)
{
return x + y;
}
```

Instead of being declared between the name of the function and its opening bracket, the parameters are declared within the parentheses of the function name itself.

All in all, the older style is simpler and easier for beginners to use, but the newer style is more reliable

At this point, after you have gotten accustomed to C programming by using the older style, the new ANSI style should not be hard for you to learn.

Formatted I/O

This book has used **printf( )** with the following special characters for formatting variables:

- **%d**—integer in decimal form
- **%f**—float
- **%c**—char
- **%s**—string

printf( ) can also be used with the following characters:

- **%o**—integer in octal form
- **%x**—integer in hexadecimal form
- **%e**—scientific(exponential) notation
- **%g**—%f or %e, whichever is shorter
- **%u**—unsigned integer

Note that many compilers support even more formatting characters than are listed here.

Printing Memory Addresses

The formatting character **%u** is particularly interesting because it can be used to print out the actual addresses of variables, as in the following program:

```
                    /* Chapter 8, Example 4 */
#include <stdio.h>

main()
{
char samplA, samplB, samplC;
static char samplD, samplE, samplF;
char *ptrA, *ptrB, *ptrC, *ptrD, *ptrE, *ptrF;

ptrA = &samplA;
ptrB = &samplB;
ptrC = &samplC;
ptrD = &samplD;
ptrE = &samplE;
ptrF = &samplF;

printf("\nThe automatic variables are stored at addresses:");
printf("\n\t%u %u %u",ptrA,ptrB,ptrC);
printf("\n\nThe static variables are stored at addresses:");
printf("\n\t%u %u %u",ptrD,ptrE,ptrF);
}
```

This program prints out the addresses of the memory locations that the system reserved for those variables, and you can to see that automatic and static variables are stored in separate areas of memory.

Printing out memory addresses can also give you a very clear sense of how pointer arithmetic works. You can see that adding one to the pointer moves you to the next memory address of that type.

For example, the following program declares two arrays, one of **ints** and the other of **doubles**. Then, the program creates a pointer of each type, makes it equal to the address of the beginning of the array of that type, and prints out the address of all the elements of both arrays by using pointer arithmetic to increment these pointers.

/* Chapter 8, Example 5 */

```
#include <stdio.h>

main()
{
int iArry[5];                    /* sample program: print */
double dArry[5];                 /* addresses using pointer */
int *iPtr;                       /* arithmetic */
double *dPtr;
int counter;

iPtr = &iArry[0];
counter = 0;                     /* print address of each */
while(counter < 5)               /* element of array of ints */
    {
    printf("\nThe address of int %d is %u",counter,iPtr);
    counter++;
    iPtr++;
    }

dPtr = &dArry[0];
counter = 0;                     /* print address of each */
while(counter < 5)               /* element of array of doubles */
    {
    printf("\nThe address of double %d is %u",counter,dPtr);
    counter++;
    dPtr++;
    }
}
```

When you run the program, note that incrementing the pointer adds 2 to the actual number of the address if the pointer points to an **int** but adds 8 to it if it points to a **double**.

Other Features of printf( )

A few additional features of **printf( )** were not previously covered earlier in the text.

Controlling the Width of the Display

You can use **printf( )**'s special formatting characters to control the minimum width of the display. Simply put the width that you want after the **%**, and the variable prints that width with blanks to fill in the extra spaces if necessary.

For example, the statement

```
printf("I%10sI","test");
```

will display

```
I      testI
```

The 'I's at the beginning and end are simply used to show that the string is right justified by default, with six spaces before the four letters of "test."

Left Justifying Text

You can also left justify it by adding a minus sign before the number that indicates the width, so that the statement

```
printf("I%-10sI","test");
```

displays

```
Itest      I
```

with the six spaces after "test."

Displaying Decimal Places

You can control how many decimal places of a **float** are displayed in a similar way. The statement

```
printf("I%8.2fI",123.45);
```

displays

```
I  123.45I
```

The formatting character **%8.2f** here causes the statement to print the value of the float to two decimal places within a character field whose total width is eight characters.

You could use **%8.2f** to left justify the number within that character field. Or you could simply use **%.2f** to print out two decimal places of the float without controlling the size of its character field.

An important use of this feature of **printf( )** is to print out amounts of money. The wages program you wrote in Chapter 3 printed out total wages with six decimal places. Now you can format the total wages properly with two decimal places, as in the following:

```
                         /* Chapter 8, Example 6 */
#include <stdio.h>

main()                          /* enter wages for each week */
{                               /* and calculate yearly wage */
float wageWk[52];
int cntr, numOfWks;
float yrlyWage;

printf("\nHow many weeks of wages do you want to enter? ");
scanf("%d",&numOfWks);

cntr = 0;                       /* get each week's wages */
while(cntr < numOfWks && cntr < 52)
     {
     printf("Enter the wage for week %d > ",cntr+1);
     scanf("%f",&wageWk[cntr]);
     cntr = cntr + 1;
     }

yrlyWage = 0;                   /* add all weekly wages */
cntr = 0;
while(cntr < numOfWks && cntr < 52)
     {
     yrlyWage = yrlyWage + wageWk[cntr];
     cntr = cntr + 1;
     }
printf("The total yearly wage is %.2f.",yrlyWage);
}
```

Note that formatting the variable in this way also removes rounding errors.

The previous examples illustrate only the most common features of **printf( )**. If you want to learn more, you should read the reference manual for your compiler.

Control Flow

This book used only two forms of control flow, the **if-else** statement (plus its expanded version, the **if-else-if** ladder) and the **while( )** loop.

As you know, you can make the program do anything using sequence, selection, and iteration. And so, for the sake of simplicity, this book used only one form of selection and one form of iteration.

This method of teaching let you begin programming quickly. Now you should look at the other forms of control flow commonly used in C, which are more convenient to use in some situations.

Looping

In Chapter 2, you learned that the **while( )** loop takes the following form:

```
while(condition)
    {
    statemt1;
    statemt2;
    statemt3;
    }
```

This form of the loop requires you to initialize the variable used in the condition before you enter the loop and to include some statement within the body of the loop that can make the condition false.

For example, the menu used for the ASCII chart program in Chapter 2 gave the user three options:

1. Look up the ASCII character for a number.
2. Look up the number for a character.
3. Quit.

Then it got the user's response, using the following loop:

```
menuOpt[0] = ' '
while(menuOpt != '1' && menuOpt != '2' && menuOpt != '3')
    {
    printf("\n\n\nWhat IS YOUR CHOICE > ");
    gets(menuOpt);
    }
```

Before entering the loop, you must initialize the variable to make sure the condition is true, which is the reason for the statement **menuOpt[0] = ' '**;.

If you do not specifically initialize the variable, the computer simply looks at whatever random piece of data happens to be in the memory location it reserved for that variable. In this case, the condition would probably be false, but there is a very small chance that there would already be a 1, 2, or 3 in that memory location. If you did not initialize the variable, it is likely that the program would work correctly for years and then, one day, would inexplicably execute one of the menu choices that happened to be in memory rather than asking the user which option he or she wants.

The do while Loop

To summarize, the **while( )** loop checks the condition before executing the statements in the loop. If you want to make sure that the loop performs at least once, as you do with menus and many other applications, you should begin with a statement that makes the condition true.

Of course, if you do very much programming, it becomes tedious initializing the variable before each loop, and so C also provides a type of loop that checks the condition after executing the statements, so you can be sure it executes at least once.

This sort of loop takes a form that is easy to understand:

```
do    {
      statemt1;
      statemt2;
      statemt3;
      }while(condition);
```

Remember that C is a free-form language, and that the code you study will often be laid out differently from the examples you see here.

To indicate that the condition is checked after the loop is executed, **while(condition)** is simply placed at the bottom of the loop instead of at the top. If you follow through the logic of the loop, you will see that the only difference this location makes is that the loop is executed at least once, whether or not the condition is true, so you do not need to worry about the preliminary initialization of the variable used in the condition.

Note that there is a semicolon after the condition here, though there is none in the ordinary **while( )** loop, because here it is at the end of the statement.

This form of loop is generally used for menus.

Computer programmers usually call the sort of loop that checks the condition before executing a **do while loop** and the sort of loop that executes before checking the condition a **do until loop**, so you should know these terms.

Early computer languages had either one or the other. Many COBOL compilers still have only what that language calls **PERFORM UNTIL**. The language automatically executes the statements once, whether the condition is true or false. If you do not want the language to execute the statements unless the condition is true, you must add an extra **IF/ELSE** statement to avoid it.

Fortunately, many languages, like C, now give you the choice of both types of loops.

The for( ) Loop

There is one other major type of loop in C, the **for( )** loop, which is typical of the condensed, cryptic statements for which C is famous.

It takes the following form:

```
for(initialization; condition; change of condition)
     {
     statemt1;
     statemt2;
     statemt3;
     }
```

The **for( )** loop is actually just an abbreviated form of the **while( )** loop. Though the **for( )** loop is difficult to learn when you first begin programming, it not be difficult for you to pick up now that you have had experience with looping.

When you are using the **while( )** loop, you must do the following:

1. Initialize the variable before the loop begins.
2. Check the condition at the top of the loop with **while(condition)**.
3. Have some statement within the body of the loop that can alter the variable to make the condition untrue.

The **for( )** loop simply squeezes all three of these actions into the parentheses following the loop.

For example, look once again at **clrscrn( )**, as it was written in this book:

```
clrscrn()                         /* clear the screen */
{                                 /* version in text */
int counter;

counter = 0;
while(counter < 25)
     {
     printf("\n");
     counter++;
     }
}
```

C programmers would actually write this function, using the **for( )** loop:

```
clrscrn()                         /* clear the screen */
{                                 /* more common version */
int counter;
for(counter=0; counter<25; counter++)
     {
     printf("\n");
     }
}
```

This loop is identical to the **while( )** loop used in this book. The initialization of the variable is squeezed into the parentheses before the testing of the condition. The addition of 1 to the variable is squeezed into the parentheses after the condition.

Within the parentheses, the initialization, condition, and change of condition are separated by semicolons. This condensed form of loop is very common in C code.

There are other refinements of the **for( )** loop that are less common and more obscure, but you should glance at them for a moment so they will not come as a surprise to you if you do run across them in code.

Initializing Multiple Variables in a for( ) Loop

You can initialize multiple variables at the beginning of a for( ) loop, as in the following example:

```
for(cntr=1, getcntr=1; cntr+getcntr < 100; cntr++)
      {
      statemt1;
      scanf("%d",&getcntr;);
      statemt2;
      }
```

Both **cntr** and **getcntr** are initialized at the beginning of the loop, and the condition involves both, but only **cntr** is incremented at the beginning of the loop, and **getcntr** is input from the user that comes within the loop.

Omitting Statements at the Beginning of a for( ) Loop

You can also omit one or more of the usual statements at the beginning of the loop, as in the following example:

```
for(cntr=0; cntr < 100;)
      {
      statemt1;
      scanf("%d",&cntr);
      statemt2;
      }
```

This loop keeps executing until the user enters a value for counter that is greater than 100.

In fact, odd as it seems, you can omit all of these statements at the beginning of the loop, as follows:

```
for(;;)
   {
     statemt1;
     scanf("%d",&cntr);
     if(cntr >= 100)
          break;
     statemt2;
   }
```

Because there is no condition at the beginning, the loop is always true. This is another way of using an infinite loop that includes a conditional **break** statement inside it, like the **while(1==1)** and the **while(1)** loops you used in the text.

Selection: the switch( ) Statement

The forms of selection available in C are not as varied as the forms of looping. Apart from the methods that you already have learned in this book, there is only one other form of selection that you will run into in C programs—the **switch( )** statement.

The **switch( )** statement generally is used in just the same way that this book has used the **if-else-if** ladder.

Several computer languages have what they call a **DO CASE** statement, which is just like the **if-else-if** ladder but is listed as a series of cases, just to emphasize the parallelism of all the options.

The **switch( )** includes one other refinement. If more than one of the conditions is true, the function executes the statements following all of the true conditions, unlike the **if-else-if**, which executes only the statement following the first condition that is true.

To make the **switch( )** execute only the first statement that is true, you must include a **break;** after each statement. C programmers often do just this.

Consider the following example of the **switch( )**. This code is from a typical menu, like many that you created earlier in this book using **if-else-if**. It assumes that the variable **menuOpt[0]** has been declared as a char, that a menu has already been displayed with '1', '2', and '3' as its valid choices, and that input has been received from the user:

```
switch(menuOpt[0])
    {
    case '1':
        statemt1;
        break;
    case '2':
        statemt2;
        break;
    case '3':
        statemt3;
        break;
    default:
        statemt4;
    }
```

The word **case** is followed by a constant, and the statements that follow it are executed if the variable following the **switch( )** is equal to that constant.

Thus case **'1':** in this switch statement is equivalent to **if(menuOpt[0] == '1')** in the menus you developed using **if-else-if** earlier in this book. The final **default** is similar to the final else in the **if-then-else** ladder. The statements following it are executed if none of the other conditions is true.

The **switch( )** is commonly used in menus in the form just given. It is probably more common than the **if-else-if** ladder, though it is no clearer or easier to use. The **break;** statements are not really needed, as the variable used to get the menu choice cannot have more than one value, but they are sometimes included for clarity.

Numeric Functions

This book has concentrated on programs that work with text, and you have learned some of the common functions for manipulating characters, such as **toupper( )**.

Most C libraries also have a rich variety of functions for working with numbers. Even programmers who will never go near a scientific or statistical application should know certain basic number-handling functions that are useful for validating numeric input.

Validating Numeric Input

You have learned to validate the length of user input by reading string input into a buffer, using a counter to check how many characters there are before the final **'\0'**, and then using the **strcpy( )** function to copy the input from the buffer into the actual string you are using, but only if the input is not too long.

There is a simple way of validating numeric input that is very similar.

First, get the input as a string.

Then use a counter to look at each character individually and make sure it is numeric. This requires a new function, **isdigit( )**, which is true if the character is one of the numbers from **'0'** to **'9'**.

Finally, if all of the characters are digits, you can use another new function, **atoi( )**, to convert the string of characters into an integer. The name **atoi( )** is short for "ASCII to Integer."

Following is a simple example of a program that validates numeric input, using this method:

```
                    /* Chapter 8, Example 7 */
#include <stdio.h>
#include <ctype.h>
#include <stdlib.h>

main()
{
char toChk[80];
int cntr;
int finalNum;

printf("\nEnter an integer > ");
gets(toChk);
cntr = 0;
while(toChk[cntr] != '\0')
    {
    if(isdigit(toChk[cntr]))
        cntr++;
    else
        {
```

```
            printf("Non-numeric input: abnormal termination.");
            exit();
            }
        }
finalNum = atoi(toChk);
printf("\n\nThank you for entering the integer %d",finalNum);
}
```

Note that the program **#includes** two new headers.

The function **isdigit( )** is declared in **ctype.h**. This header also includes a number of similar functions that are useful for testing data, such as:

- **isalpha( )**, which tests if a character is a letter of the alphabet.
- **isspace( )**, which tests if it is a white space character.
- **isupper( )**, which tests if it is upper case.
- **islower( )**, which tests if it is lower case.

The function **atoi( )** is declared in stdlib.h, along with a number of other functions for converting data types, such as **atol( )**, which converts a string of ASCII characters to a **long int** and **atof( )**, which converts a string of ASCII characters into a **float**.

When you run this program, note that because you declared **finalNum** as an **int**, the program only works properly if the number in not too large.

In an actual program, you would also test the length of the string to make sure that the number is not out of range. In most cases, ,ou would just want a one-digit integer—for example, a menu choice—and you could break out of the loop and display an error message if the counter were more than 0. In the ASCII Chart program in Chapter 2, you would need to read integers up to three digits long.

If you want the user to input a float, you could use the function **atof( )** for conversion and alter the program to accept a decimal point as well as digits, as in the following:

/* Chapter 8, Example 8 */

```
#include <stdio.h>
#include <ctype.h>
#include <stdlib.h>

main()
```

```
{
char toChk[80];
int cntr;
double finalNum;

printf("\nEnter an number > ");
gets(toChk);
cntr = 0;
while(toChk[cntr] != '\0')
      {
      if(isdigit(toChk[cntr]))
            cntr++;
      else if(toChk[cntr] == '.')
            cntr++;
      else
            {
            printf("Non-numeric input: abnormal termination.");
            exit();
            }
      }
finalNum = atof(toChk);
printf("\n\nThank you for entering the number %f",finalNum);
}
```

Note that **atof()** actually converts the string to a double-precision float, and the variable is declared as a **double**. This function is declared in both **stdlib.h** and math.h in most compilers though in some compilers it might be declared only in **math.h**.

This sort of problem is not uncommon, and the moral is that if you get error messages saying that one of the functions you used is an "undefined symbol" or something similar, look up that function in your user's manual to see what header it is declared in.

Command Line Arguments

If you work from the DOS prompt, you can start many commercial programs by either entering the command that stands for the name of the program or by entering the program name along with some **command-line argument** that tells the program what to do when it first starts.

For example, if you are using WordPerfect for word processing, you can just enter the command **WP** and start with a blank program screen. Or you can enter that command with the name of a file you want to edit, for example, **WP MYFILE.DOC**, and the program starts by displaying the file of that name.

More elementary programming languages do not have the ability to create programs that accept command-line arguments. C can accept command-line arguments as parameters of the **main( )** module, in the following way:

```
main(argc, argv)
int argc;
char *argv[];
    {
    /* BODY OF main() */
    }
```

The parameter **argc** (short for "argument count") takes as its value the number of arguments entered on the command line—that is, the number of strings separated by spaces. **argc** always is equal to 1 or more because the name of the program itself counts as one of the arguments.

The parameter **argv** (short for "argument vector" or for "argument value") contains all of the arguments entered at the command line: **argv[0]** is the command that starts the program itself, **argv[1]** is the first parameter after the command, and so on.

Specifying the Memo File To Read

In Chapter 6, you were told that in this chapter you would learn to rewrite the memo programs created in Chapter 6 (which can only create files named **memo.txt**), using command-line arguments instead.

The program to read a file is a bit simpler, and the use of command-line arguments should be easy to understand if you compare the following version of the program with the version in Chapter 6:

```
                    /* Chapter 8, Example 9 */
#include <stdio.h>

main(argc,argv)             /* read a text file */
int argc;
```

```
char *argv[];
{
FILE *filePtr;
char toWrite;
if(argc != 2)
    {
    printf("\nERROR:");
    printf("\nthe command must be used with one file name.");
    exit();
    }

filePtr = fopen(argv[1],'r');
if(filePtr== NULL)
    {
    printf("The file %s cannot be opened",argv[1]);
    exit();
    }
while(toWrite != EOF)
    {
    toWrite = getc(filePtr);
    printf("%c",toWrite);
    }
fclose(filePtr);
}
```

If you enter this program in a file named **readmemo.c** and compile it, you create a command, **READMEMO**, that you must use with the name of a file. For example, from the DOS prompt, you can enter **READMEMO MYFILE.TXT**.

There are only two significant differences between this program and the program in Chapter 6. First, this program tests to make sure that the right number of arguments have been entered: **if(argc != 2);** that is, if the user has not entered the command name plus one command-line argument, the program gives an error message and terminates. Second, this program refers to the file by using the variable **argv[1]**. Whatever string was entered following the command is the name of the file that the command tries to open.

Specifying the Memo File To Write

The program to write the memo file checks for one additional error. After making sure that the right number of arguments was entered, it checks to see if a file of that name already exists.

This program uses **fopen( )** with the mode **"w"** so that it overwrites and destroys the contents of a file of that name that already exists. To warn the user before doing this, the program takes advantage of the fact that **fopen( )** with the mode **"r"** returns a Null if a file of that name does not exist, because there is nothing for it to read. Thus, if **fopen( )** does not return a Null, a file of that name already exists, and the user is given a chance to escape from the program rather than overwrite the file.

```
                    /* Chapter 8, Example 10 */
#include <stdio.h>

main(argc,argv)               /* write a memo file */
int argc;
char *argv[];
{

FILE *filePtr;
char userInpt, confirm[2];
if(argc != 2)
     {
     printf("\nERROR:");
     printf("\nthe command must be used with one file name.");
     exit();
     }

filePtr = fopen(argv[1],'r');
if(filePtr != NULL)
     {
     fclose(filePtr);
     printf("\nA file named %s already exists.",argv[1]);
     printf("\nDo you want to destroy that file? (Y/N) > ");
     gets(confirm);
     if(toupper(confirm[0]) != 'Y')
          exit();
     }
fclose(filePtr);

filePtr = fopen(argv[1],'w');
if(filePtr== NULL)
```

```
        {
        fclose(filePtr);
        printf("\nThat file cannot be written to");
        exit();
        }

    printf("\nENTER TEXT > ");

    do  {
        scanf("%c",&userInpt);
        putc(userInpt,filePtr);
        }while(userInpt != '\n');

    fclose(filePtr);
    }
```

Note that this program uses a **do-while** loop to get the memo from the user because it must get at least one character.

Operators

So far, you have learned about the following operators:

- ✦ Arithmetic Operators
  - `+` plus
  - `-` minus
  - `*` times
  - `/` divided by
  - `%` remainder after division
- ✦ Increment and Decrement Operators
  - `++` increment
  - `--` decrement
- ✦ Logical and Relational Operators
  - `&&` and

||	or
==	is equal to
!=	is not equal to
>	is greater than
<	is less than
>=	is greater than or equal to
<=	is less than or equal to

✦ Pointer Operators

&	the address of
*****	the contents of address

The Bitwise Operators

The other major class of operators in C is the *bitwise operators*, an advanced topic that is not covered in any detail in this book.

Bitwise operators are mentioned here to give you at least a small notion of what they do and to make sure that you know what you do not know so that you do not confuse them with similar looking operators if you see them in a program.

& and **|** are the "bitwise and" and the "bitwise or." **^** is the "exclusive or" and **~** is the "one's complement." **>>** is the "shift right," and **<<** is the "shift left."

The "bitwise or," for example, makes any bit in the result equal to 1 if the corresponding bit in either of the bytes being operated on is 1. If you are using the lowest order bit of a byte as a flag and want to make it 1 to show that the condition is true, you could OR it with 1. You can visualize the operation as follows:

```
      10110110
  |   00000001
      --------
      10110111
```

In this example, the programmer wants to change just one bit of the upper byte. The bitwise OR makes a bit 1 if it is 1 either in the upper byte or in the lower byte. Thus, ORing the upper byte with 00000001 leaves its seven leftmost bits as they were and will make the lowest order bit on the right into a 1. This example gives you a basic idea of the purpose of bitwise operators.

Shorthand with Operators

There are a number of methods of using operators to write very condensed, abbreviated statements. These sometimes make the program difficult to read, but you must know them, because you will run across them frequently in C programs.

Assignment Statements

One type of shorthand is commonly used with arithmetic operators in assignment statements. The statement **x += 2;** for example, is shorthand for **x = x + 2;**.

The same shorthand works with all arithmetic operators in C. For example, **x *= 2;** is equivalent to **x = x * 2;**.

The ? and : Operators

There is also a pair of operators used to create very compressed **if-else** statements in C. The operators ? and : are used to squeeze an entire **if-else** statement onto a single line.

For example,

```
positive = numbr > 0 ? 1 : 0;
```

is equivalent to the following:

```
if(numbr > 0)
     positive = 1;
else
     positive = 0;
```

Statements using this pair of operators (**?** and **:**) are useful within a function to cause the function to use one value if the condition is true and another if it is false.

When they are used unnecessarily, however, these operators are typical of the programming style that gives C a bad reputation. The programmer saves a few seconds of typing at the expense of later programmers who must decipher and maintain the program.

The Location of Increment and Decrement Operators

Another form of shorthand is also used with the increment and decrement operators. Both of these operators can be used either before or after a variable.

Within an assignment statement, if they are used before the variable, then the program performs the increment or decrement operation before the assignment, but if they are used after the variable, then the program performs the increment or decrement operation after the assignment.

For example, after the following assignment:

```
smplNmbr = 10;
othrNmbr = ++smplNmbr;
```

the values of **smplNmbr** and **othrNmbr** are both be 11. The program increments **smplNmbr** first, making it 11, and then assigns that value to **othrNmbr**.

On the other hand, after the following assignment:

```
smplNmbr = 10;
othrNmbr = smplNmbr++;
```

the value of **smplNmbr** is 11, but the value of **othrNmbr** is still 10. The program assigns the value of **smplNmbr** to **othrNmbr** first and then increment the value of **smplNmbr**.

Condensed Style

The uses of operators that you just looked at are examples of the compressed programming style that gives C its reputation as a difficult language.

Look at some other cases where this condensed style is used.

Variables

As you learned earlier, for example, it is common to declare more than one variable at a time, with statements such as the following:

```
int cntrA, cntrB, cntrC, cntrD;
```

In addition, values are frequently assigned to more than one variable at a time, with statements such as the following:

```
cntrA = cntrB = cntrC = cntrD = 0;
```

Finally, variables are frequently declared and initialized in a single statement, as in the following:

```
int cntrA = 0;
```

All of these shortcuts are useful to save time on typing and are not difficult to understand.

Nested Statements

C programmers also tend to nest one statement inside another.

Programmers often open a file and test for an error in the same statement, for example. Instead of the following,

```
filePtr = fopen("memo.txt",'a')
if(filePtr == NULL)
     printf("ERROR");
```

C programmers almost always write

```
if( (filePtr = fopen("memo.txt",'a') )== NULL)
     printf("ERROR");
```

Note that the entire statement **filePtr = fopen("memo.txt",'a')** must be in parentheses, which are nested within the parentheses of the **if( )** statement so that there are three levels of nested parentheses.

This single line, which executes the **fopen( )** function and also tests to see if it has returned a Null indicating an error, is an example of C's cryptic style, but in this case, the technique is used so frequently that before long you will use it without thinking.

There are many cases, then, where C's abbreviated style saves time and does not cause any problems. On the other hand, some C programmers seem to take pleasure in figuring out how to write code in compressed ways that are difficult to understand—even if it takes them extra time. C is capable of more compression and terseness than other languages, but using this capability to the point where it makes a program harder to decipher is obviously bad style.

It is difficult for any programmer to maintain a program written in this way, and this style is a particular obstacle to beginners who are learning C. Now that you have become accustomed to C by using programs written in a more readable style, however, it should easier for you to go and work with programs written in a more cryptic style.

Appendix

Glossary

This glossary summarizes some of the information presented in this book in alphabetical form, for use as a reference. Any words in the definitions that have entries of their own are in bold italics, to let the reader know that there is a cross reference.

#define

A precompiler command that makes it easy to modify programs by letting you define a word (or any string of characters) as representing a constant value. For example, the statement **#define MAXWORDS 10** makes the precompiler substitute the value 10 whenever MAXWORDS appears. Note that, like other precompiler commands, this statement does not end with a semicolon. It is conventional to use all upper-case letters for the names of defined constants.

#include <stdio.h>

A precompiler instruction that reads in the standard input/output header. Note that, like other precompiler commands, this statement does not end with a semicolon.

++

The ***increment operator***, which adds 1 to a variable. With many compilers, the statement **variable++;** runs faster than **variable = variable + 1;**.

The ***decrement operator***, which subtracts 1 from a variable. With many compilers, the statement **variable- -;** will run faster than **variable = variable - 1;**.

? and : operators

Operators used to squeeze an entire ***if-else statement*** onto a single line. For example,

```
positive = numbr > 0 ? 1 : 0;
```

is equivalent to:

```
if(numbr > 0)
     positive = 1;
else
     positive = 0;
```

Statements using this pair of operators (? and :) are useful within a function to cause the function to use one value if the condition is true and another if it is false.

argc

Used as a ***parameter*** of the ***main( )*** function of a C program to pass a ***command line argument*** to the program. **argc** (short for "argument count") takes as its value the number of arguments entered on the command line—that is, the number of strings separated by spaces. **argc** always is equal to 1 or more because the name of the program itself counts as one of the arguments. Used in conjunction with ***argv***.

argv

Used as a ***parameter*** of the ***main( )*** function of a C program to pass a ***command line argument*** to the program. The parameter **argv** (short for "argument vector" or for "argument value") contains all of the arguments entered at the command line: **argv[0]** is the command that starts the program itself, **argv[1]** is the first parameter after the command, and so on. Used in conjunction with ***argc***.

Arithmetic Operators

Operators used to perform calculations. The arithmetic operators are:

+	plus
-	minus
*	times
/	divided by
%	modulo division (remainder)

Modulo division (%) gives the remainder of integer division. To do more complex calculations, you must understand ***precedence of operation***. Parentheses can be used to group operations, to change the default precedence.

Array

A group of variables that have the same name and are differentiated by their index numbers. To declare an **array**, you can use a statement such as: **char samplAry[100];**. This statement creates 100 character variables, with names ranging from **samplAry[0]** to **samplAry[99]**. Each of these variables is called an element of the array. You can create arrays of any data type by using a declaration that consists of consists of the data type followed by the name of the variable and the number of elements in the array enclosed in square brackets. In addition to this sort of one-dimensional arrays, it is also possible to create ***two-dimensional arrays*** and other higher-dimensional arrays.

Assignment Operator

= is used as an assignment operator in C. A value can be assigned to a variable, using a statement such as **SmplVar = 'A';**. A shorthand notation is often used to combine the assignment operator with arithmetic operators. For example, the statement **x += 2;** is equivalent to the statement **x = x + 2;**. The same shorthand can be used to combine = with any arithmetic operator.

atof( )

A function that returns the value of a ***string*** of ASCII characters as an ***float***. The name **atof( )** is short for "ASCII To Float."

atoi( )

A function that returns the value of a ***string*** of ASCII characters as an ***int***. The name **atoi( )** is short for "ASCII To Integer."

atol( )

A function that returns the value of a ***string*** of ASCII characters as a ***long int***. The name **atol( )** is short for "ASCII To Long."

Auto

A ***storage class***. By default—that is, if they are not explicitly declared as being in any storage type—local variables are automatic, meaning that they automatically come into existence when their function is used and go out of existence when their function is done. Some programmers declare this fact explicitly by using the storage type **auto** for most local variables.

Bitwise Operators

Operators used to perform operations on individual bits. The bitwise operators are:

& bitwise and
| bitwise or
^ exclusive or
~ one's complement
>> shift right
<< shift left

The "bitwise or," for example, makes any bit in the result equal to 1 if the corresponding bit in either of the bytes being operated on is 1. If you were using the lowest order bit of a byte as a flag and wanted to make it 1 to show that the condition is true, you could OR it with 1. You can visualize the operation as follows:

```
10110110
00000001
--------
10110111
```

In this example, the programmer wanted to change just one bit of the upper byte. The bitwise OR makes a bit 1 if it is 1 either in the upper byte or in the lower byte. Thus, ORing the upper byte with 00000001 leaves its seven leftmost bits as they were and will make the lowest order bit on the right into a 1.

break;

A statement used for ***control flow*** to break out of a control statement (such as a loop) and execute the command following its final curly bracket.

Call by Reference

A way of passing ***parameters*** that lets the called function to change the value of the variable in the calling function. For one function to change the value of a local variable of another function, it is necessary to pass the address of that variable to the function that is to change the variable's value. This is a "call by reference." By contrast, you cannot change the value of the variable in the calling function if you use a ***call by value***.

Call by Value

A way of passing ***parameters*** that does not let the called function to change the value of the variable in the calling function. You simply pass the called function the name of the variable, and the value of the variable is copied into the parameter. Thus the called function can change only its copy of the variable, not the variable in the calling function itself. To change the value of the variable in the calling function, you must use a ***call by reference***.

Char

A ***data type*** used to hold character data. An ***array*** of characters terminated by a null is a ***string***.

Command-Line Argument

An argument entered when the user enters a command at the DOS prompt, which is passed to the program and tells the program what to do when it first starts. C can accept command-line arguments as parameters of the ***main( )*** module, in the following way:

```
main(argc, argv)
int argc;
char *argv[];
      {
```

```
/* BODY OF main() */
}
```

The parameter ***argc*** (short for "argument count") takes as its value the number of arguments entered on the command line—that is, the number of strings separated by spaces. ***argc*** always is equal to 1 or more because the name of the program itself counts as one of the arguments.

The parameter ***argv*** (short for "argument vector" or for "argument value") contains all of the arguments entered at the command line: **argv[0]** is the command that starts the program itself, **argv[1]** is the first parameter after the command, and so on.

Comment

Text surrounded by /* and */, which is ignored by the compiler and included solely for the benefit of the programmer.

Compound Statement

A series of commands enclosed within a pair of curly brackets. A condition must be followed by a single statement, either simple or compound. Thus, if there is more than one instruction to be executed if the condition is true, the instructions must be enclosed in curly brackets to make them into a single compound statement. The brackets can be omitted if the condition is followed by a ***simple statement***.

continue;

A statement used for ***control flow***. It immediately returns control to the beginning of a loop and checks its condition again.

Control Flow

Statements used to redirect program control. ***Structured programming*** uses control flow based on sequence, selection, and iteration, including the ***if-else statement***, the ***if-else-if ladder***, the ***switch( )***, the ***while( ) loop***, the ***do while loop***, and the ***for( ) loop***. ***Structured programming*** avoids using the ***goto labelName*** statement for control flow.

Data Types

C includes the data types ***char*** (character), ***int*** (integer), ***long*** (long integer), ***short*** (short integer) ***float*** (number with a floating decimal point), ***double*** (double-precision, floating decimal-point number), and ***void***, which is used only to declare functions.

Database

A group of related files used to hold data, which can be connected with each other. The term *database* is often used more loosely to refer to a single file of data. One element of data in a database is called a ***field***, and a group of fields is a ***record***. Thus, a database file is a list of related records. These terms are all used generally to refer to databases and are not specific to C.

Decrement Operator

- - the ***operator*** used to decrease the value of a variable by one. The decrement operator can be used either before or after a variable: within an assignment statement, if it is used before the variable, then the program will perform the decrement operation before the assignment, but if it is used after the variable, then the program performs the decrement operation after the assignment.

do while( ) Loop

A form of ***control flow*** used in ***structured programming***. A **do while** loop executes the statement once before checking if the condition is true, then loops back to the check if the condition is true before executing it again. It takes the following form:

```
do    {
      statemt1;
      statemt2;
      statemt3;
      }while(condition);
```

though code is often laid out differently from this example. It is useful in menus and other cases where you must make sure the loop is executed at least once, because you do not have to make sure the condition is true before looping begins, as you do when you use a ***while( ) loop***.

Double

A ***data type*** used to hold double-precision, floating decimal-point numbers. A double is just like a ***float*** except that most compilers reserve 8 bytes to hold it instead of the 4 bytes used for a float. The extra width makes it precise to approximately one-trillionth of a unit, while the ordinary float is precise only to about one-millionth of a unit, and so it is used to avoid ***rounding errors***.

exit( );

A function used for ***control flow***, terminates the program and returns the user to the operating system.

Extern

A ***storage class***. Use this modifier if you want to repeat the declaration of a global variable within a function. It is necessary to use **extern** if you are compiling several files separately and intend to link the object files that are produced after compiling is finished. When you compile a file that uses a global variable declared in another file, the compiler gives you an error message saying that the variable has not been defined unless you declare it within that file as external. If you declare it without the modifier **extern**, the compiler creates a new, local variable. Thus, this modifier is necessary to let you compile one file that uses a global variable declared in another file.

fclose( )

A ***high-level disk I/O function*** that closes a file after you are done using it. **fclose( )** automatically flushes the buffer, so no input is lost. One of a family of high-level disk I/O functions, including ***fopen( )***, **fclose( )**, ***getc( )***, and ***putc( )***.

Field

An individual piece of data within a ***record***. For example, if a record holds data on an employees, the last name, the city, or the salary may be fields. Records are organized in a file of a ***database***. These terms are all used generally to refer to databases and are not specific to C.

Float

A ***data type*** used to hold floating decimal-point numbers. Most compilers reserve 4 bytes to hold a float, which makes it is precise to about one-millionth of a unit. For more precision, use a ***double*** to avoid ***rounding errors***.

fopen( )

A ***high-level disk I/O function*** that opens a file so it can be used and also returns a pointer to the beginning of the file. This function can be used with the mode "r" (read), "w" (write), and "a" (append). If the mode "a" or "w" is used, the file can be written to one character at a time by using putc(variable,filePtr); which writes the character stored in the character variable to the disk file: the mode "w" destroys any data already in the disk file, and the mode "a" adds what is written to the end of the disk file. Before opening a file in this way, you must declare a ***stream pointer***. One of a family of high-level disk I/O functions, including **fopen( )**, ***fclose( )***, ***getc( )***, and ***putc( )***.

for( ) Loop

A form of ***control flow*** used in ***structured programming***. The **for( )** loop is a condensed, cryptic statements, which takes the following form:

```
for(initialization; condition; change of condition)
     {
     statemt1;
     statemt2;
     statemt3;
     }
```

When you are using a ***while( ) loop***, you must initialize the variable used in the condition before the loop begins, include a **while(condition)** statement at the beginning of the loop to check if the condition is true, and have some statement within the body of the loop that alters the variable to make the condition untrue. The **for( )** loop simply squeezes all three of these actions into the parentheses following the loop. The initialization, condition, and change of condition are all included in parentheses following **for( )**, and are separated by semicolons. You can also initialize multiple variables at the beginning of a **for( )** loop. In addition, you can also omit one or more of the usual statements at the beginning of the loop.

Function

The modular building block of a C program. A function is made up of the function name plus one or more statements enclosed in curly brackets. The name of a function must end with parentheses, which may be empty or may include arguments. A C program must include one function named ***main( )***, which runs when the program begins. ***main( )*** can execute instructions that are built into the language, that are included as functions in libraries, or written as functions by the programmer.

getc( )

A ***high-level disk I/O function*** that reads a single character from an open file. One of a family of high level disk I/O functions, including ***fopen( )***, ***fclose( )***, **getc( )**, and ***putc( )***.

getchar( )

An unformatted I/O function used to read a character input by the user. **getchar( )** is one of a family of unformatted I/O functions that begin with **get** or **put**, including the functions ***gets( )*** and ***puts( )*** for strings and **getchar( )** and ***putchar( )*** for characters.

gets( )

An unformatted I/O function used to read a string input by the user. Unlike ***scanf( )***, **gets( )** can be used to read a string that contains blank spaces. **gets( )** is one of a family of unformatted I/O functions that begin with **get** or **put**, including the functions **gets( )** and ***puts( )*** for strings and ***getchar( )*** and ***putchar( )*** for characters.

Global Variables

Variables that are known to all of the modules of a program. C also lets you use ***local variables*** and ***parameters***.

goto labelName;

A statement used for controlling program flow. It must be used in combination with a label followed by a colon that is included elsewhere in the program, and it directs control to the location of this label. **goto** is avoided in ***structured programming***.

High-Level Disk I/O Functions

Functions that do some of the routine housekeeping tasks of disk input/output for you, such as creating a buffer. They include the functions ***fopen( )***, ***fclose( )***, ***getc( )***, and ***putc( )***.

if-else statement

A form of ***control flow*** used in ***structured programming***, which takes the form

```
if(condition)
      {
      statement;
      statement;
      }
```

```
else
      {
      statement;
      statement;
      }
```

If the condition is true, the statements in the curly brackets following it are executed. If it is false, the statements in the curly brackets following **else** are executed. The **else** may be omitted, and nothing is done if the condition is false.

if-else-if ladder

A form of ***control flow*** used in ***structured programming*** to choose among a number of options. It takes the following form:

```
if(condition)
      {
      statement;
      statement;
      }
else if(condition)
      {
      statement;
      statement;
      }
else if(condition)
      {
      statement;
      statement;
      }
else
      {
      statement;
      statement;
      }
```

The program executes the statement that follow the first condition that is true, and then the program continues after the final curly bracket. If none of the conditions is true, the program executes the statements under the final **else;** this final **else** is optional, and if it is left out, the **if-else-if** ladder does nothing if none of the conditions is true.

Increment Operator

++ the ***operator*** used to increase the value of a variable by one. The increment operators can be used either before or after a variable: within an assignment statement, if it is used before the variable, then the program will perform the increment operation before the assignment, but if they are used after the variable, then the program performs the increment operation after the assignment.

isalpha( )

A function that returns true if a character is a letter of the alphabet

isdigit( )

A function that returns true if the character is one of the numbers from '0' to '9'.

islower( )

A function that returns true if a character is lower case.

isspace( )

A function that returns true if a character is a white-space character.

isupper( )

A function that returns true if a character is upper case.

Kernigan and Ritchie

Two computer scientists who developed C at Bell Labs. Originally, the standard version of C was defined in the book *The C Programming Language* by Brian Kernighan and Dennis Ritchie (Prentice-Hall, 1978). After more than five years of study, beginning in 1983, however, the American National Standards Institute came out with a new standard for C, and Kernighan and Ritchie produced a second edition of their book that brings it into conformity with the ANSI standard.

Local Variables

Variables that are known only to the module where they are declared. If two modules have **local variables** with the same name, the program considers them to be totally different variables. This makes C a more structured and extensible language. C also lets you use ***global variables*** and ***parameters***.

Logical Operators

Operators used in conjunction with the ***relational operators*** to create complex statements that are true of false. The logical operators are:

```
&&      logical and
||      logical or
```

If && joins two statements, the combined statement is true only if both of the original statements are true. If || joins two statements, the combined statement is true if either of the two original statements is true. In more complex statements, parentheses are used for grouping, to change the default ***precedence of operation***.

main( )

The ***function*** that runs when a C program begins. You can use the ***argc*** and ***argv*** to pass ***command line arguments*** to **main( )**.

Null

The first ASCII character, which has a value of zero. The 8 bits of this character are set to 00000000. It is not to be confused with the character zero (0), which is ASCII character 48. In C, **null** is represented by the special escape character **\0**. The **null** is used to terminate a ***string***.

Operators

Used to perform operations on values. C includes ***Arithmetic Operators***, the ***Increment Operator***, the ***Decrement Operator***, ***Logical Operators*** and ***Relational Operators***, ***Pointer Operators***, and ***Bitwise Operators***.

Parameters

Variables that are passed between two functions. The names of the variables in the two functions are not related to each other. Parameters are declared as ordinary local variables within the function that passes them. Ordinarily, the values of the variables in the calling function are copied into the parameters of the function that is called, so that it can not access them or change their value in the calling function. This is a ***call by value***. To change the value of the variables in the calling function, you must use a ***call by reference***.

Pointer Arithmetic

Regardless of the data type a pointer points to, adding 1 to a pointer gives you the address that follows the memory needed to hold that data type. Pointer arithmetic is commonly used to work with arrays on a lower level: you can access the next element of an array by adding 1 to the address of the current element, regardless of its data type.

Pointer

A variable that is the address of another variable. A pointer is declared using the data type of the variable it points to plus an asterisk before its name. For example, float *pSmplVar; declares a variable that is a pointer to a float. Two operators are used to work with pointers: (&) means "the address of," and the asterisk (*), the indirection operator, means "contents of address."

Precedence of Operation—The Arithmetic Operators

The order in which calculations are performed. When arithmetic operations are evaluated, multiplication and division are given precedence over addition and subtraction, so **3 * 4 + 1** is evaluated as 13. It is possible to alter the precedence by using parentheses: **3 * (4 + 1)** would be evaluated as 15. Enclosing the addition in parentheses gives it precedence.

Precedence of Operation—The Logical Operators

The order in which logical operations are performed. By default, **&&** has precedence over ||. Parentheses can also be used to alter the precedence of logical operators. For example, **x==1 && (y==2 || z==3)** would be evaluated as true only if it is true that **x** equals 1 *and* it is true that either **y** equals 2 or **z** equals 3. On the other hand, **(x==1 && y == 2) || z==3** would be evaluated as true if it is true that **x** equals 1 and **y** equals 2 or it is true that **z** equals 3. If **x==3** was the only one of these three statements that was true, then the first example would be evaluated as false and the second would be evaluated as true.

printf( )

A function used to print output to the screen with formatting of variables. Its general form is as follows: **printf("\n The variable is %c", SmplVar);**. Ordinary characters within the quotation marks are printed on the screen. It may include special escape characters follow a backslash, such as **\n** for new line or **\t** for tab. Special characters for formatting variables follow a percent sign (**%**) and are used to format the variables named after the comma following the final quotation mark. **printf( )** can be used with the following characters for formatting variables:

%c char

%d integer in decimal form

%e scientific(exponential) notation

%f float

%g %f or %e, whichever is shorter

%o integer in octal form

%s string

%u unsigned integer

%x integer in hexadecimal form

Many compilers support even more formatting characters than are listed here. You can also use **printf( )**'s formatting characters to control the minimum width of the display: include the width that you want after the %, and the variable prints that width, using blanks to fill in the extra spaces if necessary. You can also left justify it by adding a minus sign before the number that indicates the width. You can control how many decimal places of a float are displayed in a similar way. For example, the formatting character **%8.2f** here causes the statement to print the value of the float to two decimal places within a character field whose total width is eight characters.

prn

The designation of the printer in MS-DOS systems. DOS treats the printer as a file with the name **prn**. You can print text by using the high-level file-handling functions to open the printer and write to it just as if it were a file. For example, the statement **prPtr = fopen("prn","w");** opens the printer so the program can write to it, just as ***fopen( )*** opens any file so the program can write to it.

putc( )

A ***high-level disk I/O function*** that writes a single character to an open file, and automatically maintains a buffer rather than writing the character directly to disk. One of a family of high level disk I/O functions, including ***fopen( )***, ***fclose( )***, ***getc( )***, and **putc( )**.

putchar( )

An unformatted I/O function used to display a character on the screen. putchar(7) is commonly used to make the computer beep, as ASCII character 7 is the beep character. **putchar( )** is one of a family of unformatted I/O functions that begin with **get** or **put**, including the functions ***gets( )*** and ***puts( )*** for strings and ***getchar( )*** and **putchar( )** for characters.

puts( )

An unformatted I/O function used to display a string on the screen. **puts( )** is one of a family of unformatted I/O functions that begin with **get** or **put**, including the functions ***gets( )*** and **puts( )** for strings and ***getchar( )*** and ***putchar( )*** for characters.

Random File

A disk file that can be read or changed at any point, designated by an offset from its beginning. The opposite of a ***sequential file***.

Record

A set of related data that is part of a repetitive list, for example, a name, address, and telephone number, or all of the data on a single employee. A record is made up of ***fields*** and is part of a file of a ***database***. These terms are all used generally to refer to databases and are not specific to C.

Register

A ***storage class***. It can be used as a modifier in the declaration of any variable to give it priority to be stored in a register rather than in RAM so that it can be processed more quickly. Most compilers try to optimize the performance of their code by storing some variables in registers automatically, but they are not always good at guessing which variables it is best to store there. By using the modifier **register**, you determine which variables have priority to be stored in registers.

Relational Operators

Operators used to compare values. The relational operators are:

==	is equal to
!=	is not equal to
>	is greater than
<	is less than

>= is greater than or equal to

<= is less than or equal to

return;

A statement that immediately redirects program control to the calling function, without any of the remaining instructions of the called function being executed. Using return plus some value within the called function redirects program control to the calling function and also make the called function return the specified value to the calling function. That is, the called function assumes that value in the calling function.

Rounding Error

An error in a calculation caused by the rounding of numbers. Because it uses binary arithmetic, the computer necessarily creates rounding errors when it is converting numbers to and from decimal form. If you use the ***float*** data type, results may be inaccurate by a few millionths of a unit. If you use the ***double*** data type, results may be inaccurate by a few trillionths. The accuracy of the float is adequate for dealing with money. The double is used for more precise calculations.

scanf( )

Command receives input from the keyboard. Its general form is as follows: **scanf(%c,& SmplVar);**. The characters used following the percent sign are the same as in ***printf( )***. The name of the variable to which they are assigned must be preceded by the ampersand, &, which is used to refer to an address.

Sequential File

A disk file that can only be read from beginning to end and can only be added to by appending new data onto the end. The opposite of a ***random file***, which can be read or changed at any point. The high-level file-handling functions that are built into C's standard input/output package can only access files sequentially.

Simple Statement

A one-line command terminated by a semicolon. A condition must be followed by a single statement, either simple or compound. Thus, if there is only one instruction, it is already a single statement, and the brackets can be omitted. The brackets only need to be used if the condition is followed by a ***compound statement***.

Static

A ***storage class***. Use this modifier to make a local variable remain in memory throughout the execution of a program. Most local variables exist only when the function that contains them is executing, but there are times, when you need one that remains in memory between calls of the function.

Storage Class

The declaration of a variable can include a modifier before the data type, which indicates the **storage class** of that variable. Storage classes include ***unsigned***, ***register***, ***extern***, and ***static***.

strcmp( )

A string handling function which takes two strings as its arguments and returns a 0 if the two are identical.

strcpy( )

A function used to copy a value to a string. For example, the code:

```
char name [16];
strcpy(name,"Amadeus");
```

would initialize the string name with the value Amadeus. As with most string-handling functions, the first argument of **strcpy( )** is the target that is changed. This is much easier than initializing the string one element at a time.

Stream Pointer

A pointer to a file. Before opening a file, you must declare the stream pointer as follows:

```
FILE *filePtr;
```

After this declaration, a value can be assigned to **filePtr** by using the statement **filePtr = fopen("filename","r");** so the file can be read one character at a time by using **variable = getc(filePtr);**, which assigns the character in the disk file to the variable (which should be declared as a char earlier in the program).

String

An array of characters terminated by the ***null*** character, **\0**, which C uses to work with words or text. A string is declared as an array of chars and must contain one element more than the maximum number of characters in the word that it will hold, in order to leave a space for the ***null*** terminator. String constants are enclosed in double quotation marks, unlike ***char***s, which are enclosed in single quotation marks. It is possible to assign a value to a string by initializing each ***char*** of the string individually and adding the ***null*** terminator, but it is easier to use the function ***strcpy( )***.

strlen( )

A string handling function that takes one string as its argument and returns the length of that string.

Struct

A "package of data" that lets you combine different data types. The declaration of a structure includes each of its elements after its name. For example:

```
struct employee
     {
     char fname[21];
     char lname[31];
     char address[31];
     char city[21];
     char state[3];
     char zip[6];
     char sex;
     int age;
     float salary;
     };
```

This declaration essentially creates a new data type, named **employee,** by packaging together a list of existing data types. To create variables of this data type, you can use a declaration such as **struct employee smith;**. You can also create arrays of structs, with a declaration such as **struct employee acmeEmp[100];**. To refer to individual elements of a variable that is a struct, you must use the name of the variable, plus a period, plus the name of the element, for example, **jones.salary** or **acmeEmp[10].salary** or **acmeEmp[10].lname[10]**.

Structured Programming

Programming that redirects ***control flow*** using sequence, selection, and iteration. Sequence means performing one statement after another in the same order in which the statements appear in the program. Selection means performing one of two or more C statements, and can be done using the ***if-else statement***, the ***if-else-if ladder***, or the ***switch( )***. Iteration means repeating (or reiterating) the same procedure and can be done using the ***while( ) loop***, the ***do while loop***, or the ***for ( ) loop***.

switch( )

A form of ***control flow*** used in ***structured programming***. The **switch( )** takes the following form:

```
switch(variable)
     {
     case '1':
          statemt1;
     case '2':
          statemt2;
     case '3':
          statemt3;
     default:
          statemt4;
     }
```

The statements that follow any cases whose conditions are equal to the variable are executed. If none of the cases is executed, then the statement following default is executed. Note that the **switch( )** statement can execute the statements following more than one case. The **switch( )** statement often is used in to execute only one case, like an ***if-else-if ladder***. ***break;*** is added at the end of the statement following each case, so that the program breaks out of the **switch( )** and continues with the code following it as soon as it executes the statement in one case.

tolower( )

A function which takes one ***char*** as its argument and that makes an alphabetic ***char*** lower-case but has no effect on nonalphabetic characters. The opposite of ***toupper( )***.

toupper( )

A function that takes one ***char*** as its argument and that makes an alphabetic ***char*** upper-case but has no effect on a nonalphabetic character. The opposite of ***tolower( )***.

Two-Dimensional Array

A set of variables that have the same name and are differentiated by two index numbers. To declare a one-dimensional ***array***, you use a statement such as: **char samplAry[100];**. This statement creates 100 character variables, with names ranging from **samplAry[0]** to **samplAry[99]**. Likewise, to declare a two-dimensional array, use a statement such as **char samplAry[100][5];**. This statement would create a **two-dimensional array** with 500 elements, numbered from **samplAry[0][0]** to **samplAry[99][4]**. It is easiest to think of two-dimensional arrays as tables. The example above could be visualized as a table with 5 columns across and 100 rows down.

Unsigned

A ***storage class***. It can be used as a modifier in the declaration of an ***int***, ***long***, or ***short*** to declare an unsigned integer of that type. The word unsigned can also be used alone to declare an unsigned ***int***.

Void

A data type that is used only with functions, to indicate that they do not return any value.

while( ) Loop

A form of ***control flow*** used in ***structured programming*** to repeat the same instructions, which takes the following form:

```
while(condition)
      {
      statement;
      statement;
      }
```

If the condition is true, the program performs the statements within the curly brackets. When it encounters the final bracket, it loops back up to the condition. If the condition is still true, the program performs these statements again. If the condition is false, the program continues to whatever statements follow the final curly bracket. There must be some statement within the curly brackets that eventually makes the condition false, or else the loop continues indefinitely.

Index

A

B

T

U

V

W

X

C. S. LEWIS

Prince Caspian

The return to Narnia

illustrated by
Pauline Baynes

Books UK Ltd.

This edition produced for Books UK Ltd 1997
by HarperCollins Publishers
77–85 Fulham Palace Road, Hammersmith
London W6 8JB

First published by Geoffrey Bles 1951
First published by Collins paperback 1980

1 3 5 7 9 10 8 6 4 2

ISBN 0 583 33141 6

Printed and bound in Great Britain by
Caledonian International Book Manufacturing Ltd, Glasgow

To Mary Clare Havard

CONTENTS

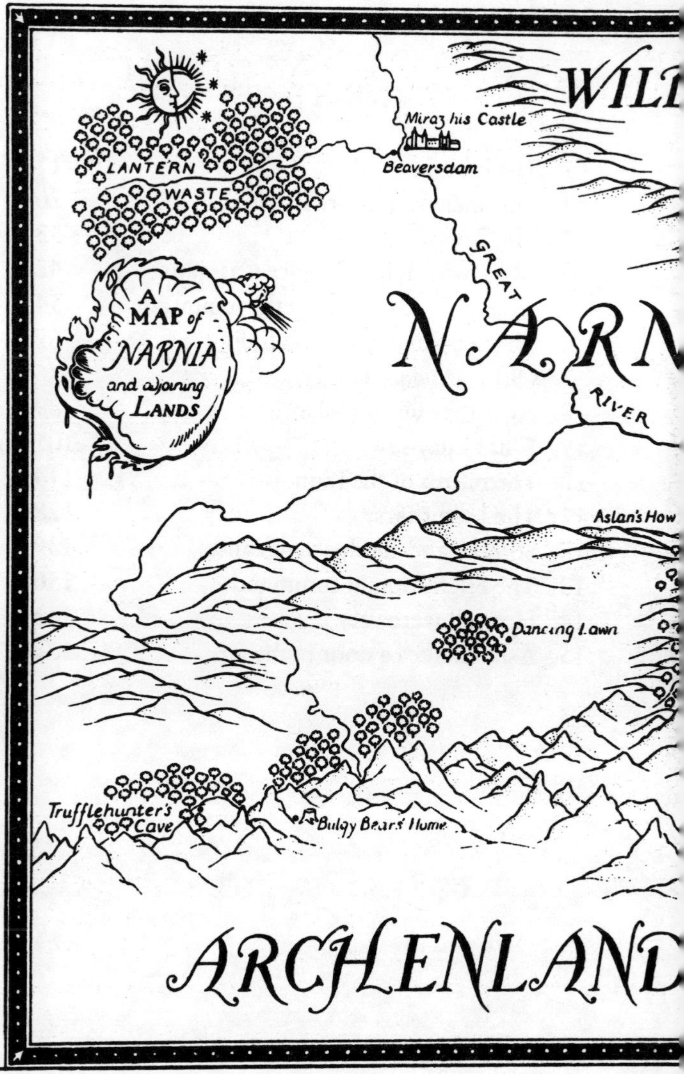
A MAP of NARNIA and adjoining LANDS
LANTERN WASTE
Miraz his Castle
Beaversdam
GREAT RIVER
NARN
WILL
Aslan's How
Dancing Lawn
Trufflehunter's Cave
Bulgy Bears' Home
ARCHENLAND

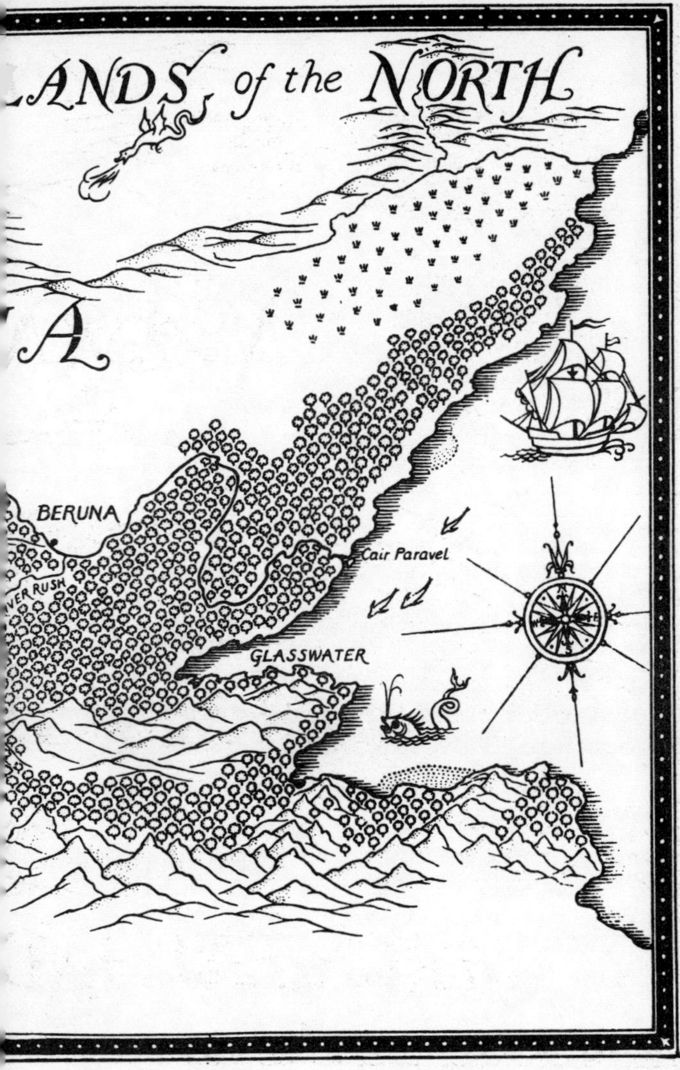
LANDS of the NORTH
BERUNA
VER RUSH
Cair Paravel
GLASSWATER

CHAPTER ONE

THE ISLAND

Once there were four children whose names were Peter, Susan, Edmund, and Lucy, and it has been told in another book called *The Lion, the Witch and the Wardrobe* how they had a remarkable adventure. They had opened the door of a magic wardrobe and found themselves in a quite different world from ours, and in that different world they had become Kings and Queens in a country called Narnia. While they were in Narnia they seemed to reign for years and years; but when they came back through the door and found themselves in England again, it all seemed to have taken no time at all. At any rate, no one noticed that they had ever been away, and they never told anyone except one very wise grown-up.

That had all happened a year ago, and now all four of them were sitting on a seat at a railway station with trunks and playboxes piled up round them. They were, in fact, on their way back to school. They had travelled together as far as this station, which was a junction; and here, in a few minutes, one train would arrive and take the girls away to one school, and in about half an hour another train would arrive and the boys would go off to another school. The first part of the journey, when they were all together, always seemed to be part of the holidays; but now when they would be saying good-bye and going different ways so soon, everyone felt that the holidays were really over and everyone felt their term-time feelings beginning again, and they were all rather gloomy and no one could think of anything to say. Lucy was going to boarding school for the first time.

It was an empty, sleepy, country station and there was hardly anyone on the platform except themselves. Suddenly Lucy gave a sharp little cry, like someone who has been stung by a wasp.

"What's up, Lu?" said Edmund – and then suddenly broke off and made a noise like "Ow!"

"What on earth –" began Peter, and then he too suddenly changed what he had been going to say. Instead, he said, "Susan, let go! What are you doing? Where are you dragging me to?"

"I'm not touching you," said Susan. "Someone is pulling *me*. Oh – oh – oh – stop it!"

Everyone noticed that all the others' faces had gone very white.

"I felt just the same," said Edmund in a breathless voice. "As if I were being dragged along. A most frightful pulling – ugh! it's beginning again."

"Me too," said Lucy. "Oh, I can't bear it."

"Look sharp!" shouted Edmund. "All catch hands and keep together. This is magic – I can tell by the feeling. Quick!"

"Yes," said Susan. "Hold hands. Oh, I do wish it would stop – oh!"

Next moment the luggage, the seat, the platform, and the station had completely vanished. The four children, holding hands and panting, found themselves standing in a woody place – such a woody place that branches were sticking into them and there was hardly room to move. They all rubbed their eyes and took a deep breath.

"Oh, Peter!" exclaimed Lucy. "Do you think we can possibly have got back to Narnia?"

"It might be anywhere," said Peter. "I can't see a yard in

all these trees. Let's try to get into the open – if there is any open."

With some difficulty, and with some stings from nettles and pricks from thorns, they struggled out of the thicket. Then they had another surprise. Everything became much brighter, and after a few steps they found themselves at the edge of the wood, looking down on a sandy beach. A few yards away a very calm sea was falling on the sand with such tiny ripples that it made hardly any sound. There was no land in sight and no clouds in the sky. The sun was about where it ought to be at ten o'clock in the morning, and the sea was a dazzling blue. They stood sniffing in the sea-smell.

"By Jove!" said Peter. "This is good enough."

Five minutes later everyone was barefooted and wading in the cool clear water.

"This is better than being in a stuffy train on the way back to Latin and French and Algebra!" said Edmund. And then for quite a long time there was no more talking, only splashing and looking for shrimps and crabs.

"All the same," said Susan presently, "I suppose we'll have to make some plans. We shall want something to eat before long."

"We've got the sandwiches Mother gave us for the journey," said Edmund. "At least I've got mine."

"Not me," said Lucy. "Mine were in my little bag."

"So were mine," said Susan.

"Mine are in my coat-pocket, there on the beach," said Peter. "That'll be two lunches among four. This isn't going to be such fun."

"At present," said Lucy, "I want something to drink more than something to eat."

Everyone else now felt thirsty, as one usually is after wading in salt water under a hot sun.

"It's like being shipwrecked," remarked Edmund. "In the books they always find springs of clear, fresh water on the island. We'd better go and look for them."

"Does that mean we have to go back into all that thick wood?" said Susan.

"Not a bit of it," said Peter. "If there are streams they're bound to come down to the sea, and if we walk along the beach we're bound to come to them."

They all now waded back and went first across the smooth, wet sand and then up to the dry, crumbly sand that sticks to one's toes, and began putting on their shoes and socks. Edmund and Lucy wanted to leave them behind and do their exploring with bare feet, but Susan said this would be a mad thing to do. "We might never find them again," she pointed out, "and we shall want them if we're still here when night comes and it begins to be cold."

When they were dressed again they set out along the shore with the sea on their left hand and the wood on their right. Except for an occasional seagull it was a very quiet place. The wood was so thick and tangled that they could hardly see into it at all; and nothing in it moved – not a bird, not even an insect.

Shells and seaweed and anemones, or tiny crabs in rock-pools, are all very well, but you soon get tired of them if you are thirsty. The children's feet, after the change from the cool water, felt hot and heavy. Susan and Lucy had raincoats to carry. Edmund had put down his coat on the station seat just before the magic overtook them, and he and Peter took it in turns to carry Peter's great-coat.

Presently the shore began to curve round to the right.

About quarter of an hour later, after they had crossed a rocky ridge which ran out into a point, it made quite a sharp turn. Their backs were now to the part of the sea which had met them when they first came out of the wood, and now, looking ahead, they could see across the water another shore, thickly wooded like the one they were exploring.

"I wonder, is that an island or do we join on to it presently?" said Lucy.

"Don't know," said Peter and they all plodded on in silence.

The shore that they were walking on drew nearer and nearer to the opposite shore, and as they came round each promontory the children expected to find the place where the two joined. But in this they were disappointed. They came to some rocks which they had to climb and from the top they could see a fair way ahead and – "Oh bother!" said Edmund, "it's no good. We shan't be able to get to those other woods at all. We're on an island!"

It was true. At this point the channel between them and the opposite coast was only about thirty or forty yards wide; but they could now see that this was its narrowest place. After that, their own coast bent round to the right again and they could see open sea between it and the mainland. It was obvious that they had already come much more than half-way round the island.

"Look!" said Lucy suddenly. "What's that?" She pointed to a long, silvery, snake-like thing that lay across the beach.

"A stream! A stream!" shouted the others, and, tired as they were, they lost no time in clattering down the rocks and racing to the fresh water. They knew that the stream would be better to drink farther up, away from the beach, so they went at once to the spot where it came out of the wood. The

trees were as thick as ever, but the stream had made itself a deep course between high mossy banks so that by stooping you could follow it up in a sort of tunnel of leaves. They dropped on their knees by the first brown, dimply pool and drank and drank, and dipped their faces in the water, and then dipped their arms in up to the elbow.

"Now," said Edmund, "what about those sandwiches?"

"Oh, hadn't we better save them?" said Susan. "We may need them far worse later on."

"I do wish," said Lucy, "now that we're not thirsty, we could go on feeling as not-hungry as we did when we *were* thirsty."

"But what about those sandwiches?" repeated Edmund. "There's no good saving them till they go bad. You've got to remember it's a good deal hotter here than in England and we've been carrying them about in pockets for hours." So they got out the two packets and divided them into four portions, and nobody had quite enough, but it was a great

deal better than nothing. Then they talked about their plans for the next meal. Lucy wanted to go back to the sea and catch shrimps, until someone pointed out that they had no nets. Edmund said they must gather gulls' eggs from the rocks, but when they came to think of it they couldn't remember having seen any gulls' eggs and wouldn't be able to cook them if they found any. Peter thought to himself that unless they had some stroke of luck they would soon be glad to eat eggs raw, but he didn't see any point in saying this out loud. Susan said it was a pity they had eaten the sandwiches so soon. One or two tempers very nearly got lost at this stage. Finally Edmund said:

"Look here. There's only one thing to be done. We must explore the wood. Hermits and knights-errant and people like that always manage to live somehow if they're in a forest. They find roots and berries and things."

"What sort of roots?" asked Susan.

"I always thought it meant roots of trees," said Lucy.

"Come on," said Peter, "Ed is right. And we must try to do something. And it'll be better than going out into the glare and the sun again."

So they all got up and began to follow the stream. It was very hard work. They had to stoop under branches and climb over branches, and they blundered through great masses of stuff like rhododendrons and tore their clothes and got their feet wet in the stream; and still there was no noise at all except the noise of the stream and the noises they were making themselves. They were beginning to get very tired of it when they noticed a delicious smell, and then a flash of bright colour high above them at the top of the right bank.

"I say!" exclaimed Lucy. "I do believe that's an apple tree."

It was. They panted up the steep bank, forced their way through some brambles, and found themselves standing round an old tree that was heavy with large yellowish-golden apples as firm and juicy as you could wish to see.

"And this is not the only tree," said Edmund with his mouth full of apple. "Look there – and there."

"Why, there are dozens of them," said Susan, throwing away the core of her first apple and picking her second. "This must have been an orchard – long, long ago, before the place went wild and the wood grew up."

"Then this was once an inhabited island," said Peter.

"And what's that?" said Lucy, pointing ahead.

"By Jove, it's a wall," said Peter. "An old stone wall."

Pressing their way between the laden branches they reached the wall. It was very old, and broken down in places, with moss and wallflowers growing on it, but it was higher than all but the tallest trees. And when they came quite close to it they found a great arch which must once have had a gate in it but was now almost filled up with the largest of all the apple trees. They had to break some of the branches to get past, and when they had done so they all blinked because the daylight became suddenly much brighter. They found themselves in a wide open place with walls all round it. In here there were no trees, only level grass and daisies, and ivy, and grey walls. It was a bright, secret, quiet place, and rather sad; and all four stepped out into the middle of it, glad to be able to straighten their backs and move their limbs freely.

CHAPTER TWO

THE ANCIENT TREASURE HOUSE

"THIS wasn't a garden," said Susan presently. "It was a castle and this must have been the courtyard."

"I see what you mean," said Peter. "Yes. That is the remains of a tower. And there is what used to be a flight of steps going up to the top of the walls. And look at those other steps – the broad, shallow ones – going up to that doorway. It must have been the door into the great hall."

"Ages ago, by the look of it," said Edmund.

"Yes, ages ago," said Peter. "I wish we could find out who the people were that lived in this castle; and how long ago."

"It gives me a queer feeling," said Lucy.

"Does it, Lu?" said Peter, turning and looking hard at her. "Because it does the same to me. It is the queerest thing that has happened this queer day. I wonder where we are and what it all means?"

While they were talking they had crossed the courtyard and gone through the other doorway into what had once been the hall. This was now very like the courtyard, for the roof had long since disappeared and it was merely another space of grass and daisies, except that it was shorter and narrower and the walls were higher. Across the far end there was a kind of terrace about three feet higher than the rest.

"I wonder, was it really the hall?" said Susan. "What is that terrace kind of thing?"

"Why, you silly," said Peter (who had become strangely

excited), "don't you see? That was the dais where the High Table was, where the King and the great lords sat. Anyone would think you had forgotten that we ourselves were once Kings and Queens and sat on a dais just like that, in our great hall."

"In our castle of Cair Paravel," continued Susan in a dreamy and rather sing-song voice, "at the mouth of the great river of Narnia. How could I forget?"

"How it all comes back!" said Lucy. "We could pretend we were in Cair Paravel now. This hall must have been very like the great hall we feasted in."

"But unfortunately without the feast," said Edmund. "It's getting late, you know. Look how long the shadows are. And have you noticed that it isn't so hot?"

"We shall need a camp-fire if we've got to spend the night here," said Peter. "I've got matches. Let's go and see if we can collect some dry wood."

Everyone saw the sense of this, and for the next half-hour they were busy. The orchard through which they had first come into the ruins turned out not to be a good place for firewood. They tried the other side of the castle, passing out of the hall by a little side door into a maze of stony humps and hollows which must once have been passages and smaller rooms but was now all nettles and wild roses. Beyond this they found a wide gap in the castle wall and stepped through it into a wood of darker and bigger trees where they found dead branches and rotten wood and sticks and dry leaves and fir-cones in plenty. They went to and fro with bundles until they had a good pile on the dais. At the fifth journey they found the well, just outside the hall, hidden in weeds, but clean and fresh and deep when they had cleared these away.

The remains of a stone pavement ran half-way round it. Then the girls went out to pick some more apples and the boys built the fire, on the dais and fairly close to the corner between two walls, which they thought would be the snuggest and warmest place. They had great difficulty in lighting it and used a lot of matches, but they succeeded in the end. Finally, all four sat down with their backs to the wall and their faces to the fire. They tried roasting some of the apples on the ends of sticks. But roast apples are not much good without sugar, and they are too hot to eat with your fingers till they are too cold to be worth eating. So they had to content themselves with raw apples, which, as Edmund said, made one realize that school suppers weren't so bad after all – "I shouldn't mind a good thick slice of bread and margarine this minute," he added. But the spirit of adventure was rising in them all, and no one really wanted to be back at school.

Shortly after the last apple had been eaten, Susan went

out to the well to get another drink. When she came back she was carrying something in her hand.

"Look," she said in a rather choking kind of voice. "I found it by the well." She handed it to Peter and sat down. The others thought she looked and sounded as if she might be going to cry. Edmund and Lucy eagerly bent forward to see what was in Peter's hand – a little, bright thing that gleamed in the firelight.

"Well, I'm – I'm jiggered," said Peter, and his voice also sounded queer. Then he handed it to the others.

All now saw what it was – a little chess-knight, ordinary in size but extraordinarily heavy because it was made of pure gold; and the eyes in the horse's head were two tiny little rubies – or rather one was, for the other had been knocked out.

"Why!" said Lucy, "it's exactly like one of the golden chessmen we used to play with when we were Kings and Queens at Cair Paravel."

"Cheer up, Su," said Peter to his other sister.

"I can't help it," said Susan. "It brought back – oh, such lovely times. And I remembered playing chess with fauns and good giants, and the mer-people singing in the sea, and my beautiful horse – and – and –"

"Now," said Peter in a quite different voice, "it's about time we four started using our brains."

"What about?" asked Edmund.

"Have none of you guessed where we are?" said Peter.

"Go on, go on," said Lucy. "I've felt for hours that there was some wonderful mystery hanging over this place."

"Fire ahead, Peter," said Edmund. "We're all listening."

"We are in the ruins of Cair Paravel itself," said Peter.

"But, I say," replied Edmund. "I mean, how do you make that out? This place has been ruined for ages. Look at all those big trees growing right up to the gates. Look at the very stones. Anyone can see that nobody has lived here for hundreds of years."

"I know," said Peter. "That is the difficulty. But let's leave that out for the moment. I want to take the points one by one. First point: this hall is exactly the same shape and size as the hall at Cair Paravel. Just picture a roof on this, and a coloured pavement instead of grass, and tapestries on the walls, and you get our royal banqueting hall."

No one said anything.

"Second point," continued Peter. "The castle well is exactly where our well was, a little to the south of the great hall; and it is exactly the same size and shape."

Again there was no reply.

"Third point: Susan has just found one of our old chessmen – or something as like one of them as two peas."

Still nobody answered.

"Fourth point. Don't you remember – it was the very day before the ambassadors came from the King of Calormen – don't you remember planting the orchard outside the north gate of Cair Paravel? The greatest of all the wood-people, Pomona herself, came to put good spells on it. It was those very decent little chaps the moles who did the actual digging. Can you have forgotten that funny old Lilygloves, the chief mole, leaning on his spade and saying, 'Believe me, your Majesty, you'll be glad of these fruit trees one day.' And by Jove he was right."

"I do! I do!" said Lucy, and clapped her hands.

"But look here, Peter," said Edmund. "This must be all rot. To begin with, we didn't plant the orchard slap up against the gate. We wouldn't have been such fools."

"No, of course not," said Peter. "But it has grown up to the gate since."

"And for another thing," said Edmund, "Cair Paravel wasn't on an island."

"Yes, I've been wondering about that. But it was a what-do-you-call-it, a peninsula. Jolly nearly an island. Couldn't it have been made an island since our time? Somebody has dug a channel."

"But half a moment!" said Edmund. "You keep on saying *since our time*. But it's only a year ago since we came back from Narnia. And you want to make out that in one year castles have fallen down, and great forests have grown up, and little trees we saw planted ourselves have turned into a big old orchard, and goodness knows what else. It's all impossible."

"There's one thing," said Lucy. "If this is Cair Paravel there ought to be a door at this end of the dais. In fact we ought to be sitting with our backs against it at this moment. You know – the door that led down to the treasure chamber."

"I suppose there *isn't* a door," said Peter, getting up.

The wall behind them was a mass of ivy.

"We can soon find out," said Edmund, taking up one of the sticks that they had laid ready for putting on the fire. He began beating the ivied wall. Tap-tap went the stick against the stone; and again, tap-tap; and then, all at once, boom-boom, with a quite different sound, a hollow, wooden sound.

"Great Scott!" said Edmund.

"We must clear this ivy away," said Peter.

"Oh, do let's leave it alone," said Susan. "We can try it in the morning. If we've got to spend the night here I don't want an open door at my back and a great big black hole that anything might come out of, besides the draught and the damp. And it'll soon be dark."

"Susan! How can you?" said Lucy with a reproachful glance. But both the boys were too much excited to take any notice of Susan's advice. They worked at the ivy with their hands and with Peter's pocket-knife till the knife broke. After that they used Edmund's. Soon the whole place where they had been sitting was covered with ivy; and at last they had the door cleared.

"Locked, of course," said Peter.

"But the wood's all rotten," said Edmund. "We can pull it to bits in no time, and it will make extra firewood. Come on."

It took them longer than they expected and, before they had done, the great hall had grown dusky and the first star or two had come out overhead. Susan was not the only one who felt a slight shudder as the boys stood above the pile of splintered wood, rubbing the dirt off their hands and staring into the cold, dark opening they had made.

"Now for a torch," said Peter.

"Oh, what *is* the good?" said Susan. "And as Edmund said –"

"I'm not saying it now," Edmund interrupted. "I still don't understand, but we can settle that later. I suppose you're coming down, Peter?"

"We must," said Peter. "Cheer up, Susan. It's no good behaving like kids now that we are back in Narnia.

You're a Queen here. And anyway no one could go to sleep with a mystery like this on their minds."

They tried to use long sticks as torches but this was not a success. If you held them with the lighted end up they went out, and if you held them the other way they scorched your hand and the smoke got in your eyes. In the end they had to use Edmund's electric torch; luckily it had been a birthday present less than a week ago and the battery was almost new. He went first, with the light. Then came Lucy, then Susan, and Peter brought up the rear.

"I've come to the top of the steps," said Edmund.

"Count them," said Peter.

"One – two – three," said Edmund, as he went cautiously down, and so up to sixteen. "And this is the bottom," he shouted back.

"Then it really must be Cair Paravel," said Lucy. "There were sixteen." Nothing more was said till all four were standing in a knot together at the foot of the stairway. Then Edmund flashed his torch slowly round.

"O – o – o – oh!!" said all the children at once.

For now all knew that it was indeed the ancient treasure chamber of Cair Paravel where they had once reigned as Kings and Queens of Narnia. There was a kind of path up the middle (as it might be in a greenhouse), and along each side at intervals stood rich suits of armour, like knights guarding the treasures. In between the suits of armour, and on each side of the path, were shelves covered with precious things – necklaces and arm rings and finger rings and golden bowls and dishes and long tusks of ivory, brooches and coronets and chains of gold, and heaps of unset stones lying piled anyhow as if they were marbles or potatoes – diamonds, rubies, carbuncles, emeralds, topazes, and amethysts. Under the shelves stood great chests of oak strengthened with iron bars and heavily padlocked. And it was bitterly cold, and so still that they could hear themselves breathing, and the treasures were so covered with dust that unless they had realized where they were and remembered most of the things, they would hardly have known they were treasures. There was something sad and a little frightening about the place, because it all seemed so forsaken and long ago. That was why nobody said anything for at least a minute.

Then, of course, they began walking about and picking things up to look at. It was like meeting very old friends. If you had been there you would have heard them saying things like, "Oh look! Our coronation rings – do you

remember first wearing this? – Why, this is the little brooch we all thought was lost – I say, isn't that the armour you wore in the great tournament in the Lone Islands? – do you remember the dwarf making that for me? – do you remember drinking out of that horn? – do you remember, do you remember?"

But suddenly Edmund said, "Look here. We mustn't waste the battery: goodness knows how often we shall need it. Hadn't we better take what we want and get out again?"

"We must take the gifts," said Peter. For long ago at a Christmas in Narnia he and Susan and Lucy had been given certain presents which they valued more than their whole kingdom. Edmund had had no gift, because he was not with them at the time. (This was his own fault, and you can read about it in the other book.)

They all agreed with Peter and walked up the path to the wall at the far end of the treasure chamber, and there, sure enough, the gifts were still hanging. Lucy's was the smallest for it was only a little bottle. But the bottle was made of diamond instead of glass, and it was still more than half full of the magical cordial which would heal almost every wound and every illness. Lucy said nothing and looked very solemn as she took her gift down from its place and slung the belt over her shoulder and once more felt the bottle at her side where it used to hang in the old days. Susan's gift had been a bow and arrows and a horn. The bow was still there, and the ivory quiver, full of well-feathered arrows, but – "Oh, Susan," said Lucy. "Where's the horn?"

"Oh bother, bother, bother," said Susan after she had thought for a moment. "I remember now. I took it with

me the last day of all, the day we went hunting the White Stag. It must have got lost when we blundered back into that other place – England, I mean."

Edmund whistled. It was indeed a shattering loss; for this was an enchanted horn and, whenever you blew it, help was certain to come to you, wherever you were.

"Just the sort of thing that might come in handy in a place like this," said Edmund.

"Never mind," said Susan, "I've still got the bow." And she took it.

"Won't the string be perished, Su?" said Peter.

But whether by some magic in the air of the treasure chamber or not, the bow was still in working order. Archery and swimming were the things Susan was good at. In a moment she had bent the bow and then she gave one little pluck to the string. It twanged: a chirruping twang that vibrated through the whole room. And that one small noise brought back the old days to the children's minds more than anything that had happened yet. All the battles and hunts and feasts came rushing into their heads together.

Then she unstrung the bow again and slung the quiver at her side.

Next, Peter took down his gift – the shield with the great red lion on it, and the royal sword. He blew, and rapped them on the floor, to get off the dust. He fitted the shield on his arm and slung the sword by his side. He was afraid at first that it might be rusty and stick to the sheath. But it was not so. With one swift motion he drew it and held it up, shining in the torchlight.

"It is my sword Rhindon," he said; "with it I killed the Wolf." There was a new tone in his voice, and the others

all felt that he was really Peter the High King again. Then, after a little pause, everyone remembered that they must save the battery.

They climbed the stair again and made up a good fire and lay down close together for warmth. The ground was very hard and uncomfortable, but they fell asleep in the end.

CHAPTER THREE

THE DWARF

THE worst of sleeping out of doors is that you wake up so dreadfully early. And when you wake you have to get up because the ground is so hard that you are uncomfortable. And it makes matters worse if there is nothing but apples for breakfast and you have had nothing but apples for supper the night before. When Lucy had said – truly enough – that it was a glorious morning, there did not seem to be anything else nice to be said. Edmund said what everyone was feeling, "We've simply got to get off this island."

When they had drunk from the well and splashed their faces they all went down the stream again to the shore and stared at the channel which divided them from the mainland.

"We'll have to swim," said Edmund.

"It would be all right for Su," said Peter (Susan had won prizes for swimming at school). "But I don't know about the rest of us." By "the rest of us" he really meant Edmund who couldn't yet do two lengths at the school baths, and Lucy, who could hardly swim at all.

"Anyway," said Susan, "there may be currents. Father says it's never wise to bathe in a place you don't know."

"But, Peter," said Lucy, "look here. I know I can't swim for nuts at home – in England, I mean. But couldn't we all swim long ago – if it was long ago – when we were Kings and Queens in Narnia? We could ride then too, and do all sorts of things. Don't you think –?"

"Ah, but we were sort of grown-up then," said Peter.

"We reigned for years and years and learned to do things. Aren't we just back at our proper ages again now?"

"Oh!" said Edmund in a voice which made everyone stop talking and listen to him.

"I've just seen it all," he said.

"Seen what?" asked Peter.

"Why, the whole thing," said Edmund. "You know what we were puzzling about last night, that it was only a year ago since we left Narnia but everything looks as if no one had lived in Cair Paravel for hundreds of years? Well, don't you see? You know that, however long we seemed to have lived in Narnia, when we got back through the wardrobe it seemed to have taken no time at all?"

"Go on," said Susan. "I think I'm beginning to understand."

"And that means," continued Edmund, "that, once you're out of Narnia, you have no idea how Narnian time is going. Why shouldn't hundreds of years have gone past in Narnia while only one year has passed for us in England?"

"By Jove, Ed," said Peter. "I believe you've got it. In that sense it really was hundreds of years ago that we lived in Cair Paravel. And now we're coming back to Narnia just as if we were Crusaders or Anglo-Saxons or Ancient Britons or someone coming back to modern England?"

"How excited they'll be to see us –" began Lucy, but at the same moment everyone else said, "Hush!" or "Look!" For now something was happening.

There was a wooded point on the mainland a little to their right, and they all felt sure that just beyond that point must be the mouth of the river. And now, round that point there came into sight a boat. When it had cleared the point,

it turned and began coming along the channel towards them. There were two people on board, one rowing, the other sitting in the stern and holding a bundle that twitched and moved as if it were alive. Both these people seemed to be soldiers. They had steel caps on their heads and light shirts of chain-mail. Their faces were bearded and hard. The children drew back from the beach into the wood and watched without moving a finger.

"This'll do," said the soldier in the stern when the boat had come about opposite to them.

"What about tying a stone to his feet, Corporal?" said the other, resting on his oars.

"Garn!" growled the other. "We don't need that, and we haven't brought one. He'll drown sure enough without a stone, as long as we've tied the cords right." With these words he rose and lifted his bundle. Peter now saw that it was really alive and was in fact a Dwarf, bound hand and foot but struggling as hard as he could. Next moment he heard a twang just beside his ear, and all at once the soldier threw up his arms, dropping the Dwarf into the bottom of

the boat, and fell over into the water. He floundered away to the far bank and Peter knew that Susan's arrow had struck on his helmet. He turned and saw that she was very pale but was already fitting a second arrow to the string. But it was never used. As soon as he saw his companion fall, the other soldier, with a loud cry, jumped out of the boat on the far side, and he also floundered through the water (which was apparently just in his depth) and disappeared into the woods of the mainland.

"Quick! Before she drifts!" shouted Peter. He and Susan, fully dressed as they were, plunged in, and before the water was up to their shoulders their hands were on the side of the boat. In a few seconds they had hauled her to the bank and lifted the Dwarf out, and Edmund was busily engaged in cutting his bonds with the pocket knife. (Peter's sword would have been sharper, but a sword is very inconvenient for this sort of work because you can't hold it anywhere lower than the hilt.) When at last the Dwarf was free, he sat up, rubbed his arms and legs, and exclaimed:

"Well, whatever they say, you don't *feel* like ghosts."

Like most Dwarfs he was very stocky and deep-chested. He would have been about three feet high if he had been standing up, and an immense beard and whiskers of coarse red hair left little of his face to be seen except a beak-like nose and twinkling black eyes.

"Anyway," he continued, "ghosts or not, you've saved my life and I'm extremely obliged to you."

"But why should we be ghosts?" asked Lucy.

"I've been told all my life," said the Dwarf, "that these woods along the shore were as full of ghosts as they were of trees. That's what the story is. And that's why, when they want to get rid of anyone, they usually bring him

down here (like they were doing with me) and say they'll leave him to the ghosts. But I always wondered if they didn't really drown 'em or cut their throats. I never quite believed in the ghosts. But those two cowards you've just shot believed all right. They were more frightened of taking me to my death than I was of going!"

"Oh," said Susan. "So that's why they both ran away."

"Eh? What's that?" said the Dwarf.

"They got away," said Edmund. "To the mainland."

"I wasn't shooting to kill, you know," said Susan. She would not have liked anyone to think she could miss at such a short range.

"Hm," said the Dwarf. "That's not so good. That may mean trouble later on. Unless they hold their tongues for their own sake."

"What were they going to drown you for?" asked Peter.

"Oh, I'm a dangerous criminal, I am," said the Dwarf cheerfully. "But that's a long story. Meantime, I was wondering if perhaps you were going to ask me to

breakfast? You've no idea what an appetite it gives one, being executed."

"There's only apples," said Lucy dolefully.

"Better than nothing, but not so good as fresh fish," said the Dwarf. "It looks as if I'll have to ask you to breakfast instead. I saw some fishing tackle in that boat. And anyway, we must take her round to the other side of the

island. We don't want anyone from the mainland coming down and seeing her."

"I ought to have thought of that myself," said Peter.

The four children and the Dwarf went down to the water's edge, pushed off the boat with some difficulty, and scrambled aboard. The Dwarf at once took charge. The oars were of course too big for him to use, so Peter rowed and the Dwarf steered them north along the channel and

presently eastward round the tip of the island. From here the children could see right up the river, and all the bays and headlands of the coast beyond it. They thought they could recognize bits of it, but the woods, which had grown up since their time, made everything look very different.

When they had come round into open sea on the east of the island, the Dwarf took to fishing. They had an excellent catch of pavenders, a beautiful rainbow-coloured fish which they all remembered eating in Cair Paravel in the old days. When they had caught enough they ran the boat up into a little creek and moored her to a tree. The Dwarf, who was a most capable person (and, indeed, though one meets bad Dwarfs, I never heard of a Dwarf who was a fool), cut the fish open, cleaned them, and said:

"Now, what we want next is some firewood."

"We've got some up at the castle," said Edmund.

The Dwarf gave a low whistle. "Beards and bedsteads!" he said. "So there really is a castle, after all?"

"It's only a ruin," said Lucy.

The Dwarf stared round at all four of them with a very curious expression on his face. "And who on earth – ?" he began, but then broke off and said, "No matter. Breakfast first. But one thing before we go on. Can you lay your hand on your hearts and tell me I'm really alive? Are you sure I wasn't drowned and we're not all ghosts together?"

When they had all reassured him, the next question was how to carry the fish. They had nothing to string them on and no basket. They had to use Edmund's hat in the end because no one else had a hat. He would have made much more fuss about this if he had not by now been so ravenously hungry.

At first the Dwarf did not seem very comfortable in the

castle. He kept looking round and sniffing and saying, "H'm. Looks a bit spooky after all. Smells like ghosts, too." But he cheered up when it came to lighting the fire and showing them how to roast the fresh pavenders in the embers. Eating hot fish with no forks, and one pocket knife between five people, is a messy business and there were several burnt fingers before the meal was ended; but, as it was now nine o'clock and they had been up since five, nobody minded the burns so much as you might have expected. When everyone had finished off with a drink from the well and an apple or so, the Dwarf produced a pipe about the size of his own arm, filled it, lit it, blew a great cloud of fragrant smoke, and said, "Now."

"You tell us your story first," said Peter. "And then we'll tell you ours."

"Well," said the Dwarf, "as you've saved my life it is only fair you should have your own way. But I hardly know where to begin. First of all I'm a messenger of King Caspian's."

"Who's he?" asked four voices all at once.

"Caspian the Tenth, King of Narnia, and long may he reign!" answered the Dwarf. "That is to say, he ought to be King of Narnia and we hope he will be. At present he is only King of us Old Narnians – "

"What do you mean by *old* Narnians, please?" asked Lucy.

"Why, that's us," said the Dwarf. "We're a kind of rebellion, I suppose."

"I see," said Peter. "And Caspian is the chief Old Narnian."

"Well, in a manner of speaking," said the Dwarf,

scratching his head. "But he's really a New Narnian himself, a Telmarine, if you follow me."

"I don't," said Edmund.

"It's worse than the Wars of the Roses," said Lucy.

"Oh dear," said the Dwarf. "I'm doing this very badly. Look here: I think I'll have to go right back to the beginning and tell you how Caspian grew up in his uncle's court and how he comes to be on our side at all. But it'll be a long story."

"All the better," said Lucy. "We love stories."

So the Dwarf settled down and told his tale. I shall not give it to you in his words, putting in all the children's questions and interruptions, because it would take too long and be confusing, and, even so, it would leave out some points that the children only heard later. But the gist of the story, as they knew it in the end, was as follows.

CHAPTER FOUR

THE DWARF TELLS OF PRINCE CASPIAN

PRINCE CASPIAN lived in a great castle in the centre of Narnia with his uncle, Miraz, the King of Narnia, and his aunt, who had red hair and was called Queen Prunaprismia. His father and mother were dead and the person whom Caspian loved best was his nurse, and though (being a prince) he had wonderful toys which would do almost anything but talk, he liked best the last hour of the day when the toys had all been put back in their cupboards and Nurse would tell him stories.

He did not care much for his uncle and aunt, but about twice a week his uncle would send for him and they would walk up and down together for half an hour on the terrace at the south side of the castle. One day, while they were doing this, the King said to him,

"Well, boy, we must soon teach you to ride and use a sword. You know that your aunt and I have no children, so it looks as if you might have to be King when I'm gone. How shall you like that, eh?"

"I don't know, Uncle," said Caspian.

"Don't know, eh?" said Miraz. "Why, I should like to know what more anyone could wish for!"

"All the same, I *do* wish," said Caspian.

"What do you wish?" asked the King.

"I wish – I wish – I wish I could have lived in the Old Days," said Caspian. (He was only a very little boy at the time.)

Up till now King Miraz had been talking in the tiresome way that some grown-ups have, which makes it quite clear

that they are not really interested in what you are saying, but now he suddenly gave Caspian a very sharp look.

"Eh? What's that?" he said. "What old days do you mean?"

"Oh, don't you know, Uncle?" said Caspian. "When everything was quite different. When all the animals could talk, and there were nice people who lived in the streams and the trees. Naiads and Dryads they were called. And there were Dwarfs. And there were lovely little Fauns in all the woods. They had feet like goats. And –"

"That's all nonsense, for babies," said the King sternly. "Only fit for babies, do you hear? You're getting too old for that sort of stuff. At your age you ought to be thinking of battles and adventures, not fairy tales."

"Oh, but there *were* battles and adventures in those days," said Caspian. "Wonderful adventures. Once there was a White Witch and she made herself Queen of the whole country. And she made it so that it was always winter. And then two boys and two girls came from somewhere and so they killed the Witch and they were made Kings and Queens of Narnia, and their names were Peter and Susan and Edmund and Lucy. And so they reigned for ever so long and everyone had a lovely time, and it was all because of Aslan –"

"Who's he?" said Miraz. And if Caspian had been a very little older, the tone of his uncle's voice would have warned him that it would be wiser to shut up. But he babbled on,

"Oh, don't you know?" he said. "Aslan is the great Lion who comes from over the sea."

"Who has been telling you all this nonsense?" said the King in a voice of thunder. Caspian was frightened and said nothing.

"Your Royal Highness," said King Miraz, letting go of Caspian's hand, which he had been holding till now, "I insist upon being answered. Look me in the face. Who has been telling you this pack of lies?"

"N – Nurse," faltered Caspian, and burst into tears.

"Stop that noise," said his uncle, taking Caspian by the shoulders and giving him a shake. "Stop it. And never let me catch you talking – or *thinking* either – about all those silly stories again. There never were those Kings and Queens. How could there be two Kings at the same time? And there's no such person as Aslan. And there are no such things as lions. And there never was a time when animals could talk. Do you hear?"

"Yes, Uncle," sobbed Caspian.

"Then let's have no more of it," said the King. Then he called to one of the gentlemen-in-waiting who were standing at the far end of the terrace and said in a cold voice, "Conduct His Royal Highness to his apartments and send His Royal Highness's nurse to me AT ONCE."

Next day Caspian found what a terrible thing he had done, for Nurse had been sent away without even being allowed to say good-bye to him, and he was told he was to have a Tutor.

Caspian missed his nurse very much and shed many tears; and because he was so miserable, he thought about the old stories of Narnia far more than before. He dreamed of Dwarfs and Dryads every night and tried very hard to make the dogs and cats in the castle talk to him. But the dogs only wagged their tails and the cats only purred.

Caspian felt sure that he would hate the new Tutor, but when the new Tutor arrived about a week later he turned

out to be the sort of person it is almost impossible not to like. He was the smallest, and also the fattest, man Caspian had ever seen. He had a long, silvery, pointed beard which came down to his waist, and his face, which was brown and covered with wrinkles, looked very wise, very ugly, and very kind. His voice was grave and his eyes were merry so that, until you got to know him really well, it was hard to know when he was joking and when he was serious. His name was Doctor Cornelius.

Of all his lessons with Doctor Cornelius the one that Caspian liked best was History. Up till now, except for Nurse's stories, he had known nothing about the History of Narnia, and he was very surprised to learn that the royal family were newcomers in the country.

"It was your Highness's ancestor, Caspian the First," said Doctor Cornelius, "who first conquered Narnia and made it his kingdom. It was he who brought all your nation into the country. You are not native Narnians at all. You are all Telmarines – that is, you all came from the Land of Telmar, far beyond the Western Mountains. That is why Caspian the First is called Caspian the Conqueror."

"Please, Doctor," asked Caspian one day, "who lived in Narnia before we all came here out of Telmar?"

"No men – or very few – lived in Narnia before the Telmarines took it," said Doctor Cornelius.

"Then who did my great-great-grandcesters conquer?"

"*Whom*, not *who*, your Highness," said Doctor Cornelius. "Perhaps it is time to turn from History to Grammar."

"Oh please, not yet," said Caspian. "I mean, wasn't

there a battle? Why is he called Caspian the Conqueror if there was nobody to fight with him?"

"I said there were very few *men* in Narnia," said the Doctor, looking at the little boy very strangely through his great spectacles.

For a moment Caspian was puzzled and then suddenly his heart gave a leap. "Do you mean," he gasped, "that there were other things? Do you mean it was like in the stories? Were there –?"

"Hush!" said Doctor Cornelius, laying his head very close to Caspian's. "Not a word more. Don't you know

your Nurse was sent away for telling you about Old Narnia? The King doesn't like it. If he found me telling you secrets, you'd be whipped and I should have my head cut off."

"But why?" asked Caspian.

"It is high time we turned to Grammar now," said Doctor Cornelius in a loud voice. "Will your Royal Highness be pleased to open Pulverulentus Siccus at the fourth page of his *Grammatical garden or the Arbour of Accidence pleasantlie open'd to Tender Wits*?"

After that it was all nouns and verbs till lunchtime, but I don't think Caspian learned much. He was too excited. He felt sure that Doctor Cornelius would not have said so much unless he meant to tell him more sooner or later.

In this he was not disappointed. A few days later his Tutor said, "Tonight I am going to give you a lesson in Astronomy. At dead of night two noble planets, Tarva and Alambil, will pass within one degree of each other. Such a conjunction has not occurred for two hundred years, and your Highness will not live to see it again. It will be best if you go to bed a little earlier than usual. When the time of the conjunction draws near I will come and wake you."

This didn't seem to have anything to do with Old Narnia, which was what Caspian really wanted to hear about, but getting up in the middle of the night is always interesting and he was moderately pleased. When he went to bed that night, he thought at first that he would not be able to sleep; but he soon dropped off and it seemed only a few minutes before he felt someone gently shaking him.

He sat up in bed and saw that the room was full of moonlight. Doctor Cornelius, muffled in a hooded robe and holding a small lamp in his hand, stood by the bedside.

Caspian remembered at once what they were going to do. He got up and put on some clothes. Athough it was a summer night he felt colder than he had expected and was quite glad when the Doctor wrapped him in a robe like his own and gave him a pair of warm, soft buskins for his feet. A moment later, both muffled so that they could hardly be seen in the dark corridors, and both shod so that they made almost no noise, master and pupil left the room.

Caspian followed the Doctor through many passages and up several staircases, and at last, through a little door in a turret, they came out upon the leads. On one side were the battlements, on the other a steep roof; below them, all shadowy and shimmery, the castle gardens; above them, stars and moon. Presently they came to another door, which led into the great central tower of the whole castle: Doctor Cornelius unlocked it and they began to climb the dark winding stair of the tower. Caspian was becoming excited; he had never been allowed up this stair before.

It was long and steep, but when they came out on the roof of the tower and Caspian had got his breath, he felt that it had been well worth it. Away on his right he could see, rather indistinctly, the Western Mountains. On his left was the gleam of the Great River, and everything was so quiet that he could hear the sound of the waterfall at Beaversdam, a mile away. There was no difficulty in picking out the two stars they had come to see. They hung rather low in the southern sky, almost as bright as two little moons and very close together.

"Are they going to have a collision?" he asked in an awe-struck voice.

"Nay, dear Prince," said the Doctor (and he too spoke in a whisper). "The great lords of the upper sky know the

steps of their dance too well for that. Look well upon them. Their meeting is fortunate and means some great good for the sad realm of Narnia. Tarva, the Lord of Victory, salutes Alambil, the Lady of Peace. They are just coming to their nearest."

"It's a pity that tree gets in the way," said Caspian. "We'd really see better from the West Tower, though it is not so high."

Doctor Cornelius said nothing for about two minutes, but stood still with his eyes fixed on Tarva and Alambil. Then he drew a deep breath and turned to Caspian.

"There," he said. "You have seen what no man now alive has seen, nor will see again. And you are right. We should have seen it even better from the smaller tower. I brought you here for another reason."

Caspian looked up at him, but the Doctor's hood concealed most of his face.

"The virtue of this tower," said Doctor Cornelius, "is that we have six empty rooms beneath us, and a long stair, and the door at the bottom of the stair is locked. We cannot be overheard."

"Are you going to tell me what you wouldn't tell me the other day?" said Caspian.

"I am," said the Doctor. "But remember. You and I must never talk about these things except here – on the very top of the Great Tower."

"No. That's a promise," said Caspian. "But do go on, please."

"Listen," said the Doctor. "All you have heard about Old Narnia is true. It is not the land of Men. It is the country of Aslan, the country of the Waking Trees and Visible Naiads, of Fauns and Satyrs, of Dwarfs and Giants, of the gods and the Centaurs, of Talking Beasts. It was against these that the first Caspian fought. It is you Telmarines who silenced the beasts and the trees and the fountains, and who killed and drove away the Dwarfs and Fauns, and are now trying to cover up even the memory of them. The King does not allow them to be spoken of."

"Oh, I do wish we hadn't," said Caspian. "And I *am* glad it was all true, even if it is all over."

"Many of your race wish that in secret," said Doctor Cornelius.

"But, Doctor," said Caspian, "why do you say *my* race? After all, I suppose you're a Telmarine too."

"Am I?" said the Doctor.

"Well, you're a Man anyway," said Caspian.

"Am I?" repeated the Doctor in a deeper voice, at the same moment throwing back his hood so that Caspian could see his face clearly in the moonlight.

All at once Caspian realized the truth and felt that he ought to have realized it long before. Doctor Cornelius was so small, and so fat, and had such a very long beard. Two thoughts came into his head at the same moment. One was a thought of terror – "He's not a real man, not a man at all, he's a *Dwarf*, and he's brought me up here to kill me." The other was sheer delight – "There are real Dwarfs still, and I've seen one at last."

"So you've guessed it in the end," said Doctor Cornelius. "Or guessed it nearly right. I'm not a pure Dwarf. I have human blood in me too. Many Dwarfs escaped in the great battles and lived on, shaving their beards and wearing high-heeled shoes and pretending to be men. They have mixed with your Telmarines. I am one of those, only a half-Dwarf, and if any of my kindred, the true Dwarfs, are still alive anywhere in the world, doubtless they would despise me and call me a traitor. But never in all these years have we forgotten our own people and all the other happy creatures of Narnia, and the long-lost days of freedom."

"I'm – I'm sorry, Doctor," said Caspian. "It wasn't my fault, you know."

"I am not saying these things in blame of you, dear Prince," answered the Doctor. "You may well ask why I say them at all. But I have two reasons. Firstly, because my old heart has carried these secret memories so long that it aches with them and would burst if I did not whisper them to you. But secondly, for this: that when you become King you may help us, for I know that you also, Telmarine though you are, love the Old Things."

"I do, I do," said Caspian. "But how can I help?"

"You can be kind to the poor remnants of the Dwarf people, like myself. You can gather learned magicians and

try to find a way of awaking the trees once more. You can search through all the nooks and wild places of the land to see if any Fauns or Talking Beasts or Dwarfs are perhaps still alive in hiding."

"Do you think there are any?" asked Caspian eagerly.

"I don't know – I don't know," said the Doctor with a deep sigh. "Sometimes I am afraid there can't be. I have been looking for traces of them all my life. Sometimes I have thought I heard a Dwarf-drum in the mountains. Sometimes at night, in the woods, I thought I had caught a glimpse of Fauns and Satyrs dancing a long way off; but when I came to the place, there was never anything there. I have often despaired; but something always happens to start me hoping again. I don't know. But at least you can try to be a King like the High King Peter of old, and not like your uncle."

"Then it's true about the Kings and Queens too, and about the White Witch?" said Caspian.

"Certainly it is true," said Cornelius. "Their reign was the Golden Age in Narnia and the land has never forgotten them."

"Did they live in this castle, Doctor?"

"Nay, my dear," said the old man. "This castle is a thing of yesterday. Your great-great-grandfather built it. But when the two sons of Adam and the two daughters of Eve were made Kings and Queens of Narnia by Aslan himself, they lived in the castle of Cair Paravel. No man alive has seen that blessed place and perhaps even the ruins of it have now vanished. But we believe it was far from here, down at the mouth of the Great River, on the very shore of the sea."

"Ugh!" said Caspian with a shudder. "Do you mean in

the Black Woods? Where all the – the – you know, the ghosts live?"

"Your Highness speaks as you have been taught," said the Doctor. "But it is all lies. There are no ghosts there. That is a story invented by the Telmarines. Your Kings are in deadly fear of the sea because they can never quite forget that in all stories Aslan comes from over the sea. They don't want to go near it and they don't want anyone else to go near it. So they have let great woods grow up to cut their people off from the coast. But because they have quarrelled with the trees they are afraid of the woods. And because they are afraid of the woods they imagine that they are full of ghosts. And the Kings and great men, hating both the sea and the wood, partly believe these stories, and partly encourage them. They feel safer if no one in Narnia dares to go down to the coast and look out to sea – towards Aslan's land and the morning and the eastern end of the world."

There was a deep silence between them for a few minutes. Then Doctor Cornelius said, "Come. We have been here long enough. It is time to go down and to bed."

"Must we?" said Caspian. "I'd like to go on talking about these things for hours and hours and hours."

"Someone might begin looking for us, if we did that," said Doctor Cornelius.

CHAPTER FIVE

CASPIAN'S ADVENTURE IN THE MOUNTAINS

After this, Caspian and his Tutor had many more secret conversations on the top of the Great Tower, and at each conversation Caspian learned more about Old Narnia, so that thinking and dreaming about the old days, and longing that they might come back, filled nearly all his spare hours. But of course he had not many hours to spare, for now his education was beginning in earnest. He learned sword-fighting and riding, swimming and diving, how to shoot with the bow and play on the recorder and the theorbo, how to hunt the stag and cut him up when he was dead, besides Cosmography, Rhetoric, Heraldry, Versification, and of course History, with a little Law, Physic, Alchemy, and Astronomy. Of Magic he learned only the theory, for Doctor Cornelius said the practical part was not proper study for princes. "And I myself," he added, "am only a very imperfect magician and can do only the smallest experiments." Of Navigation ("Which is a noble and heroical art," said the Doctor) he was taught nothing, because King Miraz disapproved of ships and the sea.

He also learned a great deal by using his own eyes and ears. As a little boy he had often wondered why he disliked his aunt, Queen Prunaprismia; he now saw that it was because she disliked him. He also began to see that Narnia was an unhappy country. The taxes were high and the laws were stern and Miraz was a cruel man.

After some years there came a time when the Queen seemed to be ill and there was a great deal of bustle and

pother about her in the castle and doctors came and the courtiers whispered. This was in early summertime. And one night, while all this fuss was going on, Caspian was unexpectedly wakened by Doctor Cornelius after he had been only a few hours in bed.

"Are we going to do a little Astronomy, Doctor?" said Caspian.

"Hush!" said the Doctor. "Trust me and do exactly as I tell you. Put on all your clothes; you have a long journey before you."

Caspian was very surprised, but he had learned to have confidence in his Tutor and he began doing what he was told at once. When he was dressed the Doctor said, "I have a wallet for you. We must go into the next room and fill it with victuals from your Highness's supper table."

"My gentlemen-in-waiting will be there," said Caspian.

"They are fast asleep and will not wake," said the Doctor. "I am a very minor magician but I *can* at least contrive a charmed sleep."

They went into the antechamber and there, sure enough, the two gentlemen-in-waiting were, sprawling on chairs and snoring hard. Doctor Cornelius quickly cut up the remains of a cold chicken and some slices of venison and put them, with bread and an apple or so and a little flask of good wine, into the wallet which he then gave to Caspian. It fitted on by a strap over Caspian's shoulder, like a satchel you would use for taking books to school.

"Have you your sword?" asked the Doctor.

"Yes," said Caspian.

"Then put this mantle over all to hide the sword and the wallet. That's right. And now we must go to the Great Tower and talk."

When they had reached the top of the Tower (it was a cloudy night, not at all like the night when they had seen the conjunction of Tarva and Alambil) Doctor Cornelius said,

"Dear Prince, you must leave this castle at once and go to seek your fortune in the wide world. Your life is in danger here."

"Why?" asked Caspian.

"Because you are the true King of Narnia: Caspian the Tenth, the true son and heir of Caspian the Ninth. Long life to your Majesty' – and suddenly, to Caspian's great surprise, the little man dropped down on one knee and kissed his hand.

"What does it all mean? I don't understand," said Caspian.

"I wonder you have never asked me before," said the Doctor, "why, being the son of King Caspian, you are not King Caspian yourself. Everyone except your Majesty knows that Miraz is a usurper. When he first began to rule he did not even pretend to be the King: he called himself Lord Protector. But then your royal mother died, the good Queen and the only Telmarine who was ever kind to me. And then, one by one, all the great lords, who had known your father, died or disappeared. Not by accident, either. Miraz weeded them out. Belisar and Uvilas were shot with arrows on a hunting party: by chance, it was pretended. All the great house of the Passarids he sent to fight giants on the northern frontier till one by one they fell. Arlian and Erimon and a dozen more he executed for treason on a false charge. The two brothers of Beaversdam he shut up as madmen. And finally he persuaded the seven noble lords, who alone among all the Telmarines did not fear the sea, to

sail away and look for new lands beyond the Eastern Ocean, and, as he intended, they never came back. And when there was no one left who could speak a word for you, then his flatterers (as he had instructed them) begged him to become King. And of course he did."

"Do you mean he now wants to kill me too?" said Caspian.

"That is almost certain," said Doctor Cornelius.

"But why now?" said Caspian. "I mean, why didn't he do it long ago if he wanted to? And what harm have I done him?"

"He has changed his mind about you because of something that happened only two hours ago. The Queen has had a son."

"I don't see what that's got to do with it," said Caspian.

"Don't see!" exclaimed the Doctor. "Have all my lessons in History and Politics taught you no more than that? Listen. As long as he had no children of his own, he was willing enough that you should be King after he died. He may not have cared much about you, but he would rather you should have the throne than a stranger. Now that he has a son of his own he will want his own son to be the next King. You are in the way. He'll clear you out of the way."

"Is he really as bad as that?" said Caspian. "Would he really murder me?"

"He murdered your Father," said Doctor Cornelius.

Caspian felt very queer and said nothing.

"I can tell you the whole story," said the Doctor. "But not now. There is no time. You must fly at once."

"You'll come with me?" said Caspian.

"I dare not," said the Doctor. "It would make your

danger greater. Two are more easily tracked than one. Dear Prince, dear King Caspian, you must be very brave. You must go alone and at once. Try to get across the southern border to the court of King Nain of Archenland. He will be good to you."

"Shall I never see you again?" said Caspian in a quavering voice.

"I hope so, dear King," said the Doctor. "What friend have I in the wide world except your Majesty? And I have a little magic. But in the meantime, speed is everything. Here are two gifts before you go. This is a little purse of gold – alas, all the treasure in this castle should be your own by rights. And here is something far better."

He put in Caspian's hands something which he could hardly see but which he knew by the feel to be a horn.

"That," said Doctor Cornelius, "is the greatest and most sacred treasure of Narnia. Many terrors I endured, many spells did I utter, to find it, when I was still young. It is the magic horn of Queen Susan herself which she left behind her when she vanished from Narnia at the end of the Golden Age. It is said that whoever blows it shall have strange help – no one can say how strange. It may have the power to call Queen Lucy and King Edmund and Queen Susan and High King Peter back from the past, and they will set all to rights. It may be that it will call up Aslan himself. Take it, King Caspian: but do not use it except at your greatest need. And now, haste, haste, haste. The little door at the very bottom of the Tower, the door into the garden, is unlocked. There we must part."

"Can I get my horse Destrier?" said Caspian.

"He is already saddled and waiting for you just at the corner of the orchard."

During the long climb down the winding staircase Cornelius whispered many more words of direction and advice. Caspian's heart was sinking, but he tried to take it all in. Then came the fresh air in the garden, a fervent handclasp with the Doctor, a run across the lawn, a welcoming whinny from Destrier, and so King Caspian the Tenth left the castle of his fathers. Looking back, he saw fireworks going up to celebrate the birth of the new prince.

All night he rode southward, choosing by-ways and bridle paths through woods as long as he was in country that he knew; but afterwards he kept to the high road. Destrier was as excited as his master at this unusual journey, and Caspian, though tears had come into his eyes at saying good-bye to Doctor Cornelius, felt brave and, in a way, happy, to think that he was King Caspian riding to seek adventures, with his sword on his left hip and Queen Susan's magic horn on his right. But when day came, with a sprinkle of rain, and he looked about him and saw on every side unknown woods, wild heaths, and blue mountains, he thought how large and strange the world was and felt frightened and small.

As soon as it was full daylight he left the road and found an open grassy place amid a wood where he could rest. He took off Destrier's bridle and let him graze, ate some cold chicken and drank a little wine, and presently fell asleep. It was late afternoon when he awoke. He ate a morsel and continued his journey, still southward, by many unfrequented lanes. He was now in a land of hills, going up and down, but always more up than down. From every ridge he could see the mountains growing bigger and blacker ahead. As the evening closed in, he was riding their lower slopes. The wind rose. Soon rain fell in torrents.

Destrier became uneasy; there was thunder in the air. And now they entered a dark and seemingly endless pine forest, and all the stories Caspian had ever heard of trees being unfriendly to Man crowded into his mind. He remembered that he was, after all, a Telmarine, one of the race who cut down trees wherever they could and were at war with all wild things; and though he himself might be

unlike other Telmarines, the trees could not be expected to know this.

Nor did they. The wind became a tempest, the woods roared and creaked all round them. There came a crash. A tree fell right across the road just behind him. "Quiet, Destrier, quiet!" said Caspian, patting his horse's neck; but he was trembling himself and knew that he had escaped death by an inch. Lightning flashed and a great crack of thunder seemed to break the sky in two just overhead.

Destrier bolted in good earnest. Caspian was a good rider, but he had not the strength to hold him back. He kept his seat, but he knew that his life hung by a thread during the wild career that followed. Tree after tree rose up before them in the dusk and was only just avoided. Then, almost too suddenly to hurt (and yet it did hurt him too) something struck Caspian on the forehead and he knew no more.

When he came to himself he was lying in a firelit place with bruised limbs and a bad headache. Low voices were speaking close at hand.

"And now," said one, "before it wakes up we must decide what to do with it."

"Kill it," said another. "We can't let it live. It would betray us."

"We ought to have killed it at once, or else let it alone," said a third voice. "We can't kill it now. Not after we've taken it in and bandaged its head and all. It would be murdering a guest."

"Gentlemen," said Caspian in a feeble voice, "whatever you do to me, I hope you will be kind to my poor horse."

"Your horse had taken flight long before we found you," said the first voice – a curiously husky, earthy voice, as Caspian now noticed.

"Now don't let it talk you round with its pretty words," said the second voice. "I still say –"

"Horns and halibuts!" exclaimed the third voice. "Of course we're not going to murder it. For shame, Nikabrik. What do you say, Trufflehunter? What shall we do with it?"

"I shall give it a drink," said the first voice, presumably

Trufflehunter's. A dark shape approached the bed. Caspian felt an arm slipped gently under his shoulders – if it was exactly an arm. The shape somehow seemed wrong. The face that bent towards him seemed wrong too. He got the impression that it was very hairy and very long nosed, and there were odd white patches on each side of it. "It's a mask of some sort," thought Caspian. "Or perhaps I'm in a fever and imagining it all." A cupful of something sweet and hot was set to his lips and he drank. At that moment one of the others poked the fire. A blaze sprang up and Caspian almost screamed with the shock as the sudden light revealed the face that was looking into his own. It was not a man's face but a badger's, though larger and friendlier and more intelligent than the face of any badger he had seen before. And it had certainly been talking. He saw, too, that he was on a bed of heather, in a cave. By the fire sat two little bearded men, so much wilder and shorter and hairier and thicker than Doctor Cornelius that he knew them at once for real Dwarfs, ancient Dwarfs with not a drop of human blood in their veins. And Caspian knew that he had found the Old Narnians at last. Then his head began to swim again.

In the next few days he learned to know them by names.

The Badger was called Trufflehunter; he was the oldest and kindest of the three. The Dwarf who had wanted to kill Caspian was a sour Black Dwarf (that is, his hair and beard were black, and thick and hard like horse-hair). His name was Nikabrik. The other Dwarf was a Red Dwarf with hair rather like a Fox's and he was called Trumpkin.

"And now," said Nikabrik on the first evening when Caspian was well enough to sit up and talk, "we still have to decide what to do with this Human. You two think you've done it a great kindess by not letting me kill it. But I suppose the upshot is that we have to keep it a prisoner for life. I'm certainly not going to let it go alive – to go back to its own kind and betray us all."

"Bulbs and bolsters! Nikabrik," said Trumpkin. "Why need you talk so unhandsomely? It isn't the creature's fault that it bashed its head against a tree outside our hole. And I don't think it looks like a traitor."

"I say," said Caspian, "you haven't yet found out whether I *want* to go back. I don't. I want to stay with you – if you'll let me. I've been looking for people like you all my life."

"That's a likely story," growled Nikabrik. "You're a Telmarine and a Human, aren't you? Of course you want to go back to your own kind."

"Well, even if I did, I couldn't," said Caspian. "I was flying for my life when I had my accident. The King wants to kill me. If you'd killed me, you'd have done the very thing to please him."

"Well now," said Trufflehunter, "you don't say so!"

"Eh?" said Trumpkin. "What's that? What have you been doing, Human, to fall foul of Miraz at your age?"

"He's my uncle," began Caspian, when Nikabrik jumped up with his hand on his dagger.

"There you are!" he cried. "Not only a Telmarine but close kin and heir to our greatest enemy. Are you still mad enough to let this creature live?" He would have stabbed Caspian then and there, if the Badger and Trumpkin had not got in the way and forced him back to his seat and held him down.

"Now, once and for all, Nikabrik," said Trumpkin. "Will you contain yourself, or must Trufflehunter and I sit on your head?"

Nikabrik sulkily promised to behave, and the other two asked Caspian to tell his whole story. When he had done so there was a moment's silence.

"This is the queerest thing I ever heard," said Trumpkin.

"I don't like it," said Nikabrik. "I didn't know there were stories about us still told among the Humans. The less they know about us the better. That old nurse, now. She'd better have held her tongue. And it's all mixed up with that Tutor: a renegade Dwarf. I hate 'em. I hate 'em worse than the Humans. You mark my words – no good will come of it."

"Don't you go talking about things you don't understand, Nikabrik," said Trufflehunter. "You Dwarfs are as forgetful and changeable as the Humans themselves. I'm a beast, I am, and a Badger what's more. We don't change. We hold on. I say great good will come of it. This is the true King of Narnia we've got here: a true King, coming back to true Narnia. And we beasts remember, even if Dwarfs forget, that Narnia was never right except when a son of Adam was King."

"Whistles and whirligigs! Trufflehunter," said

Trumpkin. "You don't mean you want to give the country to Humans?"

"I said nothing about that," answered the Badger. "It's not Men's country (who should know that better than me?) but it's a country for a man to be King of. We badgers have long enough memories to know that. Why, bless us all, wasn't the High King Peter a Man?"

"Do you believe all those old stories?" asked Trumpkin.

"I tell you, we don't change, we beasts," said Trufflehunter. "We don't forget. I believe in the High King Peter and the rest that reigned at Cair Paravel, as firmly as I believe in Aslan himself."

"As firmly as *that*, I dare say," said Trumpkin. "But who believes in Aslan nowadays?"

"I do," said Caspian. "And if I hadn't believed in him before, I would now. Back there among the Humans the people who laughed at Aslan would have laughed at stories about Talking Beasts and Dwarfs. Sometimes I did wonder if there really was such a person as Aslan: but then sometimes I wondered if there were really people like you. Yet there you are."

"That's right," said Trufflehunter. "You're right, King Caspian. And as long as you will be true to Old Narnia you shall be *my* King, whatever they say. Long life to your Majesty."

"You make me sick, Badger," growled Nikabrik. "The High King Peter and the rest may have been Men, but they were a different sort of Men. This is one of the cursed Telmarines. He has *hunted* beasts for sport. Haven't you, now?" he added, rounding suddenly on Caspian.

"Well, to tell you the truth, I have," said Caspian. "But they weren't Talking Beasts."

"It's all the same thing," said Nikabrik.

"No, no, no," said Trufflehunter. "You know it isn't. You know very well that the beasts in Narnia nowadays are different and are no more than the poor dumb, witless creatures you'd find in Calormen or Telmar. They're smaller too. They're far more different from us than the half-Dwarfs are from you."

There was a great deal more talk, but it all ended with the agreement that Caspian should stay and even the promise that, as soon as he was able to go out, he should be taken to see what Trumpkin called "the Others"; for apparently in these wild parts all sorts of creatures from the Old Days of Narnia still lived on in hiding.

CHAPTER SIX

THE PEOPLE THAT LIVED IN HIDING

Now began the happiest times that Caspian had ever known. On a fine summer morning when the dew lay on the grass he set off with the Badger and the two Dwarfs, up through the forest to a high saddle in the mountains and down on to their sunny southern slopes where one looked across the green wolds of Archenland.

"We will go first to the Three Bulgy Bears," said Trumpkin.

They came in a glade to an old hollow oak tree covered with moss, and Trufflehunter tapped with his paw three times on the trunk and there was no answer. Then he tapped again and a woolly sort of voice from inside said, "Go away. It's not time to get up yet." But when he tapped the third time there was a noise like a small earthquake from inside and a sort of door opened and out came three brown bears, very bulgy indeed and blinking their little eyes. And when everything had been explained to them (which took a long time because they were so sleepy) they said, just as Trufflehunter had said, that a son of Adam ought to be King of Narnia and all kissed Caspian – very wet, snuffly kisses they were – and offered him some honey. Caspian did not really want honey, without bread, at that time in the morning, but he thought it polite to accept. It took him a long time afterwards to get unsticky.

After that they went on till they came among tall beech trees and Trufflehunter called out, "Pattertwig! Pattertwig! Pattertwig!" and almost at once, bounding down from branch to branch till he was just above their heads, came

the most magnificent red squirrel that Caspian had ever seen. He was far bigger than the ordinary dumb squirrels which he had sometimes seen in the castle gardens; indeed he was nearly the size of a terrier and the moment you looked in his face you saw that he could talk. Indeed the difficulty was to get him to stop talking, for, like all squirrels, he was a chatterer. He welcomed Caspian at once and asked if he would like a nut and Caspian said thanks, he would. But as Pattertwig went bounding away to fetch it, Trufflehunter whispered in Caspian's ear, "Don't look. Look the other way. It's very bad manners among squirrels to watch anyone going to his store or to look as if you wanted to know where it was." Then Pattertwig came back with the nut and Caspian ate it and after that Pattertwig asked if he could take any messages to other friends. "For I can go nearly everywhere without setting foot to ground," he said. Trufflehunter and the Dwarfs thought this a very good idea and gave Pattertwig messages to all sorts of people with queer names telling them all to come to a feast and council on Dancing Lawn at midnight three nights ahead. "And you'd better tell the three Bulgies too," added Trumpkin. "We forgot to mention it to them."

Their next visit was to the Seven Brothers of Shuddering

Wood. Trumpkin led the way back to the saddle and then down eastward on the northern slope of the mountains till they came to a very solemn place among rocks and fir trees. They went very quietly and presently Caspian could feel the ground shake under his feet as if someone were hammering down below. Trumpkin went to a flat stone about the size of the top of a water-butt, and stamped on it with his foot. After a long pause it was moved away by someone or something underneath, and there was a dark, round hole with a good deal of heat and steam coming out of it and in the middle of the hole the head of a Dwarf very like Trumpkin himself. There was a long talk here and the dwarf seemed more suspicious than the Squirrel or the Bulgy Bears had been, but in the end the whole party were invited to come down. Caspian found himself descending a dark stairway into the earth, but when he came to the bottom he saw firelight. It was the light of a furnace. The whole place was a smithy. A subterranean stream ran past on one side of it. Two Dwarfs were at the bellows, another was holding a piece of red-hot metal on the anvil with a pair of tongs, a fourth was hammering it, and two, wiping their horny little hands on a greasy cloth, were coming forward to meet the visitors. It took some time to satisfy them that Caspian was a friend and not an enemy, but when they did, they all cried, "Long live the King," and their gifts were noble – mail shirts and helmets and swords for Caspian and Trumpkin and Nikabrik. The Badger could have had the same if he had liked, but he said he was a beast, he was, and if his claws and teeth could not keep his skin whole, it wasn't worth keeping. The workmanship of the arms was far finer than any Caspian had ever seen, and he gladly accepted the Dwarf-made sword instead of

his own, which looked, in comparison, as feeble as a toy and as clumsy as a stick. The seven brothers (who were all Red Dwarfs) promised to come to the feast at Dancing Lawn.

A little farther on, in a dry, rocky ravine they reached the cave of five Black Dwarfs. They looked suspiciously at Caspian, but in the end the eldest of them said, "If he is against Miraz, we'll have him for King." And the next oldest said, "Shall we go farther up for you, up to the crags? There's an Ogre or two and a Hag that we could introduce you to, up there."

"Certainly not," said Caspian.

"I should think not, indeed," said Trufflehunter. "We want none of that sort on our side." Nikabrik disagreed with this, but Trumpkin and the Badger overruled him. It gave Caspian a shock to realize that the horrible creatures out of the old stories, as well as the nice ones, had some descendants in Narnia still.

"We should not have Aslan for friend if we brought in *that* rabble," said Trufflehunter as they came away from the cave of the Black Dwarfs.

"Oh, Aslan!" said Trumpkin, cheerily but contemptuously. "What matters much more is that you wouldn't have me."

"Do *you* believe in Aslan?" said Caspian to Nikabrik.

"I'll believe in anyone or anything," said Nikabrik, "that'll batter these cursed Telmarine barbarians to pieces or drive them out of Narnia. Anyone or anything, Aslan *or* the White Witch, do you understand?"

"Silence, silence," said Trufflehunter. "You do not know what you are saying. She was a worse enemy than Miraz and all his race."

"Not to Dwarfs, she wasn't," said Nikabrik.

Their next visit was a pleasanter one. As they came lower down, the mountains opened out into a great glen or wooded gorge with a swift river running at the bottom. The open places near the river's edge were a mass of foxgloves and wild roses and the air was buzzing with bees. Here Trufflehunter called again, "Glenstorm! Glenstorm!" and after a pause Caspian heard the sound of hoofs. It grew louder till the valley trembled and at last, breaking and trampling the thickets, there came in sight the noblest creatures that Caspian had yet seen, the great Centaur Glenstorm and his three sons. His flanks were glossy chestnut and the beard that covered his broad chest was golden-red. He was a prophet and a star-gazer and knew what they had come about.

"Long live the King," he cried. "I and my sons are ready for war. When is the battle to be joined?"

Up till now neither Caspian nor the others had really been thinking of a war. They had some vague idea, perhaps, of an occasional raid on some Human farmstead or of attacking a party of hunters, if it ventured too far into these southern wilds. But, in the main, they had thought only of living to themselves in woods and caves and building up an attempt at Old Narnia in hiding. As soon as Glenstorm had spoken everyone felt much more serious.

"Do you mean a real war to drive Miraz out of Narnia?" asked Caspian.

"What else?" said the Centaur. "Why else does your Majesty go clad in mail and girt with sword?"

"Is it possible, Glenstorm?" said the Badger.

"The time is ripe," said Glenstorm. "I watch the skies,

Badger, for it is mine to watch, as it is yours to remember. Tarva and Alambil have met in the halls of high heaven, and on earth a son of Adam has once more arisen to rule and name the creatures. The hour has struck. Our council at the Dancing Lawn must be a council of war." He spoke in such a voice that neither Caspian nor the others hesitated for a moment: it now seemed to them quite possible that they might win a war and quite certain that they must wage one.

As it was now past the middle of the day, they rested with the Centaurs and ate such food as the centaurs provided – cakes of oaten meal, and apples, and herbs, and wine, and cheese.

The next place they were to visit was quite near at hand, but they had to go a long way round in order to avoid a region in which Men lived. It was well into the afternoon before they found themselves in level fields, warm between hedgerows. There Trufflehunter called at the mouth of a little hole in a green bank and out popped the last thing Caspian expected – a Talking Mouse. He was of course bigger than a common mouse, well over a foot high when

he stood on his hind legs, and with ears nearly as long as (though broader than) a rabbit's. His name was Reepicheep and he was a gay and martial mouse. He wore a tiny little rapier at his side and twirled his long whiskers as if they were a moustache. "There are twelve of us, Sire," he said with a dashing and graceful bow, "and I place all the resources of my people unreservedly at your Majesty's disposal." Caspian tried hard (and successfully) not to laugh, but he couldn't help thinking that Reepicheep and all his people could very easily be put in a washing basket and carried home on one's back.

It would take too long to mention all the creatures whom Caspian met that day – Clodsley Shovel the Mole, the three Hardbiters (who were badgers like Trufflehunter), Camillo the Hare, and Hogglestock the Hedgehog. They rested at last beside a well at the edge of a wide and level circle of grass, bordered with tall elms which now threw long shadows across it, for the sun was setting, the daisies closing, and the rooks flying home to bed. Here they supped on food they had brought with them and Trumpkin lit his pipe (Nikabrik was not a smoker).

"Now," said the Badger, "if only we could wake the spirits of these trees and this well, we should have done a good day's work."

"Can't we?" said Caspian.

"No," said Trufflehunter. "We have no power over them. Since the Humans came into the land, felling forests and defiling streams, the Dryads and Naiads have sunk into a deep sleep. Who knows if ever they will stir again? And that is a great loss to our side. The Telmarines are horribly afraid of the woods, and once the Trees moved in anger, our enemies would go mad with fright and be

chased out of Narnia as quick as their legs could carry them."

"What imaginations you Animals have!" said Trumpkin, who didn't believe in such things. "But why stop at Trees and Waters? Wouldn't it be even nicer if the stones started throwing themselves at old Miraz?"

The Badger only grunted at this, and after that there was such a silence that Caspian had nearly dropped off to sleep

when he thought he heard a faint musical sound from the depth of the woods at his back. Then he thought it was only a dream and turned over again; but as soon as his ear touched the ground he felt or heard (it was hard to tell which) a faint beating or drumming. He raised his head. The beating noise at once became fainter, but the music returned, clearer this time. It was like flutes. He saw that Trufflehunter was sitting up staring into the wood. The moon was bright; Caspian had been asleep longer than he

thought. Nearer and nearer came the music, a tune wild and yet dreamy, and the noise of many light feet, till at last, out from the wood into the moonlight, came dancing shapes such as Caspian had been thinking of all his life. They were not much taller than dwarfs, but far slighter and more graceful. Their curly heads had little horns, the upper part of their bodies gleamed naked in the pale light, but their legs and feet were those of goats.

"Fauns!" cried Caspian, jumping up, and in a moment they were all round him. It took next to no time to explain the whole situation to them and they accepted Caspian at once. Before he knew what he was doing he found himself joining in the dance. Trumpkin, with heavier and jerkier movements, did likewise and even Trufflehunter hopped and lumbered about as best he could. Only Nikabrik stayed where he was, looking on in silence. The Fauns footed it all round Caspian to their reedy pipes. Their strange faces, which seemed mournful and merry all at once, looked into his; dozens of Fauns, Mentius and Obentinus and Dumnus, Voluns, Voltinus, Girbius, Nimienus, Nausus, and Oscuns. Pattertwig had sent them all.

When Caspian awoke next morning he could hardly believe that it had not all been a dream; but the grass was covered with little cloven hoof-marks.

CHAPTER SEVEN

OLD NARNIA IN DANGER

THE place where they had met the Fauns was, of course, Dancing Lawn itself, and here Caspian and his friends remained till the night of the great Council. To sleep under the stars, to drink nothing but well water and to live chiefly on nuts and wild fruit, was a strange experience for Caspian after his bed with silken sheets in a tapestried chamber at the castle, with meals laid out on gold and silver dishes in the anteroom, and attendants ready at his call. But he had never enjoyed himself more. Never had sleep been more refreshing nor food tasted more savoury, and he began already to harden and his face wore a kinglier look.

When the great night came, and his various strange subjects came stealing into the lawn by ones and twos and threes or by sixes and sevens – the moon then shining almost at her full – his heart swelled as he saw their numbers and heard their greetings. All whom he had met were there: Bulgy Bears and Red Dwarfs and Black Dwarfs, Moles and Badgers, Hares and Hedgehogs, and others whom he had not yet seen – five Satyrs as red as foxes, the whole contingent of Talking Mice, armed to the teeth and following a shrill trumpet, some Owls, the Old Raven of Ravenscaur. Last of all (and this took Caspian's breath away), with the Centaurs came a small but genuine Giant, Wimbleweather of Deadman's Hill, carrying on his back a basketful of rather sea-sick Dwarfs who had accepted his offer of a lift and were now wishing they had walked instead.

The Bulgy Bears were very anxious to have the feast first and leave the council till afterwards: perhaps till to-morrow. Reepicheep and his Mice said that councils and feasts could both wait, and proposed storming Miraz in his own castle that very night. Pattertwig and the other Squirrels said they could talk and eat at the same time, so why not have the council and feast all at once? The Moles proposed throwing up entrenchments round the Lawn before they did anything else. The Fauns thought it would be better to begin with a solemn dance. The Old Raven, while agreeing with the Bears that it would take too long to have a full council before supper, begged to be allowed to give a brief address to the whole company. But Caspian and the Centaurs and the Dwarfs overruled all these suggestions and insisted on holding a real council of war at once.

When all the other creatures had been persuaded to sit down quietly in a great circle, and when (with more difficulty) they had got Pattertwig to stop running to and fro and saying "Silence! Silence, everyone, for the King's speech", Caspian, feeling a little nervous, got up. "Narnians!" he began, but he never got any further, for at that very moment Camillo the Hare said, "Hush! There's a Man somewhere near."

They were all creatures of the wild, accustomed to being hunted, and they all became still as statues. The beasts all turned their noses in the direction which Camillo had indicated.

"Smells like Man and yet not quite like Man," whispered Trufflehunter.

"It's getting steadily nearer," said Camillo.

"Two badgers and you three Dwarfs, with your

bows at the ready, go softly off to meet it," said Caspian.

"We'll settle 'un," said a Black Dwarf grimly, fitting a shaft to his bowstring.

"Don't shoot if it is alone," said Caspian. "Catch it."

"Why?" asked the Dwarf.

"Do as you're told," said Glenstorm the Centaur.

Everyone waited in silence while the three Dwarfs and two Badgers trotted stealthily across to the trees on the north-west side of the Lawn. Then came a sharp dwarfish cry, "Stop! Who goes there?" and a sudden spring. A moment later a voice, which Caspian knew well, could he heard saying, "All right, all right, I'm unarmed. Take my wrists if you like, worthy Badgers, but don't bite right through them. I want to speak to the King."

"Doctor Cornelius!" cried Caspian with joy, and rushed forward to greet his old tutor. Everyone else crowded round.

"Pah!" said Nikabrik. "A renegade Dwarf. A half-and-halfer! Shall I pass my sword through its throat?"

"Be quiet, Nikabrik," said Trumpkin. "The creature can't help its ancestry."

"This is my greatest friend and the saviour of my life," said Caspian. "And anyone who doesn't like his company may leave my army: at once. Dearest doctor, I *am* glad to see you again. How ever did you find us out?"

"By a little use of simple magic, your Majesty," said the Doctor, who was still puffing and blowing from having walked so fast. "But there's no time to go into that now. We must all fly from this place at once. You are already betrayed and Miraz is on the move. Before midday to-morrow you will be surrounded."

"Betrayed!" said Caspian. "And by whom?"

"Another renegade Dwarf, no doubt," said Nikabrik.

"By your horse Destrier," said Doctor Cornelius. "The poor brute knew no better. When you were knocked off, of course, he went dawdling back to his stable in the castle. Then the secret of your flight was known. I made myself scarce, having no wish to be questioned about it in Miraz's torture chamber. I had a pretty good guess from my crystal as to where I should find you. But all day – that was the day before yesterday – I saw Miraz's tracking parties out in the woods. Yesterday I learned that his army is out. I don't think some of your – um – pure-blooded Dwarfs have as much woodcraft as might be expected. You've left tracks all over the place. Great carelessness. At any rate something has warned Miraz that Old Narnia is not so dead as he had hoped, and he is on the move."

"Hurrah!" said a very shrill and small voice from somewhere at the Doctor's feet. "Let them come! All I ask is that the King will put me and my people in the front."

"What on earth?" said Doctor Cornelius. "Has your Majesty got grasshoppers – or mosquitoes – in your army?" Then after stooping down and peering carefully through his spectacles, he broke into a laugh.

"By the Lion," he swore, "it's a mouse. Signior Mouse, I desire your better acquaintance. I am honoured by meeting so valiant a beast."

"My friendship you shall have, learned Man," piped Reepicheep. "And any Dwarf – or Giant – in the army who does not give you good language shall have my sword to reckon with."

"Is there time for this foolery?" asked Nikabrik. "What are our plans? Battle or flight?"

"Battle if need be," said Trumpkin. "But we are hardly ready for it yet, and this is no very defensible place."

"I don't like the idea of running away," said Caspian.

"Hear him! Hear him!" said the Bulgy Bears. "Whatever we do, don't let's have any *running*. Especially not before supper; and not too soon after it neither."

"Those who run first do not always run last," said the Centaur. "And why should we let the enemy choose our position instead of choosing it ourselves? Let us find a strong place."

"That's wise, your Majesty, that's wise," said Trufflehunter.

"But where are we to go?" asked several voices.

"Your Majesty," said Doctor Cornelius, "and all you variety of creatures, I think we must fly east and down the river to the great woods. The Telmarines hate that region. They have always been afraid of the sea and of something that may come over the sea. That is why they have let the great woods grow up. If traditions speak true, the ancient Cair Paravel was at the river-mouth. All that part is friendly to us and hateful to our enemies. We must go to Aslan's How."

"Aslan's How?" said several voices. "We do not know what it is."

"It lies within the skirts of the Great Woods and it is a huge mound which Narnians raised in very ancient times over a very magical place, where there stood – and perhaps still stands – a very magical Stone. The Mound is all hollowed out within into galleries and caves, and the Stone is in the central cave of all. There is room in the mound for all our stores, and those of us who have most need of cover and are most accustomed to underground life can be

lodged in the caves. The rest of us can lie in the wood. At a pinch all of us (except this worthy Giant) could retreat into the Mound itself, and there we should be beyond the reach of every danger except famine."

"It is a good thing we have a learned man among us," said Trufflehunter; but Trumpkin muttered under his breath, "Soup and celery! I wish our leaders would think less about these old wives' tales and more about victuals and arms." But all approved of Cornelius's proposal and

that very night, half an hour later, they were on the march. Before sunrise they arrived at Aslan's How.

It was certainly an awesome place, a round green hill on top of another hill, long since grown over with trees, and one little, low doorway leading into it. The tunnels inside were a perfect maze till you got to know them, and they were lined and roofed with smooth stones, and on the stones, peering in the twilight, Caspian saw strange characters and snaky patterns, and pictures in which the form of a Lion was repeated again and again. It all seemed to belong

to an even older Narnia than the Narnia of which his nurse had told him.

It was after they had taken up their quarters in and around the How that fortune began to turn against them. King Miraz's scouts soon found their new lair, and he and his army arrived on the edge of the woods. And as so often happens, the enemy turned out stronger than they had reckoned. Caspian's heart sank as he saw company after company arriving. And though Miraz's men may have been afraid of going into the wood, they were even more afraid of Miraz, and with him in command they carried battle deeply into it and sometimes almost to the How itself. Caspian and other captains of course made many sorties into the open country. Thus there was fighting on most days and sometimes by night as well; but Caspian's party had on the whole the worst of it.

At last there came a night when everything had gone as badly as possible, and the rain which had been falling heavily all day had ceased at nightfall only to give place to raw cold. That morning Caspian had arranged what was his biggest battle yet, and all had hung their hopes on it. He, with most of the Dwarfs, was to have fallen on the King's right wing at daybreak, and then, when they were heavily engaged, Giant Wimbleweather, with the Centaurs and some of the fiercest beasts, was to have broken out from another place and endeavoured to cut the King's right off from the rest of the army. But it had all failed. No one had warned Caspian (because no one in these later days of Narnia remembered) that Giants are not at all clever. Poor Wimbleweather, though as brave as a lion, was a true Giant in that respect. He had broken out at the wrong time and from the wrong place, and both his party and

Caspian's had suffered badly and done the enemy little harm. The best of the Bears had been hurt, a Centaur terribly wounded, and there were few in Caspian's party who had not lost blood. It was a gloomy company that huddled under the dripping trees to eat their scanty supper.

The gloomiest of all was Giant Wimbleweather. He knew it was all his fault. He sat in silence shedding big tears which collected on the end of his nose and then fell off with a huge splash on the whole bivouac of the Mice, who had just been beginning to get warm and drowsy. They all jumped up, shaking the water out of their ears and wringing their little blankets, and asked the Giant in shrill but forcible voices whether he thought they weren't wet enough without this sort of thing. And then other people woke up and told the Mice they had been enrolled as scouts and not as a concert party, and asked why they

couldn't keep quiet. And Wimbleweather tiptoed away to find some place where he could be miserable in peace and stepped on somebody's tail and somebody (they said afterwards it was a fox) bit him. And so everyone was out of temper.

But in the secret and magical chamber at the heart of the How, King Caspian, with Cornelius and the Badger and Nikabrik and Trumpkin, were at council. Thick pillars of ancient workmanship supported the roof. In the centre was the Stone itself – a stone table, split right down the centre, and covered with what had once been writing of some kind: but ages of wind and rain and snow had almost worn them away in old times when the Stone Table had stood on the hilltop, and the Mound had not yet been built above it. They were not using the Table nor sitting round it: it was too magic a thing for any common use. They sat on logs a little way from it, and between them was a rough wooden table, on which stood a rude clay lamp lighting up their pale faces and throwing big shadows on the walls.

"If your Majesty is ever to use the Horn," said Trufflehunter, "I think the time has now come." Caspian had of course told them of his treasure several days ago.

"We are certainly in great need," answered Caspian. "But it is hard to be sure we are at our greatest. Supposing there came an even worse need and we had already used it?"

"By that argument," said Nikabrik, "your Majesty will never use it until it is too late."

"I agree with that," said Doctor Cornelius.

"And what do you think, Trumpkin?" asked Caspian.

"Oh, as for me," said the Red Dwarf, who had been listening with complete indifference, "your Majesty knows

I think the Horn – and that bit of broken stone over there – and your great King Peter – and your Lion Aslan – are all eggs in moonshine. It's all one to me when your Majesty blows the Horn. All I insist on is that the army is told nothing about it. There's no good raising hopes of magical help which (as I think) are sure to be disappointed."

"Then in the name of Aslan we will wind Queen Susan's Horn," said Caspian.

"There is one thing, Sire," said Doctor Cornelius, "that should perhaps be done first. We do not know what form the help will take. It might call Aslan himself from oversea. But I think it is more likely to call Peter the High King and his mighty consorts down from the high past. But in either case, I do not think we can be sure that the help will come to this very spot –"

"You never said a truer word," put in Trumpkin.

"I think," went on the learned man, "that they – or he – will come back to one or other of the Ancient Places of Narnia. This, where we now sit, is the most ancient and most deeply magical of all, and here, I think, the answer is likeliest to come. But there are two others. One is Lantern Waste, up-river, west of Beaversdam, where the Royal Children first appeared in Narnia, as the records tell. The other is down at the river-mouth, where their castle of Cair Paravel once stood. And if Aslan himself comes, that would be the best place for meeting him too, for every story says that he is the son of the great Emperor-over-the-Sea, and over the sea he will pass. I should like very much to send messengers to both places, to Lantern Waste and the river-mouth, to receive them – or him – or it."

"Just as I thought," muttered Trumpkin. "The first

result of all this foolery is not to bring us help but to lose us two fighters."

"Who would you think of sending, Doctor Cornelius?" asked Caspian.

"Squirrels are best for getting through enemy country without being caught," said Trufflehunter.

"All *our* squirrels (and we haven't many)," said Nikabrik, "are rather flighty. The only one I'd trust on a job like that would be Pattertwig."

"Let it be Pattertwig, then," said King Caspian. "And who for our other messenger? I know you'd go, Trufflehunter, but you haven't the speed. Nor you, Doctor Cornelius."

"I *won't* go," said Nikabrik. "With all these Humans and beasts about, there must be a Dwarf here to see that the Dwarfs are fairly treated."

"Thimbles and thunderstorms!" cried Trumpkin in a rage. "Is that how you speak to the King? Send me, Sire, I'll go."

"But I thought you didn't believe in the Horn, Trumpkin," said Caspian.

"No more I do, your Majesty. But what's that got to do with it? I might as well die on a wild goose chase as die here. You are my King. I know the difference between giving advice and taking orders. You've had my advice, and now it's the time for orders."

"I will never forget this, Trumpkin," said Caspian. "Send for Pattertwig, one of you. And when shall I blow the Horn?"

"I would wait for sunrise, your Majesty," said Doctor Cornelius. "That sometimes has an effect in operations of White Magic."

A few minutes later Pattertwig arrived and had his task explained to him. As he was, like many squirrels, full of courage and dash and energy and excitement and mischief (not to say conceit), he no sooner heard it than he was eager to be off. It was arranged that he should run for Lantern Waste while Trumpkin made the shorter journey to the river-mouth. After a hasty meal they both set off with the fervent thanks and good wishes of the King, the Badger, and Cornelius.

CHAPTER EIGHT

HOW THEY LEFT THE ISLAND

"And so," said Trumpkin (for, as you have realized, it was he who had been telling all this story to the four children, sitting on the grass in the ruined hall of Cair Paravel) – "and so I put a crust or two in my pocket, left behind all weapons but my dagger, and took to the woods in the grey of the morning. I'd been plugging away for many hours when there came a sound that I'd never heard the like of in my born days. Eh, I won't forget that. The whole air was full of it, loud as thunder but far longer, cool and sweet as music over water, but strong enough to shake the woods. And I said to myself, 'If that's not the Horn, call me a rabbit.' And a moment later I wondered why he hadn't blown it sooner –"

"What time was it?" asked Edmund.

"Between nine and ten of the clock," said Trumpkin.

"Just when we were at the railway station!" said all the children, and looked at one another with shining eyes.

"Please go on," said Lucy to the Dwarf.

"Well, as I was saying, I wondered, but I went on as hard as I could pelt. I kept on all night – and then, when it was half light this morning, as if I'd no more sense than a Giant, I risked a short cut across open country to cut off a big loop of the river, and was caught. Not by the army, but by a pompous old fool who has charge of a little castle which is Miraz's last stronghold towards the coast. I needn't tell you they got no true tale out of me, but I was a Dwarf and that was enough. But, lobsters and lollipops! it is a good thing the seneschal *was* a pompous fool. Anyone else

would have run me through there and then. But nothing would do for him short of a grand execution: sending me down 'to the ghosts' in the full ceremonial way. And then this young lady" (he nodded at Susan) "does her bit of archery – and it was pretty shooting, let me tell you – and here we are. And without my armour, for of course they took that." He knocked out and refilled his pipe.

"Great Scott!" said Peter. "So it was the horn – your own horn, Su – that dragged us all off that seat on the platform yesterday morning! I can hardly believe it; yet it all fits in."

"I don't know why you shouldn't believe it," said Lucy, "if you believe in magic at all. Aren't there lots of stories about magic forcing people out of one place – out of one world – into another? I mean, when a magician in *The Arabian Nights* calls up a Jinn, it has to come. We had to come, just like that."

"Yes," said Peter, "I suppose what makes it feel so queer is that in the stories it's always someone in our world who does the calling. One doesn't really think about where the Jinn's coming *from.*"

"And now we know what it feels like for the Jinn," said Edmund with a chuckle. "Golly! It's a bit uncomfortable to know that *we* can be whistled for like that. It's worse than what Father says about living at the mercy of the telephone."

"But we want to be here, don't we," said Lucy, "if Aslan wants us?"

"Meanwhile," said the Dwarf, "what are we to do? I suppose I'd better go back to King Caspian and tell him no help has come."

"No help?" said Susan. "But it *has* worked. And here we are."

"Um – um – yes, to be sure. I see that," said the Dwarf, whose pipe seemed to be blocked (at any rate he made himself very busy cleaning it). "But – well – I mean –"

"But don't you yet see who we are?" shouted Lucy. "You *are* stupid."

"I suppose you are the four children out of the old stories," said Trumpkin. "And I'm very glad to meet you of course. And it's very interesting, no doubt. But – no offence?' – and he hesitated again.

"Do get on and say whatever you're going to say," said Edmund.

"Well, then – no offence," said Trumpkin. "But, you know, the King and Trufflehunter and Doctor Cornelius were expecting – well, if you see what I mean, help. To put it in another way, I think they'd been imagining you as great warriors. As it is – we're awfully fond of children and all that, but just at the moment, in the middle of a war – but I'm sure you understand."

"You mean you think we're no good," said Edmund, getting red in the face.

"Now pray don't be offended," interrupted the Dwarf. "I assure you, my dear little friends – "

"*Little* from you is really a bit too much," said Edmund, jumping up. "I suppose you don't believe we won the Battle of Beruna? Well, you can say what you like about me because I know –"

"There's no good losing our tempers," said Peter. "Let's fit him out with fresh armour and fit ourselves out from the treasure chamber, and have a talk after that."

"I don't quite see the point –" began Edmund, but Lucy

whispered in his ear, "Hadn't we better do what Peter says? He is the High King, you know. And I think he has an idea." So Edmund agreed and by the aid of his torch they all, including Trumpkin, went down the steps again into the dark coldness and dusty splendour of the treasure house.

The Dwarf's eyes glistened as he saw the wealth that lay on the shelves (though he had to stand on tiptoes to do so) and he muttered to himself, "It would never do to let Nikabrik see this; never." They found easily enough a mail shirt for him, a sword, a helmet, a shield, a bow and quiverful of arrows, all of dwarfish size. The helmet was of copper, set with rubies, and there was gold on the hilt of the sword: Trumpkin had never seen, much less carried, so much wealth in all his life. The children also put on mail shirts and helmets; a sword and shield were found for Edmund and a bow for Lucy – Peter and Susan were of course already carrying their gifts. As they came back up the stairway, jingling in their mail, and already looking and feeling more like Narnians and less like schoolchildren, the two boys were behind, apparently making some plan. Lucy heard Edmund say, "No, let me do it. It will be more of a sucks for him if I win, and less of a let-down for us all if I fail."

"All right, Ed," said Peter.

When they came out into the daylight Edmund turned to the Dwarf very politely and said, "I've got something to ask you. Kids like us don't often have the chance of meeting a great warrior like you. Would you have a little fencing match with me? It would be frightfully decent."

"But, lad," said Trumpkin, "these swords are sharp."

"I know," said Edmund. "But I'll never get anywhere

near you and you'll be quite clever enough to disarm me without doing me any damage."

"It's a dangerous game," said Trumpkin. "But since you make such a point of it, I'll try a pass or two."

Both swords were out in a moment and the three others jumped off the dais and stood watching. It was well worth it. It was not like the silly fighting you see with broad swords on the stage. It was not even like the rapier fighting which you sometimes see rather better done. This was real broad-sword fighting. The great thing is to slash at your enemy's legs and feet because they are the part that have no armour. And when he slashes at yours you jump with both feet off the ground so that his blow goes under them. This gave the Dwarf an advantage because Edmund, being much taller, had to be always stooping. I don't think Edmund would have had a chance if he had fought Trumpkin twenty-four hours earlier. But the air of Narnia had been working upon him ever since they arrived on the island, and all his old battles came back to him, and his arms and fingers remembered their old skill. He was King Edmund once more. Round and round the two combatants circled, stroke after stroke they gave, and Susan (who never could learn to like this sort of thing) shouted out, "Oh, *do* be careful." And then, so quickly that no one (unless they knew, as Peter did) could quite see how it happened, Edmund flashed his sword round with a peculiar twist, the Dwarf's sword flew out of his grip, and Trumpkin was wringing his empty hand as you do after a "sting" from a cricket-bat.

"Not hurt, I hope, my dear little friend?" said Edmund, panting a little and returning his own sword to its sheath.

"I see the point," said Trumpkin drily. "You know a trick I never learned."

"That's quite true," put in Peter. "The best swordsman in the world may be disarmed by a trick that's new to him. I think it's only fair to give Trumpkin a chance at something else. Will you have a shooting match with my sister? There are no tricks in archery, you know."

"Ah, you're jokers, you are," said the Dwarf. "I begin to

see. As if I didn't know how she can shoot, after what happened this morning. All the same, I'll have a try." He spoke gruffly, but his eyes brightened, for he was a famous bowman among his own people.

All five of them came out into the courtyard.

"What's to be the target?" asked Peter.

"I think that apple hanging over the wall on the branch there would do," said Susan.

"That'll do nicely, lass," said Trumpkin. "You mean the yellow one near the middle of the arch?"

"No, not that," said Susan. "The red one up above – over the battlement."

The Dwarf's face fell. "Looks more like a cherry than an apple," he muttered, but he said nothing out loud.

They tossed up for first shot (greatly to the interest of Trumpkin, who had never seen a coin tossed before) and Susan lost. They were to shoot from the top of the steps that led from the hall into the courtyard. Everyone could see from the way the Dwarf took his position and handled his bow that he knew what he was about.

Twang went the string. It was an excellent shot. The tiny apple shook as the arrow passed, and a leaf came fluttering down. Then Susan went to the top of the steps and strung her bow. She was not enjoying her match half so much as Edmund had enjoyed his; not because she had any doubt about hitting the apple but because Susan was so tender-hearted that she almost hated to beat someone who had been beaten already. The Dwarf watched her keenly as she drew the shaft to her ear. A moment later, with a little soft thump which they could all hear in that quiet place, the apple fell to the grass with Susan's arrow in it.

"Oh, well done, Su," shouted the other children.

"It wasn't really any better than yours," said Susan to the Dwarf. "I think there was a tiny breath of wind as you shot."

"No, there wasn't," said Trumpkin. "Don't tell me. I

know when I am fairly beaten. I won't even say that the scar of my last wound catches me a bit when I get my arm well back –"

"Oh, are you wounded?" asked Lucy. "Do let me look."

"It's not a sight for little girls," began Trumpkin, but then he suddenly checked himself. "There I go talking like a fool again," he said. "I suppose you're as likely to be a great surgeon as your brother was to be a great swordsman or your sister to be a great archer." He sat down on the steps and took off his hauberk and slipped down his little shirt, showing an arm hairy and muscular (in proportion) as a sailor's though not much bigger than a child's. There was a clumsy bandage on the shoulder which Lucy proceeded to unroll. Underneath, the cut looked very nasty and there was a good deal of swelling. "Oh, poor Trumpkin," said Lucy. "How horrid." Then she carefully dripped on to it one single drop of the cordial from her flask.

"Hullo. Eh? What have you done?" said Trumpkin. But however he turned his head and squinted and whisked his beard to and fro, he couldn't quite see his own shoulder. Then he felt it as well as he could, getting his arms and fingers into very difficult positions as you do when you're trying to scratch a place that is just out of reach. Then he swung his arm and raised it and tried the muscles, and finally jumped to his feet crying, "Giants and junipers! It's cured! It's as good as new." After that he burst into a great laugh and said, "Well, I've made as big a fool of myself as ever a Dwarf did. No offence, I hope? My humble duty to your Majesties all – humble duty. And thanks for my life, my cure, my breakfast – and my lesson."

The children all said it was quite all right and not to mention it.

"And now," said Peter, "if you've really decided to believe in us –"

"I have," said the Dwarf.

"It's quite clear what we have to do. We must join King Caspian at once."

"The sooner the better," said Trumpkin. "My being such a fool has already wasted about an hour."

"It's about two days' journey, the way you came," said Peter. "For us, I mean. We can't walk all day and night like you Dwarfs." Then he turned to the others. "What Trumpkin calls Aslan's How is obviously the Stone Table itself. You remember it was about half a day's march, or a little less, from there down to the Fords of Beruna –"

"Beruna's Bridge, we call it," said Trumpkin.

"There was no bridge in our time," said Peter. "And then from Beruna down to here was another day and a bit. We used to get home about teatime on the second day, going easily. Going hard, we could do the whole thing in a day and a half perhaps."

"But remember it's all woods now," said Trumpkin, "and there are enemies to dodge."

"Look here," said Edmund, "need we go by the same way that Our Dear Little Friend came?"

"No more of that, your Majesty, if you love me," said the Dwarf.

"Very well," said Edmund. "May I say our D.L.F.?"

"Oh, Edmund," said Susan. "Don't keep *on* at him like that."

"That's all right, lass – I mean your Majesty," said

Trumpkin with a chuckle. "A jibe won't raise a blister." (And after that they often called him the D.L.F. till they'd almost forgotten what it meant.)

"As I was saying," continued Edmund, "we needn't go that way. Why shouldn't we row a little south till we come to Glasswater Creek and row up it? That brings us up behind the Hill of the Stone Table, and we'll be safe while we're at sea. If we start at once, we can be at the head of Glasswater before dark, get a few hours' sleep, and be with Caspian pretty early tomorrow."

"What a thing it is to know the coast," said Trumpkin. "None of us know anything about Glasswater."

"What about food?" asked Susan.

"Oh, we'll have to do with apples," said Lucy. "Do let's get on. We've done nothing yet, and we've been here nearly two days."

"And anyway, no one's going to have my hat for a fish-basket again," said Edmund.

They used one of the raincoats as a kind of bag and put a good many apples in it. Then they all had a good long drink at the well (for they would meet no more fresh water till they landed at the head of the Creek) and went down to the boat. The children were sorry to leave Cair Paravel, which, even in ruins, had begun to feel like home again.

"The D.L.F. had better steer," said Peter, "and Ed and I will take an oar each. Half a moment, though. We'd better take off our mail: we're going to be pretty warm before we're done. The girls had better be in the bows and shout directions to the D.L.F. because he doesn't know the way. You'd better get us a fair way out to sea till we've passed the island."

And soon the green, wooded coast of the island was falling away behind them, and its little bays and headlands were beginning to look flatter, and the boat was rising and falling in the gentle swell. The sea began to grow bigger around them and, in the distance, bluer, but close round the boat it was green and bubbly. Everything smelled salt and there was no noise except the swishing of water and the clop-clop of water against the sides and the splash of the oars and the jolting noise of the rowlocks. The sun grew hot.

It was delightful for Lucy and Susan in the bows, bending over the edge and trying to get their hands in the sea which they could never quite reach. The bottom, mostly pure, pale sand but with occasional patches of purple seaweed, could be seen beneath them.

"It's like old times," said Lucy. "Do you remember our voyage to Terebinthia – and Galma – and Seven Isles – and the Lone Islands?"

"Yes," said Susan, "and our great ship the *Splendour Hyaline*, with the swan's head at her prow and the carved swan's wings coming back almost to her waist?"

"And the silken sails, and the great stern lanterns?"

"And the feasts on the poop and the musicians."

"Do you remember when we had the musicians up in the rigging playing flutes so that it sounded like music out of the sky?"

Presently Susan took over Edmund's oar and he came forward to join Lucy. They had passed the island now and stood closer in to the shore – all wooded and deserted. They would have thought it very pretty if they had not remembered the time when it was open and breezy and full of merry friends.

"Phew! This is pretty gruelling work," said Peter.

"Can't I row for a bit?" said Lucy.

"The oars are too big for you," said Peter shortly, not because he was cross but because he had no strength to spare for talking.

CHAPTER NINE

WHAT LUCY SAW

SUSAN and the two boys were bitterly tired with rowing before they rounded the last headland and began the final pull up Glasswater itself, and Lucy's head ached from the long hours of sun and the glare on the water. Even Trumpkin longed for the voyage to be over. The seat on which he sat to steer had been made for men, not Dwarfs, and his feet did not reach the floor-boards; and everyone knows how uncomfortable that is even for ten minutes. And as they all grew more tired, their spirits fell. Up till now the children had only been thinking of how to get to Caspian. Now they wondered what they would do when they found him, and how a handful of Dwarfs and woodland creatures could defeat an army of grown-up Humans.

Twilight was coming on as they rowed slowly up the windings of Glasswater Creek – a twilight which deepened as the banks drew closer together and the over-hanging trees began almost to meet overhead. It was very quiet in here as the sound of the sea died away behind them; they could even hear the trickle of the little streams that poured down from the forest into Glasswater.

They went ashore at last, far too tired to attempt lighting a fire; and even a supper of apples (though most of them felt that they never wanted to see an apple again) seemed better than trying to catch or shoot anything. After a little silent munching they all huddled down together in the moss and dead leaves between four large beech trees.

Everyone except Lucy went to sleep at once. Lucy, being far less tired, found it hard to get comfortable. Also, she had forgotten till now that all Dwarfs snore. She knew that one of the best ways of getting to sleep is to stop trying, so she opened her eyes. Through a gap in the bracken and branches she could just see a patch of water in the Creek and the sky above it. Then, with a thrill of memory, she saw again, after all those years, the bright Narnian stars. She had once known them better than the stars of our own world, because as a Queen in Narnia she had gone to bed much later than as a child in England. And there they were – at least, three of the summer constellations could be seen from where she lay: the Ship, the Hammer, and the Leopard. "Dear old Leopard," she murmured happily to herself.

Instead of getting drowsier she was getting more awake – with an odd, night-time, dreamish kind of wakefulness. The Creek was growing brighter. She knew now that the moon was on it, though she couldn't see the moon. And now she began to feel that the whole forest was coming awake like herself. Hardly knowing why she did it, she got up quickly and walked a little distance away from their bivouac.

"This is lovely," said Lucy to herself. It was cool and fresh; delicious smells were floating everywhere.

Somewhere close by she heard the twitter of a nightingale beginning to sing, then stopping, then beginning again. It was a little lighter ahead. She went towards the light and came to a place where there were fewer trees, and whole patches or pools of moonlight, but the moonlight and the shadows so mixed that you could hardly be sure where anything was or what it was. At the same moment the nightingale, satisfied at last with his tuning up, burst into full song.

Lucy's eyes began to grow accustomed to the light, and she saw the trees that were nearest her more distinctly. A great longing for the old days when the trees could talk in Narnia came over her. She knew exactly how each of these trees would talk if only she could wake them, and what sort of human form it would put on. She looked at a silver birch: it would have a soft, showery voice and would look like a slender girl, with hair blown all about her face, and fond of dancing. She looked at the oak: he would be a wizened, but hearty old man with a frizzled beard and warts on his face and hands, and hair growing out of the warts. She looked at the beech under which she was standing. Ah! – she would be the best of all. She would be a gracious goddess, smooth and stately, the lady of the wood.

"Oh, Trees, Trees, Trees," said Lucy (though she had not been intending to speak at all). "Oh, Trees, wake, wake, wake. Don't you remember it? Don't you remember *me*? Dryads and Hamadryads, come out, come to me."

Though there was not a breath of wind they all stirred about her. The rustling noise of the leaves was almost like words. The nightingale stopped singing as if to listen to it.

Lucy felt that at any moment she would begin to understand what the trees were trying to say. But the moment did not come. The rustling died away. The nightingale resumed its song. Even in the moonlight the wood looked more ordinary again. Yet Lucy had the feeling (as you sometimes have when you are trying to remember a name or a date and almost get it, but it vanishes before you really do) that she had just missed something: as if she

had spoken to the trees a split second too soon or a split second too late, or used all the right words except one, or put in one word that was just wrong.

Quite suddenly she began to feel tired. She went back to the bivouac, snuggled down between Susan and Peter, and was asleep in a few minutes.

It was a cold and cheerless waking for them all next morning, with a grey twilight in the wood (for the sun had not yet risen) and everything damp and dirty.

"Apples, heigh-ho," said Trumpkin with a rueful grin. "I must say you ancient kings and queens don't overfeed your courtiers!"

They stood up and shook themselves and looked about. The trees were thick and they could see no more than a few yards in any direction.

"I suppose your Majesties know the way all right?" said the Dwarf.

"I don't," said Susan. "I've never seen these woods in my life before. In fact I thought all along that we ought to have gone by the river."

"Then I think you might have said so at the time," answered Peter, with pardonable sharpness.

"Oh, don't take any notice of her," said Edmund. "She always is a wet blanket. You've got that pocket compass of yours, Peter, haven't you? Well, then, we're as right as rain. We've only got to keep on going north-west – cross that little river, the what-do-you-call-it? – the Rush –"

"I know," said Peter. "The one that joins the big river at the Fords of Beruna, or Beruna's Bridge, as the D.L.F. calls it."

"That's right. Cross it and strike uphill, and we'll be at the Stone Table (Aslan's How, I mean) by eight or nine o'clock. I hope King Caspian will give us a good breakfast!"

"I hope you're right," said Susan. "I can't remember all that at all."

"That's the worst of girls," said Edmund to Peter and the Dwarf. "They never carry a map in their heads."

"That's because our heads have something inside them," said Lucy.

At first things seemed to be going pretty well. They

even thought they had struck an old path; but if you know anything about woods, you will know that one is always finding imaginary paths. They disappear after about five minutes and then you think you have found another (and hope it is not another but more of the same one) and it also disappears, and after you have been well lured out of your right direction you realize that none of them were paths at all. The boys and the Dwarf, however, were used to woods and were not taken in for more than a few seconds.

They had plodded on for about half an hour (three of them very stiff from yesterday's rowing) when Trumpkin suddenly whispered, "Stop." They all stopped. "There's something following us," he said in a low voice. "Or rather, something keeping up with us: over there on the left." They all stood still, listening and staring till their ears and eyes ached. "You and I'd better each have an arrow on the string," said Susan to Trumpkin. The Dwarf nodded, and when both bows were ready for action the party went on again.

They went a few dozen yards through fairly open woodland, keeping a sharp look-out. Then they came to a place where the undergrowth thickened and they had to pass nearer to it. Just as they were passing the place, there came a sudden something that snarled and flashed, rising out from the breaking twigs like a thunderbolt. Lucy was knocked down and winded, hearing the twang of a bowstring as she fell. When she was able to take notice of things again, she saw a great grim-looking grey bear lying dead with Trumpkin's arrow in its side.

"The D.L.F. beat you in *that* shooting match, Su," said

Peter, with a slightly forced smile. Even he had been shaken by this adventure.

"I – I left it too late," said Susan, in an embarrassed voice. "I was so afraid it might be, you know – one of our kind of bears, a *talking* bear." She hated killing things.

"That's the trouble of it," said Trumpkin, "when most of the beasts have gone enemy and gone dumb, but there are still some of the other kind left. You never know, and you daren't wait to see."

"Poor old Bruin," said Susan. "You don't think he *was*?"

"Not he," said the Dwarf. "I saw the face and I heard the snarl. He only wanted Little Girl for his breakfast. And talking of breakfast, I didn't want to discourage your Majesties when you said you hoped King Caspian would give you a good one: but meat's precious scarce in camp. And there's good eating on a bear. It would be a shame to leave the carcass without taking a bit, and it won't delay us more than half an hour. I dare say you two youngsters – Kings, I should say – know how to skin a bear?"

"Let's go and sit down a fair way off," said Susan to Lucy. "I know what a horrid messy business *that* will be." Lucy shuddered and nodded. When they had sat down she said: "Such a horrible idea has come into my head, Su."

"What's that?"

"Wouldn't it be dreadful if some day, in our own world, at home, men started going wild inside, like the animals here, and still looked like men, so that you'd never know which were which?"

"We've got enough to bother about here and now in

Narnia," said the practical Susan, "without imagining things like that."

When they rejoined the boys and the Dwarf, as much as they thought they could carry of the best meat had been cut off. Raw meat is not a nice thing to fill one's pockets with, but they folded it up in fresh leaves and made the best of it. They were all experienced enough to know that they would feel quite differently about these squashy and unpleasant parcels when they had walked long enough to be really hungry.

On they trudged again (stopping to wash three pairs of hands that needed it in the first stream they passed) until the sun rose and the birds began to sing, and more flies than they wanted were buzzing in the bracken. The stiffness from yesterday's rowing began to wear off. Everybody's spirits rose. The sun grew warmer and they took their helmets off and carried them.

"I suppose we *are* going right?" said Edmund about an hour later.

"I don't see how we can go wrong as long as we don't bear too much to the left," said Peter. "If we bear too much to the right, the worst that can happen is wasting a little time by striking the great River too soon and not cutting off the corner."

And again they trudged on with no sound except the thud of their feet and the jingle of their chain shirts.

"Where's this bally Rush got to?" said Edmund a good deal later.

"I certainly thought we'd have struck it by now," said Peter. "But there's nothing to do but keep on." They both knew that the Dwarf was looking anxiously at them, but he said nothing.

And still they trudged on and their mail shirts began to feel very hot and heavy.

"What on earth?" said Peter suddenly.

They had come, without seeing it, almost to the edge of a small precipice from which they looked down into a gorge with a river at the bottom. On the far side the cliffs rose much higher. None of the party except Edmund (and perhaps Trumpkin) was a rock climber.

"I'm sorry," said Peter. "It's my fault for coming this way. We're lost. I've never seen this place in my life before."

The Dwarf gave a low whistle between his teeth.

"Oh, do let's go back and go the other way," said Susan. "I knew all along we'd get lost in these woods."

"Susan!" said Lucy, reproachfully, "don't nag at Peter like that. It's so rotten, and he's doing all he can."

"And don't you snap at Su like that, either," said Edmund. "I think she's quite right."

"Tubs and tortoiseshells!" exclaimed Trumpkin. "If we've got lost coming, what chance have we of finding our way back? And if we're to go back to the Island and begin all over again – even supposing we could – we might as well give the whole thing up. Miraz will have finished with Caspian before we get there at that rate."

"You think we ought to go on?" said Lucy.

"I'm not sure the High King *is* lost," said Trumpkin. "What's to hinder this river being the Rush?"

"Because the Rush is not in a gorge," said Peter, keeping his temper with some difficulty.

"Your Majesty says *is*," replied the Dwarf, "but oughtn't you to say *was*? You knew this country hundreds – it may be a thousand – years ago. Mayn't it

have changed? A landslide might have pulled off half the side of that hill, leaving bare rock, and there are your precipices beyond the gorge. Then the Rush might go on deepening its course year after year till you get the little precipices this side. Or there might have been an earthquake, or anything."

"I never thought of that," said Peter.

"And anyway," continued Trumpkin, "even if this is not the Rush, it's flowing roughly north and so it must

fall into the Great River anyway. I think I passed something that might have been it, on my way down. So if we go downstream, to our right, we'll hit the Great River. Perhaps not so high as we'd hoped, but at least we'll be no worse off than if you'd come my way."

"Trumpkin, you're a brick," said Peter. "Come on, then. Down this side of the gorge."

"Look! Look! Look!" cried Lucy.

"Where? What?" said everyone.

"The Lion," said Lucy. "Aslan himself. Didn't you

see?" Her face had changed completely and her eyes shone.

"Do you really mean –?" began Peter.

"Where did you think you saw him?" asked Susan.

"Don't talk like a grown-up," said Lucy, stamping her foot. "I didn't *think* I saw him. I saw him."

"Where, Lu?" asked Peter.

"Right up there between those mountain ashes. No, this side of the gorge. And up, not down. Just the opposite of the way you want to go. And he wanted us to go where he was – up there."

"How do you know that was what he wanted?" asked Edmund.

"He – I – I just know," said Lucy, "by his face."

The others all looked at each other in puzzled silence.

"Her Majesty may well have seen a lion," put in Trumpkin. "There are lions in these woods, I've been told. But it needn't have been a friendly and talking lion any more than the bear was a friendly and talking bear."

"Oh, don't be so stupid," said Lucy. "Do you think I don't know Aslan when I see him?"

"He'd be a pretty elderly lion by now," said Trumpkin, "if he's one you knew when you were here before! And if it could be the same one, what's to prevent him having gone wild and witless like so many others?"

Lucy turned crimson and I think she would have flown at Trumpkin, if Peter had not laid his hand on her arm. "The D.L.F. doesn't understand. How could he? You must just take it, Trumpkin, that we do really know about Aslan; a little bit about him, I mean. And you mustn't talk about him like that again. It isn't lucky for one thing: and it's all nonsense for

another. The only question is whether Aslan was really there."

"But I know he was," said Lucy, her eyes filling with tears.

"Yes, Lu, but we don't, you see," said Peter.

"There's nothing for it but a vote," said Edmund.

"All right," replied Peter. "You're the eldest, D.L.F. What do you vote for? Up or down?"

"Down," said the Dwarf. "I know nothing about Aslan. But I do know that if we turn left and follow the gorge up, it might lead us all day before we found a place where we could cross it. Whereas if we turn right and go down, we're bound to reach the Great River in about a couple of hours. And if there *are* any real lions about, we want to go away from them, not towards them."

"What do you say, Susan?"

"Don't be angry, Lu," said Susan, "but I do think we should go down. I'm dead tired. Do let's get out of this wretched wood into the open as quick as we can. And none of us except you saw *anything*."

"Edmund?" said Peter.

"Well, there's just this," said Edmund, speaking quickly and turning a little red. "When we first discovered Narnia a year ago – or a thousand years ago, whichever it is – it was Lucy who discovered it first and none of us would believe her. I was the worst of the lot, I know. Yet she was right after all. Wouldn't it be fair to believe her this time? I vote for going up."

"Oh, Ed!" said Lucy and seized his hand.

"And now it's your turn, Peter," said Susan, "and I do hope –"

"Oh, shut up, shut up and let a chap think,"

interrupted Peter. "I'd much rather not have to vote."

"You're the High King," said Trumpkin sternly.

"Down," said Peter after a long pause. "I know Lucy may be right after all, but I can't help it. We must do one or the other."

So they set off to their right along the edge, downstream. And Lucy came last of the party, crying bitterly.

CHAPTER TEN

THE RETURN OF THE LION

To keep along the edge of the gorge was not so easy as it had looked. Before they had gone many yards they were confronted with young fir woods growing on the very edge, and after they had tried to go through these, stooping and pushing for about ten minutes, they realized that, in there, it would take them an hour to do half a mile. So they came back and out again and decided to go round the fir wood. This took them much farther to their right than they wanted to go, far out of sight of the cliffs and out of sound of the river, till they began to be afraid they had lost it altogether. Nobody knew the time, but it was getting to the hottest part of the day.

When they were able at last to go back to the edge of the gorge (nearly a mile below the point from which they had started) they found the cliffs on their side of it a good deal lower and more broken. Soon they found a way down into the gorge and continued the journey at the river's edge. But first they had a rest and a long drink. No one was talking any more about breakfast, or even dinner, with Caspian.

They may have been wise to stick to the Rush instead of going along the top. It kept them sure of their direction: and ever since the fir wood they had all been afraid of being forced too far out of their course and losing themselves in the wood. It was an old and pathless forest, and you could not keep anything like a straight course in it. Patches of hopeless brambles, fallen trees, boggy places and dense undergrowth would be always getting in your way. But the gorge of the Rush was not at all a nice place

for travelling either. I mean, it was not a nice place for people in a hurry. For an afternoon's ramble ending in a picnic tea it would have been delightful. It had everything you could want on an occasion of that sort – rumbling waterfalls, silver cascades, deep, amber-coloured pools, mossy rocks, and deep moss on the banks in which you could sink over your ankles, every kind of fern, jewel-like dragon flies, sometimes a hawk overhead and once (Peter and Trumpkin both thought) an eagle. But of course what

the children and the Dwarf wanted to see as soon as possible was the Great River below them, and Beruna, and the way to Aslan's How.

As they went on, the Rush began to fall more and more steeply. Their journey became more and more of a climb and less and less of a walk – in places even a dangerous climb over slippery rock with a nasty drop into dark chasms, and the river roaring angrily at the bottom.

You may be sure they watched the cliffs on their left eagerly for any sign of a break or any place where they

could climb them; but those cliffs remained cruel. It was maddening, because everyone knew that if once they were out of the gorge on that side, they would have only a smooth slope and a fairly short walk to Caspian's head-quarters.

The boys and the Dwarf were now in favour of lighting a fire and cooking their bear-meat. Susan didn't want this; she only wanted, as she said, "to get *on* and finish it and get out of these beastly woods". Lucy was far too tired and miserable to have any opinion about anything. But as there was no dry wood to be had, it mattered very little what anyone thought. The boys began to wonder if raw meat was really as nasty as they had always been told. Trumpkin assured them it was.

Of course, if the children had attempted a journey like this a few days ago in England, they would have been knocked up. I think I have explained before how Narnia was altering them. Even Lucy was by now, so to speak, only one-third of a little girl going to boarding school for the first time, and two-thirds of Queen Lucy of Narnia.

"At last!" said Susan.

"Oh, hurray!" said Peter.

The river gorge had just made a bend and the whole view spread out beneath them. They could see open country stretching before them to the horizon and, between it and them, the broad silver

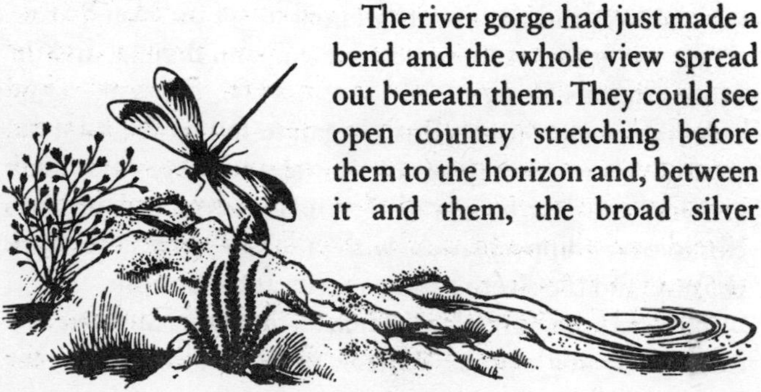

ribbon of the Great River. They could see the specially broad and shallow place which had once been the Fords of Beruna but was now spanned by a long, many-arched bridge. There was a little town at the far end of it.

"By Jove," said Edmund. "We fought the Battle of Beruna just where that town is!"

This cheered the boys more than anything. You can't help feeling stronger when you look at a place where you won a glorious victory not to mention a kingdom, hundreds of years ago. Peter and Edmund were soon so busy talking about the battle that they forgot their sore feet and the heavy drag of their mail shirts on their shoulders. The Dwarf was interested too.

They were all getting on at a quicker pace now. The going became easier. Though there were still sheer cliffs on their left, the ground was becoming lower on their right. Soon it was no longer a gorge at all, only a valley. There were no more waterfalls and presently they were in fairly thick woods again.

Then – all at once – *whizz*, and a sound rather like the stroke of a woodpecker. The children were still wondering where (ages ago) they had heard a sound just like that and why they disliked it so, when Trumpkin shouted, "Down', at the same moment forcing Lucy (who happened to be next to him) flat down into the bracken. Peter, who had been looking up to see if he could spot a squirrel, had seen what it was – a long cruel arrow had sunk into a tree trunk just above his head. As he pulled Susan down and dropped himself, another came rasping over his shoulder and struck the ground at his side.

"Quick! Quick! Get back! *Crawl*!" panted Trumpkin.

They turned and wriggled along uphill, under the

bracken amid clouds of horribly buzzing flies. Arrows whizzed round them. One struck Susan's helmet with a sharp ping and glanced off. They crawled quicker. Sweat poured off them. Then they ran, stooping nearly double. The boys held their swords in their hands for fear they would trip them up.

It was heart-breaking work – all uphill again, back over the ground they had already travelled. When they felt that they really couldn't run any more, even to save their lives,

they all dropped down in the damp moss beside a waterfall and behind a big boulder, panting. They were surprised to see how high they had already got.

They listened intently and heard no sound of pursuit.

"So *that's* all right," said Trumpkin, drawing a deep breath. "They're not searching the wood. Only sentries, I expect. But it means that Miraz has an outpost down there. Bottles and battledores! though, it was a near thing."

"I ought to have my head smacked for bringing us this way at all," said Peter.

"On the contrary, your Majesty," said the Dwarf. "For one thing it wasn't you, it was your royal brother, King Edmund, who first suggested going by Glasswater."

"I'm afraid the D.L.F.'s right," said Edmund, who had quite honestly forgotten this ever since things began going wrong.

"And for another," continued Trumpkin, "if we'd gone my way, we'd have walked straight into that new outpost, most likely; or at least had just the same trouble avoiding it. I think this Glasswater route has turned out for the best."

"A blessing in disguise," said Susan.

"Some disguise!" said Edmund.

"I suppose we'll have to go right up the gorge again now," said Lucy.

"Lu, you're a hero," said Peter. "That's the nearest you've got today to saying *I told you so*. Let's get on."

"And as soon as we're well up into the forest," said Trumpkin, "whatever anyone says, I'm going to light a fire and cook supper. But we must get well away from here."

There is no need to describe how they toiled back up the gorge. It was pretty hard work, but oddly enough everyone felt more cheerful. They were getting their second wind; and the word *supper* had had a wonderful effect.

They reached the fir wood which had caused them so much trouble while it was still daylight, and bivouacked in a hollow just above it. It was tedious gathering the firewood; but it was grand when the fire blazed up and they began producing the damp and smeary parcels of bear-meat which would have been so very unattractive to

anyone who had spent the day indoors. The Dwarf had splendid ideas about cookery. Each apple (they still had a few of these) was wrapped up in bear's meat – as if it was to be apple dumpling with meat instead of pastry, only much thicker – and spiked on a sharp stick and then roasted. And the juice of the apple worked all through the meat, like apple sauce with roast pork. Bear that has lived too much on other animals is not very nice, but bear that has had plenty of honey and fruit is excellent, and this turned out to be that sort of bear. It was a truly glorious meal. And, of course, no washing up – only lying back and watching the smoke from Trumpkin's pipe and stretching one's tired legs and chatting. Everyone felt quite hopeful now about finding King Caspian tomorrow and defeating Miraz in a few days. It may not have been sensible of them to feel like this, but they did.

They dropped off to sleep one by one, but all pretty quickly.

Lucy woke out of the deepest sleep you can imagine, with the feeling that the voice she liked best in the world had been calling her name. She thought at first it was her father's voice, but that did not seem quite right. Then she thought it was Peter's voice, but that did not seem to fit either. She did not want to get up; not because she was still tired – on the contrary she was wonderfully rested and all the aches had gone from her bones – but because she felt so extremely happy and comfortable. She was looking straight up at the Narnian moon, which is larger than ours, and at the starry sky, for the place where they had bivouacked was comparatively open.

"Lucy," came the call again, neither her father's voice nor Peter's. She sat up, trembling with excitement but not

with fear. The moon was so bright that the whole forest landscape around her was almost as clear as day, though it looked wilder. Behind her was the fir wood; away to her right the jagged cliff-tops on the far side of the gorge; straight ahead, open grass to where a glade of trees began about a bow-shot away. Lucy looked very hard at the trees of that glade.

"Why, I do believe they're moving," she said to herself. "They're walking about."

She got up, her heart beating wildly, and walked towards them. There was certainly a noise in the glade, a noise such as trees make in a high wind, though there was no wind tonight. Yet it was not exactly an ordinary tree-noise either. Lucy felt there was a tune in it, but she could not catch the tune any more than she had been able to catch the words when the trees had so nearly talked to her the night before. But there was, at least, a lilt; she felt her own feet wanting to dance as she got nearer. And now there was no doubt that the trees were really moving – moving in and out through one another as if in a complicated country dance. ("And I suppose," thought Lucy, "when trees dance, it must be a very, very country dance indeed.') She was almost among them now.

The first tree she looked at seemed at first glance to be not a tree at all but a huge man with a shaggy beard and great bushes of hair. She was not frightened: she had seen such things before. But when she looked again he was only a tree, though he was still moving. You couldn't see whether he had feet or roots, of course, because when trees move they don't walk on the surface of the earth; they wade in it as we do in water. The same thing happened with every tree she looked at. At one moment they seemed

to be the friendly, lovely giant and giantess forms which the tree-people put on when some good magic has called them into full life: next moment they all looked like trees again. But when they looked like trees, it was like strangely human trees, and when they looked like people, it was like strangely branchy and leafy people – and all the time that queer lilting, rustling, cool, merry noise.

"They are almost awake, not quite," said Lucy. She knew she herself was wide awake, wider than anyone usually is.

She went fearlessly in among them, dancing herself as she leaped this way and that to avoid being run into by these huge partners. But she was only half interested in them. She wanted to get beyond them to something else; it was from beyond them that the dear voice had called.

She soon got through them (half wondering whether she had been using her arms to push branches aside, or to take hands in a Great Chain with big dancers who stooped to reach her) for they were really a ring of trees round a central open place. She stepped out from among their shifting confusion of lovely lights and shadows.

A circle of grass, smooth as a lawn, met her eyes, with dark trees dancing all round it. And then – oh joy! For *he* was there: the huge Lion, shining white in the moonlight, with his huge black shadow underneath him.

But for the movement of his tail he might have been a stone lion, but Lucy never thought of that. She never stopped to think whether he was a friendly lion or not. She rushed to him. She felt her heart would burst if she lost a moment. And the next thing she knew was that she was kissing him and putting her arms as far round his neck as

she could and burying her face in the beautiful rich silkiness of his mane.

"Aslan, Aslan. Dear Aslan," sobbed Lucy. "At last."

The great beast rolled over on his side so that Lucy fell, half sitting and half lying between his front paws. He bent forward and just touched her nose with his tongue. His warm breath came all round her. She gazed up into the large wise face.

"Welcome, child," he said.

"Aslan," said Lucy, "you're bigger."

"That is because you are older, little one," answered he.

"Not because you are?"

"I am not. But every year you grow, you will find me bigger."

For a time she was so happy that she did not want to speak. But Aslan spoke.

"Lucy," he said, "we must not lie here for long. You have work in hand, and much time has been lost today."

"Yes, wasn't it a shame?" said Lucy. "*I* saw you all right. They wouldn't believe me. They're all so –"

From somewhere deep inside Aslan's body there came the faintest suggestion of a growl.

"I'm sorry," said Lucy, who understood some of his moods. "I didn't mean to start slanging the others. But it wasn't my fault anyway, was it?"

The Lion looked straight into her eyes.

"Oh, Aslan," said Lucy. "You don't mean it was? How could I – I couldn't have left the others and come up to you alone, how could I? Don't look at me like that . . . oh well, I suppose I *could*. Yes, and it wouldn't have been alone, I know, not if I was with you. But what would have been the good?"

Aslan said nothing.

"You mean," said Lucy rather faintly, "that it would have turned out all right – somehow? But how? Please, Aslan! Am I not to know?"

"To know what *would* have happened, child?" said Aslan. "No. Nobody is ever told that."

"Oh dear," said Lucy.

"But anyone can find out what *will* happen," said Aslan. "If you go back to the others now, and wake them up; and tell them you have seen me again; and that you must all get up at once and follow me – what will happen? There is only one way of finding out."

"Do you mean that is what you want me to do?" gasped Lucy.

"Yes, little one," said Aslan.

"Will the others see you too?" asked Lucy.

"Certainly not at first," said Aslan. "Later on, it depends."

"But they won't believe me!" said Lucy.

"It doesn't matter," said Aslan.

"Oh dear, oh dear," said Lucy. "And I was so pleased at finding you again. And I thought you'd let me stay. And I thought you'd come roaring in and frighten all the enemies away – like last time. And now everything is going to be horrid."

"It is hard for you, little one," said Aslan. "But things never happen the same way twice. It has been hard for us all in Narnia before now."

Lucy buried her head in his mane to hide from his face. But there must have been magic in his mane. She could feel lion-strength going into her. Quite suddenly she sat up.

"I'm sorry, Aslan," she said. "I'm ready now."

"Now you are a lioness," said Aslan. "And now all Narnia will be renewed. But come. We have no time to lose."

He got up and walked with stately, noiseless paces back to the belt of dancing trees through which she had just come: and Lucy went with him, laying a rather tremulous hand on his mane. The trees parted to let them through and for one second assumed their human forms completely. Lucy had a glimpse of tall and lovely wood-gods and wood-goddesses all bowing to the Lion; next moment they were trees again, but still bowing, with such graceful sweeps of branch and trunk that their bowing was itself a kind of dance.

"Now, child," said Aslan, when they had left the trees behind them, "I will wait here. Go and wake the others and tell them to follow. If they will not, then you at least must follow me alone."

It is a terrible thing to have to wake four people, all older than yourself and all very tired, for the purpose of telling them something they probably won't believe and making them do something they certainly won't like. "I mustn't think about it, I must just do it," thought Lucy.

She went to Peter first and shook him. "Peter," she whispered in his ear, "wake up. Quick. Aslan is here. He says we've got to follow him at once."

"Certainly, Lu. Whatever you like," said Peter unexpectedly. This was encouraging, but as Peter instantly rolled round and went to sleep again it wasn't much use.

Then she tried Susan. Susan did really wake up, but only to say in her most annoying grown-up voice, "You've been dreaming, Lucy. Go to sleep again."

She tackled Edmund next. It was very difficult to wake

him, but when at last she had done it he was really awake and sat up.

"Eh?" he said in a grumpy voice. "What are you talking about?"

She said it all over again. This was one of the worst parts of her job, for each time she said it, it sounded less convincing.

"Aslan!" said Edmund, jumping up. "Hurray! Where?"

Lucy turned back to where she could see the Lion waiting, his patient eyes fixed upon her. "There," she said, pointing.

"Where?" asked Edmund again.

"There. There. Don't you see? Just this side of the trees."

Edmund stared hard for a while and then said, "No. There's nothing there. You've got dazzled and muddled with the moonlight. One does, you know. I thought I saw something for a moment myself. It's only an optical what-do-you-call-it."

"I can see him all the time," said Lucy. "He's looking straight at us."

"Then why can't I see him?"

"He said you mightn't be able to."

"Why?"

"I don't know. That's what he said."

"Oh, bother it all," said Edmund. "I do wish you wouldn't keep on seeing things. But I suppose we'll have to wake the others."

CHAPTER ELEVEN

THE LION ROARS

WHEN the whole party was finally awake Lucy had to tell her story for the fourth time. The blank silence which followed it was as discouraging as anything could be.

"I can't see anything," said Peter after he had stared his eyes sore. "Can you, Susan?"

"No, of course I can't," snapped Susan. "Because there isn't anything to see. She's been dreaming. Do lie down and go to sleep, Lucy."

"And I do hope," said Lucy in a tremulous voice, "that you will all come with me. Because – because I'll have to go with him whether anyone else does or not."

"Don't talk nonsense, Lucy," said Susan. "Of course you can't go off on your own. Don't let her, Peter. She's being downright naughty."

"I'll go with her, if she *must* go," said Edmund. "She's been right before."

"I know she has," said Peter. "And she may have been right this morning. We certainly had no luck going down the gorge. Still – at this hour of the night. And why should Aslan be invisible to us? He never used to be. It's not like him. What does the D.L.F. say?"

"Oh, I say nothing at all," answered the Dwarf. "If you all go, of course, I'll go with you; and if your party splits up, I'll go with the High King. That's my duty to him and King Caspian. But, if you ask my private opinion, I'm a plain dwarf who doesn't think there's much chance of finding a road by night where you couldn't find one by day. And I have no use for magic lions which are talking

lions and don't talk, and friendly lions though they don't do us any good, and whopping big lions though nobody can see them. It's all bilge and beanstalks as far as I can see."

"He's beating his paw on the ground for us to hurry," said Lucy. "We must go *now*. At least I must."

"You've no right to try to force the rest of us like that. It's four to one and you're the youngest," said Susan.

"Oh, come on," growled Edmund. "We've got to go. There'll be no peace till we do." He fully intended to back Lucy up, but he was annoyed at losing his night's sleep and was making up for it by doing everything as sulkily as possible.

"On the march, then," said Peter, wearily fitting his arm into his shield-strap and putting his helmet on. At any other time he would have said something nice to Lucy, who was his favourite sister, for he knew how wretched she must be feeling, and he knew that, whatever had happened, it was not her fault. But he couldn't help being a little annoyed with her all the same.

Susan was the worst. "Supposing *I* started behaving like Lucy," she said. "I might threaten to stay here whether the rest of you went on or not. I jolly well think I shall."

"Obey the High King, your Majesty," said Trumpkin, "and let's be off. If I'm not to be allowed to sleep, I'd as soon march as stand here talking."

And so at last they got on the move. Lucy went first, biting her lip and trying not to say all the things she thought of saying to Susan. But she forgot them when she fixed her eyes on Aslan. He turned and walked at a slow pace about thirty yards ahead of them. The others had only Lucy's directions to guide them, for Aslan was not only

invisible to them but silent as well. His big cat-like paws made no noise on the grass.

He led them to the right of the dancing trees – whether they were still dancing nobody knew, for Lucy had her eyes on the Lion and the rest had their eyes on Lucy – and nearer the edge of the gorge. "Cobbles and kettledrums!" thought Trumpkin. "I hope this madness isn't going to end in a moonlight climb and broken necks."

For a long way Aslan went along the top of the precipices. Then they came to a place where some little trees grew right on the edge. He turned and disappeared among them. Lucy held her breath, for it looked as if he had plunged over the cliff; but she was too busy keeping him in sight to stop and think about this. She quickened her pace and was soon among the trees herself. Looking down, she could see a steep and narrow path going slantwise down into the gorge between rocks, and Aslan descending it. He turned and looked at her with his happy eyes. Lucy clapped her hands and began to scramble down after him. From behind her she heard the voices of the others shouting, "Hi! Lucy! Look out, for goodness' sake. You're right on the edge of the gorge. Come back – " and then, a moment later, Edmund's voice saying, "No, she's right. There *is* a way down."

Half-way down the path Edmund caught up with her.

"Look!" he said in great excitement. "Look! What's that shadow crawling down in front of us?"

"It's *his* shadow," said Lucy.

"I do believe you're right, Lu," said Edmund. "I can't think how I didn't see it before. But where is he?"

"With his shadow, of course. Can't you see him?"

"Well, I almost thought I did – for a moment. It's such a rum light."

"Get on, King Edmund, get on," came Trumpkin's voice from behind and above: and then, farther behind and still nearly at the top, Peter's voice saying, "Oh, buck up, Susan. Give me your hand. Why, a baby could get down here. And do stop grousing."

In a few minutes they were at the bottom and the roaring of water filled their ears. Treading delicately, like a cat, Aslan stepped from stone to stone across the stream. In the middle he stopped, bent down to drink, and as he raised his shaggy head, dripping from the water, he turned to face them again. This time Edmund saw him. "Oh, Aslan!" he cried, darting forward. But the Lion whisked round and began padding up the slope on the far side of the Rush.

"Peter, Peter," cried Edmund. "Did you see?"

"I saw something," said Peter. "But it's so tricky in this moonlight. On we go, though, and three cheers for Lucy. I don't feel half so tired now, either."

Aslan without hesitation led them to their left, farther up the gorge. The whole journey was odd and dream-like – the roaring stream, the wet grey grass, the glimmering cliffs which they were approaching, and always the glorious, silently pacing Beast ahead. Everyone except Susan and the Dwarf could see him now.

Presently they came to another steep path, up the face of the farther precipices. These were far higher than the ones they had just descended, and the journey up them was a long and tedious zig-zag. Fortunately the Moon shone right above the gorge so that neither side was in shadow.

Lucy was nearly blown when the tail and hind legs of Aslan disappeared over the top: but with one last effort she

scrambled after him and came out, rather shaky-legged and breathless, on the hill they had been trying to reach ever since they left Glasswater. The long gentle slope (heather and grass and a few very big rocks that shone white in the moonlight) stretched up to where it vanished in a glimmer of trees about half a mile away. She knew it. It was the hill of the Stone Table.

With a jingling of mail the others climbed up behind her. Aslan glided on before them and they walked after him.

"Lucy," said Susan in a very small voice.

"Yes?" said Lucy.

"I see him now. I'm sorry."

"That's all right."

"But I've been far worse than you know. I really believed it was him – he, I mean – yesterday. When he warned us not to go down to the fir wood. And I really believed it was him tonight, when you woke us up. I mean, deep down inside. Or I could have, if I'd let myself. But I just wanted to get out of the woods and – and – oh, I don't know. And what ever am I to say to him?"

"Perhaps you won't need to say much," suggested Lucy.

Soon they reached the trees and through them the children could see the Great Mound, Aslan's How, which had been raised over the Table since their days.

"Our side don't keep very good watch," muttered Trumpkin. "We ought to have been challenged before now –"

"Hush!" said the other four, for now Aslan had stopped and turned and stood facing them, looking so majestic that they felt as glad as anyone can who feels afraid, and as afraid as anyone can who feels glad. The boys strode

forward: Lucy made way for them: Susan and the Dwarf shrank back.

"Oh, Aslan," said King Peter, dropping on one knee and raising the Lion's heavy paw to his face, "I'm so glad. And I'm so sorry. I've been leading them wrong ever since we started and especially yesterday morning."

"My dear son," said Aslan.

Then he turned and welcomed Edmund. "Well done," were his words.

Then, after an awful pause, the deep voice said, "Susan." Susan made no answer but the others thought she was crying. "You have listened to fears, child," said Aslan. "Come, let me breathe on you. Forget them. Are you brave again?"

"A little, Aslan," said Susan.

"And now!" said Aslan in a much louder voice with just a hint of roar in it, while his tail lashed his flanks. "And now, where is this little Dwarf, this famous swordsman and archer, who doesn't believe in lions? Come here, son of Earth, come HERE!" – and the last word was no longer the hint of a roar but almost the real thing.

"Wraiths and wreckage!" gasped Trumpkin in the ghost of a voice. The children, who knew Aslan well enough to see that he liked the Dwarf very much, were not disturbed; but it was quite another thing for Trumpkin, who had never seen a lion before, let alone this Lion. He did the only sensible thing he could have done; that is, instead of bolting, he tottered towards Aslan.

Aslan pounced. Have you ever seen a very young kitten being carried in the mother cat's mouth? It was like that. The Dwarf, hunched up in a little, miserable ball, hung from Aslan's mouth. The Lion gave him one shake and all

his armour rattled like a tinker's pack and then – hey-presto – the Dwarf flew up in the air. He was as safe as if he had been in bed, though he did not feel so. As he came down the huge velvety paws caught him as gently as a

mother's arms and set him (right way up, too) on the ground.

"Son of Earth, shall we be friends?" asked Aslan.

"Ye – he – he – hes," panted the Dwarf, for it had not yet got its breath back.

"Now," said Aslan. "The Moon is setting. Look behind you: there is the dawn beginning. We have no time to lose. You three, you sons of Adam and son of Earth, hasten into the Mound and deal with what you will find there."

The Dwarf was still speechless and neither of the boys dared to ask if Aslan would follow them. All three drew their swords and saluted, then turned and jingled away into the dusk. Lucy noticed that there was no sign of weariness in their faces: both the High King and King Edmund looked more like men than boys.

The girls watched them out of sight, standing close beside Aslan. The light was changing. Low down in the east, Aravir, the morning star of Narnia, gleamed like a little moon. Aslan, who seemed larger than before, lifted his head, shook his mane, and roared.

The sound, deep and throbbing at first like an organ beginning on a low note, rose and became louder, and then far louder again, till the earth and air were shaking with it. It rose up from that hill and floated across all Narnia. Down in Miraz's camp men woke, stared palely in one another's faces, and grasped their weapons. Down below that in the Great River, now at its coldest hour, the heads and shoulders of the nymphs, and the great weedy-bearded head of the river-god, rose from the water. Beyond it, in every field and wood, the alert ears of rabbits rose from their holes, the sleepy heads of birds came out from under wings, owls hooted, vixens barked, hedgehogs grunted, the trees stirred. In towns and villages mothers pressed babies close to their breasts, staring with wild eyes, dogs whimpered, and men leaped up groping for lights. Far away on the northern frontier the mountain giants peered from the dark gateways of their castles.

What Lucy and Susan saw was a dark something coming to them from almost every direction across the hills. It looked first like a black mist creeping on the ground, then

like the stormy waves of a black sea rising higher and higher as it came on, and then, at last, like what it was – woods on the move. All the trees of the world appeared to be rushing towards Aslan. But as they drew nearer they looked less like trees, and when the whole crowd, bowing and curtsying and waving thin long arms to Aslan, were all around Lucy, she saw that it was a crowd of human shapes. Pale birch-girls were tossing their heads, willow-women pushed back their hair from their brooding faces to gaze on Aslan, the queenly beeches stood still and adored

him, shaggy oak-men, lean and melancholy elms, shock-headed hollies (dark themselves, but their wives all bright with berries) and gay rowans, all bowed and rose again, shouting, "Aslan, Aslan!" in their various husky or creaking or wave-like voices.

The crowd and the dance round Aslan (for it had become a dance once more) grew so thick and rapid that Lucy was confused. She never saw where certain other people came from who were soon capering about among the trees. One was a youth, dressed only in a fawn-skin, with vine-leaves wreathed in his curly hair. His face would have been almost too pretty for a boy's, if it had not looked

so extremely wild. You felt, as Edmund said when he saw him a few days later, "There's a chap who might do anything – absolutely anything." He seemed to have a great many names – Bromios, Bassareus, and the Ram were three of them. There were a lot of girls with him, as wild as he. There was even, unexpectedly, someone on a donkey. And everybody was laughing: and everybody was shouting out, "Euan, euan, eu-oi-oi-oi."

"Is it a Romp, Aslan?" cried the youth. And apparently it was. But nearly everyone seemed to have a different idea as to what they were playing. It may have been Tig, but Lucy never discovered who was It. It was rather like Blind Man's Buff, only everyone behaved as if they were blindfolded. It was not unlike Hunt the Slipper, but the slipper was never found. What made it more complicated was that the man on the donkey, who was old and enormously fat, began calling out at once, "Refreshments! Time for refreshments," and falling off his donkey and being bundled on to it again by the others, while the donkey was under the impression that the whole thing was a circus and tried to give a display of walking on its hind legs. And all the time there were more and more vine leaves everywhere. And soon not only leaves but vines. They were climbing up everything. They were running up the legs of the tree people and circling round their necks. Lucy put up her hands to push back her hair and found she was pushing back vine branches. The donkey was a mass of them. His tail was completely entangled and something dark was nodding between his ears. Lucy looked again and saw it was a bunch of grapes. After that it was mostly grapes – overhead and underfoot and all around.

"Refreshments! Refreshments," roared the old man.

Everyone began eating, and whatever hothouses your people may have, you have never tasted such grapes. Really good grapes, firm and tight on the outside, but bursting into cool sweetness when you put them into your mouth, were one of the things the girls had never had quite enough of before. Here, there were more than anyone could possibly want, and no table-manners at all. One saw sticky and stained fingers everywhere, and, though mouths were full, the laughter never ceased nor the yodelling cries of *Euan, euan, eu-oi-oi-oi-oi*, till all of a sudden everyone felt at the same moment that the game (whatever it was), and the feast, ought to be over, and everyone flopped down breathless on the ground and turned their faces to Aslan to hear what he would say next.

At that moment the sun was just rising and Lucy remembered something and whispered to Susan,

"I say, Su, I know who they are."

"Who?"

"The boy with the wild face is Bacchus and the old one on the donkey is Silenus. Don't you remember Mr Tumnus telling us about them long ago?"

"Yes, of course. But I say, Lu –"

"What?"

"I wouldn't have felt safe with Bacchus and all his wild girls if we'd met them without Aslan."

"I should think not," said Lucy.

CHAPTER TWELVE

SORCERY AND SUDDEN VENGEANCE

MEANWHILE Trumpkin and the two boys arrived at the dark little stone archway which led into the inside of the Mound, and two sentinel badgers (the white patches on their cheeks were all Edmund could see of them) leaped up with bared teeth and asked them in snarling voices, "Who goes there?"

"Trumpkin," said the Dwarf. "Bringing the High King of Narnia out of the far past."

The badgers nosed at the boys' hands. "At last," they said. "At last."

"Give us a light, friends," said Trumpkin.

The badgers found a torch just inside the arch and Peter lit it and handed it to Trumpkin. "The D.L.F. had better lead," he said. "We don't know our way about this place."

Trumpkin took the torch and went ahead into the dark tunnel. It was a cold, black, musty place, with an occasional bat fluttering in the torchlight, and plenty of cobwebs. The boys, who had been mostly in the open air since that morning at the railway station, felt as if they were going into a trap or a prison.

"I say, Peter," whispered Edmund. "Look at those carvings on the walls. Don't they look old? And yet we're older than that. When we were last here, they hadn't been made."

"Yes," said Peter. "That makes one think."

The Dwarf went on ahead and then turned to the right, and then to the left, and then down some steps, and then to the left again. Then at last they saw a light ahead – light

from under a door. And now for the first time they heard voices, for they had come to the door of the central chamber. The voices inside were angry ones. Someone was talking so loudly that the approach of the boys and the Dwarf had not been heard.

"Don't like the sound of that," whispered Trumpkin to Peter. "Let's listen for a moment." All three stood perfectly still on the outside of the door.

"You know well enough," said a voice ("That's the

King," whispered Trumpkin), "why the Horn was not blown at sunrise this morning. Have you forgotten that Miraz fell upon us almost before Trumpkin had gone, and we were fighting for our lives for the space of three hours and more? I blew it when first I had a breathing space."

"I'm not likely to forgot it," came the angry voice, "when my Dwarfs bore the brunt of the attack and one in five of them fell." ("That's Nikabrik," whispered Trumpkin.)

"For shame, Dwarf," came a thick voice ("Trufflehunter's," said Trumpkin). "We all did as much as the Dwarfs and none more than the King."

"Tell that tale your own way for all I care," answered

Nikabrik. "But whether it was that the Horn was blown too late, or whether there was no magic in it, no help has come. You, you great clerk, you master magician, you know-all; are you still asking us to hang our hopes on Aslan and King Peter and all the rest of it?"

"I must confess – I cannot deny it – that I am deeply disappointed in the result of the operation," came the answer. ("That'll be Doctor Cornelius," said Trumpkin.)

"To speak plainly," said Nikabrik, "your wallet's empty, your eggs addled, your fish uncaught, your promises broken. Stand aside then and let others work. And that is why –"

"The help will come," said Trufflehunter. "I stand by Aslan. Have patience, like us beasts. The help will come. It may be even now at the door."

"Pah!" snarled Nikabrik. "You badgers would have us wait till the sky falls and we can all catch larks. I tell you we *can't* wait. Food is running short; we lose more than we can afford at every encounter; our followers are slipping away."

"And why?" asked Trufflehunter. "I'll tell you why. Because it is noised among them that we have called on the Kings of old and the Kings of old have not answered. The last words Trumpkin spoke before he went (and went, most likely, to his death) were, 'If you must blow the Horn, do not let the army know why you blow it or what you hope from it.' But that same evening everyone seemed to know."

"You'd better have shoved your grey snout in a hornets' nest, Badger, than suggest that I am the blab," said Nikabrik. "Take it back, or –"

"Oh, stop it, both of you," said King Caspian. "I want

to know what it is that Nikabrik keeps on hinting we should do. But before that, I want to know who those two strangers are whom he has brought into our council and who stand there with their ears open and their mouths shut."

"They are friends of mine," said Nikabrik. "And what better right have you yourself to be here than that you are a friend of Trumpkin's and the Badger's? And what right has that old dotard in the black gown to be here except that he is your friend? Why am I to be the only one who can't bring in his friends?"

"His Majesty is the King to whom you have sworn allegiance," said Trufflehunter sternly.

"Court manners, court manners," sneered Nikabrik. "But in this hole we may talk plainly. You know – and he knows – that this Telmarine boy will be king of nowhere and nobody in a week unless we can help him out of the trap in which he sits."

"Perhaps," said Cornelius, "your new friends would like to speak for themselves? You there, who and what are you?"

"Worshipful Master Doctor," came a thin, whining voice. "So please you, I'm only a poor old woman, I am, and very obliged to his Worshipful Dwarfship for his friendship, I'm sure. His Majesty, bless his handsome face, has no need to be afraid of an old woman that's nearly doubled up with the rheumatics and hasn't two sticks to put under her kettle. I have some poor little skill – not like yours, Master Doctor, of course – in small spells and cantrips that I'd be glad to use against our enemies if it was agreeable to all concerned. For I hate 'em. Oh yes. No one hates better than me."

"That is all most interesting and – er – satisfactory," said Doctor Cornelius. "I think I now know what you are, Madam. Perhaps your other friend, Nikabrik, would give some account of himself?"

A dull, grey voice at which Peter's flesh crept replied, "I'm hunger. I'm thirst. Where I bite, I hold till I die, and even after death they must cut out my mouthful from my enemy's body and bury it with me. I can fast a hundred years and not die. I can lie a hundred nights on the ice and not freeze. I can drink a river of blood and not burst. Show me your enemies."

"And it is in the presence of these two that you wish to disclose your plan?" said Caspian.

"Yes," said Nikabrik. "And by their help that I mean to execute it."

There was a minute or two during which Trumpkin and the boys could hear Caspian and his two friends speaking in low voices but could not make out what they were saying. Then Caspian spoke aloud.

"Well, Nikabrik," he said, "we will hear your plan."

There was a pause so long that the boys began to wonder if Nikabrik was ever going to begin; when he did, it was in a lower voice, as if he himself did not much like what he was saying.

"All said and done," he muttered, "none of us knows the truth about the ancient days in Narnia. Trumpkin believed none of the stories. I was ready to put them to the trial. We tried first the Horn and it has failed. If there ever was a High King Peter and a Queen Susan and a King Edmund and a Queen Lucy, then either they have not heard us, or they cannot come, or they are our enemies –"

"Or they are on the way," put in Trufflehunter.

"You can go on saying that till Miraz has fed us all to his dogs. As I was saying, we have tried one link in the chain of old legends, and it has done us no good. Well. But when your sword breaks, you draw your dagger. The stories tell of other powers beside the ancient Kings and Queens. How if we could call *them* up?"

"If you mean Aslan," said Trufflehunter, "it's all one calling on him and on the Kings. They were his servants. If he will not send them (but I make no doubt he will), is he more likely to come himself?"

"No. You're right there," said Nikabrik. "Aslan and the Kings go together. Either Aslan is dead, or he is not on our side. Or else something stronger than himself keeps him back. And if he did come – how do we know he'd be our friend? He was not always a good friend to Dwarfs by all that's told. Not even to all beasts. Ask the Wolves. And anyway, he was in Narnia only once that I ever heard of, and he didn't stay long. You may drop Aslan out of the reckoning. I was thinking of someone else."

There was no answer, and for a few minutes it was so still that Edmund could hear the wheezy and snuffling breath of the Badger.

"Who do you mean?" said Caspian at last.

"I mean a power so much greater than Aslan's that it held Narnia spellbound for years and years, if the stories are true."

"The White Witch!" cried three voices all at once, and from the noise Peter guessed that three people had leaped to their feet.

"Yes," said Nikabrik very slowly and distinctly, "I mean the Witch. Sit down again. Don't all take fright at a name as if you were children. We want power: and we want a

power that will be on our side. As for power, do not the stories say that the Witch defeated Aslan, and bound him, and killed him on that very stone which is over there, just beyond the light?"

"But they also say that he came to life again," said the Badger sharply.

"Yes, they *say*," answered Nikabrik, "but you'll notice that we hear precious little about anything he did afterwards. He just fades out of the story. How do you explain that, if he really came to life? Isn't it much more likely that he didn't, and that the stories say nothing more about him because there was nothing more to say?"

"He established the Kings and Queens," said Caspian.

"A King who has just won a great battle can usually establish himself without the help of a performing lion," said Nikabrik. There was a fierce growl, probably from Trufflehunter.

"And anyway," Nikabrik continued, "what came of the Kings and their reign? They faded too. But it's very different with the Witch. They say she ruled for a hundred years: a hundred years of winter. There's power, if you like. There's something practical."

"But, heaven and earth!" said the King, "haven't we always been told that she was the worst enemy of all? Wasn't she a tyrant ten times worse than Miraz?"

"Perhaps," said Nikabrik in a cold voice. "Perhaps she *was* for you humans, if there were any of you in those days. Perhaps she was for some of the beasts. She stamped out the Beavers, I dare say; at least there are none of them in Narnia now. But she got on all right with us Dwarfs. I'm a Dwarf and I stand by my own people. *We're* not afraid of the Witch."

"But you've joined with us," said Trufflehunter.

"Yes, and a lot of good it has done my people, so far," snapped Nikabrik. "Who is sent on all the dangerous raids? The Dwarfs. Who goes short when the rations fail? The Dwarfs. Who –?"

"Lies! All lies!" said the Badger.

"And so," said Nikabrik, whose voice now rose to a scream, "if you can't help my people, I'll go to someone who can."

"Is this open treason, Dwarf?" asked the King.

"Put that sword back in its sheath, Caspian," said Nikabrik. "Murder at council, eh? Is that your game? Don't be fool enough to try it. Do you think I'm afraid of you? There's three on my side, and three on yours."

"Come on, then," snarled Trufflehunter, but he was immediately interrupted.

"Stop, stop, stop," said Doctor Cornelius. "You go on too fast. The Witch is dead. All the stories agree on that. What does Nikabrik mean by calling on the Witch?"

That grey and terrible voice which had spoken only once before said, "Oh, *is* she?"

And then the shrill, whining voice began, "Oh, bless his heart, his dear little Majesty needn't mind about the White Lady – that's what *we* call her – being dead. The Worshipful Master Doctor is only making game of a poor old woman like me when he says that. Sweet Master Doctor, learned Master Doctor, who ever heard of a witch that really died? You can always get them back."

"Call her up," said the grey voice. "We are all ready. Draw the circle. Prepare the blue fire."

Above the steadily increasing growl of the Badger and

Cornelius's sharp "What?" rose the voice of King Caspian like thunder.

"So that is your plan, Nikabrik! Black sorcery and the calling up of an accursed ghost. And I see who your companions are – a Hag and a Wer-Wolf!"

The next minute or so was very confused. There was an animal roaring, a clash of steel; the boys and Trumpkin rushed in; Peter had a glimpse of a horrible, grey, gaunt creature, half man and half wolf, in the very act of leaping

upon a boy about his own age, and Edmund saw a badger and a Dwarf rolling on the floor in a sort of cat fight. Trumpkin found himself face to face with the Hag. Her nose and chin stuck out like a pair of nut-crackers, her dirty grey hair was flying about her face and she had just got Doctor Cornelius by the throat. At one slash of Trumpkin's sword her head rolled on the floor. Then the light was knocked over and it was all swords, teeth, claws, fists, and boots for about sixty seconds. Then silence.

"Are you all right, Ed?"

"I – I think so," panted Edmund. "I've got that brute Nikabrik, but he's still alive."

"Weights and water-bottles!" came an angry voice. "It's *me* you're sitting on. Get off. You're like a young elephant."

"Sorry, D.L.F.," said Edmund. "Is that better?"

"Ow! No!" bellowed Trumpkin. "You're putting your boot in my mouth. Go away."

"Is King Caspian anywhere?" asked Peter.

"I'm here," said a rather faint voice. "Something bit me."

They all heard the noise of someone striking a match. It was Edmund. The little flame showed his face, looking pale and dirty. He blundered about for a little, found the candle (they were no longer using the lamp, for they had run out of oil), set it on the table, and lit it. When the flame rose clear, several people scrambled to their feet. Six faces blinked at one another in the candlelight.

"We don't seem to have any enemies left," said Peter. "There's the Hag, dead." (He turned his eyes quickly away from her.) "And Nikabrik, dead too. And I suppose this thing is a Wer-Wolf. It's so long since I've seen one. Wolf's head and man's body. That means he was just turning from man into wolf at the moment he was killed. And you, I suppose, are King Caspian?"

"Yes," said the other boy. "But I've no idea who you are."

"It's the High King, King Peter," said Trumpkin.

"Your Majesty is very welcome," said Caspian.

"And so is *your* Majesty," said Peter. "I haven't come to take your place, you know, but to put you into it."

"Your Majesty," said another voice at Peter's elbow. He turned and found himself face to face with the Badger.

Peter leaned forward, put his arms round the beast and kissed the furry head: it wasn't a girlish thing for him to do, because he was the High King.

"Best of badgers," he said. "You never doubted us all through."

"No credit to me, your Majesty," said Trufflehunter. "I'm a beast and we don't change. I'm a badger, what's more, and we hold on."

"I am sorry for Nikabrik," said Caspian, "though he hated me from the first moment he saw me. He had gone sour inside from long suffering and hating. If we had won quickly he might have become a good Dwarf in the days of peace. I don't know which of us killed him. I'm glad of that."

"You're bleeding," said Peter.

"Yes, I'm bitten," said Caspian. "It was that – that wolf thing." Cleaning and bandaging the wound took a long time, and when it was done Trumpkin said, "Now. Before everything else we want some breakfast."

"But not here," said Peter.

"No," said Caspian with a shudder. "And we must send someone to take away the bodies."

"Let the vermin be flung into a pit," said Peter. "But the Dwarf we will give to his people to be buried in their own fashion."

They breakfasted at last in another of the dark cellars of Aslan's How. It was not such a breakfast as they would have chosen, for Caspian and Cornelius were thinking of venison pasties, and Peter and Edmund of buttered eggs and hot coffee, but what everyone got was a little bit of cold bear-meat (out of the boys' pockets), a lump of hard cheese, an onion, and a mug of water. But, from the way they fell to, anyone would have supposed it was delicious.

CHAPTER THIRTEEN

THE HIGH KING IN COMMAND

"Now," said Peter, as they finished their meal, "Aslan and the girls (that's Queen Susan and Queen Lucy, Caspian) are somewhere close. We don't know when he will act. In his time, no doubt, not ours. In the meantime he would like us to do what we can on our own. You say, Caspian, we are not strong enough to meet Miraz in pitched battle."

"I'm afraid not, High King," said Caspian. He was liking Peter very much, but was rather tongue-tied. It was much stranger for him to meet the great Kings out of the old stories than it was for them to meet him.

"Very well, then," said Peter, "I'll send him a challenge to single combat." No one had thought of this before.

"Please," said Caspian, "could it not be me? I want to avenge my father."

"You're wounded," said Peter. "And anyway, wouldn't he just laugh at a challenge from you? I mean, we have seen that you are a king and a warrior but he thinks of you as a kid."

"But, Sire," said the Badger, who sat very close to Peter and never took his eyes off him. "Will he accept a challenge even from you? He knows he has the stronger army."

"Very likely he won't," said Peter, "but there's always the chance. And even if he doesn't, we shall spend the best part of the day sending heralds to and fro and all that. By then Aslan may have done something. And at least I can inspect the army and strengthen the position. I will send

the challenge. In fact I will write it at once. Have you pen and ink, Master Doctor?"

"A scholar is never without them, your Majesty," answered Doctor Cornelius.

"Very well, I will dictate," said Peter. And while the Doctor spread out a parchment and opened his ink-horn and sharpened his pen, Peter leant back with half-closed eyes and recalled to his mind the language in which he had written such things long ago in Narnia's golden age.

"Right," he said at last. "And now, if you are ready, Doctor?"

Doctor Cornelius dipped his pen and waited. Peter dictated as follows:

"*Peter, by the gift of Aslan, by election, by prescription, and by conquest, High King over all Kings in Narnia, Emperor of the Lone Islands and Lord of Cair Paravel, Knight of the Most Noble Order of the Lion, to Miraz, Son of Caspian the Eighth, sometime Lord Protector of Narnia and now styling himself King of Narnia, Greeting.* Have you got that?"

"*Narnia, comma, greeting,*" muttered the Doctor. "Yes, Sire."

"Then begin a new paragraph," said Peter. "*For to prevent the effusion of blood, and for the avoiding all other inconveniences likely to grow from the wars now levied in our realm of Narnia, it is our pleasure to adventure our royal person on behalf of our trusty and well-beloved Caspian in clean wager of battle to prove upon your Lordship's body that the said Caspian is lawful King under us in Narnia both by our gift and by the laws of the Telmarines, and your Lordship twice guilty of treachery both in withholding the dominion of Narnia from the said*

Caspian and in the most abhominable, – don't forget to spell it with an H, Doctor – *bloody, and unnatural murder of your kindly lord and brother King Caspian Ninth of that name. Wherefore we most heartily provoke, challenge, and defy your Lordship to the said combat and monomachy, and have sent these letters by the hand of our well beloved and royal brother Edmund, sometime King under us in Narnia, Duke of Lantern Waste and Count of the Western March, Knight of the Noble Order of the Table, to whom we have given full power of determining with your Lordship all the conditions of the said battle. Given at our lodging in Aslan's How this XII day of the month Greenroof in the first year of Caspian Tenth of Narnia.*

"That ought to do," said Peter, drawing a deep breath. "And now we must send two others with King Edmund. I think the Giant ought to be one."

"He's – he's not very clever, you know," said Caspian.

"Of course not," said Peter. "But any giant looks impressive if only he will keep quiet. And it will cheer him up. But who for the other?"

"Upon my word," said Trumpkin, "if you want someone who can kill with looks, Reepicheep would be the best."

"He would indeed, from all I hear," said Peter with a laugh. "If only he wasn't so small. They wouldn't even see him till he was close!"

"Send Glenstorm, Sire," said Trufflehunter. "No one ever laughed at a Centaur."

An hour later two great lords in the army of Miraz, the Lord Glozelle and the Lord Sopespian, strolling along

their lines and picking their teeth after breakfast, looked up and saw coming down to them from the wood the Centaur and Giant Wimbleweather, whom they had seen before in battle, and between them a figure they could not recognize. Nor indeed would the other boys at Edmund's school have recognized him if they could have seen him at that moment. For Aslan had breathed on him at their meeting and a kind of greatness hung about him.

"What's to do?" said the Lord Glozelle. "An attack?"

"A parley, rather," said Sopespian. "See, they carry green branches. They are coming to surrender most likely."

"He that is walking between the Centaur and the Giant has no look of surrender in his face," said Glozelle. "Who can he be? It is not the boy Caspian."

"No indeed," said Sopespian. "This is a fell warrior, I warrant you, wherever the rebels have got him from. He is (in your Lordship's private ear) a kinglier man than ever Miraz was. And what mail he wears! None of our smiths can make the like."

"I'll wager my dappled Pomely he brings a challenge, not a surrender," said Glozelle.

"How then?" said Sopespian. "We hold the enemy in our fist here. Miraz would never be so hair-brained as to throw away his advantage on a combat."

"He might be brought to it," said Glozelle in a much lower voice.

"Softly," said Sopespian. "Step a little aside here out of earshot of those sentries. Now. Have I taken your Lordship's meaning aright?"

"If the King undertook wager of battle," whispered Glozelle, "why, either he would kill or be killed."

"So," said Sopespian, nodding his head.

"And if he killed we should have won this war."

"Certainly. And if not?"

"Why, if not, we should be as able to win it without the King's grace as with him. For I need not tell your Lordship that Miraz is no very great captain. And after that, we should be both victorious and kingless."

"And it is your meaning, my Lord, that you and I could hold this land quite as conveniently without a King as with one?"

Glozelle's face grew ugly. "Not forgetting," said he, "that it was we who first put him on the throne. And in all the years that he has enjoyed it, what fruits have come our way? What gratitude has he shown us?"

"Say no more," answered Sopespian. "But look – here comes one to fetch us to the King's tent."

When they reached Miraz's tent they saw Edmund and his two companions seated outside it and being entertained with cakes and wine, having already delivered the challenge, and withdrawn while the King was considering

it. When they saw them thus at close quarters the two Telmarine lords thought all three of them very alarming.

Inside, they found Miraz, unarmed and finishing his breakfast. His face was flushed and there was a scowl on his brow.

"There!" he growled, flinging the parchment across the table to them. "See what a pack of nursery tales our jackanapes of a nephew has sent us."

"By your leave, Sire," said Glozelle. "If the young warrior whom we have just seen outside is the King Edmund mentioned in the writing, then I would not call him a nursery tale but a very dangerous knight."

"King Edmund, pah!" said Miraz. "Does your Lordship believe those old wives' fables about Peter and Edmund and the rest?"

"I believe my eyes, your Majesty," said Glozelle.

"Well, this is to no purpose," said Miraz, "but as touching the challenge, I suppose there is only one opinion between us?"

"I suppose so, indeed, Sire," said Glozelle.

"And what is that?" asked the King.

"Most infallibly to refuse it," said Glozelle. "For though I have never been called a coward, I must plainly say that to meet that young man in battle is more than my heart would serve me for. And if (as is likely) his brother, the High King, is more dangerous than he – why, on your life, my Lord King, have nothing to do with him."

"Plague on you!" cried Miraz. "It was not that sort of council I wanted. Do you think I am asking you if I should be afraid to meet this Peter (if there is such a man)? Do you think I fear him? I wanted your counsel on the policy of the matter; whether we,

having the advantage, should hazard it on a wager of battle."

"To which I can only answer, your Majesty," said Glozelle, "that for all reasons the challenge should be refused. There is death in the strange knight's face."

"There you are again!" said Miraz, now thoroughly angry. "Are you trying to make it appear that I am as great a coward as your Lordship?"

"Your Majesty may say your pleasure," said Glozelle sulkily.

"You talk like an old woman, Glozelle," said the King. "What say you, my Lord Sopespian?"

"Do not touch it, Sire," was the reply. "And what your Majesty says of the policy of the thing comes in very happily. It gives your Majesty excellent grounds for a refusal without any cause for questioning your Majesty's honour or courage."

"Great Heaven!" exclaimed Miraz, jumping to his feet. "Are *you* also bewitched today? Do you think I am *looking* for grounds to refuse it? You might as well call me coward to my face."

The conversation was going exactly as the two lords wished, so they said nothing.

"I see what it is," said Miraz, after staring at them as if his eyes would start out of his head, "you are as lily-livered as hares yourselves and have the effrontery to imagine my heart after the likeness of yours! Grounds for a refusal, indeed! Excuses for not fighting! Are you soldiers? Are you Telmarines? Are you men? And if I do refuse it (as all good reasons of captaincy and martial policy urge me to do) you will think, and teach others to think, I was afraid. Is it not so?"

"No man of your Majesty's age," said Glozelle, "would be called coward by any wise soldier for refusing the combat with a great warrior in the flower of his youth."

"So I'm to be a dotard with one foot in the grave, as well as a dastard," roared Miraz. "I'll tell you what it is, my Lords. With your womanish counsels (ever shying from the true point, which is one of policy) you have done the very opposite of your intent. I had meant to refuse it. But I'll accept it. Do you hear, accept it! I'll not be shamed because some witchcraft or treason has frozen both your bloods."

"We beseech your Majesty –" said Glozelle, but Miraz had flung out of the tent and they could hear him bawling out his acceptance to Edmund.

The two lords looked at one another and chuckled quietly.

"I knew he'd do it if he were properly chafed," said Glozelle. "But I'll not forget he called me coward. It shall be paid for."

There was a great stirring at Aslan's How when the news came back and was communicated to the various creatures. Edmund, with one of Miraz's captains, had already marked out the place for the combat, and ropes and stakes had been put round it. Two Telmarines were to stand at two of the corners, and one in the middle of one side, as marshals of the lists. Three marshals for the other two corners and the other side were to be furnished by the High King. Peter was just explaining to Caspian that he could not be one, because his right to the throne was what they were fighting about, when suddenly a thick, sleepy voice said, "Your Majesty, please." Peter turned and there stood the eldest of the Bulgy Bears.

"If you please, your Majesty," he said, "I'm a bear, I am."

"To be sure, so you are, and a good bear too, I don't doubt," said Peter.

"Yes," said the Bear. "But it was always a right of the bears to supply one marshal of the lists."

"Don't let him," whispered Trumpkin to Peter. "He's a good creature, but he'll shame us all. He'll go to sleep and he *will* suck his paws. In front of the enemy too."

"I can't help that," said Peter. "Because he's quite right. The Bears had that privilege. I can't imagine how it has been remembered all these years, when so many other things have been forgotten."

"Please, your Majesty," said the Bear.

"It is your right," said Peter. "And you shall be one of the marshals. But you *must* remember not to suck your paws."

"Of course not," said the Bear in a very shocked voice.

"Why, you're doing it this minute!" bellowed Trumpkin.

The Bear whipped his paw out of his mouth and pretended he hadn't heard.

"Sire!" came a shrill voice from near the ground.

"Ah – Reepicheep!" said Peter after looking up and down and round as people usually did when addressed by the Mouse.

"Sire," said Reepicheep. "My life is ever at your command, but my honour is my own. Sire, I have among my people the only trumpeter in your Majesty's army. I had thought, perhaps, we might have been sent with the challenge. Sire, my people are grieved. Perhaps if it were your pleasure that I should be a marshal of the lists, it would content them."

A noise not unlike thunder broke out from somewhere overhead at this point, as Giant Wimbleweather burst into one of those not very intelligent laughs to which the nicer sorts of Giant are so liable. He checked himself at once and looked as grave as a turnip by the time Reepicheep discovered where the noise came from.

"I am afraid it would not do," said Peter very gravely. "Some humans are afraid of mice –"

"I had observed it, Sire," said Reepicheep.

"And it would not be quite fair to Miraz," Peter continued, "to have in sight anything that might abate the edge of his courage."

"Your Majesty is the mirror of honour," said the Mouse with one of his admirable bows. "And on this matter we have but a single mind. . . . I thought I heard someone laughing just now. If anyone present wishes to make me the subject of his wit, I am very much at his service – with my sword – whenever he has leisure."

An awful silence followed this remark, which was

broken by Peter saying, "Giant Wimbleweather and the Bear and the Centaur Glenstorm shall be our marshals. The combat will be at two hours after noon. Dinner at noon precisely."

"I say," said Edmund as they walked away, "I suppose it *is* all right. I mean, I suppose you can beat him?"

"That's what I'm fighting him to find out," said Peter.

CHAPTER FOURTEEN

HOW ALL WERE VERY BUSY

A LITTLE before two o'clock Trumpkin and the Badger sat with the rest of the creatures at the wood's edge looking across at the gleaming line of Miraz's army which was about two arrow-shots away. In between, a square space of level grass had been staked for the combat. At the two far corners stood Glozelle and Sopespian with drawn swords. At the near corners were Giant Wimbleweather and the Bulgy Bear, who in spite of all their warnings was sucking his paws and looking, to tell the truth, uncommonly silly. To make up for this, Glenstorm on the right of the lists, stock-still except when he stamped a hind hoof occasionally on the turf, looked much more imposing than the Telmarine baron who faced him on the left. Peter had just shaken hands with Edmund and the Doctor, and was now walking down to the combat. It was like the moment before the pistol goes at an important race, but very much worse.

"I wish Aslan had turned up before it came to this," said Trumpkin.

"So do I," said Trufflehunter. "But look behind you."

"Crows and crockery!" muttered the Dwarf as soon as he had done so. "What are they? Huge people – beautiful people – like gods and goddesses and giants. Hundreds and thousands of them, closing in behind us. What are they?"

"It's the Dryads and Hamadryads and Silvans," said Trufflehunter. "Aslan has waked them."

"Humph!" said the Dwarf. "That'll be very useful if the

enemy try any treachery. But it won't help the High King very much if Miraz proves handier with his sword."

The Badger said nothing, for now Peter and Miraz were entering the lists from opposite ends, both on foot, both in chain shirts, with helmets and shields. They advanced till they were close together. Both bowed and seemed to speak, but it was impossible to hear what they said. Next moment the two swords flashed in the sunlight. For a second the clash could be heard but it was immediately drowned because both armies began shouting like crowds at a football match.

"Well done, Peter, oh, well done!" shouted Edmund as he saw Miraz reel back a whole pace and a half. "Follow it up, quick!" And Peter did, and for a few seconds it looked as if the fight might be won. But then Miraz pulled himself together – began to make real use of his height and weight. "Miraz! Miraz! The King! The King!" came the roar of the Telmarines. Caspian and Edmund grew white with sickening anxiety.

"Peter is taking some dreadful knocks," said Edmund.

"Hullo!" said Caspian. "What's happening now?"

"Both falling apart," said Edmund. "A bit blown, I expect. Watch. Ah, now they're beginning again, more scientifically this time. Circling round and round, feeling each other's defences."

"I'm afraid this Miraz knows his work," muttered the Doctor. But hardly had he said this when there was such a clapping and baying and throwing up of hoods among the Old Narnians that it was nearly deafening.

"What was it? What was it?" asked the Doctor. "My old eyes missed it."

"The High King has pricked him in the arm-pit," said

Caspian, still clapping. "Just where the arm-hole of the hauberk let the point through. First blood."

"It's looking ugly again now, though," said Edmund. "Peter's not using his shield properly. He must be hurt in the left arm."

It was only too true. Everyone could see that Peter's shield hung limp. The shouting of the Telmarines redoubled.

"You've seen more battles than I," said Caspian. "Is there any chance now?"

"Precious little," said Edmund. "I suppose he might *just* do it. With luck."

"Oh, why did we let it happen at all?" said Caspian.

Suddenly all the shouting on both sides died down. Edmund was puzzled for a moment. Then he said, "Oh, I see. They've both agreed to a rest. Come on, Doctor. You and I may be able to do something for the High King." They ran down to the lists and Peter came outside the ropes to meet them, his face red and sweaty, his chest heaving.

"Is your left arm wounded?" asked Edmund.

"It's not exactly a wound," Peter said. "I got the full weight of his shoulder on my shield – like a load of bricks – and the rim of the shield drove into my wrist. I don't think it's broken, but it might be a sprain. If you could tie it up very tight I think I could manage."

While they were doing this, Edmund asked anxiously, "What do you think of him, Peter?"

"Tough," said Peter. "Very tough. I have a chance if I can keep him on the hop till his weight and short wind come against him – in this hot sun too. To tell the truth, I haven't much chance else. Give my love to – to everyone at home, Ed, if he gets me. Here he comes into the lists again.

So long, old chap. Good-bye, Doctor. And I say, Ed, say something specially nice to Trumpkin. He's been a brick."

Edmund couldn't speak. He walked back with the Doctor to his own lines with a sick feeling in his stomach.

But the new bout went well. Peter now seemed to be able to make some use of his shield, and he certainly made good use of his feet. He was almost playing Tig with Miraz now, keeping out of range, shifting his ground, making the enemy work.

"Coward!" booed the Telmarines. "Why don't you stand up to him? Don't you like it, eh? Thought you'd come to fight, not dance. Yah!"

"Oh, I do hope he won't listen to them," said Caspian.

"Not he," said Edmund. "You don't know him – Oh!" – for Miraz had got in a blow at last, on Peter's helmet. Peter staggered, slipped sideways, and fell on one knee. The roar of the Telmarines rose like the noise of the sea. "Now, Miraz," they yelled. "Now. Quick! Quick! Kill him." But indeed there was no need to egg the usurper on. He was on top of Peter already. Edmund bit his lips till the blood came, as the sword flashed down on Peter. It looked as if it would slash off his head. Thank heavens! it had glanced down his right shoulder. The Dwarf-wrought mail was sound and did not break.

"Great Scott!" cried Edmund. "He's up again. Peter, go it, Peter."

"I couldn't see what happened," said the Doctor. "How did he do it?"

"Grabbed Miraz's arm as it came down," said Trumpkin, dancing with delight. "There's a man for you! Uses his enemy's arm as a ladder. The High King! The High King! Up, Old Narnia!"

"Look," said Trufflehunter. "Miraz is angry. It is good."

They were certainly at it hammer and tongs now: such a flurry of blows that it seemed impossible for either not to be killed. As the excitement grew, the shouting almost died away. The spectators were holding their breath. It was most horrible and most magnificent.

A great shout arose from the Old Narnians. Miraz was down – not struck by Peter, but face downwards, having tripped on a tussock. Peter stepped back, waiting for him to rise.

"Oh bother, bother, bother," said Edmund to himself. "Need he be as gentlemanly as all that? I suppose he must. Comes of being a Knight *and* a High King. I suppose it is what Aslan would like. But that brute will be up again in a minute and then –"

But "that brute" never rose. The Lords Glozelle and Sopespian had their own plans ready. As soon as they saw their King down they leaped into the lists crying, "Treachery! Treachery! The Narnian traitor has stabbed him in the back while he lay helpless. To arms! To arms, Telmar!"

Peter hardly understood what was happening. He saw two big men running towards him with drawn swords. Then the third Telmarine had leaped over the ropes on his left. "To arms, Narnia! Treachery!" Peter shouted. If all three had set upon him at once he would never have spoken again. But Glozelle stopped to stab his own King dead where he lay: "That's for your insult, this morning," he whispered as the blade went home. Peter swung to face Sopespian, slashed his legs from under him and, with the back-cut of the same stroke, walloped off his head. Edmund was now at his side crying, "Narnia, Narnia! The Lion!" The whole Telmarine army was rushing towards

them. But now the Giant was stamping forward, stooping low and swinging his club. The Centaurs charged. *Twang, twang* behind and *hiss, hiss* overhead came the archery of Dwarfs. Trumpkin was fighting at his left. Full battle was joined.

"Come back, Reepicheep, you little ass!" shouted Peter. "You'll only be killed. This is no place for mice." But the ridiculous little creatures were dancing in and out among the feet of both armies, jabbing with their swords. Many a Telmarine warrior that day felt his foot suddenly pierced as if by a dozen skewers, hopped on one leg cursing the pain, and fell as often as not. If he fell, the mice finished him off; if he did not, someone else did.

But almost before the Old Narnians were really warmed to their work they found the enemy giving way. Tough-looking warriors turned white, gazed in terror not on the Old Narnians but on something behind them, and then flung down their weapons, shrieking, "The Wood! The Wood! The end of the world!"

But soon neither their cries nor the sound of weapons could be heard any more, for both were drowned in the ocean-like roar of the Awakened Trees as they plunged through the ranks of Peter's army, and then on, in pursuit of the Telmarines. Have you ever stood at the edge of a great wood on a high ridge when a wild south-wester broke over it in full fury on an autumn evening? Imagine that sound. And then imagine that the wood, instead of being fixed to one place, was rushing *at* you; and was no longer trees but huge people; yet still like trees because their long arms waved like branches and their heads tossed and leaves fell round them in showers. It was like that for the Telmarines. It was a little alarming even for the

Narnians. In a few minutes all Miraz's followers were running down to the Great River in the hope of crossing the bridge to the town of Beruna and there defending themselves behind ramparts and closed gates.

They reached the river, but there was no bridge. It had disappeared since yesterday. Then utter panic and horror fell upon them and they all surrendered.

But what had happened to the bridge?

Early that morning, after a few hours' sleep, the girls had

waked, to see Aslan standing over them and to hear his voice saying, "We will make holiday." They rubbed their eyes and looked round them. The trees had all gone but could still be seen moving away towards Aslan's How in a dark mass. Bacchus and the Maenads – his fierce, madcap girls – and Silenus were still with them. Lucy, fully rested, jumped up. Everyone was awake, everyone was laughing, flutes were playing, cymbals clashing. Animals, not Talking Animals, were crowding in upon them from every direction.

"What is it, Aslan?" said Lucy, her eyes dancing and her feet wanting to dance.

"Come, children," said he. "Ride on my back again today."

"Oh, lovely!" cried Lucy, and both girls climbed on to the warm golden back as they had done no one knew how many years before. Then the whole party moved off – Aslan leading, Bacchus and his Maenads leaping, rushing, and turning somersaults, the beasts frisking round them, and Silenus and his donkey bringing up the rear.

They turned a little to the right, raced down a steep hill, and found the long Bridge of Beruna in front of them. Before they had begun to cross it, however, up out of the water came a great wet, bearded head, larger than a man's, crowned with rushes. It looked at Aslan and out of its mouth a deep voice came.

"Hail, Lord," it said. "Loose my chains."

"Who on earth is *that*?" whispered Susan.

"I think it's the river-god, but hush," said Lucy.

"Bacchus," said Aslan. "Deliver him from his chains."

"That means the bridge, I expect," thought Lucy. And so it did. Bacchus and his people splashed forward into the shallow water, and a minute later the most curious things began happening. Great, strong trunks of ivy came curling up all the piers of the bridge, growing as quickly as a fire grows, wrapping the stones round, splitting, breaking, separating them. The walls of the bridge turned into hedges gay with hawthorn for a moment and then disappeared as the whole thing with a rush and a rumble collapsed into the swirling water. With much splashing, screaming, and laughter the revellers waded or swam or danced across the ford ("Hurrah! It's the Ford of Beruna again now!" cried the girls) and up the bank on the far side and into the town.

Everyone in the streets fled before their faces. The first house they came to was a school: a girls' school, where a lot of Narnian girls, with their hair done very tight and ugly tight collars round their necks and thick tickly stockings on their legs, were having a history lesson. The sort of "History" that was taught in Narnia under Miraz's rule was duller than the truest history you ever read and less true than the most exciting adventure story.

"If you don't attend, Gwendolen," said the mistress, "and stop looking out of the window, I shall have to give you an order-mark."

"But please, Miss Prizzle –" began Gwendolen.

"Did you hear what I said, Gwendolen?" asked Miss Prizzle.

"But please, Miss Prizzle," said Gwendolen, "there's a LION!"

"Take two order-marks for talking nonsense," said Miss Prizzle. "And now –" A roar interrupted her. Ivy came curling in at the windows of the classroom. The walls

became a mass of shimmering green, and leafy branches arched overhead where the ceiling had been. Miss Prizzle found she was standing on grass in a forest glade. She clutched at her desk to steady herself, and found that the desk was a rose-bush. Wild people such as she had never even imagined were crowding round her. Then she saw the Lion, screamed and fled, and with her fled her class, who were mostly dumpy, prim little girls with fat legs. Gwendolen hesitated.

"You'll stay with us, sweetheart?" said Aslan.

"Oh, *may* I? Thank you, thank you," said Gwendolen. Instantly she joined hands with two of the Maenads, who whirled her round in a merry dance and helped her take off some of the unnecessary and uncomfortable clothes that she was wearing.

Wherever they went in the little town of Beruna it was the same. Most of the people fled, a few joined them. When they left the town they were a larger and a merrier company.

They swept on across the level fields on the north bank, or left bank, of the river. At every farm animals came out to join them. Sad old donkeys who had never known joy grew suddenly young again; chained dogs broke their chains; horses kicked their carts to pieces and came trotting along with them – clop-clop – kicking up the mud and whinnying.

At a well in a yard they met a man who was beating a boy. The stick burst into flower in the man's hand. He tried to drop it, but it stuck to his hand. His arm became a branch, his body the trunk of a tree, his feet took root. The boy, who had been crying a moment before, burst out laughing and joined them.

At a little town half-way to Beaversdam, where two rivers met, they came to another school, where a tired-looking girl was teaching arithmetic to a number of boys who looked very like pigs. She looked out of the window and saw the divine revellers singing up the street and a stab of joy went through her heart. Aslan stopped right under the window and looked up at her.

"Oh, don't, don't," she said. "I'd love to. But I mustn't. I

must stick to my work. And the children would be frightened if they saw you."

"Frightened?" said the most pig-like of the boys. "Who's she talking to out of the window? Let's tell the inspector she talks to people out of the window when she ought to be teaching us."

"Let's go and see who it is," said another boy, and they all came crowding to the window. But as soon as their mean little faces looked out, Bacchus gave a great cry of *Euan, euoi-oi-oi-oi* and the boys all began howling with

fright and trampling one another down to get out of the door and jumping out of the windows. And it was said afterwards (whether truly or not) that those particular little boys were never seen again, but that there were a lot of very fine little pigs in that part of the country which had never been there before.

"Now, Dear Heart," said Aslan to the Mistress: and she jumped down and joined them.

At Beaversdam they re-crossed the river and came east again along the southern bank. They came to a little cottage where a child stood in the doorway crying. "Why are you crying, my love?" asked Aslan. The child, who had never seen a picture of a lion, was not afraid of him. "Auntie's very ill," she said. "She's going to die." Then Aslan went to go in at the door of the cottage, but it was too small for him. So, when he had got his head through, he pushed with his shoulders (Lucy and Susan fell off when he did this) and lifted the whole house up and it fell backwards and apart. And there, still in her bed, though the bed was now in the open air, lay a little old woman who looked as if she had Dwarf blood in her. She was at death's door, but when she opened her eyes and saw the bright, hairy head of the lion staring into her face, she did not scream or faint. She said, "Oh, Aslan! I knew it was true. I've been waiting for this all my life. Have you come to take me away?"

"Yes, Dearest," said Aslan. "But not the long journey yet." And as he spoke, like the flush creeping along the underside of a cloud at sunrise, the colour came back to her white face and her eyes grew bright and she sat up and said, "Why, I do declare I feel *that* better. I think I could take a little breakfast this morning."

"Here you are, mother," said Bacchus, dipping a pitcher in the cottage well and handing it to her. But what was in it now was not water but the richest wine, red as red-currant jelly, smooth as oil, strong as beef, warming as tea, cool as dew.

"Eh, you've done something to our well," said the old woman. "That makes a nice change, that does." And she jumped out of bed.

"Ride on me," said Aslan, and added to Susan and Lucy, "You two queens will have to run now."

"But we'd like that just as well," said Susan. And off they went again.

And so at last, with leaping and dancing and singing, with music and laughter and roaring and barking and neighing, they all came to the place where Miraz's army stood flinging down their swords and holding up their hands, and Peter's army, still holding their weapons and breathing hard, stood round them with stern and glad faces. And the first thing that happened was that the old woman slipped off Aslan's back and ran across to Caspian and they embraced one another; for she was his old nurse.

CHAPTER FIFTEEN

ASLAN MAKES A DOOR IN THE AIR

AT the sight of Aslan the cheeks of the Telmarine soldiers became the colour of cold gravy, their knees knocked together, and many fell on their faces. They had not believed in lions and this made their fear greater. Even the Red Dwarfs, who knew that he came as a friend, stood with open mouths and could not speak. Some of the Black Dwarfs, who had been of Nikabrik's party, began to edge away. But all the Talking Beasts surged round the Lion, with purrs and grunts and squeaks and whinneys of delight, fawning on him with their tails, rubbing against him, touching him reverently with their noses and going to and fro under his body and between his legs. If you have ever seen a little cat loving a big dog whom it knows and trusts, you will have a pretty good picture of their behaviour. Then Peter, leading Caspian, forced his way through the crowd of animals.

"This is Caspian, Sir," he said. And Caspian knelt and kissed the Lion's paw.

"Welcome, Prince," said Aslan. "Do you feel yourself sufficient to take up the Kingship of Narnia?"

"I – I don't think I do, Sir," said Caspian. "I'm only a kid."

"Good," said Aslan. "If you had felt yourself sufficient, it would have been a proof that you were not. Therefore, under us and under the High King, you shall be King of Narnia, Lord of Cair Paravel, and Emperor of the Lone Islands. You and your heirs while your race lasts. And your coronation – but what have we here?" For at that

moment a curious little procession was approaching – eleven Mice, six of whom carried between them something on a litter made of branches, but the litter was no bigger than a large atlas. No one has ever seen mice more woebegone than these. They were plastered with mud – some with blood too – and their ears were down and their whiskers drooped and their tails dragged in the grass, and their leader piped on his slender pipe a melancholy tune. On the litter lay what seemed little better than a damp heap of fur; all that was left of Reepicheep. He was still breathing, but more dead than alive, gashed with innumerable wounds, one paw crushed, and, where his tail had been, a bandaged stump.

"Now, Lucy," said Aslan.

Lucy had her diamond bottle out in a moment. Though only a drop was needed on each of Reepicheep's wounds, the wounds were so many that there was a long and anxious silence before she had finished and the Master Mouse sprang from the litter. His hand went at once to his sword hilt, with the other he twirled his whiskers. He bowed.

"Hail, Aslan!" came his shrill voice. "I have the honour –" But then he suddenly stopped.

The fact was that he still had no tail – whether that Lucy had forgotten it or that her cordial, though it could heal wounds, could not make things grow again. Reepicheep became aware of his loss as he made his bow; perhaps it altered something in his balance. He looked over his right shoulder. Failing to see his tail, he strained his neck further till he had to turn his shoulders and his whole body followed. But by that time his hind-quarters had turned too and were out of sight. Then he strained his

neck looking over his shoulder again, with the same result. Only after he had turned completely round three times did he realize the dreadful truth.

"I am confounded," said Reepicheep to Aslan. "I am completely out of countenance. I must crave your indulgence for appearing in this unseemly fashion."

"It becomes you very well, Small One," said Aslan.

"All the same," replied Reepicheep, "if anything could

be done . . . Perhaps her Majesty?" and here he bowed to Lucy.

"But what do you want with a tail?" asked Aslan.

"Sir," said the Mouse, "I can eat and sleep and die for my King without one. But a tail is the honour and glory of a Mouse."

"I have sometimes wondered, friend," said Aslan, "whether you do not think too much about your honour."

"Highest of all High Kings," said Reepicheep, "permit me to remind you that a very small size has been

bestowed on us Mice, and if we did not guard our dignity, some (who weigh worth by inches) would allow themselves very unsuitable pleasantries at our expense. That is why I have been at some pains to make it known that no one who does not wish to feel this sword as near his heart as I can reach shall talk in my presence about Traps or Toasted Cheese or Candles: no, Sir – not the tallest fool in Narnia!" Here he glared very fiercely up at Wimbleweather, but the Giant, who was always a stage behind everyone else, had not yet discovered what was being talked about down at his feet, and so missed the point.

"Why have your followers all drawn *their* swords, may I ask?" said Aslan.

"May it please your High Majesty," said the second Mouse, whose name was Peepiceek, "we are all waiting to cut off our own tails if our Chief must go without his. We will not bear the shame of wearing an honour which is denied to the High Mouse."

"Ah!" roared Aslan. "You have conquered me. You have great hearts. Not for the sake of your dignity, Reepicheep, but for the love that is between you and your people, and still more for the kindness your people showed me long ago when you ate away the cords that bound me on the Stone Table (and it was then, though you have long forgotten it, that you began to be *Talking* Mice), you shall have your tail again."

Before Aslan had finished speaking the new tail was in its place. Then, at Aslan's command, Peter bestowed the Knighthood of the Order of the Lion on Caspian, and Caspian, as soon as he was knighted, himself bestowed it on Trufflehunter and Trumpkin and Reepicheep, and

made Doctor Cornelius his Lord Chancellor, and confirmed the Bulgy Bear in his hereditary office of Marshal of the Lists. And there was great applause.

After this the Telmarine soldiers, firmly but without taunts or blows, were taken across the ford and all put under lock and key in the town of Beruna and given beef and beer. They made a great fuss about wading in the river, for they all hated and feared running water just as much as they hated and feared woods and animals. But in the end the nuisance was over: and then the nicest parts of that long day began.

Lucy, sitting close to Aslan and divinely comfortable, wondered what the trees were doing. At first she thought they were merely dancing; they were certainly going round slowly in two circles, one from left to right and the other from right to left. Then she noticed that they kept throwing something down in the centre of both circles. Sometimes she thought they were cutting off long strands of their hair; at other times it looked as if they were breaking off bits of their fingers – but, if so, they had plenty of fingers to spare and it did not hurt them. But whatever they were throwing down, when it reached the ground, it became brushwood or dry sticks. Then three or four of the Red Dwarfs came forward with their tinder boxes and set light to the pile, which first crackled, and then blazed, and finally roared as a woodland bonfire on midsummer night ought to do. And everyone sat down in a wide circle round it.

Then Bacchus and Silenus and the Maenads began a dance, far wilder than the dance of the trees; not merely a dance for fun and beauty (though it was that too) but a magic dance of plenty, and where their hands touched,

and where their feet fell, the feast came into existence – sides of roasted meat that filled the grove with delicious smell, and wheaten cakes and oaten cakes, honey and many-coloured sugars and cream as thick as porridge and as smooth as still water, peaches, nectarines, pomegranates, pears, grapes, strawberries, raspberries – pyramids and cataracts of fruit. Then, in great wooden cups and bowls and mazers, wreathed with ivy, came the wines; dark, thick ones like syrups of mulberry juice, and clear red ones like red jellies liquefied, and yellow wines

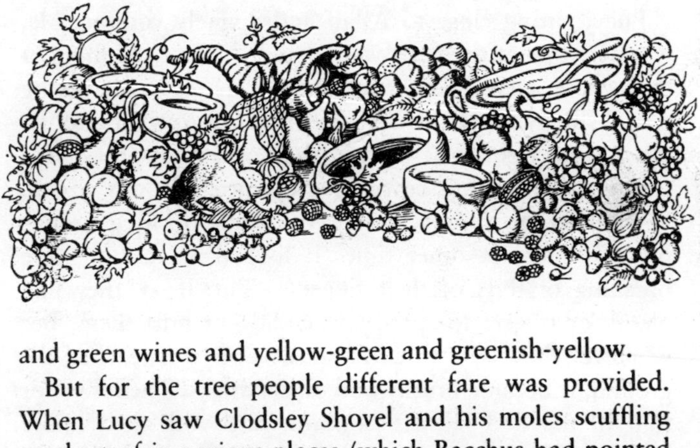

and green wines and yellow-green and greenish-yellow.

But for the tree people different fare was provided. When Lucy saw Clodsley Shovel and his moles scuffling up the turf in various places (which Bacchus had pointed out to them) and realized that the trees were going to eat *earth* it gave her rather a shudder. But when she saw the earths that were actually brought to them she felt quite different. They began with a rich brown loam that looked almost exactly like chocolate; so like chocolate, in fact, that Edmund tried a piece of it, but he did not find it at all nice. When the rich loam had taken the edge off their

hunger, the trees turned to an earth of the kind you see in Somerset, which is almost pink. They said it was lighter and sweeter. At the cheese stage they had a chalky soil, and then went on to delicate confections of the finest gravels powdered with choice silver sand. They drank very little wine, and it made the Hollies very talkative: for the most part they quenched their thirst with deep draughts of mingled dew and rain, flavoured with forest flowers and the airy taste of the thinnest clouds.

Thus Aslan feasted the Narnians till long after the

sunset had died away, and the stars had come out; and the great fire, now hotter but less noisy, shone like a beacon in the dark woods, and the frightened Telmarines saw it from far away and wondered what it might mean. The best thing of all about this feast was that there was no breaking up or going away, but as the talk grew quieter and slower, one after another would begin to nod and finally drop off to sleep with feet towards the fire and good friends on either side, till at last there was silence all round the circle, and the chattering of water over stone at the Ford of Beruna could be heard once more. But all night Aslan and the

Moon gazed upon each other with joyful and unblinking eyes.

Next day messengers (who were chiefly squirrels and birds) were sent all over the country with a proclamation to the scattered Telmarines – including, of course, the prisoners in Beruna. They were told that Caspian was now King and that Narnia would henceforth belong to the Talking Beasts and the Dwarfs and Dryads and Fauns and other creatures quite as much as to the men. Any who

chose to stay under the new conditions might do so; but for those who did not like the idea, Aslan would provide another home. Anyone who wished to go there must come to Aslan and the Kings at the Ford of Beruna by noon on the fifth day. You may imagine that this caused plenty of head-scratching among the Telmarines. Some of them, chiefly the young ones, had, like Caspian, heard stories of the Old Days and were delighted that they had come back. They were already making friends with the creatures. These all decided to stay in Narnia. But most of the older men, especially those who had been important under Miraz, were sulky and had no wish to live in a

country where they could not rule the roost. "Live here with a lot of blooming performing animals! No fear," they said. "And ghosts too," some added with a shudder. "That's what those there Dryads really are. It's not canny." They were also suspicious. "I don't trust 'em," they said. "Not with that awful Lion and all. He won't keep his claws off us long, *you'll* see." But then they were equally suspicious of his offer to give them a new home. "Take us off to his den and eat us one by one most likely," they muttered. And the more they talked to one another the sulkier and more suspicious they became. But on the appointed day more than half of them turned up.

At one end of the glade Aslan had caused to be set up two stakes of wood, higher than a man's head and about three feet apart. A third, and lighter, piece of wood was bound across them at the top, uniting them, so that the whole thing looked like a doorway from nowhere into nowhere. In front of this stood Aslan himself with Peter on his right and Caspian on his left. Grouped round them were Susan and Lucy, Trumpkin and Trufflehunter, the Lord Cornelius, Glenstorm, Reepicheep, and others. The children and the Dwarfs had made good use of the royal wardrobes in what had been the castle of Miraz and was now the castle of Caspian, and what with silk and cloth of gold, with snowy linen glancing through slashed sleeves, with silver mail shirts and jewelled sword-hilts, with gilt helmets and feathered bonnets, they were almost too bright to look at. Even the beasts wore rich chains about their necks. Yet nobody's eyes were on them or the children. The living and strokable gold of Aslan's mane outshone them all. The rest of the Old Narnians stood down each side of the glade. At the far end stood the

Telmarines. The sun shone brightly and pennants fluttered in the light wind.

"Men of Telmar," said Aslan, "you who seek a new land, hear my words. I will send you all to your own country, which I know and you do not."

"We don't remember Telmar. We don't know where it is. We don't know what it is like," grumbled the Telmarines.

"You came into Narnia out of Telmar," said Aslan. "But you came into Telmar from another place. You do not belong to this world at all. You came hither, certain generations ago, out of that same world to which the High King Peter belongs."

At this, half the Telmarines began whimpering, "There you are. Told you so. He's going to kill us all, send us right out of the world," and the other half began throwing out their chests and slapping one another on the back and whispering, "There you are. Might have guessed we didn't belong to this place with all its queer, nasty, unnatural creatures. We're of royal blood, you'll see." And even Caspian and Cornelius and the children turned to Aslan with looks of amazement on their faces.

"Peace," said Aslan in the low voice which was nearest to his growl. The earth seemed to shake a little and every living thing in the grove became still as stone.

"You, Sir Caspian," said Aslan, "might have known that you could be no true King of Narnia unless, like the Kings of old, you were a son of Adam and came from the world of Adam's sons. And so you are. Many years ago in that world, in a deep sea of that world which is called the South Sea, a shipload of pirates were driven by storm on an island. And there they did as pirates would: killed the

natives and took the native women for wives, and made palm wine, and drank and were drunk, and lay in the shade of the palm trees, and woke up and quarrelled, and sometimes killed one another. And in one of these frays six were put to flight by the rest and fled with their women into the centre of the island and up a mountain, and went, as they thought, into a cave to hide. But it was one of the magical places of that world, one of the chinks or chasms between that world and this. There were many chinks or chasms between worlds in old times, but they have grown rarer. This was one of the last: I do not say *the* last. And so they fell, or rose, or blundered, or dropped right through, and found themselves in this world, in the Land of Telmar which was then unpeopled. But why it was unpeopled is a long story: I will not tell it now. And in Telmar their descendants lived and became a fierce and proud people; and after many generations there was a famine in Telmar and they invaded Narnia, which was then in some disorder (but that also would be a long story), and conquered it and ruled it. Do you mark all this well, King Caspian?"

"I do indeed, Sir," said Caspian. "I was wishing that I came of a more honourable lineage."

"You come of the Lord Adam and the Lady Eve," said Aslan. "And that is both honour enough to erect the head of the poorest beggar, and shame enough to bow the shoulders of the greatest emperor on earth. Be content."

Caspian bowed.

"And now," said Aslan, "you men and women of Telmar, will you go back to that island in the world of men from which your fathers first came? It is no bad place. The race of those pirates who first found it has died

out, and it is without inhabitants. There are good wells of fresh water, and fruitful soil, and timber for building, and fish in the lagoons; and the other men of that world have not yet discovered it. The chasm is open for your return; but this I must warn you, that once you have gone through, it will close behind you for ever. There will be no more commerce between the worlds by that door."

There was silence for a moment. Then a burly, decent-looking fellow among the Telmarine soldiers pushed forward and said:

"Well, I'll take the offer."

"It is well chosen," said Aslan. "And because you have spoken first, strong magic is upon you. Your future in that world shall be good. Come forth."

The man, now a little pale, came forward. Aslan and his court drew aside, leaving him free access to the empty doorway of the stakes.

"Go through it, my son," said Aslan, bending towards him and touching the man's nose with his own. As soon as the Lion's breath came about him, a new look came into the man's eyes – startled, but not unhappy – as if he were trying to remember something. Then he squared his shoulders and walked into the Door.

Everyone's eyes were fixed on him. They saw the three pieces of wood, and through them the trees and grass and sky of Narnia. They saw the man between the doorposts: then, in one second, he had vanished utterly.

From the other end of the glade the remaining Telmarines set up a wailing. "Ugh! What's happened to him? Do you mean to murder us? We won't go that way." And then one of the clever Telmarines said:

"We don't see any other world through those sticks. If

you want us to believe in it, why doesn't one of *you* go? All your own friends are keeping well away from the sticks."

Instantly Reepicheep stood forward and bowed. "If *my* example can be of any service, Aslan," he said, "I will take eleven mice through that arch at your bidding without a moment's delay."

"Nay, little one," said Aslan, laying his velvety paw ever so lightly on Reepicheep's head. "They would do dreadful things to you in that world. They would show you at fairs. It is others who must lead."

"Come on," said Peter suddenly to Edmund and Lucy. "Our time's up."

"What do you mean?" said Edmund.

"This way," said Susan, who seemed to know all about it. "Back into the trees. We've got to change."

"Change what?" asked Lucy.

"Our clothes, of course," said Susan. "Nice fools we'd look on the platform of an English station in *these*."

"But our other things are at Caspian's castle," said Edmund.

"No, they're not," said Peter, still leading the way into the thickest wood. "They're all here. They were brought down in bundles this morning. It's all arranged."

"Was that what Aslan was talking to you and Susan about this morning?" asked Lucy.

"Yes – that and other things," said Peter, his face very solemn. "I can't tell it to you all. There were things he wanted to say to Su and me because we're not coming back to Narnia."

"Never?" cried Edmund and Lucy in dismay.

"Oh, you two are," answered Peter. "At least, from what he said, I'm pretty sure he means you to get back some day. But not Su and me. He says we're getting too old."

"Oh, Peter," said Lucy. "What awful bad luck. Can you bear it?"

"Well, I think I can," said Peter. "It's all rather different from what I thought. You'll understand when it comes to your last time. But, quick, here are our things."

It was odd, and not very nice, to take off their royal clothes and to come back in their school things (not very fresh now) into that great assembly. One or two of the nastier Telmarines jeered. But the other creatures all cheered and rose up in honour of Peter the High King,

and Queen Susan of the Horn, and King Edmund, and Queen Lucy. There were affectionate and (on Lucy's part) tearful farewells with all their old friends – animal kisses, and hugs from Bulgy Bears, and hands wrung by Trumpkin, and a last tickly, whiskerish embrace with Trufflehunter. And of course Caspian offered the Horn back to Susan and of course Susan told him to keep it. And then, wonderfully and terribly, it was farewell to

Aslan himself, and Peter took his place with Susan's hands on his shoulders and Edmund's on hers and Lucy's on his and the first of the Telmarine's on Lucy's, and so in a long line they moved forward to the Door. After that came a moment which is hard to describe, for the children seemed to be seeing three things at once. One was the mouth of a cave opening into the glaring green and blue of an island in the Pacific, where all the Telmarines would find themselves the moment they were through the Door. The second was a glade in Narnia, the faces of Dwarfs

and Beasts, the deep eyes of Aslan, and the white patches on the Badger's cheeks. But the third (which rapidly swallowed up the other two) was the grey, gravelly surface of a platform in a country station, and a seat with luggage round it, where they were all sitting as if they had never moved from it – a little flat and dreary for a moment after all they had been through, but also, unexpectedly, nice in its own way, what with the familiar railway smell and the English sky and the summer term before them.

"Well!" said Peter. "We *have* had a time."

"Bother!" said Edmund. "I've left my new torch in Narnia."

The Chronicles of Narnia
by C. S. Lewis

C. S. Lewis's wit and wisdom, his blend of excitement and adventure with fantasy, have made this magnificent series beloved of many generations of readers. The final book, *The Last Battle*, won the Carnegie Medal for 1956.

Each of the seven titles is a complete story in itself, but all take place in the magical land of Narnia. Guided by the noble Lion Aslan, the children learn that evil and treachery can only be overcome by courage, loyalty and great sacrifice.

The titles, in suggested reading order, are as follows:

The Magician's Nephew
The Lion, the Witch and the Wardrobe
The Horse and His Boy
Prince Caspian
The Voyage of the Dawn Treader
The Silver Chair
The Last Battle

all at £3.50

The Chronicles of Narnia

C. S. Lewis

Each of the seven titles is a complete story in itself, but all take place in the magical land of Narnia. Guided by the noble Lion Aslan, the children learn that evil and treachery can only be overcome by courage, loyalty and great sacrifice.

In reading order:

The Magician's Nephew	**£3.50**
The Lion, The Witch and the Wardrobe	**£3.50**
The Horse and His Boy	**£3.50**
Prince Caspian	**£3.50**
The Voyage of the *Dawn Treader*	**£3.50**
The Silver Chair	**£3.50**
The Last Battle	**£3.50**
Narnia Gift Pack	**£25.00**
(all seven titles in a slipcase)	

The Chronicles of Narnia are also available in larger format editions, price £3.50 each (the slipcase is £25.00, and contains all seven titles) and in hardback, price £6.95 each. The boxed hardback set is £50.00.

THE CHRONICLES OF NARNIA

are all available in Lions

In reading order

The Magician's Nephew

The Lion, the Witch and the Wardrobe

The Horse and his Boy

Prince Caspian

The Voyage of the *Dawn Treader*

The Silver Chair

The Last Battle

CW01650122

PRINCE CASPIAN

Full of gloom, the Pevensie children are waiting at the railway station for the train to take them back to school. Lucy feels a sudden tug, then Edmund does, and a minute later Peter and Susan do too. In a trice the station has vanished, and they find themselves in an overgrown wood near the sea, close by the ruins of their former castle, Cair Paravel. They are back in the magical land of Narnia where they had such wonderful times when they ruled as Kings and Queens (in *The Lion, the Witch and the Wardrobe*).

But something is very wrong. Their glorious castle lies in ruins and everywhere is strangely silent and empty. With the startling arrival of the Dwarf, they learn of the sad fate that has befallen Narnia. Civil war is now destroying the land as brave Prince Caspian, realising his uncle King Miraz's evil ways, is trying to regain the kingdom that is rightfully his. But Caspian needs help and, with the guidance of Aslan, the children take up the challenge to save Narnia and restore the long lost days of freedom and happiness.